A SPECIAL RELATIONSHIP?

American Influences on Public Law in the UK

A SPECIAL RELATIONSHIP?

American Influences on Public Law in the UK

IAN LOVELAND

CLARENDON PRESS · OXFORD

Oxford University Press, Walton Street, Oxford OX2 6DP
Oxford New York
Athens Auckland Bangkok Bombay
Calcutta Cape Town Dar es Salaam Delhi
Florence Hong Kong Istanbul Karachi
Kuala Lumpur Madras Madrid Melbourne
Mexico City Nairobi Paris Singapore
Taipei Tokyo Toronto
and associated companies in
Berlin Ibadan

Oxford is a trade mark of Oxford University Press

Published in the United States
by Oxford University Press Inc., New York

First published 1995
Reprinted (with corrections) 1996

British Library Cataloguing in Publication Data
Data available

Library of Congress Cataloging in Publication Data
A special relationship?: American influences on public law in the UK
[edited by] Ian Loveland.
p. cm.
Includes index.
1. Public law—Great Britain. 2. Public law—United States.
I. Loveland, Ian.
KD3930.A75S68 1995
342.41—dc20
[344.102]
ISBN 0–19–826014–8

Printed in Great Britain
on acid-free paper by
The Ipswich Book Company Ltd., Suffolk

Acknowledgements

This is the second edited collection to emerge from my brief tenure as Faculty Seminar Organizer at Queen Mary and Westfield College. As with the first, I owe particular thanks to Professor Hazel Genn, who provided the intellectual and (from the Faculty's limited funds) financial impetus for both projects. In respect of this collection, I must also thank her for indulging my somewhat esoteric wish several years ago to introduce an LLB course at Queen Mary and Westfield College on the Constitutional Law of the USA. There are perhaps few Heads of Department who would allow a substantial amount of a junior colleague's teaching load to be spent on a course which initially attracted only six students. (Any other Heads out there who receive a similar request might note the course rapidly attracted forty students each year.) My experience of teaching that course, and indulging that interest, in large part explains my motivation for organizing this volume.

I must also give extensive thanks to all my contributors, some of whom travelled a considerable distance to present the first versions of their chapters in our 1994 seminar series. A special mention should be given to Professor Eric Barendt, whose *Freedom of Speech* further sharpened my own interest in comparative US/UK public law scholarship, and who offered me considerable assistance with the introductory chapter; and to Professors Genevra Richardson and Roger Cotterrell, for being enthusiastic and ever-present participants in the series itself.

My thanks finally to Richard Hart whose initial enthusiasm for my original proposal led me to produce a rather better second version, and who thereafter was constantly helpful and supportive as the book made its way through Oxford University Press.

Ian Loveland

London
Spring 1995

Contents

List of Contributors

T. R. S. ALLAN
Fellow of Pembroke College, University of Cambridge

ERIC BARENDT
Professor of Media Law, University College London

PETER CANE
Fellow of Corpus Christi College, University of Oxford

ROGER COTTERRELL
Professor of Law, Queen Mary and Westfield College, London

PAUL CRAIG
Fellow of Worcester College, University of Oxford

KEITH EWING
Professor of Law, Kings College London

PETER FITZPATRICK
Professor of Law, University of Kent

CAROL HARLOW
Professor of Public Law, London School of Economics and Political Science

IAN LOVELAND
Professor of Law, Brunel University

RICHARD RAWLINGS
Lecturer in Law, London School of Economics and Political Science

GENEVRA RICHARDSON
Professor of Public Law, Queen Mary and Westfield College, London

MARTIN WASIK
Professor of Law, University of Manchester

Introduction: Should We Take Lessons from America?

IAN LOVELAND[1]

As we approach the twenty-first century, we will find few supporters for the proposition that the academic study of British public law, whether in its constitutional or administrative manifestation, can plausibly operate as a closed system, its borders securely fastened against incursion from the cross-disciplinary insights offered by historians, political scientists, and public administrators. The broad question underlying this collection of essays is to ask whether the time has now come for Parliamentary, judicial, and academic analyses of vexatious legal problems to engage in a more systematic process of border crossing in the geographical as well as interdisciplinary senses. It is now quite clear that that process of 'internationalization' is firmly established in our domestic law in respect of matters pertaining to the European Community. The contributors to this book have however cast their gaze in a rather different direction, to alight on certain aspects of the legal order of the United States of America.

An immediate impetus for such a study is provided by two recent decisions of the House of Lords, on matters of considerable political and moral significance, which were much influenced by the jurisprudence of the United States Supreme Court. In *Times Newspapers Ltd* v. *Derbyshire County Council*,[2] the House of Lords relied primarily on American case-law (rather than, as had the Court of Appeal, on an—in British terms—innovative application of the European Convention on Human Rights) in concluding that the public policy interests served by the common law prevented a local authority maintaining an action in libel to protect its political reputation.[3] The US precedents on which the House of Lords relied are, in American terms, long established principles which have subsequently undergone substantial extension and refinement.[4] This not

[1] My thanks to Trevor Allan, Carol Harlow, and especially Eric Barendt for making extensive comments on earlier drafts of this introduction.

[2] [1993] 1 All ER 1011.

[3] The propriety of the court doing so is discussed in Barendt's chapter in this volume, and also in E. Barendt, 'Libel and Freedom of Speech in English Law', [1993] *PL* 449: . Loveland, 'Defamation of Government: Taking Lessons from America', (1994a) 14 *Legal Studies* 22.

[4] For a brief guide see Loveland (1994a) *op. cit.*

unnaturally prompts one to wonder how much further domestic defamation law will be judicially reformed in the immediate future, and to what extent that reform will follow US developments. Having accepted counsel's invitation to open the First Amendment door, the House of Lords may soon find itself staking out a rather more expansive constitutional landscape.[5]

The House of Lords conducted a rather more extensive survey of American precedent in *Airedale NHS Trust* v. *Bland*.[6] Mr Bland was a victim of the Hillsborough football stadium tragedy, whose injuries had left him in a persistent vegetative state. The action had been brought by the Trust, with the support of Mr Bland's family, to seek a declaration that it was not unlawful for a doctor to withhold life preserving treatment in such circumstances. Lord Keith drew 'some comfort' from the fact that jurisdictions in the United States 'have with near unanimity concluded that it is not unlawful to discontinue medical treatment and care, including artificial feeding, to persistent vegetative state patients'.[7] Lords Goff, Mustill and Browne-Wilkinson made rather wider resort to both federal and State US precedent, in judgments which seemed to regard both American and Commonwealth decisions as authorities which could be interspersed unproblematically with decisions of British courts.

That the House of Lords has twice chosen in recent years to seek guidance from Supreme Court decisions is not in itself sufficient reason to assume that more wide-ranging scrutiny of American public law principle and practice is a worthwhile task.[8] To be more than a mere indulgence of academic curiosity, or an opportunistic search for speculative arguments to buttress counsel's opinions in apparently hopeless or novel causes, comparative analysis must demonstrate firstly a climate of receptivity in its host legal system—that legislators and judges are open in principle to non-domestic influences (whatever their source); and secondly a high degree of familiarity—that one's favoured foreign field has a landscape sufficiently similar to one's own to make exploration a worthwhile task. In respect of comparative US/UK analysis, the first precondition is a matter of present practice; the second one of historical principle.

[5] See A. Lester, 'No Place for a Politician to Hide', *The Guardian* 22 Nov. 1994.

[6] [1993] 1 All ER 821.

[7] *Id.*, 861–2.

[8] One might note that Lord Browne-Wilkinson's use of comparative analysis might impliedly be limited to cases (such as *Bland*) where the court faced 'a wholly new series of ethical and social problems'. [1993] 1 All ER 821, 878. Although one might then suggest that such a limitation in turn raises large questions as to the meanings of ethics and social ordering in a cross-cultural perspective.

RECEPTIVITY—EUROPEANIZATION AND INTERNATIONALIZATION

There is little doubt that the United Kingdom's membership of the EC, and its accession to the European Convention on Human Rights, have produced the first precondition. A substantial, if not the dominant cause of the judiciary's increasing willingness to look towards Europe as a source for public law principles is clearly the political reality of EC membership and European Convention on Human Rights accession, and the institutional realities therein of two supranational Courts.

These new realities have had (to borrow from the European Court of Justice's jurisprudential phrase book) direct and indirect effects on academic[9] and judicial understandings both of the current substance of the constitution's legal rules, and of the processes through which that substance may now legitimately be changed. The most dramatic departures from conventional constitutional orthodoxies have been the abandonment of the doctrine of implied repeal in relation to British statutes dealing with matters within the competence of the European Community;[10] the emergence of the principle that British courts may 'disapply' domestic legislation which contravenes our EU obligations;[11] and the acceptance of proportionality (via the European Court Justice's general principles of law) as a substantive ground of judicial review of government action in respect of matters with an EC dimension.[12]

The indirect effect of EC membership on domestic public law is harder to gauge, but in the long term may prove even more significant. One might wonder, for example, if the radical shift in techniques of statutory interpretation approved by the House of Lords in *Pepper* v. *Hart*[13] would have happened (at least so quickly) if our judges had not for the previous

[9] Indeed, the first two chapters of the third edition of Jeffrey Jowell & Dawn Oliver, *The Changing Constitution* (Oxford, 1994) are now Vernon Bogdanor's 'Britain and the European Community' and Anthony Lester's 'European Human Rights and the British Constitution'.

[10] *MacCarthys* v. *Smith* [1979] 3 All ER 325; *Garland* v. *British Rail Engineering Ltd* [1983] 2 AC 751.

[11] *R* v. *Secretary of State for Transport, ex parte Factortame* [1989] 2 CMLR 353: [1990] 2 AC 85: *(No. 2)* [1991] 1 All ER 70.

[12] See J. Jowell & A. Lester, 'Proportionality: Neither Novel Nor Dangerous', in Jowell J. & Oliver D. (eds.), *New Directions in Judicial Review* (London, 1988): M. Dauses, 'The Protection of Fundamental Rights in the Community Legal Order' (1985) 10 *ELR* 398: R. Dallen, 'An Overview of European Community Protection of Human Rights, with Some Special References to the UK' [1990] 27 *CMLR* 761: N. Grief, 'The Domestic Impact of the ECHR as Mediated Through Community Law' [1991] *PL* 555.

[13] [1992] 3 WLR 1032. The decision permits courts in some limited circumstances to make reference to Ministerial statements in the Commons or Lords as an aid to interpreting obscure or ambiguous statutory language, and thus represents a radical departure from the traditional principle that judges were to 'find' the intentions of Parliament only in the text of the statute they were interpreting.

twenty years been exposed to the teleological strategies of the European Court of Justice;[14] or if their Lordships' innovative decision in *In re M*[15] would have appeared if not for the previous acceptance of similar principles in relation to EC matters in *Factortame (No. 2)*.

Furthermore, in recent years, British judges and British courts[16] have become increasingly receptive to the idea that they might legitimately have explicit regard to the legal principles espoused by the domestic legal systems of our partner nations in the European Community, as well as to the jurisprudence of the European Court of Human Rights, when deciding the extent to which governmental and legislative activity of a purely domestic nature should be subject to judicial control.[17] For example, it now seems to be an orthodox principle of British administrative law that our courts should allow themselves to be guided by the Convention when faced with ambiguous questions of common law principle or statutory interpretation.[18] Some members of the judiciary also appear willing to accept that the Convention has been indirectly incorporated in respect of matters falling within the purview of EU law.[19]

But our domestic courts have (in some respects) gone further than the bare minimum required to uphold the UK's Treaty obligations. Neither Article 5 of the Treaty of Rome, nor sections 2–3 of the European Communities Act 1972, compel any spill over or ripple effect of EC derived principles into matters of purely domestic law, which seems to

[14] See e.g. the comments of Lord Denning in *Bulmer* v. *Bollinger* [1974] 3 WLR 202, 216 on the norms British judges would have to apply when interpreting the Treaty or EEC legislation: 'They must follow the European pattern. No longer must they examine the words in meticulous detail. No longer must they argue about the precise grammatical sense. They must look to the purpose or intent. . . . They must divine the spirit of the Treaty and gain inspiration from it. If they find a gap, they must fill it as best they can'. Denning immediately imported this principle into the interpretation of other international agreements: *Buchanan and Co Ltd* v. *Babco Forwarding and Shipping (UK) Ltd* [1977] 2 WLR 107. It nevertheless took the courts fifteen further years to accept that they could legitimately apply such interpretive techniques to domestic legislation in areas of EC competence: see *Pickstone* v. *Freemans plc* [1988] 2 All ER 213, a case much relied upon in *Pepper* v. *Hart*, which adopted precisely the methodology condemned by Viscount Simonds in *Magor and St. Mellens* v. *Newport Corporation* [1951] 2 All ER 839 as 'a naked usurpation of the legislative function'.

[15] [1994] 1 AC 377. *M* departed from traditional understandings as to the Crown's immunity from injunctive relief and the contempt jurisdiction.

[16] The distinction is drawn to reflect the fact that views a judge might hold as a matter of personal moral or political taste, and express through academic or popular writings, may not find their way into her judgments for what she regards as reasons of legal orthodoxy or constitutional conformity.

[17] The most influential recent expositions of the personal viewpoint being Lord Browne-Wilkinson, 'The Infiltration of a Bill of Rights' [1992] *PL* 397; and Sir John Laws, 'Is the High Court the Guardian of Fundamental Constitutional Rights?' [1993] *PL* 59.

[18] See the judgment of the Court of Appeal in *Derbyshire County Council* v. *Times Newspapers Ltd* [1992] 3 All ER 65.

[19] Browne-Wilkinson *op. cit.*

have been the case in decisions such as *Pepper* v. *Hart* and *In re M*, or, less significantly, the suggestion in *Doody* that the ECJ doctrine of 'transparency' might sensibly inform notions of procedural fairness in relation to domestic issues.[20] This indicates that the courts may on occasion be persuaded to see intrinsic attractions, not simply instrumental compulsions, in a greater receptivity to principles espoused in foreign jurisdictions.

Such attitudinal shifts need not amount to anything so grand as the reconstruction of the 'separation of powers' on a transnational basis, in which judges in all countries find that they share more philosophical and constitutional common ground with their continental colleagues than with their own respective legislatures and governments. They may however be seen as part of a more diffuse trend towards the 'internationalization' of the role played by law and the legal process in regulating citizen/state relations in modern western democracies.[21]

'Internationalization' may be regarded as a somewhat glib term, invoked as an expedient label to explain away developments in domestic legal theory which have no readily discernible root. To lend the concept a more tangible base, one might point to certain institutional factors, such as more frequent interchanges between politicians and lawyers, in which all are exposed more often and more deeply to the others' constitutional orthodoxies. Such influences are rather amorphous however. Similarly, one might highlight the increasing presence in domestic courts, whether as counsel or judge, of lawyers whose past appearances before the European Court of Justice or the European Court of Human Rights have made hitherto heterodox ideas an integral element of their legal armoury. The 'ideological baggage' carried (with admittedly varying degrees of enthusiasm) by legislators and lawyers has become increasingly cosmopolitan. If 'internationalization' is a glib term, it may be because the process itself is unavoidably elusive, amounting perhaps to little more than a state of mind or, alternatively, to an idea whose time has come.

The attitude taken in this volume towards 'Americanization' as a sub-current within the (to misquote Lord Denning) incoming internationalist tide is perhaps best characterized as 'open-minded scepticism'. As will become evident to the reader, some of the contributors are considerably more sceptical than others. The approach is much influenced by Otto

[20] *Doody* v. *Home Secretary* [1993] 3 All ER 92, per Lord Mustill 107.

[21] J. Koopmans, 'European Public Law—Reality and Prospects' [1991] *PL* 53: J. Schwarze, 'Tendencies Towards a Common Administrative Law in Europe' (1991) 16 *ELR* 3. Nor is the cross-fertilization limited to matters of public law. For a useful insight into the Europeanization of areas of private law see B. Markesenis (ed.), *The Gradual Convergence* (Oxford, 1994).

Kahn-Freund's celebrated 1974 article, 'On Uses and Misuses of Comparative Law'.[22] In particular, care has been taken to accommodate the observation that: 'The use of comparative law for practical purposes becomes an abuse only if it is informed by a legalistic spirit which ignores [the social and above all the political context] of the law'.[23] Kahn-Freund was concerned in part to emphasize that the growing convergence of political, economic, social, and cultural factors among the western democracies had undermined Montesqiueu's blunt warning that: '*Les lois politiques et civile de chaque nation . . . doivent être tellement propres au peuple pour lequel elles sont faites, que c'est un grand hazard si celles d'une nation peuvent convenir a une autre*'.[24]

In the twenty years since Kahn-Freund delivered his message, that convergence has proceeded apace, and so increased the chance that an international process of free trade in jurisprudential ideas will yield mutually beneficial results. The appearance of the 'global village' has further softened the jagged edges of transnational cultural pluralism, to the extent that one may now plausibly suggest, as Sir John Laws has recently done, that the countries of the western world are drifting in matters of public law towards a mutual recognition[25] in their respective legal systems of axiomatic democratic principles 'about whose desirability there can be no serious argument'.[26]

As a broad technique, selectively indulged, the search for axiomatic principles across national boundaries may appeal both to Parliament and the courts, and may with varying degrees of apparent legitimacy be resorted to by either branch of government. A sovereign legislature may look wherever it pleases for guidance to influence the contents of the laws it enacts. That Parliament has chosen sometimes to look to the United States is evidenced most clearly by its bequests to former colonies of constitutions containing supra-legislative protection of basic democratic and civil rights. Apparently, while the United Kingdom Parliament must be trusted always to uphold such timeless moral values as the rule of law and respect for individual liberty, and so may safely retain its legal sovereignty, such faith could not be placed in the emerging rulers of newly independent colonies. For their people, additional safeguards were required, ideally topped by a supra-legislative Supreme Court in the shape of the Privy Council. Observers familiar with the genesis of American revolutionary philosophy might find this trend particularly ironic, given that the elaborate vertical and horizontal separations of powers

[22] [1974] 37 *MLR* 1.
[23] *Id.*, 27.
[24] Quoted in Kahn-Freund *op. cit.*, 6.
[25] Itself of course the term used to describe the EC's approach to harmonization since 1986.
[26] *Op. cit.*, 60.

institutionalized in the 1787–1791 constitutional settlement reflected the colonists' assumption that all political cultures (but especially Britain's) were far too corrupt to allow its legislators unlimited legal power to enact any measure which commanded simple majority support.[27]

In the domestic sphere, the most pertinent modern example of Parliament importing American experience is perhaps the Race Relations Act 1976. In terms both of its substance, and its methods of enforcement, that legislation drew heavily (but not uncritically) on the USA's long and often painful entanglement in the problems posed by racial discrimination.[28] Several of the chapters in this volume suggest that that practice might usefully be repeated in respect of some currently controversial legal matters. Genevra Richardson addresses the issue of legal regulation of privatized prisons, Ian Loveland considers the desirability of creating a specific criminal offence of racist violence, while Martin Wasik assesses the benefits that might accrue from a selective importation of the principles informing American sentencing policy. In contrast, the chapters by Ewing and Barendt argue in forceful terms that in such important areas as freedom of expression and the regulation of political parties Parliament would be well advised to reject any proposals for thorough reform along American lines.

Parliamentary acceptance of invitations to legislate in imitation of American law raise obvious questions of constitutional legitimacy, notwithstanding the rigour with which legislators evaluate the ideas before them, insofar it may be construed as betokening a cultural deference which dilutes a nation's *de facto* 'sovereignty' in the modern world. For **Parliament**, the questions of legality are, in contrast, generally straightforward. But no such assumption can be made in respect of the use the **courts** might make of US law. Legitimacy may be much the larger issue whenever British judges produce innovative decisions, but rather narrower questions of legality also arise. A recurrent theme of this collection of essays, however, is that judicial room for manoeuvre in both respects is often substantially underestimated.

Irrespective of the impact of EC membership on the judiciary's legitimate scope for constitutional innovation, we should not permit the dull orthodoxy of traditional theories of legislative supremacy to blind us to the extraordinary level of autonomy which our courts have exercised in

[27] E. Corwin, 'The Higher Law Background of American Constitutional Law (Part II)' (1929) 42 *Harvard LR* 365: L. Levy, 'Introduction—the Making of the Constitution', in Levy L. *The Making of the Constitution* (New York, 1987): B. Bailyn, *The Ideological Origins of the American Revolution* esp. 199–227 (Cambridge, Mass., 1967).

[28] J. Solomos, 'Equal Opportunites Policies and Racial Inequality: the Role of Public Policy', (1989) 67 *Public Administration* 79: A. Lester, 'Discrimination: What Lawyers can Learn From History' [1994a] *PL* 224.

developing the common law and interpreting statutory criteria. Parliament may reverse judicial decisions of which it disapproves, but it places no pre-emptive controls on the dynamicism of the common law. That process remains a matter for the courts. It may be shaped by internal factors, such as the recognition of new norms of business/consumer relationships (*Donoghue* v. *Stevenson*[29]), or the rediscovery of long neglected principles of constitutional propriety (*Woolwich Building Society* v. *Inland Revenue*[30]); by (*MacCarthys* v. *Smith and Factortame (No. 2)*) entirely external influences; as well as (*M* and *Pepper* v. *Hart*) a mixture of the two. And if we accept that the clear blue waters surrounding our island kingdom constitute only a physical and not a jurisprudential frontier—that our legal system satisfies the criterion of receptivity—we might wonder if our attention might just as sensibly be directed westwards as well as to the south, to alight on the already matured United States of America rather than the nascent united states of Europe, in the expectation that what we find there meets the test of familiarity.

FAMILIARITY—ENGLISH COMMON LAW AND THE AMERICAN CONSTITUTION: A SPECIAL (LEGAL) RELATIONSHIP?

Prior to the aforementioned decisions in *Derbyshire* and *Bland*, British courts had made scant reference to principles drawn from the jurisprudence of Federal or State courts in the United States as a guide for the exercise of judicial discretion in relation to public law matters. So sweeping a generalization has rather less force in the academic sphere. Wade and Schwarz's comparative study of administrative law in the early 1970s is an obvious exception to the rule.[31] Equally significant was Jerome Elkind's rather more wide-ranging 1978 work, *The Impact of American Law on English and Commonwealth Law*.[32] In his introduction to Elkind's volume, Leonard Leigh suggested it was a 'first and worthwhile step' on a potentially fruitful journey.[33] But since then, the comparative pickings have been rather thin. Notable contributions can be identified, foremost among them Eric Barendt's *Freedom of Speech* and Paul Craig's *Public Law and Democracy in Britain and the USA*.[34] Relatedly, Craig's *Administrative Law* and Carol Harlow and Rick Rawlings' *Law and Administration*[35] each dwell at sufficient length on American jurisprudence

[29] [1932] AC 562.
[30] [1993] AC 70.
[31] H. W. R. Wade & B. Schwarz, *Legal Control of Government: Administrative Law in Britain and the United States* (London, 1972).
[32] (St. Paul, Minnesota).
[33] *Id.*, viii.
[34] (Oxford, 1987); and (Oxford, 1990) respectively.
[35] (London, 1994 3rd ed.); and (London, 1984) respectively.

in their early stages to make their subsequent resort to comparative critique a fluent and pertinent aid to understanding the strengths or weaknesses of indigenous principles. One might also point to a small number of influential articles on explicitly comparative themes, generally focusing on questions of supra-legislative fundamental rights.[36]

But the sparsely populated nature of this particular academic field is perhaps surprising, for a number of reasons. The first of these, all too easily forgotten when one views the profound institutional divergences between the US and UK systems of government, is that the political ends each country's constitution is presumed to serve derive from the same political roots.[37] The concern of such philosopher revolutionaries as Franklin, Madison, and Jefferson was not to abandon the common and natural law principles they assumed the British constitution existed to protect, but to fashion practical safeguards to minimize the chances of those principles being corrupted by the invariably venal reality of the government process. The 'self-evident truths' adverted to in the Declaration of Independence did not spring Athena-like from Jefferson's brow, but were firmly rooted in a coherent and forceful strand of (radical) British constitutional theory.[38] Bernard Bailyn's wonderful study of the gradual consolidation of the American revolutionary consciousness illustrates this point with startling force across the entire sweep of the Constitution's subsequent structure;[39] although from a lawyer's perspective, the influence of *Dr Bonham's Case* on the emergence of the doctrine of judicial review may provide a more accessible reference point.[40]

The difficulties and attractions of comparative US/UK analysis are pursued at length by Roger Cotterrell and T. R. S. Allan in chapters one and two. Cotterrell's essay dwells on the symbolic role performed by constitutional structures to suggest that the US model is an inapposite tool

[36] S. Lee 'Bicentennial Bork, Tercentennial Spycatcher: Do the British Need a Bill of Rights?' (1988) 49 *U Pitt. LR* 777: P. Fitzgerald, 'An English Bill of Rights: Some Observations from Her Majesty's Former Colonies in America', (1982) 70 *Georgetown LJ* 1229: J. Skelly Wright, 'The Bill of Rights in Britain and America: a Not Quite Full Circle', (1981) 55 *Tulane LR* 291. In the area of administrative law, R. Baldwin & K. Hawkins, 'Discretionary Justice: Davis Reconsidered' [1984] *PL* 570 provides considerable insight into the potential and limits of cross-national theoretical analysis, while among contributions of a slightly older vintage, the outstanding example is J. Jowell, 'The Legal Control of Administrative Discretion' [1973] *PL* 178.

[37] See especially on this point Corwin *op. cit.* A more sceptical contemporaneous view is offered in T. Plucknett, 'Bonham's Case and Judicial Review' (1926) 39 *Harvard LR* 30.

[38] See particularly D. Rabban, 'The Original Meaning of the Free Speech Clause of the First Amendment', in R. Simmons (ed.), *The US Constitution—the First Two Hundred Years* (Manchester, 1988): P. Maier, 'John Wilkes and American Disillusionment with Britain' (1963) *William and Mary Quarterly* 373.

[39] *Op. cit.*

[40] Corwin *op. cit.*: Plucknett *op. cit.*: S. Thorne, 'Dr Bonham's Case' (1938) 54 *LQR* 543.

for the development of UK public law. Allan, in contrast, in focusing on the somewhat narrower task of identifying common political principles which courts might deploy to regulate both legislative and executive autonomy, suggests that a considerable degree of interchangeability is both possible and desirable. This theme is lent a sharper, more legalistic focus, by Paul Craig, in a chapter which assesses the efforts of the Supreme Court and the House of Lords to fashion coherent answers to the difficult question of how to define the jurisdiction of executive bodies; and by Peter Cane's analysis of the issue of *locus standi* in administrative law. Peter Fitzpatrick then addresses questions of jurisdiction and *locus standi* at a considerably more rarefied level, and identifies an area of constitutional jurisprudence so clearly specific to the USA, yet so central to the development of its public law, that one might begin to wonder if any meaningful transatlantic congress is possible. Carol Harlow also offers, like Cotterrell, a sceptical viewpoint, in suggesting that the disparities in the government structures the two countries have adopted severely undermine the utility of cross-fertilization in many areas of administrative law.

A second, more pragmatic justification for careful perusal of the American experience is that the United States has long been grappling with issues which are now being forced on to the British political agenda, and might thus be thought to offer valuable guidance (be it positive or negative) to British lawmakers. The aforementioned chapters by Richardson, Wasik, Loveland, Ewing, and Barendt all embrace this source of knowledge in respect of specific issues. But American experience might also now be thought of great value to the development of British constitutional and administrative law in a rather more pervasive, practical sense.

The debate over 'federalism' within the EU is the obvious example. The arguments advanced by contemporary British Euro-sceptics bear a startling similarity to those offered by the Anti-Federalists in the United States during the struggle to ratify the Constitution in the late 1780s.[41] The parallels between British Euro-sceptics' desire for a loose alliance of Sovereign European States, and the system of United States government existing under the Articles of Confederation are too precise to ignore—from grandiose concerns over the location of 'sovereignty', to detailed issues such as the desirability of a single currency, common military forces, and the protection of indigenous fishing industries. One also sees seductive

[41] J. Main, 'The Anti-Federalists', in B. Ollman & J. Birmbaum (eds.), *The United States Constitution* (New York, 1990). For a contemporaneous critique see *The Federalist Papers Nos. 10, 14, 19, 20, 45, & 46*. In the modern British context see I. Loveland, *Constitutional Law* ch. 12 (London, 1996 forthcoming).

similarities in contemporary European protestations about the 'creeping competence' of the ECJ, and the fury of Southern States in the 1950s and 1960s at the Warren Court's 'nationalization' of civil liberties issues.[42]

Relatedly, the now plausible prospect of a Blair-led Labour government promising some degree of internal federalization of the United Kingdom, a non-hereditary second chamber for the central legislature, and the incorporation (if not entrenchment) of the European Convention on Human Rights, all speak to matters which the USA accepted as fundamental constitutional principles over two hundred years ago. It is perhaps a crude analogy to find in Blair's vision of community echoes of Madison's overriding fear of factional government, or in Delors' vision of an ever closer union of European states similar echoes of Madison's forceful arguments on federalism.[43] But it would be extraordinarily myopic to assume we had nothing of value to learn from the political principles underlying the formative stages of America's constitutional settlement.

Such myopia would be even less forgivable in respect of subsequent US developments. *Pepper* v. *Hart* has opened the door in this country for the development of the doctrine of original intent to play a major part in the art of statutory interpretation. There is surely no better guide to the potential and the limitations of that doctrine than the jurisprudence of the US Supreme Court.[44] Some British commentators have latterly identified that need, but the task itself has yet to be begun.[45] More broadly, one should not forget that the drafters of the European Convention on Human Rights were much influenced by US principles and practice, and therefore at one further step removed, by common law entitlements.[46] To that extent, at least, we have unknowingly absorbed many invisible lessons from America into our legal system.[47]

[42] See particularly the decisions of the German Federal Constitutional Court in *Internationale Handelsgesellschaft* [1972] 2 CMLR 540 and of the French Conseil D'Etat in *Cohin-Bendit* [1980] 1 CMLR 543. In the American context, the obvious reference points are *Brown* v. *Board of Education* (1954) 347 US 438 and *Cooper* v. *Aaron* (1958) 358 US 1.

[43] Respectively in *The Federalist Papers* Nos. 10 & 39.

[44] See H. Powell, 'Rules for Originalists' (1987) 73 *Virginia LR* 659: P. Brest, 'The Misconceived Quest for Original Understanding', (1980) 60 *Boston ULR* 204. And there is perhaps no more fascinating question within that topic than whether our courts will be attracted to Earl Warren's concept of 'evolving purpose', whereby the 'intent' behind legislation would not be that of the Parliament which introduced the Act, but of the Parliament which tolerated its continued existence; see Warren's judgments in *McGowan* v. *Maryland* (1961) 366 US 420; *Braunfield* v. *Brown* (1961) 366 US 599, and fn. 79 below and accompanying text.

[45] R. Rawlings, 'Legal Politics: the United Kingdom and the Ratification of the Treaty on European Union (Part One)' [1994] *PL* 254, 256 & n.7.

[46] A. Lester, 'The Overseas Trade in the American Bill of Rights' (1988) 88 *Columbia LR* 537.

[47] *Id.*: W. Brennan (1989) 'Why Have a Bill of Rights?', (1989) 9 *OJLS* 425.

AN EBBING TIDE OF JUDICIAL HOSTILITY?

This is not to say that, prior to 1990, one cannot discern instances of our judges paying explicit attention to US principles: the reception has however often been less than welcoming. One of the most memorable judicial references to the American public law experience is Lord Reid's blunt rejection of principles limiting the government's tortious liability in respect of property damage caused by absconding prisoners in *Dorset Yacht Co Ltd* v. *Home Office*.[48] Lord Reid's suggestion that we British were made of sterner stuff than our American counterparts, and thus had no need of public law rules according government agencies protection over and above that extended to private citizens, can be seen in one sense as a reiteration of Dicey's hostility towards any suggestion that the British constitution needed to develop a distinctive 'public law' to regulate governmental action. But it also betokens a more pervasive judicial arrogance concerning the superiority of our political and thence constitutional culture.

An obvious, recent illustration of this attitude is Lord Donaldson MR's refusal even to address counsel's suggestion in *R* v. *Boundary Commission, ex parte Foot* that US litigation on constituency apportionment might offer helpful principles with which to resolve ambiguities in the UK's own legislation.[49] Similar insularity was displayed in Lord Ackner's dismissive reference during the *Spycatcher* saga to the suggestion made by the *Guardian's* counsel that the common law solution to the problem before the court might sensibly draw on the lessons offered by the USA's prolonged and closely argued experience with balancing the competing claims of press freedom and national security. Ackner, noted, somewhat acerbically, that:

> [American] courts, by virtue of the First Amendment, are, I understand, powerless to control the press. Fortunately the press in this country is, as yet, not above the law, although like some other organisations they would like that to be so, that is, until they require the law's protection.[50]

Lord Ackner's statement exemplifies a tradition of somewhat ill informed constitutional isolationism. One might immediately question his Lordship's evident attachment to the Diceyan fiction that no one in Britain was above the law: *Spycatcher* was decided at a time (prior to *Factortame* and *M*)

[48] [1970] AC 1004.

[49] [1983] 1 QB 600. For detailed comment see I. Loveland, 'Positive Discrimination and Fair Electoral Representation in the United States', [1994] *PL* 332.

[50] *Attorney-General* v. *Guardian Newspapers* [1987] 1 WLR 1248, 1306.

when Ministers of the Crown were clearly 'above' the law in respect of their immunity from injunctions and the contempt jurisdiction.

Furthermore, Lord Ackner's evidently blunt denial that comparative US/UK analysis could have any value at all to resolving the problem before him seems to be premised on a quite inadequate understanding of the comparators presented. Lord Ackner's suggestion that the press, or any other institution or individual, whether in the governmental or private sectors, is 'above the law' in the United States is difficult to understand. It reveals more about the occasionally stunted nature of the British judicial consciousness than it does about the realities of press freedom in America. The First Amendment is no less 'law' because it occupies a superior constitutional position to Congressional legislation, Presidential fiat, or any State activity. On the contrary, insofar as one sees 'law' as a behavioural code which commands respect because of the intrinsic merit of its substantive ideas, rather than its mere source in a legislature or a court, the First Amendment is law in an unusually pure form. If the First Amendment cannot be construed as 'law' within the British constitutional paradigm, it is because its status as law in the United States depends more on its legitimacy than its legality. Had Lord Ackner said that the First Amendment placed press freedom above those 'laws' made by intolerant or irrational politicians enjoying a bare legislative majority, his view would have been defensible. He would also, one assumes, be describing the constitutional position adopted by many western democracies—but not, of course, his own.

It is similarly difficult to sustain the argument that the First Amendment is somehow beyond judicial control. One can readily point to decisions in which federal courts have upheld restraints on press freedom in defence of other countervailing constitutional pressures; the complex line of case law regulating press freedom to publicize matters which may jeopardize the impartial administration of justice is an obvious example.[51] Nor does it demand an intimate familiarity with the First Amendment to appreciate the force of Holmes J's observation that free expression could never extend to the right to shout 'Fire' in a crowded theatre or to the right to publish details of troop movements in time of war.[52]

The shortcomings of such attitudes are perhaps more methodological than substantive (insofar as questions of process and outcome can meaningfully be separated). As suggested above, a guiding theme of this book is the presumption that while the constitutions of modern western democracies may share a good deal of common ground, the details of their public law cartography will inevitably vary, as those legal rules are

[51] *Gannet Co* v. *DePasquale* (1979) 443 US 368: *Richmond Newspapers Inc* v. *Virginia* (1980) 448 US 555.

[52] *Schenck* v. *United States* (1919) 249 US 47.

designed to express the heterogeneity of their respective nation's 'culture, history, and political structure'.[53] One should not therefore expect that overseas solutions to given problems can simply be integrated unmodified into our domestic law. Consequently, a penchant for reasoned dismissal of foreign experience is something to be welcomed in our highest court when it is addressing contentious political issues. It might thus be argued that the 'seamless web' approach to the integration of American precedent into the English common law adopted by some members of the House of Lords in *Bland* amounts to an overly-enthusiastic embrace of foreign influence.

More evidently defensible judicial strategies can be identified however, in which foreign precedents are used not mechanistically to determine the outcome of domestic litigation, but: 'to promote a higher degree of judicial consciousness of the importance of fundamental liberties in the shaping of the common law'.[54] The most sophisticated example of such a technique is perhaps Lord Scarman's dissenting opinion in *Home Office* v. *Harman*.[55] To American eyes, the notion that there was a triable issue on the facts of *Harman* would seem quite bizarre. For the majority of the House of Lords however, the presumption that a solicitor could be in contempt of court for providing a journalist with documents that had been read out in open court was evidently an entirely orthodox proposition of British law.

In dissent, Scarman carefully explained why he attached 'powerfully persuasive' influence to American case law which would preclude any legal sanction being attached to an action such as Harman's if undertaken in the United States. He emphasized the shared foundations of the common law (as he perceived it) and the USA's constitutional jurisprudence by drawing on Milton's *Aeropagitica*, the sentiments of which ('Give me the liberty to know to utter, and to argue freely according to conscience, above all liberties') are frequently invoked as the philosophical root of the First Amendment in both judicial and academic writings.[56] Lord Scarman continued by observing that the US Bill of Rights did not reject British constitutional 'tradition', but rejected the institutional structure which left 'tradition' at the mercy of a sovereign legislature: 'Americans made into fundamental constitutional law what they saw as the basic rights vouchsafed to them by their heritage of the common law'.[57] Scarman's claim precisely echoes the sentiment of Justice Holmes in *Gompers* v. *United States*: 'The provisions of the Constitution are not mathematical formulas having their essence in their form: they are organic living

[53] Brennan *op. cit.*, 425.

[54] H. Lee, 'The Australian High Court and Implied Fundamental Guarantees' [1993] *PL* 606, 616.

[55] [1983] 4 AC 280.

[56] e.g. L. Fisher, *Constitutional Rights: Civil Rights and Civil Liberties* (New York, 1990) ch. 11: L. Levy, *Emergence of a Free Press* (New York, 1985), 93–7.

[57] At 311.

institutions transplanted from English soil'.[58] As such, basic principles (if not the detailed superstructure) of First Amendment jurisprudence should be considered a pertinent guide to the development of English law.

Furthermore, Lord Scarman recognized, (as Lord Ackner in *Spycatcher* did not), that the First Amendment did not make press freedom an absolute value, but one that would have to be balanced against (and occasionally give way to) countervailing constitutional interests. Preventing Harman's disclosure served no such compelling cause. Thus while her behaviour would have been constitutionally protected in the USA, it would be so as a matter of its relative, not absolute, importance.

As the previous discussion of *Times Newspapers* v. *Derbyshire County Council* would suggest, the present majority in the House of Lords appears rather more approving of Scarman's approach when it is faced with free speech issues. Eric Barendt argues in chapter 9 that there is much scope for judicial importation of First Amendment jurisprudence into British law. Whether the outcomes produced by such principles would be desirable in the British context is, Barendt suggests, far from clear. There is however little doubt that one justifiably might have more confidence in the rectitude of one's own country's response to a given public law problem if alternative solutions have been rejected after careful and informed consideration.

The need for such detailed scrutiny becomes all the more apparent when one recalls that many of the American principles which this book examines are highly contested as matters of United States law. This highlighting of the marked contingency of the solutions to particular problems adopted in the USA emphasizes the point that the comparative public lawyer, whether her focus is on abstract matters of constitutional principle, on legislative policy choices, or on the intricacies of judicial precedent, is well advised to remind herself that her effort is better directed towards a search for ideas than a hunt for authorities.

It may however be that such a cautious methodology is in itself insufficient to convince Anglo-centric observers that the US Supreme Court could ever be an appropriate source of substantive inspiration for domestic lawmakers. That the Americans fought a revolution to free themselves from the British constitution, and thereafter fashioned both a federal division of powers and a supra-legislative Supreme Court, might suggest that the United States is simply too 'different' from Britain to permit meaningful comparison. One might seek to assuage, if not dispel, such scepticism by pointing to the way US precedents have been used in legal systems whose detachment from the British constitution was the result of consensual negotiation rather than violent revolution, and within

[58] (1914) 233 US 604, 610.

which the structure and style of government corresponds far more closely to a Westminster-like model of Parliamentary democracy.

BRIDGING THE GAP? LESSONS FROM AMERICA IN INDIA, CANADA AND AUSTRALIA

The limited impact of American jurisprudence on British public law litigation is perhaps the more surprising when one considers the enthusiasm with which United States' case-law has been embraced by other ('new' and 'old') Commonwealth countries in recent years. As Anthony Lester has observed, Indian public law has had no qualms about allowing its evolution to be guided by American rather than British constitutional principles.[59] The deep penetration of American orthodoxies into India's public law culture is neatly illustrated by the opening paragraphs of a recent survey of developments in Indian administrative law. Soli Sorabjee, formerly Attorney General of India, couches 'the problem' the Indian judiciary faces in explicitly Madisonian terms: '[Y]ou must first enable the government to control the governed: and in the next place oblige it to control itself'.[60]

The 'discovery' of a supra-legislative right to procedural due process in the *Manneka Gandhi*[61] case is a shining example of the Americanesque 'controls' fashioned by the Indian judiciary. More significant perhaps, as an example of an importing jurisdiction's awarenss of the historical context on which it draws, was the Indian Supreme Court's resort in *Gujarat* v. *Shri Ambica Mills*[62] to its US counterpart's landmark pro-New Deal decision *West Coast Hotel* v. *Parish*[63] to rebut substantive due process objections to government regulation of economic affairs.

In a more pervasive vein, Lester cites the Indian Supreme Court's explanation in *Uttar Pradesh* v. *Deoman Puadhyaya* of its frequent resort to US jurisprudence when interpreting its own constitution's equal protection provisions:

> It may reasonably be assumed that our Constituent Assembly when it enshrined the guarantee of equal protection . . . was aware of its content delimited by judicial interpretation in the United States of America. In considering the authorities of the superior courts in the United States, we would not therefore be incorporating principles foreign to our constitution.[64]

[59] (1988) *op. cit.*

[60] S. Sorabjee, 'Obliging Government to Control Itself: Recent Developments in Indian Administrative Law', [1994] *PL* 39.

[61] *Maneka Gandhi* v. *Union* (1978) 2 SCR 621.

[62] (1974) 61 AIR (SC) 1300.

[63] (1936) 300 US 379.

[64] (1960) 47 AIR (SC) 1125; cited in Lester (1994) *op. cit.*, 547.

British devotees of First Amendment jurisprudence, whose expectations of influencing domestic law on matters affecting freedom of expression were afforded a perhaps unexpected legitimacy by the *Derbyshire* judgment, will no doubt also point to the 1994 Indian Supreme Court decision in *Rajogopal* v. *State of Tamil Nadu*.[65] In *Rajagopal*, the Court amended Indian common law rules on defamation in order to preclude any such action by government bodies. Furthermore, actions by politicians or government officials in respect of accounts of their official conduct would not succeed, even if the accounts contained factual errors 'unless the official establishes that the publication was made [by the defendant] with reckless disregard for truth'.[66]

The judgment quoted extensively from Brennan J.'s opinion in *New York Times* v. *Sullivan*.[67] *Sullivan* had concluded that the English common law rules on defamation which most States retained were incompatible with the First Amendment's protection of free speech. Henceforth, politicans and government officials would succeed in such actions only if they proved both the falsity of the impugned report and recklessness as to its truth on the defendant's part; any test which was more favourable to the plaintiff would unacceptably 'chill' public debate over governmental issues. The Indian Supreme Court in *Rajagopal* concluded that while the details of the *Sullivan* doctrine could not unthinkingly be transplanted into the Indian context, the 'major premises' underlying both countries' attitudes to freedom of discussion of government affairs were sufficiently similar for *Sullivan* to serve as a point of departure for reform of domestic common law.

The degree to which American legal principle has permeated Indian culture has also recently been demonstrated by Vikram Seth's epic novel of post-independence India, *A Suitable Boy*.[68] A key element of the plot concerns the constitutionality of state land redistribution legislation. The case-law presented at the trial is characterized as 'an ecumenical fricassee of Hodge v The Queen, Jatindra Nath Gupta v Province of Bihar, and Schechter Poultry Corp v the United States';[69] a key line of authority is US Supreme Court decisions on the equal protection clause of the Fourteenth Amendment; and the principal reference point for guidance on the legitimate scope of legislative delegation is Cooley's *Constitutional Limitations*. Seth brilliantly illustrates the conceptual and cultural difficulties facing judges reared on British traditions when faced with novel American-inspired ideas when the Chief Justice cautions counsel against

[65] The case was decided on 7 Oct. For early comment see A. Noorani, 'Rights and Wrongs: Issues of Libel and Press Freedom', *Frontline* 30 Dec. 1994, 100–2.

[66] *Id.*, 101.

[67] (1964) 376 US 254.

[68] (London, 1993).

[69] *Id.*, 691.

'crossing the Atlantic for your arguments'. As counsel points out in response, one would more rationally cross the Pacific, not the Atlantic, to reach the USA from India.[70] A further illustration of the cultural force of Anglo–American principles within India's constitutional tradition is adverted to a little later in the book, when a troubled civil servant draws on Harold Laski's analysis of the separation of powers in rebutting a Congress official's efforts to use government resources to boost his party's campaign funds.

Laski, of course, remained intimately connected throughout his academic and political life with the prevailing currents of American public law jurisprudence. His lengthy correspondence with Oliver Wendell Holmes is an illustration of the Anglo–American 'special relationship' in its most human and intimate form.[71] There is however, no need to equate easy familiarity with American ideas with uncritical acceptance of the principles and practices they espouse. This is perhaps best illustrated by the controversy currently engendered in Canada as to the legitimacy of Canadian courts using American interpretations of the US Bill of Rights to structure interpretation of Canada's recently introduced Charter of Rights.[72] Canada is a more appropriate bridge than India from a UK perspective, insofar as such 'fundamental' provisions which the Canadian Constitution has contained since 1982 are entrenched only against *implied* statutory repeal, and not against explicit legislative intrusion.[73]

Since the enactment of the Charter of Rights, Canadian courts have looked with growing frequency to US Supreme Court decisions.[74] In broad terms, much of the Canadian debate has centred on the fear that American constitutional jurisprudence is underpinned by a distinctively individualist ethos, an ethos ill suited to settling constitutional issues in Canada's arguably more communitarian political environment.[75] Such concerns

[70] (London, 1993), 690.

[71] M. Howe, *Holmes—Laski Letters Volumes I and II* (London, 1953).

[72] P. Manfredi,'The Canadian Supreme Court and American Judicial Review: United States Constitutional Jurisprudence and the Canadian Charter of Rights and Freedoms', (1992) 86 *American J. of Comparative Law* 213: P. Bender, 'The Canadian Charter of Rights and Freedoms and the United States Bill of Rights: a Comparison' (1983) 28 *McGill LJ* 811.

[73] On the parallels between this situation and the UK courts' initial reponse to s.2 of the European Communities Act 1972 see T. R. S. Allan, 'Parliamentary Sovereignty: Lord Denning's Dexterous Revolution' (1983) 3 *OJLS* 23.

[74] S. Bushnell, 'The Use of American Cases' (1986) 35 *U. of North Brunswick LJ* 157.

[75] P. Hogg, 'The Charter of Rights and American Theories of Interpretation', (1987) 25 *Osgoode Hall LJ* 87. If correct, that view would perhaps increase the applicability of US law to the British context. Those members of the British judiciary who have of late shown themselves more assertive in controlling governmental power have been so in defence of individual rather than collective rights; Browne-Wilkinson LJ's dissenting speech in *Wheeler* v. *Leicester City Council* [1985] AC 1054 being perhaps the paradigmatic example. See A. Hutchinson & M. Jones, '*Wheeler*-Dealing: an Essay on Law, Politics and Speech' (1988) 15 *JLS* 263.

seem somewhat overstated, since the Canadian Supreme Court appears to deploy the detail of US case law more as a point of departure than a final destination. That is not to say, however, that the Canadian judiciary has not enthusiastically welcomed some broad American principles.

The first Supreme Court judgment in the post-Charter era, *Law Society of Upper Canada* v. *Skapinker*[76] drew approvingly on Marshall CJ's celebrated characterization of judicial review as an expansive tool, and of constitutions as substantively dynamic legal norms, in *McCulloch* v. *Maryland*.[77] In so doing, the Supreme Court claimed for itself (as did Marshall for his own court) rather more constitutional authority than the Framers of the 1982 settlement may have envisaged. Subsequently, in *Hunter* v. *Southam*, Dickson CJ expounded a manifestly teleological theory of Charter interpretation which would seem almost to compel, not merely empower, the Supreme Court to take heed of the jurisprudence of other western democracies. Canadian courts should adopt: 'a broad purposive analysis, which interprets specific provisions of a constitutional document in the light of its larger objects'.[78] The Court has not suggested that the USA is the sole overseas supplier of such 'larger objects'. Moreover on those occasions when it has perused American case law, the results—in terms of whether American rules are appropriate regulators for Canadian behaviour—have been mixed. However the methodology has been uniformly thorough and searching; adoption or rejection of US precedent has entailed a reasoned, contextualized discussion of its applicability to Canadian society.

A cogent example (with both UK and EC resonance) is provided by the Court's treatment of Canada's Sunday Trading laws. Rather than approach the controversy as a uniquely Canadian problem, the Court made copious reference to the Warren Court's exploration of the issue some twenty-five years earlier. Warren had used these cases to articulate the so-called 'evolving purpose' doctrine.[79] When **introduced**, the legislation before the Court had been motivated by religious discrimination. But that legislation was now **retained** for the avowedly secular objective of limiting the total hours that employees in certain industries could be compelled to work. The initial motive contravened the First Amendment, the current motive did not. In upholding the statutes in question, the Warren Court in effect concluded that the evolving purpose doctrine allowed 'creeping secularization' to wash away the taint of religious bigotry which would have rendered the legislation incompatible with the First Amendment.

In *R* v. *Big M Drug Mart*,[80] the Canadian Supreme Court produced a

[76] (1984) 9 DLR (4th) 161.

[77] (1819) 17 US 316.

[78] (1984) 11 DLR (4th) 641, 650; cited in Manfredi *op. cit.*, 216.

[79] *McGowan* v. *Maryland* (1961) 366 US 420: *Braunfield* v. *Brown* (1961) 366 US 599.

[80] (1985) 18 DLR (4th) 321.

reasoned rejection (premised on Canada's history as a Parliamentary form of democracy) of the 'evolving purpose' interpretive technique as a general principle, and the substantive outcomes to which it led in Sabbath observance cases. The Court's decision in *Retail, Wholesale and Department Store Union* v. *Dolphin Delivery Ltd*[81] employed a similar methodology in outlining the fundamental tenets underpinning the First Amendment's protection of picketing during labour disputes, and then explaining why the combined impact of the text of the Charter and Canada's differing perceptions of public policy led to the conclusion that a prohibition on secondary picketing was a legitimate interference with freedom of speech.

In contrast, the Court adopted the US concept of 'commercial free speech' in *Ford* v. *Quebec*[82] to invalidate a Quebec law requiring business to advertise only in French. Similarly, the Court empathized with American rather than British precedent in determining the limits of 'justiciability' in the *Operation Dismantle* judgment.[83] The Candian judiciary has also made frequent and critical use of US law in respect of criminal procedure,[84] while observing that 'American decisions can be transplanted to the Canadian context only with the greatest caution'.[85] This is perhaps most evident in respect of the the *Sullivan* v. *New York Times* doctrine referred to so approvingly by Lord Keith in the *Derbyshire* case and by the Indian Supreme Court in *Rajagopal*. Canadian courts have consistently declined invitations to import *Sullivan*, whether directly into the common law, or via the Charter of Rights, in order to amend domestic defamation laws.[86] Once again, however, the substantive outcome is perhaps of less significance than the process through which it was reached: namely a carefully reasoned rather than simply instinctive rejection of American principle.

Recent Australian experience provides a further illustration of the general exportability of American doctrine for use as an evaluative tool. In constitutional terms, Australia may be distinguished from Canada in several important respects. The Australian High Court has, for example, long recognized an implied (and thus judicially created) legal barrier to federal legislative attempts to reallocate power between the central and state governments.[87] In Canada, in contrast, any such barrier enjoyed only

[81] (1986) 33 DLR (4th) 174.

[82] (1988) 54 DLR (4th) 577.

[83] *Operation Dismantle* v. *The Queen* (1985) 18 DLR (4th) 481.

[84] R. Harvie & H. Foster, 'Ties That Bind? The Supreme Court of Canada, American Jurisprudence, and the Revision of Canadian Criminal Law under the Charter', (1990) 28 *Osgoode Hall LJ* 729.

[85] Per Dickson CJ, quoted in Manfredi *op. cit.*, 231.

[86] *Coates* v. *The Citizen* (1988) NSR (2d.) 146: *Derrickson* v. *Tomat* (1992) 88 DLR 4th 401.

[87] *Western Australia* v. *Commonwealth* (1975) 134 CLR 202: *Queensland* v. *Commonwealth* (1977) 139 CLR 585.

conventional status prior to the 1982 reforms.[88] Equally importantly, Australia does not as yet possess an explicit supra-Parliamentary Bill of Rights, such as those contained in Canada's Charter. Yet while (pre-Charter) the Canadian courts firmly resisted invitations to fashion an 'implied bill of rights' to constrain federal legislative autonomy,[89] the Australian High Court has lately been pursuing that path with considerable (American influenced) enthusiasm.

The federal legislation at issue in *Nationwide News Party Ltd* v. *Wills*,[90] section 299 of the Industrial Relations Act 1988, bore an uncanny resemblance to the notorious 1798 Sedition Act employed by John Adams' Federalists to silence the dissent of Jeffersonian Republicans.[91] Section 299 criminalized any written or oral expression, even if true, designed to bring the Australian Industrial Relations Commission or its members into disrepute. The Sedition Act was repealed before its constitutionality was tested by the Supreme Court. Section 299 suffered a more ignominious fate: a unanimous High Court invalidated it. The minority found the statute unconstitutional by applying orthodox principles of constitutional interpretation. The majority, however, advanced a more radical theory, premised on the assumption that an implied right of free expression could be extracted from the constitution's attachment to the basic political principle that Australia was to be governed as a representative democracy. Toohey and Deane JJ adverted explicitly to 'the seminal judgment of the United States Supreme Court (delivered by Miller J) in *Crandall* v. *State of Nevada*'[92] to buttress their conclusion.

The High Court's contemporaneous decision in *Australian Capital Television Pty Ltd* v. *Commonwealth of Australia*[93] is perhaps of even greater relevance to debate about the internationalization of public law principles. The case centred on the constitutionality of provisions of the Political Broadcast and Political Disclosures Act 1992, which tightly regulated television and radio advertising on 'political matters' in the run up to federal elections or referenda. In a section of his opinion titled 'Freedom of communication as an indispensable element in representative government', Mason CJ embarked on a *tour de force* of comparative legal exploration, alighting upon judgments of the European Convention on

[88] *Reference Re Amendment of the Constitution of Canada* [1981] 1 SCR 753. For comment see T. Allan, 'Law, Convention and Prerogative: Reflections Prompted by the Canadian Constitutional Case', (1986) 45 *CLJ* 305.

[89] *AG Canada and Dupond* v. *Montreal* [1978] 2 SCR 770.

[90] (1992) 108 ALR 681.

[91] See particularly Fisher *op. cit.*, 638–43: Rabban *op. cit.*

[92] (1867) 73 US 35.

[93] (1992) 66 AJLR 695. For comment see K. Ewing, 'New Constitutional Constraints in Australia' [1993] *PL* 256: Lee *op. cit.* The case is also discussed *infra* by Barendt, and by Ewing.

Human Rights, the First Amendment case law of both the Warren and Burger Courts, and post-Charter Canadian decisions which had themselves drawn extensively on US principles.[94] In combination with domestic case law and academic analysis, this heterogeneous collection of authority led the Court to find an implied right to freedom of communication within the Australian Constitution, which precluded the types of media regulation introduced by the 1992 Act.

Nationwide and *Capital Television* prompted a fierce debate, at least in academic circles, over the constitutional legitimacy of the High Court's reasoning process.[95] But searching analysis of US precedent is by no means a novel feature of the High Court's jurisprudence. In contrast to Lord Donaldson MR's dismissal of American principles in *Foot*, the High Court paid them careful attention in *Attorney General of the Commonwealth, ex rel McKinlay* v. *Commonwealth*.[96] *McKinlay* addressed the meaning of section 24 of the Constitution, which provides that the lower house of the Federal legislature be 'directly chosen by the people of the Commonwealth'. While noting the obvious American influence on the design of section 24, the Court then explained in some detail why Australia's Constitution did not demand that voting rights be premised on the 'one woman one vote one value' interpretation of those principles expounded by the US Supreme Court in *Wesberry* v. *Sanders*.[97]

Finally, one might make brief reference to the High Court's decision in *Theophanous* v. *The Herald and Weekly Times Ltd.*[98] Theophanous was decided at almost exactly the same time as the Indian Supreme Court's judgment in *Rajagopal*, and came to virtually the same conclusion. Theophanous, the Chair of the House of Representatives' Standing Committee on Migration took exception to a newspaper report accusing him of pro-Greek bias, anti-Australian sentiments, and general idiocy. The majority opinion drew heavily on *Sullivan* and subsequent US case law (as well as on the European Convention on Human Rights and the UK's *Derbyshire* judgment) to guide their search for the 'correct' answer, in the Australian context, to the question of what obstacles a politician should have to surmount to succeed in a defamation action relating to speech on political matters. *Theophanous* concluded that the disseminator may successfully defend such an action not by having to discharge the onerous burden of proving her speech was true, but merely by establishing either that she took reasonable steps to ascertain the accuracy of the report, or that in the circumstances such inquiries were not reasonably required. In formal terms, this test is less protective of speech than *Sullivan*, which

[94] See especially 594–7.
[95] For a summary of which see H. Lee *op. cit.*
[96] (1975) 135 CLR 1.
[97] (1964) 376 US 1.
[98] High Court of Australia, Canberra, 12 Oct. 1994.

places the burden of proof on the plaintiff. However the *Theophanous* test would seem easily surmountable by any reputable media organisation. It would thus seem that in effect, Australian politicians, like their Indian and American counterparts, can no longer rely on a compliant common law as a means to stifle political criticism.

CONCLUSION

India, Canada, and Australia have all made extensive resort, in rather different ways, and with rather different outcomes, to US institutional structures and Supreme Court case-law. In doing so, these Commonwealth jurisdictions are most assuredly not assuming the role of jurisprudential colonial outposts, cringing before the advance of American constitutional imperialism. Nor can their judges convincingly be accused of seeking a spurious cloak to legitimize a judicial usurpation of political power hitherto presumed to rest with other branches of government. Some of their recent decisions may indeed be controversial, but all are rooted in a plausible domestic base. Moreover, such judgments have shared a certain methodological rigour, in which judges engage in selective and informed scrutiny of those American ideas which are seen as potential aids to the resolution of domestic problems: US law is presumed to offer valuable organizing principles and extensive practical experience, but not universality and omniscience.

It would thus be something of an exaggeration to suggest that judicial importation of American principles into British law would transform the legal system into an alternate or additional political process,[99] any more than Parliamentary copying of American initiatives would entail an abdication of national sovereignty. More accurately, one might claim that reference to US litigation or legislation would trigger an explicit 'constitutionalization' of disputes before the courts and issues before Parliament, which in turn highlights the falsity of the formal law versus politics dichotomy maintained by conservative analyses of British public law. The collection of essays presented in this volume is intended to make a further contribution to the fostering and maintenance of such a critically constructive climate among policymakers, lawyers, academics, and students in this country.

[99] Although this is an argument which both Rawlings and Cane pursue in this volume.

1

The Symbolism of Constitutions: Some Anglo–American Comparisons

ROGER COTTERRELL

CONSTITUTIONS provide and define authority for a society's principal organs of government. This is assumed to be the fundamental reason for their existence.[1] Where comparisons are made between constitutions it is usually on the basis of the form in which they express this authority, the kind of allocation of governmental powers for which they provide, and the legal limits that they impose on government action. This essay[2] argues, however, that constitutions not only 'constitute' government in these ways, mapping structures of authority and normative relationships between various arms and agencies of government, as well as their specific powers, responsibilities, and jurisdictional limits. They also typically contribute to 'constitute', in a certain sense, **the governed society** itself, and this contribution is one of their most important aspects.

My argument is that, in order to provide authority for the government of a political society, constitutional thought evokes, reinforces, or proclaims certain cultural characteristics of that society which are favourable to the establishment and maintenance of political authority. Specifically, constitutional ideas help to affirm the identity of the political society made up of those from whom the constitution demands allegiance.[3] Insofar as constitutions are themselves considered authoritative this is because they construct, focus, organize, or affirm in certain ways plausible images of the general nature of the society comprized of those whose allegiance to the constitution is required.

How is this evocation of images of society achieved? In many so-called 'programmatic' national constitutions[4] the appeal to symbols of the nation is blatant. Descriptions in constitutional provisions of the symbolic

[1] See e.g. S. De Smith & R. Brazier, *Constitutional and Administrative Law* (London, 1989, 6th ed.), 6–7.

[2] This essay is adapted and abbreviated from 'Some Aspects of the Communication of Constitutional Authority' in D. Nelken (ed.), *Law and Communication* (Aldershot, forthcoming).

[3] Cf. B. Thompson, *Textbook on Constitutional and Administrative Law* (London, 1993), 12–13.

[4] Cf. De Smith & Brazier *op. cit.*, 4.

meaning of the colours of the national flag[5] or the design of the national emblem, evocations of the political history, values and aspirations of the nation,[6] or perhaps specifications of the national language or languages or even of the music to be recognized as the national anthem[7] appeal to or are calculated to influence a collective national consciousness. But symbolic aspects of constitutional communication are not limited to these easily recognized forms. Constitutional symbols can be regarded as all those features or objects of constitutional discourse and constitutional practice that are powerfully (if often ambiguously) evocative in some way of assumed fundamental characteristics of the political society as a whole.

Symbolic aspects of constitutions are recognized in British constitutional law texts but are usually firmly marginalized. The predominant conception of a constitution in British legal literature is that of a set of rules about government, comparable in form with legislative rules.[8] Nevertheless, what constitutions communicate about the nature of the political society in which they exist may or may not be conveyed through the medium of rules or legal principles. Hence symbolic aspects of constitutions tend to appear in legal reasoning and legal theory as peripheral insofar as they are not understandable in terms of the typical substance and forms of legal doctrine. They appear as matters of rhetoric rather than constitutional substance of concern to lawyers.

This paper uses comparisons between British and United States constitutional structures to suggest that this view is too narrow. The particular legal form of constitutional ideas (including the manner in which and even the extent to which they are expressed in constitutional documents) may be much less significant than the ideas themselves. And their significance may often lie in profound ambiguity rather than in the kind of interpretive clarity which lawyers try to find in law. Indeed, constitutional communication may be impossible to confine within specific modern legal forms with which lawyers typically feel at ease. The attempt to so confine it may account for some enduring dilemmas of contemporary constitutional interpretation.

In American literature the idea of the constitution as symbolically constituting society is much more familiar and widely discussed than in British writing.[9] According to some recent commentators, the United

[5] See e.g. Constitution of Angola 1975 (revised 1980), Part 4; and see Thompson *op. cit.*, 12.

[6] See Constitution of Algeria, Preamble; cf. Thompson *op. cit.*, 13–14.

[7] On the significance of national anthems in symbolizing the nature of the political society see K. A. Cerullo, 'Sociopolitical Control and the Structure of National Symbols: An Empirical Analysis of National Anthems' (1989) 68 *Social Forces* 76.

[8] See e.g. C. Munro, 'What is a Constitution?' [1983] *PL* 567.

[9] For early discussions see E. S. Corwin, 'The Constitution as Instrument and as Symbol' (1936) 30 *American Political Science Review* 1071; M. Lerner, 'Constitution and Court as Symbols' (1937) 46 *Yale Law Journal* 1290.

States constitution's role is that of 'the "constituent agent" of our identity as Americans';[10] the constitutional document 'assumes the identity of the nation itself';[11] it represents 'the lifeblood of the American nation, its supreme symbol and manifestation . . . so intimately welded with the national existence itself that the two have become inseparable'.[12] The American legal scholar Sanford Levinson quotes the following statement: 'To be an American means to be a member of the "covenanting community" in which the commitment to freedom under law, having transcended the "natural" bonds of race, religion, and class, itself takes on transcendent importance', and he adds that the 'central "covenant" of the community, from this perspective, is the Constitution'.[13] A major recent study of United States constitutional law begins with the declaration that 'Americans revere their Constitution',[14] often treating it as sacred.[15] The frequent suggestion is that in some sense Americans are 'made' by it; it creates their identity as members of the political society. They recognize themselves as citizens, seeing their image as members of society through a kind of double mirror effect[16] reflecting the image of the society which the constitution and associated instruments of symbolic power—such as the flag and the Declaration of Independence—help to shape and sustain.[17]

Constitutions both convey authority and require authority. Januslike, they face two ways—towards the **cultural sources** that provide their moral and political authority and stability, and that in certain ways they represent symbolically, and towards the **agencies of government** for which they provide legal authority. A constitution can hardly provide authority for government unless it attracts authority and respect to itself. The bases of the authority of constitutions may differ in different political societies. This essay argues that the fundamentally different, though historically related, bases of authority of the British and United States constitutions are reflected in the different kinds of authority that these constitutions provide for government. These differences register also in the contrasting ways that the British and American constitutions contribute towards the symbolic representation of the nature of the societies in which they exist.

I have tried to show elsewhere that modern legal thought, at least in Britain and the United States, contains presuppositions about the

[10] S. Levinson, *Constitutional Faith* (Princeton NJ, 1988), 5.

[11] M. Foley, *The Silence of Constitutions* (London, 1989), 37.

[12] H. Kohn, quoted in Foley *op. cit.*, 37.

[13] Levinson *op. cit.*, 5.

[14] C. Sunstein, *The Partial Constitution* (Cambridge, Mass., 1993), v.

[15] E. S. Corwin, 'The Worship of the Constitution' in R. Loss (ed.), *Corwin on the Constitution* (Ithaca NY, 1981), 47–55; T. C. Grey, 'The Constitution as Scripture' (1984) 37 *Stanford Law Review* 21; Levinson *op. cit.*, ch. 1.

[16] Cf. L. Althusser 'Ideology and Ideological State Apparatuses' in *Essays in Ideology* (London, 1984), 54.

[17] Cf. Levinson *op. cit.*, 11.

regulatory structure of the society to which it relates—that is, legal discourse expresses or assumes certain very general images of the structure of the regulated population. In broad terms two kinds of images of the regulated society seem identifiable in modern legal thought in the Anglo–American context. One is an image of *imperium*—essentially an image of hierarchical political organization and of individuals as subjects of centralized political authority. The other is an image of *community*—essentially the image of a social group whose members are linked in voluntary association as autonomous political actors by their allegiance to shared group values.[18] Contrasts in legal philosophy and judicial rhetoric[19] and in certain patterns of judicial decision making[20] can be understood, to some extent, in the light of the power of these contrasting images of the regulatory or normative character of society. It seems reasonable to suggest that these images may also be reflected and presented, in part, through the symbolism of constitutions. In other words, insofar as the British and American constitutions do more than map and guarantee the authority of government—insofar as they contribute towards constituting the idea of the political society as such—they might be supposed to do this in ways that are understandable in terms of these images of community and imperium.

The different authority bases of the British and American constitutions ultimately determine the different ways in which constitutions in these countries provide authority for government. And identifying the differences has practical significance. Indeed, a comparison of these authority bases may cast light on possibilities for constitutional change in Britain in a situation in which British public lawyers have increasingly 'come to doubt the stability and adequacy of our constitutional heritage'.[21]

THE NATURE OF CONSTITUTIONAL SYMBOLISM

Before developing this comparison it is important to recognize some important general problems of the analysis of constitutional symbolism. Law operates not merely through the calculated attempt (especially in legislative enactments and judicial discourse) to establish legal understanding as a field of authoritative certainties but also through the creation of

[18] R. Cotterrell, *Law's Community: Legal Theory in Sociological Perspective* (Oxford, 1995), ch. 11.

[19] *Ibid.*, 222–240.

[20] Cotterrell, 'Judicial Review and Legal Theory' in G. Richardson & H. Genn (eds.), *Administrative Law and Government Action: The Courts and Alternative Mechanisms of Review* (Oxford, 1994).

[21] N. Walker, 'The Middle Ground in Public Law' in W. Finnie *et al.* (eds.), *Edinburgh Essays in Public Law* (Edinburgh, 1991), 57.

infinitely suggestive ambiguities which seem by their nature open to an indefinite range of levels of interpretation[22] and to serve as a focus or stimulus for a myriad of cultural references, understandings, and emotions.[23]

Symbolism in law entails such ambiguities of meaning (an openness to contrasting interpretations of what is being communicated). Thus, many recent inquiries about legal symbolism are concerned to recognize the indefinitely wide ramifications of the ambiguity of symbols, and to emphasize the rich overlay of symbolic references that provide the 'irrational', contradictory, or mystificatory foundations of modern legal rationality.[24]

These kinds of inquiries are worthwhile but the cost of pursuing them needs emphasizing. The overlap of symbolic references that spill out from and beyond legal texts creates a dense texture of signification in which possibilities of meaning and interpretation are potentially almost unlimited and yet narrowly local in origin. The 'forest of symbols'[25] envelops those who inhabit it, so that the difficulty of gaining a broad perspective on the terrain of symbolic communication is acute and the temptation is to give up systematic attempts to do so. Interpretations of symbolic meaning necessarily remain indeterminate and are permanently controversial.[26]

To let light into the 'darkness' of the symbolic forest it may be necessary to provide guidance for these interpretations from the conceptual frameworks that are suggested by studies of legal ideology. For example, it may be especially useful to analyse the ways in which ambiguous symbols are interpreted in popular and legal professional consciousness so as to reinforce the assumed certainties of ideological thought. Emblematic institutions, elements of ritual, or certain ideas and references presented in or associated with constitutional doctrine may be analysed in terms of the ways in which they are understood by citizens so as to reinforce and complete ideological representations or images of the 'essential' nature of the political society to which these symbols relate. But this is always a matter of studying symbols for **particular** purposes, **conceptualizing** the represented 'reality' sociologically, and hence **choosing** the symbolic meanings that are to be considered significant.

The problems of interpreting symbols parallel problems of interpreting

22 Cf. V. Turner, *The Forest of Symbols: Aspects of Ndembu Ritual* (Ithaca NY, 1967), 44.

23 See E. Sapir, 'Symbols' in E. R. A. Seligman (ed.), *Encyclopedia of the Social Sciences* Vol 14 (New York, 1934), 493.

24 See e.g. P. Fitzpatrick, *The Mythology of Modern Law* (London, 1992).

25 Cf. Turner *op. cit.*

26 Cf. Carl Jung's statement that 'a symbol is always the best possible expression of a relatively *unknown* fact, a fact, however, which is none the less recognized or postulated as existing' (quoted in Turner *op. cit.*, 26).

the legal nature of constitutions. It is said that the 'defining feature of legal modernity lies in the attempt to make law self-founding'.[27] The peculiarity of law as a normative system, according to Hans Kelsen, is that it regulates its own creation;[28] it can be portrayed as a self-reproducing rule system.[29] Whatever the general problems of this understanding of law, there are serious problems in applying it to constitutional law. Constitutions may indeed regulate their own creation or inhabit a self-reproducing legal system in the limited sense of providing procedures for modification of their own documentary provisions, or even for replacement of their entire written text. But, in the graphic Kelsenian image, the (historically first) constitution provides the legal foundation of the legal system as a whole. As such, however, it is necessarily only ambiguously legal in quality itself, for its norms—at least according to Kelsen's instructive analysis—are derived not by imputation from other legal norms but from the fabric of **cultural elements** expressed for the limited purposes of legal theory in the fictional idea of the basic norm.[30] Indeed, whether or not anything like the Kelsenian perspective is adopted, the specifically **legal** character of constitutions remains difficult to define because constitutions significantly defy the project of making law 'self-founding'. They are the conduit by which elements of social authority (attributed, for example, to a social contract, popular will, or the political virtues of the rule of law) or transcendental authority (attributed, for example, to notions of natural law, divine right, or religious origins of government or society) are carried into law and legal interpretation as the basis of their legitimacy.

Much follows from this. Constitutions are not to be seen as bounded by the orthodox forms of positive law but extend through and beyond these legal forms. Their character as simultaneously legal, moral, and political institutions and as bridges or conduits between the cultural conditions of existence of the political society, on the one hand, and positive legal doctrine, on the other, suggests that their scope is never confined to the contents of constitutional **documents**. On the one hand, they are expressed in familiar forms of enacted positive law (statements of rules, rights, and duties, principles or procedures, or formal definitions and authorizations of governmental structures, set out in a constitutional document or documents). On the other, they include elements of signification not necessarily conveyed or conveyable in familiar legal forms, and certainly not constrained in meaning by such forms. In particular, these elements of

[27] P. Goodrich, 'Fate as Seduction: The Other Scene of Legal Judgment' in A. Norrie (ed.), *Closure or Critique? New Directions in Legal Theory* (Edinburgh, 1993), 116.
[28] H. Kelsen, *The Pure Theory of Law* (Berkeley, Cal., 1967), 71, 221.
[29] H. L. A. Hart, *The Concept of Law* (Oxford, 1961).
[30] Kelsen, 'The Function of a Constitution' in R. Tur and W. Twining (eds.), *Essays on Kelsen* (Oxford, 1986).

signification may include symbolic representations of the culture of the regulated political society insofar as that culture provides the identity of the society to which the constitution as a foundation of governmental authority appeals and from which it is considered to draw its own authority.

These representations might be identified through the analysis of a wide range of phenomena: for example, constitutional documents themselves; judicial decisions and pronouncements and other professional and lay commentary on particular constitutional issues; established practices and traditions in the conduct of government and public affairs; the literature of constitutional theory and constitutional history, including popular (non-specialist) writings; lay opinion about the constitution and about questions of government; and public rituals, procedures, ceremonies, and celebrations linked with matters of governmental continuity and authority. Thus, symbolic elements of the constitution are identifiable in both its 'written' (documentary) and 'unwritten' components.

POPULAR SOVEREIGNTY AND FUNDAMENTAL LAW

The aim in what follows is to illustrate two (apart from many other) different ways in which constitutional thought can contribute to 'constitute' the society in which it exists; in other words, two different ways in which constitutions reinforce cultural sources of their authority through symbolic representations that help to establish a particular image of the nature of the regulated society. For this purpose the focus is limited to some crucial distinctions between the bases of constitutional authority in the United Kingdom and the United States.

In a classic essay of 1928 Edward Corwin remarked that: 'It is customary nowadays to ascribe the **legality** as well as the **supremacy** of the [United States] constitution—the one is, in truth, but the obverse of the other—exclusively to the fact that, in its own phraseology, it was "ordained" by "the people of the United States" '. Corwin notes that two important ideas are thereby brought into play. 'One is the so-called "positive" conception of law as a general expression merely for the particular commands of a human lawgiver, as a series of acts of human will; the other is that the highest possible source of such commands, because the highest possible embodiment of human will, is "the people".'[31]

Corwin appropriately pinpoints the essential intellectual development that enabled a specific constitutional document, or small group of

[31] E. S. Corwin, 'The "Higher Law" Background of American Constitutional Law' (1928) 62 *Harvard Law Review* 151.

documents, to achieve recognition as fundamental law, superior to all other law, in the United States. To be law in the modern positivist conception that was becoming established in the common law world in the late eighteenth and nineteenth centuries, especially as a result of Jeremy Bentham's and John Austin's ideas, the constitution had to be seen as 'posited' by a human legislator, and no such legislator could have greater law-making authority than 'the people', treated as a political unity. Thus the theory of the constitution as a superior positive legal creation of 'the people' simultaneously established the centrality of the popularly enacted constitutional document in the idea of the constitution and enabled the constitution, understood in this sense, to dominate all other law conceived in similarly positive terms. 'The people' is thus the image of the regulated population which underpins constitutional authority and is promoted in constitutional thought.

The idea of a special popular authority of some kind underlying the constitution is carried through to the most recent debates about American constitutional law. Bruce Ackerman's[32] analysis of what he calls America's 'dualist democracy' distinguishes between, on the one hand, the authority of ordinary legislation conferred by the popular mandate to govern, given to legislators by periodic elections, and, on the other, the popular foundations of the constitution. These foundations consist in the notion that the constitution was established by a convention of the people and can be altered by decisions of the American people as a whole (rather than their elected representatives) registered in ways (formal or informal) outside the mundane political processes of representative democracy. Thus, amendments to the constitution are no ordinary acts of legislation. They are expressions of a popular authority distinct from that which authorizes legislators to develop law through everyday processes of legislative amendment. Ackerman declares: 'Americans have not been "born equal" through some miraculous act of immaculate conception. To the extent that we have gained equality, we have won it through energetic debate, popular decision, and constitutional creativity.'[33] The message is that the values and structure of the constitution are popularly defined and capable of being changed or developed by popular will. For Ackerman 'the people' refers to individuals who can through collective action bring about constitutional change.

The idea of popular sovereignty focused on the image of a polity of active citizens is strongly present also in the resurgence of the idea, in the American context, of deliberative democracy.[34] This involves the advocacy

[32] B. Ackerman, *We the People. Volume 1: Foundations* (Cambridge, Mass., 1991).

[33] Ackerman *op. cit.*, 27.

[34] See especially J. S. Fishkin, *Democracy and Deliberation: New Directions for Democratic Reform* (New Haven, Conn., 1991).

of a kind of informed and dynamic conversation among the populace at large about the fundamentals and directions of the polity, as well as the closely related insistence that determination of the meaning of the constitution is not to be treated as a monopoly of judicial wisdom.[35] Indeed, the debate over who should have authority to interpret the constitution acquires a prominence comparable to, and explicitly compared with, theological disputes as to who should have the authority to interpret holy scripture. The tradition of popular sovereignty sometimes seems to inform the drawing of analogies between judges and priests as interpreters and to inspire a 'protestant' suspicion of both insofar as they claim unique authority, through their access to an 'expert' tradition of doctrine that supplements the words of the written text, to fix the meaning of ideas that should belong to the whole people.[36]

But in what way specifically, can 'the people' act except through legislative representatives? If they act through such representatives it seems appropriate to speak of legislative supremacy rather than popular sovereignty, and the idea of the superiority of a constitution, founded on popular sovereignty, over mere legislative majorities becomes incoherent. However, James Fishkin's recent analysis of mechanisms of deliberative democracy[37] is an attempt to demonstrate how even in a large, complex polity such as the United States certain procedures can be created to allow democratic deliberation as a form of action by the people as a whole. Some other modern writers, too, are concerned to ask hard questions about the mechanisms through which 'the people' can act, but in much literature the possibilities remain startlingly unclear. How, for example, is 'protestant' interpretation of the constitution by ordinary citizens able to compete with judicial interpretation? Is it in the end unimportant unless it creates civil disturbance or revolt? Again, adopting Ackerman's own question about America's 'dualist democracy': how can a process be organized to mark out 'the rare occasions' when a political movement is to be recognized as acting in the name of the people as a whole?[38]

Such problems of popular or direct democracy are familiar in the history of political thought. How is popular government possible except through representatives? One way to avoid this practical *cul-de-sac* is simply to ignore the implication in the idea of popular sovereignty that the question requires an answer. Thus, while the popular basis of government is treated as fundamental it can be assumed to be adequately safeguarded through the ordinary processes of representative democracy. Ackerman asserts that this kind of denial of dualist democracy has in fact become 'dominant

[35] Sunstein *op. cit.*; R. Dworkin, *Taking Rights Seriously* (London, 1977), ch. 8.

[36] Levinson *op. cit.*, 27–8; cf. Grey *loc. cit.*

[37] Fishkin *op. cit.*

[38] Ackerman *op. cit.*, 7.

among serious constitutionalists over the course of the last century'.[39] The consequence of such a denial, however, is that the idea of the constitution as fundamental law, superior to ordinary legislation, has to be sought in some source other than that of popular sovereignty.

American constitutional history shows that such other sources have always seemed available. Many writers have traced the origins of American constitutional thought in ideas of natural law and natural rights, in general traditions and principles associated with English common law, and in documentary sources such as Magna Carta. It has been claimed that the United States has always had an unwritten constitution existing alongside the written one;[40] that the Framers of the documentary constitution assumed that the unwritten elements of constitutional thought and tradition would continue to coexist with the constitutional document which they now saw as invested with popular authority[41] and that the documentary constitution presupposed these unwritten elements as necessary to the completion of its meaning. On this view the idea of popular sovereignty was never the sole basis of the constitution's authority. On the other hand, the unwritten elements of the constitution are organized around and given coherence and focus through the existence and status of the constitutional document, which gains its special authority as the creation of 'the people'.

The recognition of the continuing significance of non-documentary components of the constitution, located in ideology, inherited values, and legal and cultural traditions raises, in itself, interesting questions about the possibility of popular interpretation of the constitution. On one view, since the words of the constitutional document cannot be understood without reference to a tradition of values, interpretations, and understandings external to the document itself it must be accepted that constitutional interpretation is necessarily the monopoly of experts (such as judges of a specialist constitutional court) who are learned in that tradition. On the other hand, this 'catholic' view[42] of the necessary qualifications to be an interpreter is not inevitable. Ronald Dworkin, for example, asserts that there is no reason why ordinary citizens should not be able to involve themselves in the process of interpretation of the underlying value structures of the constitution.[43] In general, however, as a matter of

[39] Ackerman *op. cit.*, 3.

[40] T. C. Grey, 'Do We Have an Unwritten Constitution?' (1975) 27 *Stanford Law Review* 703; Grey, 'The Origins of the Unwritten Constitution: Fundamental Law in American Revolutionary Thought' (1978) 30 *Stanford Law Review* 843.

[41] S. Sherry, 'The Founders' Unwritten Constitution' (1987) 54 *University of Chicago Law Review* 1127.

[42] Levinson *op. cit.*, 27; Grey, 'Constitution as Scripture' *supra*.

[43] Dworkin *op. cit.*, ch. 8.

practicality, judges monopolize constitutional interpretation. The idea of popular sovereignty accommodates this situation insofar as the judiciary can be seen as guardians of and spokespersons for the values and traditions that unite 'the people' as a political community, and that complete the meaning of the popularly created documentary constitution.

The above discussion indicates that the idea of popular sovereignty may be interpreted in various ways, and that it is not necessary to treat it as the sole basis of current constitutional authority in the United States. Nevertheless it remains the distinguishing idea that makes possible the special character of the written United States constitution as fundamental law. Because of this, the question remains: in what way and by what means do 'the people' give authority to the constitution? In answering this question the nature of 'the people' presupposed in the idea of popular sovereignty is of the greatest importance. As has been noted, 'the people' is not a democratic majority. It is rather the entire nation viewed as a single community. Much literature suggests that 'the people' is not necessarily restricted to the citizens existing at any particular moment but refers also to the continuity of the political society through time.

How then can 'the people' be conceptualized as a historical actor? At the most mundane level it can be treated as the electorate, but acting through special procedures (those which the constitution provides for its own amendment), distinguished from the procedures that give popular sanction to ordinary legislation. The amendment process preserves a separation between expressions of popular authority for the creation of constitutional provisions, on the one hand, and of ordinary legislation, on the other. But this conceptualization of 'the people' as an actor is relatively weak. 'The people' appear primarily as the legislative representatives of the electorate acting through exceptional procedures.[44]

Much more powerful conceptualizations of 'the people' are rooted in the 'exceptional process'[45] of the constitution's creation. 'The people' are symbolized most significantly in constitutional history by the Framers, the few dozen delegates of the thirteen states, whose deliberations at Philadelphia leading to the signing of the constitution in 1787 are evoked and analysed in an immense popular and scholarly literature. Creators of a constitutional agreement based on principled deliberation, easily treated as symbolizing a social contract on which the nation was founded, the Framers—'superb democratic politicians'[46]—are seen by some historians as heroic, having had the infinite wisdom to craft 'a perfect and complete political theory, adequate to all our future needs'.[47]

[44] United States Constitution Art. V.

[45] Munro *loc. cit.*, 656.

[46] J. P. Roche, 'The Convention as a Case Study in Democratic Politics' in L. W. Levy (ed.), *Essays on the Making of the Constitution* (New York, 1987 2nd ed.), 179.

[47] Daniel Boorstin, quoted in Foley *op. cit.*, 37.

Charles Beard's thesis of the economic origins of the constitution[48] 'appeared to demonstrate irrefutably and with all the paraphernalia of scientific scholarship'[49] the unrepresentative character of the Framers in relation to the populations of the states and the extent to which they had framed the constitution in pursuit of their personal economic interests. But the issue of how far the Framers represented—in any sense of formal political representation—the diversity of the actual populations of the states seems unimportant. In one sense, the Framers are not legislative representatives of an electorate at all; their representative status is cultural, not political. They **symbolize** in constitutional thought the nation as a diverse but unified cultural entity. But the symbol is ambiguous. The Framers are also seen as political representatives of the thirteen existing states; that is, they represented as historical actors political societies already established and agreeing together a 'compact' for a government to unite them, this unity being recognized as essential to remedy major crises of government arising in relationships between the states.[50] In negotiating this compact the Framers are seen as having established the basis of a new political society.

'The people' is thus ambiguously represented as a community based on free agreement and shared values. The status of the constitution as fundamental law remains dependent on the coherence of the idea of popular sovereignty; constitutional thought and tradition reinforce the image of the people as sovereign. But constitutional thought, lay and professional, helps to constitute 'the people', partly through symbolic representations derived from traditions of the constitution's origins. It imagines the nation as a **community**, a morally cohesive association of politically autonomous people, related through natural, spontaneous, or freely chosen association on the basis of values held in common.[51] It might be suggested that the need for the constitutional promotion of the image of the people has increased as the constitution has itself required stronger authority, gradually becoming recognized less as the consequence of a limited compact between small states and more clearly as the sole guarantor of legal authority for an increasingly powerful central government[52] directing economic and social policy in a huge, complex, and perhaps—given its ethnic and other diversity—potentially disunified nation.

[48] C. A. Beard, *An Economic Interpretation of the Constitution of the United States* (New York, 1913). [49] L. W. Levy (ed.) *op. cit.*, 3.

[50] See Levy, 'Introduction: The Making of the Constitution, 1776–89' in Levy (ed.) *op. cit.*

[51] Cf. Cotterrell, *Law's Community op. cit.*, 222–3.

[52] Cf. L. H. Tribe, *Constitutional Choices* (Cambridge, Mass., 1985), ch. 9.

PARLIAMENTARY SOVEREIGNTY AND FUNDAMENTAL LAW

By contrast to American constitutional thought the British constitution is characterized by an almost total absence of the idea of popular sovereignty. The British constitution, however defined, represents symbolically the nature of the political society in which it exists in radically different ways from those typical of American constitutional thought. In what follows the concern is not with constitutional history as such but with identifying the dominant image of British society represented in constitutional thought and some of the symbolic means of this representation.

Many writers have remarked on 'the United Kingdom's attachment to *ad hoc* solutions and its lack of interest in general constitutional issues'.[53] The constitution does not occupy the place in popular consciousness that the United States constitution seems to have. A sophisticated and ironic passivity infuses the notion that, lacking a supreme constitutional document, the United Kingdom has no constitution. Foreign observers are struck by the 'failure of politicians and civil servants to think constitutionally'.[54] Ultimately, this constitutional passivity is rooted in the cultural acceptance of legislative supremacy, associated with the idea of parliamentary sovereignty. If parliamentary sovereignty means what it says, writes Terence Daintith, 'there is certainly no room for any constitutional principles, since the maintenance of any rule, principle or body of practice is wholly contingent upon parliamentary abstinence from its alteration.'[55] Parliamentary sovereignty, and thus legislative supremacy, **is** the constitution, according to this view. For many constitutional commentators this situation has become the central theoretical problem of government in Britain. The solution is generally seen in constructing—either through constitutional enactments or judicial activity—principles to limit or modify parliamentary sovereignty. An object is to devise means of controlling the governmental power of transient political majorities, which may represent only social minorities given the limitations of electoral arrangements.

But a prerequisite for understanding possibilities for engrafting new constitutional principle on an unprincipled constitution is to understand the basis of authority of the constitution. As Dicey correctly noted, the British constitution is firmly rooted in the tradition of common law thought. One of the most striking consequences of this is that constitutional documents which, in other circumstances, might have become

[53] Gillian Peele, quoted in Foley *op. cit.*, 97.

[54] J. Cornford, quoted in Foley *op. cit.*, 126.

[55] T. C. Daintith, 'Political Programmes and the Content of the Constitution' in Finnie *et al.* (eds.) *op. cit.*, 46.

established as fundamental law have often been treated as expressions of already existing common law principle. In the English context common law thought provided both a folk and a professional legal philosophy that eventually became the only significant potential source of fundamental law. Magna Carta for a time, especially in the fourteenth century, assumed immense status as a fundamental basis of English legal freedoms,[56] but when revived as such by Edward Coke in the seventeenth century as 'fountain of all the fundamental laws of the realm',[57] its significance was as declaratory of the unchanging heritage of common law freedoms.

As J. G. A. Pocock has shown,[58] the doctrine of the 'ancient constitution' in the seventeenth century presented, in an important tradition of English legal and political thought, the common law as immemorial and unchanging, except through processes of elaboration reflecting the timeless wisdom of the community—a wisdom entrusted to the professional common lawyers and necessarily expressed as the 'artificial reason' of the law. The doctrine of the ancient constitution was a powerful weapon against royal power since, according to Pocock, it enabled the common lawyers to argue that all political authority in the realm derived from unimaginably ancient cultural sources, still present in an unbroken legal tradition; indeed, a tradition unbroken by any political change, including that of the Norman Conquest itself.

The assumed supremacy of the common law tradition, graphically illustrated in the doctrine of the ancient constitution, is most dramatically presented in Coke's assertion, especially in the context of *Bonham's Case*, of the common law's authority to control Acts of Parliament and declare them void 'as against common right and reason, or repugnant, or impossible to be performed'.[59] Natural law enters the discourse of English law, if only briefly and impractically,[60] as the substance of common law principle. But of greater importance is the example of common law method available to be used, with no such dramatic rhetoric, in everyday judicial decision making, not necessarily opposed to political law making but usually allied with it. The tradition of common law thought enabled courts to attach the authority of the supposed immemorial wisdom of the community to principle fashioned for the moment and consciously shaped by the judges.[61] It allowed them also to recognize that legislation could be accepted as an expression of the common law tradition. A common law judge, writes Pocock, elaborating the implications of his original thesis,

[56] Corwin, ' "Higher Law" Background' *loc. cit.*, 178.

[57] 1 Co. Inst. 81.

[58] J. G. A. Pocock, *The Ancient Constitution and the Feudal Law* extended ed. (Cambridge, 1987).

[59] 8 Co. 118a (1610).

[60] See J. W. Gough, *Fundamental Law in English Constitutional History* (Oxford, 1955).

[61] Pocock *op. cit.*, 268–9.

'was not in the least precluded from thinking of law as decreed by the king's authority in the king's courts, from discerning the affinity between what he was doing and the sovereign reason by which the king-in-parliament made statutes binding on him and the whole nation . . .'.[62] Behind such reasoning, however, is the idea that the common law gives authority to all who professionally or officially interpret or develop law, whether courts or legislators, and no other source of ultimate authority is available to do this.[63]

These ideas suggest that common law principle should remain, at least, a subordinate source of constitutional principle, as in the United States where it is treated by exponents of the 'unwritten constitution' as supplementing the documentary constitution positively established on the basis of popular sovereignty. A fundamental difference between the British and American contexts, however, is that, in the former no doctrine of popular sovereignty—no image of 'the people' as an active law-making collectivity—was available to become attached to the contents of a specific **document** as fundamental constitutional law and become an enduring reference point in constitutional thought. Thus, the common law tradition subsumed specific enactments within itself as exemplifications of common law principle while validating the processes of parliamentary legislation.

Undoubtedly something more was necessary to provide an intellectual foundation of parliamentary sovereignty as long as the authority of the political legislator was treated as located in the superior authority of common law. John Figgis' classic thesis on the transition from religious to modern secular understandings of ultimate political authority describes processes by which mystical ideas of the 'sacredness' of monarchical authority provided a climate of thought which paved the way for the acceptance of modern theories of sovereignty.[64] In England, especially in the seventeenth century, a tradition of religious ideas about authority was transformed into a secular conception of political sovereignty, which in its early development, at least, could receive aid from the common law's ambivalence about the appropriate location of authority in the State and its convenient emphasis on communal sources of all regulatory power.

As parliamentary processes acquired an independent political legitimacy, they inevitably freed themselves of all elements of common law tutelage. On the basis of Figgis' arguments, it can be suggested that the concept of parliamentary sovereignty succeeded to similar assumptions about government (as a hierarchical, 'top-down' relationship of superiors and subordinates) as those surrounding earlier ideas of monarchical authority.

[62] *Ibid.*, 269. [63] *Ibid.*, 269–71.
[64] J. N. Figgis, *The Divine Right of Kings* 2nd ed. (Cambridge, 1913).

Further, the vague authority base of common law in the idea of immemorial communal wisdom—accessible only to lawyers—could hardly compete with that of a parliament not only having established law-making power but also gradually coming to possess some democratic credentials. In the United States, elements of common law principle, together with many other value elements derived from a variety of ideological sources, could find a focus for constitutional relevance as part of an 'unwritten constitution' given secure existence by its connection with the documentary constitution founded by political acts of 'the people'. In Britain, such elements could acquire no relevance in constitutional interpretation, since no independent constitutional focus to compete with a legislative sovereignty aspiring to democratic legitimation had been established. In the absence of such a focus common law could not impose limitations of principle on parliamentary legislation.

Thus, it may, indeed, be said that parliamentary sovereignty and the associated idea of legislative supremacy, in the British context, amount to the constitution. The authority of the constitution, once given by the common law tradition, is now found in representative democracy. And common law is revealed as lacking any authority to limit parliamentary legislative activity. Legislative supremacy founded in parliamentary sovereignty seems constitutionally unchallengeable.

As has been seen, American constitutional thought portrays 'the people' as a unified creator of law, though the problems of this idea lead to contrasting emphases and formulations. British constitutional thought portrays the regulated population symbolically in a quite different way. Certainly classical common law, as typified by the seventeenth century writings of Matthew Hale and Coke, embodied an image of the regulated population as a community linked by shared values, history and traditions.[65] The mythical ancient constitution was understood as the national heritage of the English people, whose cultural unity and homogeneity had defied all political disturbances that might have threatened it. Yet this pre-modern image of community is very different from the image of the active law-creating community of American constitutional thought. The community of classical common law thought coexists with royal power and its law confers authority on the king's courts and the king-in-Parliament. The symbolic representation of the regulated population in classical common law thought is not that of an active law-creating community but of a unified nation of loyal English subjects, content with the legal structures which they have inherited from a shared past and with which they collectively identify.[66] Hence the terms community, nation and realm are

[65] See e.g. G. J. Postema, *Bentham and the Common Law Tradition* (Oxford, 1986), 73.
[66] *Ibid.*, 73–4.

interchangeable. The popular will or reason of the community does not make law. Law is the 'artificial reason' of professional lawyers given force by the institutions of the monarchical state.

Hence, as common law sustains and ultimately subordinates itself to parliamentary sovereignty in English history, citizens are not recognizable in legal thought as part of a unified law-making community but are either individual **objects** of regulation (since Parliament, not citizens, creates law) or individual electors who choose their parliamentary representatives—who put their legal sovereign in place. In either case they are passive in their specific relation to law: delegating to others the creation of regulation, or submitting themselves to it. The image of society that the British constitution implies is thus one of *imperium*; of individual subjects of a superior political authority.[67] Certainly this authority may be conceived in abstract terms. It may, for example, be taken to be the authority of law itself, as in the idea of the Rule of Law. But nothing in the constitution suggests the idea of a unified law-making community. The democratic foundation of parliamentary sovereignty does not require symbolization in terms of a population actively involved in the shaping of its law.

Anachronistic as the claim may seem, in this light the central constitutional symbol at present in the constitution of the United Kingdom might appropriately be considered to be that of the monarch. Walter Bagehot, one of the few classic writers on the constitution to have attached due significance to its purely symbolic—or, as he termed them, 'dignified'—elements, suggested as much.[68] The monarch and the monarch's family represent many aspects of the political society in the ambiguous manner characteristic of constitutional symbols. The image of hierarchy and of the relation of sovereign and subject, underlying and preceding the idea of a democratic polity of free citizens, is coupled with that of the universal family and its cycle of births, marriages, and deaths as the foundation of social life.[69] Again, monarchy symbolizes the elements of privilege and class deeply rooted in society, yet also the authority that renders all members of society equal in their subjection. Bagehot thought that in a political society whose unity centred on common adherence of subjects to a sovereign authority, the monarchy provided an easily intelligible focus of allegiance. A constitutional partnership of Church and

[67] Cotterrell, *Law's Community op. cit.*, 223; 'Judicial Review and Legal Theory' *loc. cit.*

[68] W. Bagehot, *The English Constitution* (London, 1963), ch. 2: 'The use of the Queen, in a dignified capacity, is incalculable. Without her in England, the present English government would fail and pass away' (at 82). See further T. Nairn, *The Enchanted Glass: Britain and its Monarchy* (London, 1988) and, for recognition of the symbolic significance of monarchy in recent discussion of constitutional law, De Smith & Brazier *op. cit.*, 111.

[69] Bagehot *op. cit.*, 85–6.

State is also evoked in coronation rituals and other events and in the official allegiance of the monarch to a declared religious faith. In a regulated population represented constitutionally as a society of onlookers who do not participate in government but, as in classical common law thought, 'identify' with it, the monarch and the royal family are symbols of the minimal social structure (individuals within families) and, as such, are easily seen as a microcosm and exemplification of the nation's moral character, its strengths, and weaknesses. Monarchy, finally, symbolizes in its dynastic continuity the historical continuity of the political society and the endlessly self-renewing character of authority. Yet nothing is fixed and unchanging: as political and social conditions change so the significance and power of all of these symbols may change too.

CONSTITUTIONAL SYMBOLISM AND LEGAL ANALYSIS

Two examples of constitutional symbolism—the symbolism of the Framers in American constitutional thought and that of the institution of monarchy in modern British constitutional thought—have been emphasized above. Many other constitutional symbols could be considered. As noted earlier, a central problem for this kind of analysis is that the interpretation of symbols remains indeterminate and unlimited because of their inherent ambiguity and uncontrollable proliferation. For this reason it requires guidance and control within a theoretically structured inquiry.

If such an inquiry is about **law**, we must ask: how, specifically, does the identification and interpretation of constitutional symbols help in understanding law and in structuring the problems addressed by constitutional lawyers? Consider first the idea of the Framers as a symbolic representation of the people as makers of the United States Constitution. In constitutional interpretation the concentration on the Framers' intentions as the basis of the Constitution's meaning is explicable once it is understood that the Framers are the symbolic representation of the fundamental authority of the constitutional document. A recent writer such as Ronald Dworkin might insist that the fiction of seeking the Framers' intention should be replaced with an overt recognition that constitutional lawyers, like other lawyers, are engaged in the task of interpreting the political and moral meaning of the legal order as a whole.[70] But if we recognize that such interpretation must often become a political battle about deeply controversial values, a battle that continually threatens to burst beyond the constraints of constitutional discourse and challenge the idea of a constitutional (legal) framework for politics,[71] the

[70] R. Dworkin, *Law's Empire* (London, 1986).
[71] See e.g. Tribe *op. cit.*, ch. 1.

appeal to Framers' intentions may be the most plausible claim to a constitutional authority founded on shared values or legal traditions.[72] It presents itself as an appeal to the powerful symbols of a popular agreement whose controversial origins are blurred by history. It avoids the difficult question of who 'the people' presently are and in what way the constitution continues to express 'their' values as a unified collectivity.

Consider also the symbolic significance of monarchy in the British context. Orthodox constitutional analysis typically treats the monarchy as a relatively insignificant element in the constitutional structure. Legal discussions focus on conventions and legal powers associated with the monarch's role in relation to government.[73] But it seems important to consider evidence of transformations of monarchy's symbolic significance as well as its role as a specific agent in decision making within the state structure or in organising the exercise of governmental and especially law-making powers. A focus on constitutional symbolism might locate monarchy, for reasons noted earlier, close to the heart of constitutional concerns because of its symbolic importance as part of the constitution's evocation of an image of the regulatory structure of society which, in turn, underpins the authority which the constitution provides for government. Legal provisions that link the institution of monarchy with governmental processes harness to these processes the complex symbolic representations of authority that monarchy provides. Since constitutional interpretation is concerned with locating and defining authority for government action it cannot realistically ignore symbolic forms as conduits of that authority. Specifically, therefore, an analysis of the legal significance to be attached to monarchy must include a recognition of symbolic elements that help to infuse the 'constitution as hard law'[74] with a wider culture of constitutional thought.

Again, the significance of bills of rights should be seen not only in terms of their utility as positive law available for invocation by citizens, but also in terms of symbolic aspects. The United States Bill of Rights can be considered to express not only a set of rights available for enforcement through the courts, but also a powerful symbol of the centrality of the idea of individual autonomy in the structure of the American polity. The Bill of Rights helps to evoke the idea of the political society as one of individuals joined in civil society on the basis of free mutual agreement. It adds further

[72] R. Post, 'Theories of Constitutional Interpretation' in Post (ed.) *Law and the Order of Culture* (Berkeley, Cal., 1991), 21, discussing the claim that 'the Constitution is the fundamental will of the people; that is why it is the fundamental law' and arguing that the most common form of this claim 'regards the intentions of the Framers as the best evidence of the agreement represented by the Constitution'.

[73] See e.g. G. Marshall, *Constitutional Conventions* (Oxford, 1984), ch. 2.

[74] Cf. Post *loc. cit.*, 19.

symbolism to the idea of 'the people' as an association of autonomous citizens, whose rights as such are fundamental to the entire structure of political authority.

As discussion earlier in this essay has suggested, constitutional symbolism contributes to reinforce images of the nature of the political society, which, in turn, can be seen as informing the constitution and defining the nature of its authority as fundamental law. Constitutional symbolism must, therefore, to this extent be consistent with the cultural basis of authority at the heart of the constitutional structure. In the British context we have noted the absence of a culture of popular sovereignty independent of parliamentary sovereignty. For this reason there is no easy answer to the question raised in much recent discussion of constitutional reform in Britain as to how elements of a written (documentary) constitution or bill of rights might be entrenched as fundamental law, even if such constitutional innovations were thought desirable.[75] In the United States context the authority of the people provides the essential **independent** authority of the written constitution which makes it supreme over all other legal authority including that of legislation produced by democratic majorities. Interestingly, the Preamble of a recent elaborate draft written constitution for Britain[76] begins with the declaration that 'We the People of the United Kingdom . . .' affirm and respect certain principles of government and social justice, which are to inform the constitution. The need to protect these principles justifies constitutional limitations on ordinary legislative activity and the requirement that all agencies of the state conform to the requirements of a Bill of Rights set out in chapter 2 of the draft. But the American idea of 'We the People' is alien to British constitutional thought. Without the appeal to popular sovereignty, or some equivalent foundational authority, the problem of the legal impossibility of entrenchment arises.

No claim is being made here that the image of community—of popular sovereignty arising from free association of citizens establishing some kind of morally unified collectivity—is essential as the image of society which **any** documentary constitution must somehow appeal to in order to secure its status as fundamental law. As a substitute for 'the people' one might envisage the charismatic 'saviour' who gives law, probably in time of emergency and danger to bring order and justice to the polity. The image of a society structured by the inspiration of such a charismatic figure or figures—perhaps charismatic only because of the circumstances of the times—is likely to be an *imperium* image of some kind. It might well found

[75] Cf. J. Jaconelli, *Enacting a Bill of Rights: the Legal Problems* (Oxford, 1980).

[76] Institute for Public Policy Research, *The Constitution of the United Kingdom* (London, 1991).

the authority of a documentary constitution, perhaps through the kind of process which Max Weber described as the routinization of charisma.[77] In modern times this process might be seen in the establishment of constitutions at the beginnings of the independent existence of nations or after periods of crisis or war. Again the idea of 'the past as present'—the timelessness of tradition—might found the authority of a documentary constitution, although the best illustration of the constitutional appropriation of this authority would seem to lie in the idea of the 'unwritten' ancient constitution of common law.

We have noted, however, how the imagery of the regulated society in British constitutional thought reinforces the specific form of constitutional authority embodied in parliamentary sovereignty. It seems that common law cannot easily be invoked to provide principles that could limit or challenge parliamentary sovereignty since this sovereignty is itself given legitimacy by the common law. The image of society symbolized in British constitutional thought encompasses the idea of the Rule of Law (of law, once created, having authority over all within the realm) but envisages the citizen as passive in relation to the processes of law creation.

The symbolic significance of components of the British constitution is most obvious and consistent when viewed in connection with the image of *imperium*—the image of a hierarchically ordered society of individuals united only in their allegiance to superior authority. It might be appropriate to conclude with two further instances of this powerful symbolism. The survival of the House of Lords as a second chamber can undoubtedly be explained or defended on functional grounds—in terms of what Bagehot called 'efficient' elements of the constitution. Yet in its present form its main constitutional significance—more central than its specific legislative or governmental powers—might be considered to be the permanent symbolic rejection at the very heart of the constitutional structure of the idea of popular sovereignty—of the image of society as a free association of autonomous citizens agreeing together on the nature of their (self-) government. Hereditary peers do not sit as representatives within the Lords but are the traditional élite class of the realm incorporated **directly** in Parliament. Their constitutional importance is primarily as a symbol of *imperium*; of a society founded on hierarchy, deference, and distant, unchallenged political authority.

Again, the legal necessity for the recording of the monarch's assent to legislation is regarded as a matter of pure formality in most discussions of British constitutional law. Yet the symbolism of the requirement for the monarch's assent to legislation as the final element in the parliamentary legislative process insists—again at the very heart of

[77] M. Weber, *Economy and Society* (Berkeley, Cal., 1978), 246ff.

the constitutional process of law creation—that royal power (and thus established hierarchical structures of political society, immune from democratic modification and carrying the weight of ancient privilege) is necessary in order to confer final authority as law on anything proposed through democratic processes. In practice the conferring of this authority will not be refused.[78] But the provision for its formal conferment reinforces in every democratic legislative act the symbolism of hierarchy and subjection—evoking the image of *imperium* implicit in law, and the cultural source from which the constitution continues to draw its ultimate authority.

[78] See e.g. Marshall *op. cit.*, 21–3.

2

Equality and Moral Independence: Private Morality and Public Law

T. R. S. ALLAN

> That only is a free government, in the American sense of the term, under which the inalienable right of every citizen to pursue his happiness is unrestrained, except by just, equal, and impartial laws.
>
> *Slaughter-House Cases* 16 Wall. (83 US) 36 (1972), Field J (dissenting), citing Blackstone as authority.

PUBLIC lawyers generally assume that the British and American Constitutions dictate radically different answers to fundamental questions concerning political authority and individual rights. The written constitution's status as higher law is contrasted with the sovereignty of Parliament, a contrast suggesting a familiar opposition between the supremacy of natural law, on the one hand, and the unchallenged dominion of positive law, on the other. As Roger Cotterrell suggested in chapter one, it may be wise to exercise caution in drawing parallels, in the sphere of constitutional fundamentals, between the two systems of government. There are none the less reasons for seeking common ground in the protection of individual rights. Beneath the surface of constitutional arrangements, which seem to flaunt their contrasting philosophies of government, lie profoundly difficult questions whose answers I shall argue depend more on political theory, and less on settled tradition, than is often acknowledged. If constitutional theory is always a segment of political philosophy, issues of legal interpretation must ultimately turn as much on underlying visions of liberal democracy as on more prosaic analysis of legal text and precedent.[1]

Several recent British and American cases raise in acute form an important question of political theory, concerning the extent to which the law may properly enforce conventional or popular morality.[2] Considerations of both liberty and equality argue in favour of stringent limitations on

[1] Cf. R. Dworkin, *Taking Rights Seriously* (London, 1977), ch. 5; and *A Matter of Principle* (Oxford, 1986), chs. 1–2. See also P. Craig, *Public Law and Democracy in the UK and the USA* (Oxford, 1990), esp. ch. 1. Craig examines the implications of several theories of justice and democracy for judicial review (while warning against exclusive focus on the judicial role).

[2] For general discussion see H. Hart, *Law, Liberty, and Morality* (Oxford, 1963): P. Devlin *The Enforcement of Morals* (Oxford, 1965): N. MacCormick, *Legal Right and Social Democracy* (Oxford, 1982), ch. 2.

the power of a democratic majority to translate its own moral preferences into criminal law. If, with John Stuart Mill, we favour an independent criterion of 'harm' as justification for legal enforcement—a criterion of 'critical' as opposed to 'positive' morality[3]—we may doubt the legitimacy, and perhaps also the legality, of restrictions on individual freedom which serve only to satisfy popular sentiment in matters of personal morality.

The idea that the United States Constitution should be understood in accordance with Mill's thesis about the limits of legitimate government has often been rejected by judges and commentators.[4] It is well established that government may lawfully impose restrictions on people's conduct to further general public interests, or protect public values, which cannot be justified as preventing harm to particular individuals. Scalia J has been one of the foremost champions of the power to enforce conventional morality, even for its own sake. In concurring with the Supreme Court's judgment in *Barnes* v. *Glen Theatre*,[5] upholding a statute which proscribed nude dancing, where no likelihood existed that any viewer would be offended, Scalia J insisted that such activities could be prohibited in the absence of any harm to others on the ground that they were considered '*contra bonos mores*'.[6]

However, Scalia J's view is plainly controversial. The four dissentients, who held that the statute's improper purpose was to proscribe the message which nude dancing communicated, in breach of the First Amendment, held a more restricted view of permissible legislative purposes.[7] White J observed that the statute discriminated between expressive and non-expressive conduct of the same type: it did not enact a **general** prohibition on nudity. Scalia J's response, which stressed the distinction between forbidden nudity in public and permissible nudity in private, might be thought to require some further justification. Since the legal enforcement of conventional morality must always be compatible with those individual rights which the Constitution affirms, the legitimacy of any restriction of freedom, in the service of some collective interest or value, must depend on what constitutional rights are implicated and how they are understood. The minority in *Barnes* considered that regulation of the sort in question could be justified only as a means of preventing public conduct from causing offence to others.

Mill's principle of limited government, suitably interpreted, may offer useful guidance in fashioning an appropriate vision of the Constitution as a charter for government of a free society. The due process clause of the

[3] Cf. Hart *op. cit.*, 17–24. See J. Mill, *On Liberty* (first published in 1859).
[4] See e.g. L. Tribe, *American Constitutional Law* (Mineola, NY, 1988, 2nd ed.), 1302–6.
[5] (1991) 115 L Ed. 2d. 504.
[6] *Id.*, 517.
[7] White J's dissent was joined by Marshall, Blackmun, & Stevens JJ.

Fourteenth Amendment can readily be viewed as embodying limitations on the power of a State to enforce conventional morality. It can clearly be argued that such an interpretation is supported by the First Amendment, protecting freedom of conscience by safeguarding the free exercise of religion and entrenching the separation of Church and State.[8] Although inevitably a morally-laden concept, invoking contested notions of benefit and detriment, we should seek a sense of 'harm' to the interests of persons which does not appeal to religious or ethical convictions which many people would reasonably reject. The effort to distinguish between legitimate considerations of 'public decency', on the one hand, and matters of 'private immorality', on the other, may reasonably be thought a necessary feature of a liberal democracy based on principles of equal citizenship and religious tolerance.[9] Freedom of conscience, if genuine, arguably entails at least a limited sphere of liberty of independent action as well as belief. It would otherwise be a somewhat abstract liberty, lacking all connection to a person's autonomy in the practical matter of living his life.

Admittedly, Mill's defence of the harm principle was ultimately grounded in utilitarian ethics. It might therefore be understood primarily as a warning to elected representatives that legislating on the basis of popular morality is generally unwise, rather than as affording the grounds of a constitutional right to moral independence. It is difficult to derive such a right, with appropriate force, from utilitarian arguments alone.[10] While British lawyers adhere to the dogma of unlimited parliamentary sovereignty, of course, the harm principle can never function as a constitutional restraint which is enforceable in the courts.

However, Mill's persuasive denunciation of criminal laws which constrain people's conduct on the basis of conventional morality, where their acts inflict no concrete harm on particular persons, cannot easily be relegated to the legislative sphere, as if his principle had nothing to say to courts. Good reasons exist for regarding Mill's principle as expressing a right to moral independence lying at the heart of modern constitutionalism, and which is therefore pertinent to British and American constitutional theory. Suitably elaborated, such a right assists in making sense of the (derivative) right to privacy which forms the basis of the Supreme Court's decisions on contraception and abortion; and these decisions have lessons (I shall argue) for a better understanding of the general ideal of equality which underpins the rule of law.

[8] Cf. D. Richards, *Toleration and the Constitution (*New York, 1986).

[9] Cf. Hart *op. cit.*, 38–48.

[10] See generally J. Rawls, *A Theory of Justice (*New York, 1977), ch. 1: Dworkin (1977) *op. cit.* esp. chs. 6–7. For a defence of the harm principle based on government's duty to promote, not violate, autonomy, see J. Raz, *The Morality of Freedom* (Oxford, 1986), ch. 15.

In *Griswold* v. *Connecticut*,[11] a constitutional right of privacy was invoked to deny the validity of a State prohibition on the use of contraceptives within marriage; and in *Roe* v. *Wade*,[12] the Court held that the right to privacy encompassed the decision to choose an abortion. A woman's right to decide to terminate her pregnancy could be restricted only by a compelling State interest; the State interest in preserving the life of the foetus became compelling only when the foetus was capable of surviving outside the womb. These decisions safeguard personal autonomy by insulating the individual's 'right of decision' about procreation from State interference, protecting the decision to enjoy sexual relations without begetting or bearing a child.[13] The underlying principle of self-determination in matters of conscience—or 'private morality'—is plainly part of a wider political theory of liberal constitutionalism.

Contemporary Supreme Court jurisprudence concerning fundamental rights provides a fascinating insight into the implications of liberal political theory for modern constitutional government. Its chief significance lies in the nature of the conflict revealed between rival visions of the constitutional order. American constitutional theory is quite as much concerned with determining the requirements of the rule of law, or foundations of constitutionalism, as with the meaning of the Bill of Rights: in practice, the two matters are scarcely possible to distinguish. It may be strongly argued, then, that constitutional doctrine inevitably depends on considerations of political theory, which resist resolution on the basis of textual analysis alone. Conflicting interpretations of the Bill of Rights reflect different theories of the nature of constitutional government.

It may therefore be wrong to assume that appropriate answers to fundamental questions of political authority and legitimacy necessarily depend on the existence or absence of a written constitution entrenching basic rights. Different constitutional arrangements may none the less be consistent with a broadly common approach to the most important questions about individual freedom. If, then, a right to moral independence—encompassing related ideas of liberty, privacy, and self-determination or autonomy—can be defended as part of an attractive interpretation of American constitutionalism, it is reasonable to suggest that British lawyers may have something to learn from the American experience of protecting basic rights. The present essay sketches the outlines of such an argument, drawing attention to some recent decisions of interest in each jurisdiction.

[11] 381 US 479 (1965).

[12] 410 US 113 (1973).

[13] See *Carey* v. *Population Services International* 431 US 678 (1977), esp. 687: 'Read in the light of its progeny, the teaching of *Griswold* is that the Constitution protects individual decisions in matters of childbearing from unjustified intrusion by the State'; (Brennan J).

THE RULE OF LAW, EQUALITY, AND MORAL INDEPENDENCE

As a constitutional principle the rule of law clearly means more than formal legality, in the jejune sense in which government actions must be properly authorized. It would hardly be satisfied by a constitution which placed unlimited powers in the hands of government officials, permitting unfettered discretion in the conduct of public affairs. As a constitutional principle, the rule of law demands some form of separation of powers, so that the propriety of government actions may ultimately be tested by independent judges against limits established by valid legislation or accepted constitutional norms.[14]

The chief point of such an arrangement, however, must be to curtail the opportunities for unfair or discriminatory government action against particular groups or identifiable individuals—particularly those who might oppose government policies, or constitute unpopular minorities whose oppression would pose little threat to the ruling party's hold on power. The separation of powers entails a division between legislative and executive powers in order to ensure both generality and equality. If laws are sufficiently general, in the sense that they apply to all on equal terms, no one can be singled out for special treatment or hostile discrimination.[15]

It is this, essentially formal, conception of equality—the governance of laws which apply to everyone, including the legislators themselves—which Scalia J has invoked in his interpretation of American constitutionalism. He was, for example, prepared to recognize only one limit on the power of a State to override a patient's choice to decline medical treatment.[16] The Fourteenth Amendment's equal protection clause required the democratic majority to accept for themselves whatever they imposed on everyone else. The weakness of that requirement, however, is at once apparent. If the principle of generality were not supplemented by further constraints on the **content** of the laws, there would be equality—in any genuine sense, affording real protection—only for those who formed the majority or shared its convictions and aspirations.

The Court's equal protection jurisprudence, in particular the special scrutiny attracted by laws which infringe fundamental rights or employ 'suspect classifications', plainly repudiates a formal conception of equality, confined to generality. Even the lesser requirement that legislative classifications should have a fair rational basis serves a more fundamental

[14] See T. Allan, *Law, Liberty & Justice* (Oxford, 1993), ch. 3.

[15] Cf. F. Hayek, *The Constitution of Liberty* (London, 1960) 278–9, and *Law, Legislation and Liberty* (London, 1982) III, esp. ch. 13.

[16] *Cruzan* v. *Director, Missouri Department of Health* 497 US 261, 300 (1990).

ideal of equality by placing significant constraints on the content of general laws.[17]

We should reject a purely formal conception of equality, as an interpretation of the rule of law, on the ground that it is morally deficient and even arbitrary. A virtuous legal form could too easily disguise a vicious political substance. If we are anxious to prevent oppression of minorities by overtly discriminatory legislation, it is difficult to see how we could consistently tolerate laws which, though general in their terms, inevitably penalize such groups in practice. The governing ideal of equality, which explains and justifies the basic constitutional division of powers, also imposes constraints on the content of general laws in order to protect unpopular groups. Are we not driven inexorably, by our commitment to the essential idea of equality, towards the acceptance of constitutional limits on the purposes which regulation may seek to achieve, and the manner in which it pursues them?

The miscegenation laws struck down in *Loving* v. *Virginia*[18] applied equally to black and white: the State sought to support the validity of statutes prohibiting interracial marriages on the basis that they punished equally the white and Negro parties. The Court rightly repudiated such a defence on the ground that the Fourteenth Amendment barred all official State sources of invidious racial discrimination; the obvious purpose of the statutes was to prevent intermarriage which threatened 'white supremacy'. The formal equality between black and white, secured by equal punishment for equivalent conduct, could not justify a measure which, in substance, reflected and reinforced assumptions of white racial superiority.

Once the necessity for distinguishing between legitimate and illegitimate purposes is accepted, legislation or government action penalizing those whose lives, beliefs, or conduct are widely thought immoral or unworthy seems a primary candidate for special scrutiny. In the absence of criteria of harm, which retain some independence from popular morality, there is nothing to insulate the victims of popular prejudice from hostile discrimination. No useful distinction can be drawn between popular morality and popular prejudice, even if it were thought legitimate to impose the former. Popular morality—even if consistent and articulate[19]—will inevitably reflect ethical or religious principles whose imposition on everyone would violate the fundamental equality which freedom of conscience seems designed to secure. Freedom to reject constraints on conduct which form no part of one's own moral code, where those constraints serve no interests which can be generally acknowledged on the basis of reasons all can understand, should therefore be considered a

[17] See generally P. Polyviou, *The Equal Protection of the Laws* (London, 1980), ch. 2.
[18] 388 US 1 (1967).
[19] Cf. Dworkin (1977) *op. cit.*, 248–55.

constituent of equal citizenship.[20] The damage to the freedom and dignity of those whose conduct is regulated by laws enforcing conventional morality can be fairly assessed only in the light of their own values and aspirations. No assessment which discounted such values and aspirations, even if not widely shared, could be consistent with a genuine commitment to equal citizenship.[21]

In practice, attempts to force everyone to comply with the moral code of the majority, even in matters of 'private morality', serve only to legitimate and foster hatred and contempt for those who resist. Moreover, it will generally be impossible to distinguish between the enforcement of popular morality, for its own sake, and the deliberate repression of dissenting minorities. Hostility to a minority may be too easily disguised as a moral aversion to its practices. Only a commitment to the impartial protection of freedoms widely regarded as central to personal fulfilment and human dignity, whatever form their exercise may take, at least in private, can give the idea of equal citizenship real substance and content.

Equality and sexual autonomy

It follows that, in denying the existence of any constitutional right of homosexuals to engage in acts of sodomy, the majority judgment in *Bowers* v. *Hardwick*[22] denied legitimate claims to equality as well as liberty or privacy. In overturning the Court of Appeals' holding that a Georgia statute, which made it a criminal offence to commit sodomy, violated rights of privacy protected by the Ninth Amendment and by the due process clause of the Fourteenth, the Supreme Court majority sanctioned the imposition of conventional sexual morality on those who would reject its demands. The right of privacy which explained the Court's decisions on contraception and abortion was distinguished on the ground that those decisions acknowledged a fundamental right to decide whether or not to beget or bear a child. There had been no connection established 'between family, marriage, or procreation on the one hand and homosexual activity on the other'.[23]

This reasoning failed to confront the relevant questions of principle at an appropriate level of generality—one which prevents the repression of a minority masquerading as the suppression of immoral conduct.[24] As Blackmun J's powerful dissenting opinion emphasized, the grounds of the right of privacy, which acknowledge the central role that marriage and

[20] Cf. Richards *op. cit.*, (1986) esp. ch. 8.
[21] See generally Dworkin *op. cit.*, (1986) chs. 2, 9, & 17.
[22] 478 US 186 (1986). [23] *Id.*, 191 (White J).
[24] Cf. Tribe, *op. cit.*, 1421–35.

procreation play in individuals' personal lives, support recognition of the right of every person to control the nature of his intimate associations with others. Nor was it pertinent that condemnation of homosexual conduct was 'firmly rooted in Judaeo-Christian moral and ethical standards'.[25] Blackmun J rightly insisted that such legislation could not properly be justified by its conformity to religious doctrine, or by the antiquity of traditional hostility. He could not accept that 'either the length of time a majority has held its convictions or the passions with which it defends them' could deprive the Court of its duty of scrutiny.[26]

The House of Lords' decision in *Brown*[27] is open to similar objections, even if in that case no question arose concerning the validity of the statute. It was not suggested that the court's role could go beyond its interpretative function, determining the meaning and scope of the Offences against the Person Act 1861 according to accepted canons of judicial construction. Even within that narrower sphere, however, it may be argued that the majority mistook the nature of their duty toward the rule of law.

The issue in *Brown* was whether a person's consent to minor injuries caused during sado-masochistic homosexual practices constituted a defence to charges of assault and wounding under sections 20 and 47 of the 1861 Act. In refusing to acknowledge such a defence, the majority chose to penalize private, consensual activities which they considered morally repugnant. The judges thereby usurped Parliament's role by effectively widening the scope of the criminal law on the basis of their own perceptions of the public interest.[28] By contrast, Lords Mustill and Slynn showed better appreciation of the courts' constitutional role by allowing the defendants the benefit of the law's uncertainty. Lord Mustill observed that, though formally a case about the criminal law relating to violence, it was in reality a case concerning private sexual relations.[29] Rejecting a view of the law which condemned all infliction of bodily harm above the level of common assault, permitting a defence of consent only in special circumstances, he declined to 'impress upon section 47 an interpretation which penalizes the relevant level of harm irrespective of consent'.[30]

Lord Slynn's dissent was coupled with an acceptance that the case raised questions of policy which lay beyond the courts' legitimate sphere. It was a matter of policy for the legislature to decide: 'If society takes the view that this kind of behaviour, even though sought after and done in private, is either so new or so extensive or so undesirable that it should be brought now for the first time within the criminal law, then it is for the legislature to decide.'[31] Lord Mustill's approach, however, appears more radical,

[25] 478 US 196 (Burger CJ, concurring).
[26] *Id.*, 210 (Blackmun J).
[27] [1993] 2 All ER 75.
[28] See esp. Lord Jauncy, 92.
[29] *Id.*, 101.
[30] *Id.*, 116.
[31] *Id.*, 124.

denying the legitimacy of legislative intrusion into matters of 'private morality'. Asserting that the State should interfere with an individual's right to choose his own lifestyle no more than is necessary, he denied that the proper standards for judging the defendants' conduct were those of the criminal law. The individual must apply his own moral standards, or be subject to the 'moral pressures exerted by whatever religious or other community to whose ethical ideals he responds'.[32]

Our analysis of the rule of law suggests that we should not treat Lord Mustill's remarks as indicating only reasons for legislative restraint. If we can ultimately make most sense of our adherence to the rule of law in terms of a commitment to equality, which grounds a fundamental right to moral independence, we may be driven to deny legislative competence altogether as a matter of constitutional morality. The conventional view that parliamentary sovereignty cannot be made to bow to such considerations in the absence of a Fourteenth Amendment, or its equivalent, must therefore at least be open to question. If parliamentary sovereignty is ultimately inconsistent with a reasonable interpretation of the point and substance of our constitutional tradition, it should perhaps be repudiated in deference to better legal doctrine and more persuasive political theory.[33]

If we accept the idea that law and politics in the liberal democratic state should be grounded in a **public morality**—one in which all citizens can join in upholding as a fair basis of co-operation, permitting a wide range of different conceptions of the good life for human beings—laws which proscribe private behaviour on the sole ground that the majority find it repugnant or disgusting are indefensible. They are in practice indistinguishable from the grosser forms of prejudice based on class or sex or race. Laws prohibiting conduct which causes only minor physical harm to consenting adults of sound mind reflect an impermissibly partisan, moralistic outlook at odds with a society based on the co-operation of equals for mutual advantage. If, then, we embrace the rule of law as an ideal worth striving to preserve, and acknowledge the roots of that ideal in a conception of equality between citizens, we should be gravely suspicious of laws whose only rationale is to enforce conventional morality. *Brown* was not only wrongly decided, according to accepted canons of judicial construction: it was contrary to a proper understanding of liberal constitutionalism.

Parliamentary sovereignty can only be defended on the basis of some conception of democracy. But democracy itself assumes a public conception of political morality which denies the authority of moral views dependent solely on particular religious convictions, or reflecting beliefs about personal conduct, which cannot be defended on the basis of reasons

[32] *Id.*, 116.

[33] Further see Allan, *op. cit.*, chs. 3 & 11.

everyone can understand. If democracy is not to consist merely in the imposition on unwilling minorities of the moral attitudes of an intransigent majority, there must be scope for genuine public discourse, aimed at facilitating agreement on features of the general good, but relatively neutral or impartial between conflicting views about personal morality. In the absence of independent criteria of harm which all can understand, reflecting principles which all are capable of applying, such minorities are effectively excluded from the political process. Their participation is hollow since they cannot engage the attention of the majority by appealing to common aspirations. There is no shared, common territory on which argument can take place about the appropriate course of public policy.[34]

The argument must not be overstated. It is undoubtedly reasonable to conclude that there is no general principle either of American or British constitutional law which forbids the enactment or enforcement of laws based on, or reflecting, conventional morality—even if the conventional morality is repudiated by some of those whose conduct is regulated. But it does not follow that **all** such laws are legitimate, in either polity. It can be strongly argued that there is (or, at least, **ought** to be) a principle which requires the suffering such laws cause to those whose freedom is curbed or denied to be justified by—reasonably proportionate to—the public benefits which are alleged to be sought or secured. Some such principle seems to be a concomitant of the rule of law, in the sense explained, because where such alleged public benefits are (wholly) disproportionate to the burdens imposed, those whose conduct is regulated are not treated fairly as equal citizens.

Laws proscribing private homosexual activity offend equality because they give insufficient weight to individual freedom and personal fulfilment. Even if such laws reflect sincere moral conviction, as opposed to prejudice against and hostility towards an unpopular group, the suffering they inflict is not proportionate to, or justified by, any resulting, **legitimate** public benefit. The public good allegedly served by laws proscribing private conduct between consenting adults of which the majority disapproves is not legitimate because it appeals to sectarian religious or ethical doctrine—sectarian in the sense that it invokes no values which those whose conduct is regulated could reasonably be expected to share or even, perhaps, to understand. A genuine commitment to equal citizenship must entail at least the attempt to assess the suffering imposed, from the perspective of

[34] Cf. D. Lyons, *Ethics and the Rule of Law* (Cambridge, 1984), 191. See also J. Rawls, *Political Liberalism* (New York, 1993), esp. Lecture VI. Rawls argues that 'exercise of political power is proper and hence justifiable only when it is exercised in accordance with a constitution the essentials of which all citizens may reasonably be expected to endorse in the light of principles and ideals acceptable to them as reasonable and rational' (217).

the goals and aspirations of those who suffer, in the context of a public good susceptible of appreciation on grounds of public reason, available to all (conscientious) citizens.[35]

Michael Perry has argued that laws against homosexual sodomy discriminate against homosexuals, in breach of the Fourteenth Amendment, because such laws are, in practice, the only instances of the enforcement of private sexual morality.[36] He cites a judgment of the Kentucky Supreme Court, which noted that all non-marital sexual activity violated traditional morality:

> The issue . . . is not whether sexual activity traditionally viewed as immoral can be punished by society, **but whether it can be punished solely on the basis of sexual preference** . . . The question is whether a society that no longer criminalizes adultery, fornication, or [sodomy] between heterosexuals, has a rational basis to single out homosexual acts for different treatment.[37]

Perry contends that the predicate of a law which proscribes homosexual activity is undoubtedly that persons of homosexual orientation are inferior—less worthy of respect and concern—to those of heterosexual orientation.

It is doubtful, however, if Perry's argument is ultimately consistent with his view that it may be sufficient justification that a law is 'expressive'—expressing a State's judgment that prohibited conduct is immoral. (He thinks that the law in issue in *Griswold* might have been defended successfully as expressing a judgment about the immorality of contraception; and, accordingly, that *Eisenstadt* v. *Baird*,[38] concerning Massachusetts' judgment that the distributing of contraceptives to unmarried people was immoral, was wrongly decided.) Perry overlooks the possibility that homosexual activity might sincerely be thought more gravely immoral than other activities which flout traditional sexual morality. His assumption that laws against homosexual sodomy reflect only prejudice against homosexuals is certainly plausible, but not incontrovertible. But such laws are truly objectionable because, even if they **do** reflect or express genuine moral conviction, they inflict suffering wholly disproportionate to any public gain. Laws which may destroy the happiness of those affected merely in order to 'express' moral distaste or condemnation violate any notion of equal citizenship acceptable in a morally pluralistic, but fair, society.

[35] On public reason, see Rawls, n.34 *supra*. Compare relevant decisions of the European Court of Human Rights: *Dudgeon* v. *UK* (1981) 4 EHRR 149; *Norris* v. *Ireland* (1988) 13 EHRR 186.

[36] M. Perry, *The Constitution in the Courts: Law or Politics?* (New York, 1994), 174–9.

[37] *Commonwealth [of Kentucky]* v. *Wasson* 842 SW 2d 487, 499–501 (1992); emphasis added.

[38] 405 US 238 (1972).

Perry's argument is thus incomplete: it lacks an appropriate conception of public benefit or public reason—an account of the sort of considerations which may legitimately be taken into account, and their appropriate weight, in justifying restrictions on personal freedom. Perry is also able to conclude that laws restricting abortion achieve sufficient public benefit only because he ignores considerations of context and weight. He dismisses as ridiculous the suggestion that no legislator could reasonably conclude that in saving foetal life—a legitimate public benefit—restrictive legislation is proportionate to the 'undeniably great' costs to women affected. But does not the reasonableness of that conclusion depend on the nature and severity of the restrictions? Should the courts really abstain altogether from enquiring whether such legislation is truly justified by a 'compelling State interest', and sufficiently narrowly drawn, leaving the matter entirely to the legislature?

It is not necessary to defend the decision in *Roe* v. *Wade*, as Perry does, on the grounds that some restrictions on abortion may be thought to express 'sex-selective sympathy and indifference'.[39] Legislation which (for example) permits a woman to abort a pregnancy, at any stage, only where it is necessary to save her life, or prevent grievous harm to her physical health, arguably attempts to secure an alleged public benefit at a wholly disproportionate cost. It accords that benefit a **weight** which, in view of its deeply controversial nature, reflecting divided religious and ethical views, denies the equality of those women who conscientiously dissent. Such legislation, unless suitably qualified, seems to flout basic constitutional values in a society which acknowledges freedom of conscience as well as the principle of the sanctity of human life. The legitimacy of a restriction on freedom must be assessed in the light of the nature and scale of both the benefit secured and the obligations imposed; and where the benefit is fiercely contested, the burden of justification would seem the greater.[40]

These considerations indicate the close connection between the Fourteenth Amendment's due process clause, as interpreted by the Court, and the values served by the equal protection clause. Some of the cases concerned with rights to liberty or privacy could as well be explained by considerations of equality; and the principles of equality which underlie liberal constitutionalism can be fully understood only by analysis of those interests which seem crucial to the autonomy or self-determination of all citizens. Accordingly, much of the equal protection case-law itself focuses attention on the special nature of the personal interests shielded from legislative intrusions based on conventional or popular morality.

[39] *Op. cit.*, 185.

[40] Perry wishes to restrict judicial review on the ground of proportionality or reasonableness because of the 'competing assumptions, values and priorities characteristic of pluralistic American society'. See below for an argument to the opposite effect.

Although the Court declined to decide, in *Eisenstadt* v. *Baird*,[41] whether legislation could be based solely on the view that use of contraceptives was immoral, its insistence on equality of rights for married and single persons provided the necessary protection from laws which prohibited socially harmless conduct. The right of privacy recognized in *Griswold* could not be confined to marriage, which was an association of two individuals 'each with a separate intellectual and emotional make-up':

> If the right of privacy means anything, it is the right of the **individual**, married or single, to be free from unwarranted governmental intrusion into matters so fundamentally affecting a person as the decision whether to bear or beget a child.[42]

I have suggested that the right to moral independence, as an aspect of individual autonomy, derives from a more fundamental conception of equality. From this perspective, there is an obvious analogy between discriminatory laws against minority sexual practices, on the one hand, and those suspect classifications which are acknowledged as invoking strict judicial scrutiny, on the other. Once it is accepted that criminal laws reflecting conventional morality may be illegitimate where they derive no support from principles which all citizens could fairly be expected to approve or apply, the relevant distinctions between persons become as dubious as those based on race or class or sex. Equality as an ideal clearly implies that certain differences are inherently inappropriate as a basis for regulation, and that legislation which utilizes such distinctions flouts the human dignity of those affected.[43]

Moreover, many of the reasons generally offered in defence of this form of strict scrutiny apply to those whose sexual morality is widely condemned. Homosexuals are invariably in a minority, as regards the exercise of political power in the field of sexual morality, and to that extent as vulnerable to prejudice as other 'discrete and insular minorities'.[44] And laws enforcing sexual morality also reinforce the stigma of inferiority attaching to such minorities, just as racial discrimination reflects and generates perceptions of inferiority.[45] No doubt the requirements of equal citizenship are controversial, and the proper limits of majoritarian legislative power hard to define; but it hardly follows that the demands of justice can be met in the absence of judicial review. The complex equal

[41] 405 US 238 (1972).
[42] *Id.*, 453 (Brennan J). For useful analysis of *Eisenstadt*, see Polyviou *op. cit.*, 221.
[43] Cf. Polyviou, *op. cit.*, 235–6.
[44] *US* v. *Carolene Products* 304 US 144, 152 n. 4 (1938) (Stone J). See Note, 'The Constitutional Status of Sexual Orientation: Homosexuality as a Suspect Classification', (1985) 98 *Harvard LR* 1285.
[45] *Brown* v. *Board of Education* 347 US 483, 494, (1954) (Warren CJ). Cf. Tribe *op. cit.*, 1516–8.

protection jurisprudence shows that the Court has considered it necessary to travel beyond mere rationality review in the case of various sorts of discrimination with 'deep social and legal roots', whose fairness is now considered questionable.[46]

The ideal of equality seeks both to secure the independence of those who repudiate aspects of conventional morality in their private lives, and to protect unpopular minorities from hostile discrimination at the hands of the majority. The two purposes are independent but connected: legislation may often reflect hostility and contempt towards those whose freedom is curbed in response to popular pressure for conformity. Where the autonomy and dignity of citizens are especially vulnerable, there are often grounds to doubt the legitimacy of legislative restrictions on their freedom. The requirement of equal respect, which government should show towards all citizens, is violated by laws which express moral condemnation without also preventing genuine social harm, impartially and even-handedly assessed.

In *Skinner* v. *Oklahoma*,[47] the Court invalidated a State law providing for the sterilization of persons twice convicted of 'felonies involving moral turpitude'. While someone twice convicted of larceny came within the scope of the statute, a person convicted of embezzlement (and certain other specified offences) was expressly excluded. The tendency to penalize a particular class of common (as opposed to white-collar) criminals was a matter of grave concern, given the implications of the statute for personal autonomy. The power to sterilize, if abused, could 'cause races or types which are inimical to the dominant group to wither and disappear'.[48] Such a measure must raise serious questions of legitimacy in any modern constitutional democracy: 'When the law lays an unequal hand on those who have committed intrinsically the same quality of offence and sterilizes one and not the other, it has made an invidious a discrimination as if it had selected a particular race or nationality for oppressive treatment.'[49]

Freedoms of speech and conscience

Although the idea of equality, as a constitutional fundamental, is rarely given explicit consideration by British courts, it may constitute an important component of their appeal to principles of justice and fairness. Moreover, the underlying role of equality in judgments about the rationality of administrative regulations was acknowledged by Lord Russell of Killowen in 1898. In *Kruse* v. *Johnson*,[50] he suggested by-laws

46 *San Antonio School District* v. *Rodriguez* 411 US 1, 107 (1973) (Marshall J, dissenting).
47 316 US 535 (1942). 48 *Id.*, 541. 49 *Id.*
50 [1898] 2 QB 91, 99.

which were 'partial and unequal in their operation as between different classes' as an example of delegated legislation which would be struck down as invalid and unreasonable. On close inspection, considerations of equality are found to underlie many instances of judicial review of administrative action, where the court has intervened in defence of fairness or rationality.

Wheeler v. *Leicester City Council*[51] is an illuminating example. The Council was held to have acted unlawfully by denying a local rugby football club access to a recreation ground which it administered. It had sought to strengthen its policy in respect of apartheid by inducing the club to oppose a forthcoming tour of South Africa by the English Rugby Football Union. In his judgment in the Court of Appeal, dissenting from the majority decision in favour of the Council, Browne-Wilkinson LJ condemned the Council's action as an impermissible constraint on fundamental freedoms of speech and conscience—freedoms which could be curtailed only by express legislative provision.

In not explicitly affirming that approach, the House of Lords seemed to rest its decision on a wider basis. The Council's action amounted to an improper attempt to punish the club, which had itself acted lawfully and reasonably. Although there had therefore been an abuse of statutory powers, in the sense that powers of management of public property were not given to punish dissenters from the Council's policies, further explanation still seems required: the problem remains of distinguishing between permissible and impermissible purposes. The Council's action was ultimately wrong because it violated rights to equality: rights not to be punished, or treated adversely, in consequence of a public authority's disapproval or resentment or dislike.

Despite the House of Lords' apparent reluctance to endorse Browne-Wilkinson LJ's reliance on rights of speech and conscience, we can see that the two approaches were actually complementary rather than opposed. If freedoms of speech and conscience are held in special regard in liberal democracies, it is ultimately because they are an ineradicable component of equal citizenship. The notion of co-operation among equals for mutual benefit could make no sense without these rights. Without free speech and freedom of conscience there would be no opportunity to influence the terms of social co-operation, and no possibility of pursuing private goals and interests with a stable legal framework, suitably neutral between diverse individual needs and aspirations. To punish someone for expressing an unwelcome opinion, or for failing to endorse the policy of a public

[51] [1985] 2 All ER 151 (CA); [1985] AC 1054 (HL).

agency, is to deny his fundamental right as an equal citizen to moral independence—to express his own judgements both in word and deed.

Thomas Scanlon has argued, extending Mill's thesis, that at the core of our convictions about freedom of speech lies the principle that restrictions are illegitimate if their purpose is to prevent the acceptance of certain beliefs. A legitimate government is 'one whose authority citizens can recognize while still regarding themselves as equal, autonomous, rational agents'.[52] To be autonomous in the relevant sense, a person must be free to decide what to believe and in weighing competing reasons for action. He may still rely on the judgement of others, but only where he is able to advance independent reasons for trusting their judgement, and can weigh their advice against contrary evidence. An equal, rational citizen could not concede to the State the power to curtail his ability to distinguish truth from error, by restricting speech. Nor could he allow the State to prevent debate about whether its restrictions on conduct were justified. A citizen is entitled to form an independent judgement, based on full information and open discussion, as to whether the law should be obeyed.

Scanlon illuminates the close association between freedom of speech and questions of obedience, showing how the legitimacy of the State's authority rests on the preservation of that freedom. The right to freedom of speech, however, should not be understood to rest on the citizen's need for full information alone. The connection with the issue of obedience suggests a further ground of protection. Freedom of speech is guaranteed in liberal societies as the expression of conscience: it enables those who reject the values and interests of others, including the majority, to voice their dissent.

The Supreme Court's decision in *West Virginia State Board of Education* v. *Barnette*[53] is a fine illustration. Schoolchildren could not lawfully be required to salute the flag and recite a pledge of allegiance, as a means of promoting national unity by instilling feelings of patriotism, because forcing a person publicly to profess a statement of belief 'invades the sphere of intellect and spirit' which it was the purpose of the First Amendment to reserve from official control. Coercion of affirmations of loyalty was inconsistent with the fundamental idea of government by consent of the governed.[54]

In the light of these reflections on the legitimacy of government and freedom of speech, the reference by both House of Lords and Court of Appeal in *Derbyshire County Council* v. *Times Newspapers*[55] to leading American authorities on the importance of political speech is of some significance. The view expressed by the Supreme Court of Illinois in *City of*

[52] T. Scanlon, 'A Theory of Freedom of Expression', (1972) 1 *Philosophy & Public Affairs* 214.

[53] 319 US 624 (1943).

[54] *Id.*, 641 (Jackson J). See also *Wooley* v. *Maynard* 430 US 705 (1977).

[55] [1992] 3 All ER 65; [1993] 1 All ER 1011.

Chicago v. *Tribune*,[56] and those of the United States Supreme Court in *New York Times* v. *Sullivan*,[57] were invoked in support of the conclusion that an English local authority could not maintain an action for damages for defamation; the threat of civil actions for libel would have an unacceptable 'chilling effect' on the right to criticize. The untrammelled freedom to criticize in good faith the conduct of government is plainly a central element of equal citizenship, constituting a condition of the State's legitimacy and the citizen's obligation to obey the law.[58]

The close association of freedoms of speech and conscience, and their special status as conditions of legitimate government, underlie and explain the modern American jurisprudence concerning the advocacy of unlawful action. In *Brandenburg* v. *Ohio,*[59] the Supreme Court held that a State was not permitted to proscribe speech advocating resort to force or illegal action unless such advocacy was intended, and likely, to incite imminent lawless action. If the idea of moral independence envisages every citizen making his own judgements about whether or not his government should ultimately be obeyed, or whether its iniquity demands active resistance or rebellion, it must be wrong for the State to censor the expression of pertinent opinions. It is only where the circumstances allow no time for proper reflection, and for the interposition of reasoned debate, that proscription of 'subversive advocacy' can be justified. In *Whitney* v. *California*,[60] Brandeis J drew a clear distinction between advocacy of lawbreaking which is likely to have immediate consequences, and such advocacy in circumstances where opportunity existed for full discussion. The founders, 'believing in the power of reason as applied through public discussion', had 'eschewed silence coerced by law—the argument of force in its worst form'.[61]

The principle of moral independence, however, acknowledging the equal right of every citizen to form his own judgements about questions of morality and justice, supports a wider scope of constitutional protection than that for political speech alone. It demands a similar protection for all forms of speech which express or contribute to the formation of people's convictions about matters of personal and moral integrity. Just as the right to moral independence is incompatible with restrictions on conduct which causes no harm, in an appropriately neutral, non-sectarian, sense of 'harm', it is inconsistent with restrictions on speech which enforce State judgements about the truth or value of certain opinions. Censorship of

[56] 307 Ill 595 (1923).
[57] 376 US 254 (1964).
[58] For a fuller discussion see Barendt's chapter in this volume. As Loveland notes in the introductory chapter, the *Sullivan* principle is currently crossing a good many geographical boundaries; see 16–23 above.
[59] 395 US 444 (1969).
[60] 274 US 357 (1927).
[61] *Id.*, 375–6. Cf. Rawls *op. cit.*, (1993), 340–56.

speech on the ground of its worthlessness, as determined by either official or majority opinion, denies the independence which equality requires.[62]

Even speech which disparages people on grounds of their race or religion, however unwelcome and distasteful, can be curbed only on the illegitimate assumption that government is entitled to decide which moral and political convictions people can be allowed to consider or endorse. It is one thing for government to condemn racial or religious bigotry, and promote legislation to counter discrimination; it is surely another for the State to ban the expression of views which challenge the social and political vision on which its legitimacy is grounded.[63] As Harlan J observed, in a case which restricted the scope of the 'fighting words' doctrine,[64] freedom of expression was designed not only 'in the hope that use of such freedom will ultimately produce a more capable citizenry and more perfect polity', but also 'in the belief that no other approach would comport with the premise of individual dignity and choice' upon which the political system rested. It follows that the stringent conditions placed by the Court on permissible legislative proscriptions of offensive speech may be required, not merely by the most plausible interpretation of the First Amendment, but by the nature of legitimate constitutional government.

Speech as action

However, the expression of conscience is not confined to the spoken or written word. The right of moral independence, which equality demands, entails at least a limited freedom to **act** in accordance with one's own moral judgement. A person can ultimately express his own considered opinions about the sort of life he wishes to lead, and the sorts of moral constraints he accepts, only by acting accordingly. The protection of a realm of private morality from legal constraint, preventing government interference with private conduct whose only vice is to offend those who have different moral or religious convictions, is therefore demanded by the principles which underlie the protection of speech. An autonomous citizen will resist restrictions on conduct which causes no harm, in a sense of 'harm' amenable to justification in terms of public reason, just as he will deny the State authority to censor the ideas and information which form the basis of his beliefs.

Reflection on the decision in *Stanley* v. *Georgia*[65] undermines reliance on sharp distinctions between word and conduct in the context of matters of conscience. In holding that the mere private possession of obscene matter could not constitutionally be made a crime, the Court stressed the

[62] Cf. Richards *op. cit.*, ch. 6.
[63] *Id.*, 189–95.
[64] *Cohen* v. *California* 403 US 15, 24 (1971), citing *Whitney* v. *California* 274 US 357 (1927), 377 (Brandeis J).
[65] 394 US 557 (1969).

'added dimension' of the right to receive information and ideas supplied by the appellant's right to privacy. He was 'asserting the right to read or observe what he pleases—the right to satisfy his intellectual and emotional needs in the privacy of his own home'.[66]

The majority's attempt, in *Bowers*, to confine *Stanley* to its grounding in the First Amendment was therefore unconvincing: as Blackmun J pointed out, *Stanley* rested as much on the Fourth Amendment as on the First.[67] It would hardly show genuine respect for a right of moral independence, if such a right is acknowledged, to restrict the protection of privacy to the reading of obscene materials and deny it to consensual sexual activity. If the 'right to be let alone' is truly the 'most comprehensive of rights and the right most valued by civilized man',[68] it surely encompasses either activity in the confines of a person's home.[69]

It is ultimately because freedom of speech is a necessary component of the idea of equal citizenship that consistency requires respect for individual autonomy in many matters of conduct as well. Freedom of conscience, for similar reasons, cannot be confined, in matters of religion, to conventional expressions of religious faith; it must extend to protect forms of religious worship which, while posing no harm (in an appropriately neutral sense of harm) may yet cause offence to others. In *Church of the Lukumi Babalu Aye* v. *City of Hialeah*,[70] the Supreme Court struck down as unconstitutional various municipal ordinances whose intended effect was to outlaw the Santerian religion, whose practice, which included the sacrifice of animals, had provoked local opposition.

Although the regulations were defended as contributing to animal welfare and the protection of public health, the Court held that they discriminated against the Santerians by having a plainly selective impact on their activities: the regulations lacked the neutrality and 'general applicability' necessary to comply with the First Amendment. The texts of the ordinances had been 'gerrymandered with care to proscribe religious killings of animals but to exclude almost all secular killings'. The First Amendment had been infringed because the restrictions imposed denied the equality of those affected: the regulations could not be justified on grounds which applied fairly to all members of the community.[71]

Although the First Amendment identifies freedoms of special significance, the underlying conception of equality needs no formal bill of rights to provide it with a constitutional anchorage. It is a conception implicit in the idea of government by consent—the consent of every citizen, in so far as that can be secured by appeal to reasonable principles, widely accepted.

66 *Id.*, 565.

67 478 US 186 (1986), 207.

68 *Olmstead* v. *US* 277 US 438 (1928), 478 (Brandeis J).

69 Cf. Tribe *op. cit.*, 1425–6.

70 124 L Ed. 2d. 472 (1993).

71 The relevance of equal protection analysis was explicitly recognized at 495.

English principles of administrative law, which seek to inhibit abuses of power by preventing unfair discrimination against those lawfully resisting the policy ambitions of public authorities, proceed from the same underlying conception of the rule of law. The *Wheeler* case has been followed in subsequent challenges to the decisions of local authorities, where those decisions have been shown to reflect an attempt to punish or coerce commercial companies whose policies have earned disapproval.[72]

Even if British courts are unable or unwilling to review the legality of primary legislation, unlike their American counterparts, they can properly be expected to interpret statutes, so far as possible, in a manner which limits the scope for discrimination by public authorities against those who lawfully dissent from the political vision currently endorsed by a majority of the electorate or its representatives. And if the legitimacy of such a style of interpretation is granted, on grounds of political theory, it may reasonably be conjectured that there are ultimate limits even to parliamentary authority, which stem from commitments to liberty and justice considered as fundamental.

The fundamental right to equality—or equal concern and respect—prevents arbitrary discrimination against particular groups, where 'arbitrary' denotes the lack of a convincing basis of government action in pursuit of the public interest. The equal protection of the laws serves a wider goal of individual liberty or autonomy than that secured by respect for fundamental rights of expression or conscience: it prohibits imposition of unfair burdens on unpopular groups, and precludes coercion of those who lawfully withhold co-operation from public agencies. The identification of a threat to liberties of speech or conscience, however, justifies the more rigorous scrutiny of State action alleged to violate equality. This is because what constitutes unfairness, or illegitimate coercion, can only be determined in the context of government purposes and those private interests or aspirations regarded as threatened.

The idea of equality, if it is to be more than an indeterminate aspiration without practical legal force, entails a concept of proportionality. The more significant the purposes which government seeks to pursue, in the sense of their importance to the well-being of the whole community, the greater the sacrifice it may be reasonable to impose on minorities whose freedom may have to be curtailed. By the same token, State intrusions into the enjoyment of those rights or interests regarded as fundamental require greater justification than those which make more modest demands on the citizen's duty of obedience. Infringement of fundamental civil and political rights, or restriction of the freedoms they protect, poses the more serious threat to the citizen's self-esteem. Such infringement or restriction, by

[72] See *R* v. *Lewisham LBC ex p. Shell* [1988] 1 All ER 938; *R* v. *Ealing LB, ex p. Times Newspapers* (1986) 85 LGR 316; Allan *op. cit.*, ch. 7.

constituting the most serious challenge to his claim to equal citizenship, undermines his obligation of obedience by impugning the basis of his consent to authority.

It is reasonable to infer a right of moral independence, as a companion right to those of freedoms of speech and conscience, from the general idea of equality in view of the fundamental interests it would protect. Insofar as a right of moral independence enhances a person's autonomy, by safeguarding his freedom to choose a lifestyle or moral commitments and ideals of which the government may disapprove, it enables him more readily to accept the State's authority. And in acknowledging the critical role in a person's self-conception and self-fulfilment of such matters as sexual identity and personal morality, and in restricting governmental interference, the State gives substance to the ideal of equality which it professes to honour. The consequent limitations on the powers of the democratic majority to achieve their own aspirations are the price of a society based on genuine respect for minorities and tolerance of their conflicting ambitions.

The right to moral independence cannot be absolute, any more than those of speech or conscience. Restrictions on the public exhibition of conduct which may cause widespread moral offence may be a legitimate concession to majority sensibilities. But it does not follow that restrictions on private conduct, on similar grounds, would be compatible with equal respect. A principle of proportionality is necessary to ensure that those whose conduct is regulated, contrary to their desire, can acknowledge such regulation as a reasonable accommodation—one which does not by its oppressive nature deny their equality, or impugn the value and point of their citizenship.

The requirement that State interference with a fundamental right should be proportionate to a legitimate governmental objective—justified by a 'compelling State interest' and adopting 'means narrowly tailored' to achieve it—explains why Souter J was correct, in *Church of Lukumi*, to reject a conception of 'formal neutrality'. Questioning the Court's adherence to the rule formulated in an earlier case,[73] whereby a neutral and generally applicable law need not to be so justified even it had the incidental **effect** of restricting a particular religious practice, Souter J insisted on the importance of **substantive** neutrality. In addition to requiring a secular objective, not designed to discriminate against any religion, the Free Exercise Clause of the First Amendment generally required government 'to accommodate religious differences by exempting religious practices from formally neutral laws'.[74]

[73] *Employment Division, Dept of Human Resources of Oregon* v. *Smith* 494 US 872 (1990).

[74] (1993) 124 L Ed. 2d. 472, 509. See also the concurring opinion of Blackmun & O'Connnor JJ, 519–21.

A rigid distinction between laws whose **object** was to prohibit religious exercise, on the one hand, and laws with that **effect**, on the other, would hardly be compatible with a genuine commitment to equal citizenship. An impediment to religious observance is no less an impediment because it is not imposed as a means of deliberate suppression. Whether or not it can be justified—and is capable of justification to those affected—must depend on its importance or necessity to the attainment of a legitimate public interest. While freedom of conscience cannot be invoked to prevent every governmental measure which might incidentally inhibit religious observance, its claims must nevertheless receive proper attention: that is, state interference must be no more than is proportionate to pressing social needs. A narrower, more formal interpretation of the Free Exercise Clause, permitting incidental restraints on religious observance without any test of compelling State interest, plainly weakens the ideal of government by consent. Souter J noted the crucial importance of the issue for the integrity of those citizens affected: 'neutral, generally applicable' laws, drafted from the perspective of the non-adherent, had 'the unavoidable potential of putting the believer to a choice between God and government'.[75]

The sanctity of life and moral independence

The failure of the joint opinion of O'Connor, Kennedy, and Souter JJ, in *Planned Parenthood of Southeastern Pensylvania* v. *Casey*,[76] to invalidate some of the restrictions on the availability of abortion imposed by Pennsylvania demonstrated the complexity of many judgments about the scope or weight of fundamental rights. Those justices upheld requirements for the provision of advice designed to dissuade a woman from proceeding to an abortion, and for a twenty-four hour delay to enable her to consider it, which Stevens and Blackmun JJ thought unconstitutional. They nevertheless affirmed that a woman's right to seek an abortion in the early stages of pregnancy was grounded in the conception of privacy which underlay the freedom to use contraception. The State could not impose its own vision of appropriate conduct: 'The destiny of the woman must be shaped to a large extent on her own conception of her spiritual imperatives and her place in society'.[77]

Since *Roe* v. *Wade*[78] had acknowledged the State's legitimate interest in protecting the potentiality of human life, as well as its concern with the woman's health, regulations should not be struck down merely because they had the incidental effect of making an abortion more difficult or expensive

[75] *Id.*, 519.
[76] 120 L Ed. 2d. 683 (1992).
[77] *Id.*, 699.
[78] 410 US 113 (1973).

to obtain: 'Only where State regulation imposes an undue burden on a woman's ability to make this decision does the power of the State reach into the heart of the liberty protected by the Due Process Clause.'[79] A statute would be invalid if it placed a 'substantial obstacle' in the path of a woman seeking an abortion, where the foetus had not yet obtained any chance of survival outside the womb. Although Stevens and Blackmun JJ denied the power of the State to seek to dissuade a woman from choosing abortion, they agreed with the joint opinion that the State could properly express a preference for 'normal childbirth' and take steps to ensure that the woman's choice was 'thoughtful and informed'.

The emphasis given by the joint opinion to the importance of respect for precedent may appear to diminish its significance for political theory. O'Connor, Kennedy, and Souter JJ buttressed their argument from principles of liberty and privacy by a lengthy exposition of the contribution made by consistency to the Court's legitimacy. There had been no evolution of legal principle since *Roe* which could justify its overruling as a 'mere survivor of obsolete constitutional thinking'. That decision had sought to resolve an intensely divisive controversy on the basis of constitutional analysis. In such circumstances, its repudiation would appear as a surrender to political pressure: 'A decision to overrule *Roe's* essential holding . . . would address error, if error there was, at the cost of both profound and unnecessary damage to the Court's legitimacy, and to the Nation's commitment to the rule of law.'[80]

The strength of this appeal to the rule of law is somewhat diminished, however, by the cogent objections expressed in the dissenting speeches. There is force in the observations of Rehnquist and Scalia JJ that, despite its affirmation of *Roe's* 'central holding', regarding a woman's right to choose abortion before 'viability', the Court's adoption of the 'undue burden' formula, together with the joint opinion's repudiation of *Roe's* strict trimester framework for regulation of abortion, amounts to a substantial weakening of that right.

Moreover, the joint opinion's warning of the danger of retreating from a decision in response to popular protest is hardly conclusive: it could be no more legitimate to 'adhere to the decision at all costs least it **seem** to be retreating under fire'.[81] The Chief Justice was surely correct to assert that the Court's duty was to ignore public opinion in deciding constitutional questions. In any event, as he noted, a decision to **affirm** *Roe* could as easily be construed as a response to popular demonstrations in its support. If the Court was right to overrule *Plessey* v. *Ferguson*, which upheld the 'separate but equal' treatment of racial minorities, and *Lochner* v. *New*

[79] 120 L Ed. 2d. 683 (1992), 713.
[80] 120 L Ed. 2d. 683 (1992), 709.
[81] *Id.*, 769 (Rehnquist CJ).

York, protecting contractual freedom, it must be right to overrule *Roe* if persuaded that that decision was clearly wrong.

Casey's contribution to an understanding of the nature and scope of a right of moral independence must lie in the Court's recognition of the close association between abortion and other, more widely accepted, aspects of privacy and autonomy. *Stare decisis* was important only in the sense of the Court's commitment to a consistent scheme of legal principle, which could justify a range of other decisions concerning related rights and interests. Even if a State is permitted to assert an interest in the protection of potential life, which exists from the start of pregnancy, equality precludes denial of a woman's right to choose an abortion altogether, at least under appropriate conditions. As Stevens J emphasized, it is a matter of conscience which necessarily implicates the rights of privacy and personhood; and it is in this sense that the Court's decision primarily serves the basic ideal of the rule of law (in the sense of constitutional government). It seems wrong to enforce an official view about essentially ethical or religious matters against women who dissent, when that view is deeply controversial and the interference with the woman's liberty and autonomy plainly severe.[82]

Scalia, J's objection that the Court begs the whole question by assuming that the foetus is only **potential** human life misfires. If the foetus were accorded the right to life enjoyed by a 'person', within the meaning of the Fourteenth Amendment, abortion would not be a legitimate procedure even to protect the life or health of the mother. And if the foetus were a person, in the appropriate sense, the States would hardly be free, if they wished, to permit 'abortion on demand', as Scalia J also asserts. It is hard to accept that the regulation of abortion could be **wholly** left to the democratic process as if it raised no questions of constitutional propriety at all: could a court which accepted responsibility for protecting fundamental rights to life and liberty properly leave their reconciliation entirely to majority vote? Scalia J's plea for the Court to relinquish its jurisdiction in favour of the operation of ordinary politics is hardly more plausible than his objection to a process of constitutional adjudication dependent on the making of 'value judgements', even if his plea would be widely accepted in Britain.[83]

Although *Casey* does not clearly define the nature of the State's interest in regulating abortion—Stevens J mentioned the 'offence' caused to many

[82] Cf. R. Dworkin, *Life's Dominion: An Argument about Abortion and Euthanasia* (London, 1993), ch. 6. Rejecting theistic belief as a necessary element of religion, Dworkin describes people's beliefs about the intrinsic value of human life as '**essentially** religious'.

[83] 120 L Ed. 2d. (1992), 795–6. Tribe denies that fundamental rights can properly be reduced to political interests, even if that is 'the case under a parliamentary government where the legislative will is supreme'; *op. cit.*, 1351–2.

people by the practice of abortion—it seems clear that it consists in an ethical or religious concern which, even if not commanding universal assent, is none the less widely shared. While the State's intervention may be largely confined to ensuring that the woman's choice is well-informed and thoughtfully made, the legality of even those restrictions assumes the legitimacy of a governmental endorsement of the value of protecting potential human life. It would follow that government may adhere to an abstract principle of the sanctity of life, whose scope transcends its application to any particular individual person.[84] 'Neutrality' on a matter of such general moral concern is not demanded.[85] The principle of equality—in the form of the right to moral independence—merely limits the scope of permissible State action, in defence of a fundamental value, in deference to the dignity and autonomy of those who dissent.[86]

Even if equality is not denied by legal provision to protect the developing foetus, however, it does not follow that an abstract governmental interest in the sanctity of life may justify laws which compel submission to unwanted medical treatment, or even laws proscribing suicide. Respect for personal autonomy arguably requires more stringent limitations on the powers of the State: in the absence of any bodily harm to anyone (or any potential human being) who does not knowingly consent, governmental intervention in harder to justify. In *Cruzan* v. *Director, Missouri Department of Health*,[87] the Supreme Court acknowledged a constitutionally protected liberty interest in refusing unwanted medical treatment, but held that Missouri was entitled to require 'clear and convincing' evidence of a patient's wishes, even in the case of a person diagnosed to be in a persistent vegetative state who had no prospect of improvement or recovery. Evidence of the patient's probable attitude, as provided by previous statements to a friend, could lawfully be rejected as insufficient: a patient's liberty must be balanced against a State's unqualified interest in the preservation of life, regardless of the quality of life that that person might enjoy.

Although O'Connor J qualified her concurrence with the majority judgment by observing that a State may be bound to give effect to the

[84] Dworkin examines the idea of the sanctity or 'inviolability' of life in *Life's Dominion*. The importance of protecting potential human life is implicit in recognition of the special significance of the woman's autonomy in this sphere: see Tribe *op. cit.*, 1348–9.

[85] The State is not, e.g., required to pay for abortions even if it funds health care incident to childbirth: it may make 'a value judgement favouring childbirth over abortion, and . . . implement that judgement by the allocation of public funds'; (*Maher* v. *Roe* 432 US 464 (1977)).

[86] The significance of 'viability', as the point at which the life of the foetus becomes the paramount consideration, may lie in the fact that, until viability, the foetus is wholly dependent on the woman's body, whose autonomy is therefore uniquely vulnerable: see Tribe *op. cit.*, 1357–8.

[87] 497 US 261 (1990).

decisions of a surrogate decision maker, where one had been appointed, the Court's deference to State policy (as expressed in Missouri's 'Living Will' statutes) might be thought exaggerated. Brennan J (with whom Marshall and Blackmun JJ agreed) denied that the State had any legitimate interest in a person's life abstracted from his interest in living it. There was accordingly nothing which could outweigh that person's choice to abstain from medical treatment, insofar as it could be accurately ascertained. In applying its 'clear and convincing' evidence standard, the Missouri Supreme Court had imposed an illegitimate obstacle to the exercise of a fundamental right.

Even if there can be no objection to the assertion of an abstract governmental interest in the preservation of life in the context of abortion, where that interest amounts to safeguarding potential life, in the present context such an assertion arguably lacks a suitably impartial, or commonly accepted, moral foundation. For Stevens J (also dissenting in *Cruzan*); personal choice in matters concerning one's own life or death touched the core of personal liberty, so that the Court's decision drove an illegitimate wedge between the patient's life, on the one hand, and her liberty or happiness on the other. In the circumstances of the case, the State's intervention amounted to an 'effort to define life's meaning' rather than an attempt to preserve its sanctity. Disregarding the patient's own interests, the State sought to equate her life with the biological persistence of her bodily functions.[88]

A study of these recent American cases suggests that, properly understood, the legal debate is less about the requirements of the Constitution, in any technical sense, than the morality of abortion or euthanasia, on the one hand, and the (moral) legitimacy of enforcing the collective judgements on those matters against dissentients, on the other. The divergence of judicial opinion was not confined to the meaning of the sanctity of life. Its roots lay in conflicting conceptions of democratic authority—divided views about the legitimacy of attempts to enforce the conventional or collective morality in this sphere. Stevens J, in *Cruzan*, emphasized the role of individual conscience, which indicated the inappropriateness of governmental interference. The Court's distinction between life in the abstract and the quality of life enjoyed by any particular individual could only be defended as a matter of religious faith. Whatever its justification in theology or 'speculative philosophy', it was 'radically inconsistent with the foundation of all legitimate government'.[89]

[88] *Id.*, 344–6. Stevens J observes that the patient's fate was 'in the hands of the State legislature instead of in those of her family, her independent neutral guardian *ad litem*, and an impartial judge—all of whom agree on the course of action that is in her best interests'; (339).

[89] *Id.*, 356. See also Stevens J at 343: 'not much may be said with confidence about death unless it is said from faith, and that alone is reason enough to protect the freedom to conform

In *Cruzan*, as in *Casey*, Scalia J's plea for the Court to withdraw from the field begs too many questions about the nature of constitutional government. He considered that the federal courts had no legitimate power to interfere with State decisions. Even when the patient's wishes **were** demonstrated by clear and convincing evidence, she had no protected constitutional right. Just as Missouri's Supreme Court had declared that 'broad policy questions bearing on life and death are more properly addressed by representative assemblies' than judicial bodies,[90] Scalia J considered that it was for the citizens of Missouri, through their elected representatives, to decide whether the patient's wish to die should be honoured. Judges could not overrule the wishes of the majority because the Constitution was silent on the matter.[91]

Scalia J's reliance on the Constitution's literal text simply sidesteps the important arguments of political theory on which the dissentients relied. It is not merely that a positivistic adherence to the 'literal' text is incompatible with a genuine attempt to confront the complex moral issues which abstract guarantees of equality and due process necessarily raise.[92] The crucial point is that the fundamental nature of the issues inherently resists resolution on the basis of **textual** analysis (unless abstract moral argument is **dressed** as textual interpretation).

Given the inevitable constraints of language, and continuing controversy about how to reconcile the conflicting indications of theory and tradition, the content of **any** constitution—whether given formal textual expression or not—will be heavily dependent on the moral and political judgements of its interpreter. And the more important the question—the more fundamental an issue of interpretation to the underlying idea of government by consent of the governed—the greater that dependence will inevitably become. For the meaning of constitutional provisions, and the scope of constitutional doctrines, are inextricably related to the nature of the enterprise which the interpreter understands constitutional theory to be.

The radical error of lawyers who emphasize 'original intent' as a means of resolving serious controversy, or purport to rely wholly on textual analysis, is shared by those who doubt the relevance of American case-law to British or European legal debate. They overlook the necessary dependence of constitutional interpretation on moral and political values

choices about death to individual conscience'. It was not, he thought, 'within the province of secular government to circumscribe the liberties of the people by regulations designed wholly for the purpose of establishing a sectarian definition of life'; (350).

[90] *Cruzan* v. *Harmon* 760 SW 2d. 408 (1988), 426.

[91] 497 US 261, 293. Cf. *Airedale NHS Trust* v. *Bland* [1993] 1 All ER 821, 888–9 (Lord Mustill).

[92] See esp. Dworkin *op. cit.* (1993), ch. 5.

which can serve to explain and justify the practice of interpretation itself. The submission of questions of political authority and individual right to judges—even in the course of ordinary litigation—is not a self-evident good. It can be defended and understood only in the light of a general theory about the nature and merits of constitutional government, and about the meaning and value of the rule of law.

Perry's recent defence of the 'originalist' approach to judicial review—treating the constitutional text **as originally understood** as authoritative—is coupled with an important distinction between textual interpretation and the specification of norms.[93] Hans-Georg Gadamer's objection to any distinction between (historical) understanding and practical application is met by distinguishing instead between ascertaining the original meaning of a constitutional provision, on the one hand, and the specification (for purposes in hand) of an indeterminate norm, on the other.[94] Since a provision will often be indeterminate, a judge's understanding of the judicial role and his wider political morality will govern his choice between plausible outcomes. Moreover, the judge's political morality will also be likely to influence his resolution of contested questions of constitutional interpretation—where historical materials render plausible more than one conclusion about original meaning. Perry concludes that, contrary to the assumption of many of its adherents, that originalism provides a weak basis for doubting the legitimacy of the Supreme Court's more expansive protection of individual rights: the crucial debate concerns 'the role the Court should play in confronting the indeterminacy both of constitutional history and of constitutional morality'.[95]

Despite Hoffman LJ's observation, in *Airedale National Health Service Trust* v. *Bland*,[96] that it was a 'somewhat unusual enterprise' for a judge 'to argue from moral rather than purely legal principles', he recognized that the legality of the decision to terminate treatment, in the case of a patient whose cerebral cortex (affording consciousness) had been destroyed, depended on the resolution of fundamental moral questions. His attempt to reconcile the conflicting principles of the sanctity of life and the patient's right of self-determination, in the circumstances of that case, drew expressly for support on the dissenting judgments in *Cruzan*. Stevens J's judgment was also cited by Butler-Sloss LJ in support of her view that considerations of quality of life, and the nature of a patient's death, must be weighed against the general principle of the sanctity and inviolability of life. Although Lord Goff drew a sharper distinction between the English criterion of the patient's best interests and the American 'substituted

[93] Perry *op. cit.* esp. chs. 1–6.
[94] *Id.*, 74–6, citing Gadamer, *Truth and Method* (Eng. trans, 1975), 275.
[95] *Id.*, 69.
[96] [1993] 1 All ER 821.

judgment' test, he stated none the less that he derived support from American decisions; and he entertained 'a strong sense that a community of view on the legal principles applicable in cases of discontinuing life support is in the course of development and acceptance throughout the common law world'.[97]

Admittedly, Lord Browne-Wilkinson doubted whether resolution of the underlying moral and ethical issues lay within the proper scope of common law development: he thought it the judges' function 'to apply the principles which society, through the democratic process, adopts' rather than 'to impose their standards on society'.[98] If, however, there is force in Stevens J's objections, in *Cruzan*, to the unhindered application of public policy, where it would deny the liberty of an incompetent patient on ethical grounds he rejects, it should not be assumed that unqualified judicial deference to the popular will is always legitimate, even in Britain.

Lord Browne-Wilkinson also observed that a doctor's decision to withhold medical treatment from an insensate patient with no prospect of recovery could properly be influenced by his own attitude to the sanctity of life. But if society must respect the conscientious convictions of the doctor, it should also defer, in some degree, to those of the patient, where these have been expressed, or to those of close relatives where they have not. As with abortion, the meaning of the sanctity of life and its requirements in the present context are deeply controversial. It is doubtful whether any government can legitimately impose a collective judgement which contradicts a patient's own considered opinion about how and when to die in the circumstances of cases like *Cruzan* and *Bland*.[99] Nor is it credible that Parliament might properly impose an 'absolute obligation' to prolong a patient's life by any means available, regardless of the quality of his life: 'common humanity requires otherwise'.[100]

CONCLUSION

In Britain, conflict between rival visions of liberal democracy, and their implications for both legal and political decision making, remains largely submerged: the sovereignty of Parliament, as generally understood, appears to strip such conflict of any practical importance. By contrast, the American practice of constitutional judicial review gives theoretical debate

[97] [1993] 1 All ER 873.

[98] *Id.*, 879. Lord Mustill also called for legislation: 'The formulation of the necessary broad social and moral policy is an enterprise which the courts have neither the means nor the right to perform'; (at 888).

[99] Cf. Dworkin *op. cit.* (1993), ch. 7.

[100] [1993] 1 All ER 868 (Lord Goff).

a central role in adjudication. It would be as foolish to ignore the American experience of shaping and protecting individual rights, however, as to think that the American jurisprudence is readily available for adoption or adaptation in Britain. Beneath the differences of constitutional tradition lie more abstract questions of political theory, whose contemplation, as they arise in either country, can inform our understanding of the rule of law and can thereby contribute to the evolution of public law in both.

Moreover, the degree to which ordinary common law adjudication is insulated from political theory is widely exaggerated, and to that extent the standard contrasts between the two systems of government over-drawn. Principles which favour a more restricted or more generous sphere of popular decision making in the United States may dictate a correspondingly more robust, or alternatively deferential, style of statutory interpretation in Britain; and the relevance (at least) of American decisions to wise development of the common law scarcely needs demonstration. The scope for judicial choice in Britain is attested by the cases examined; and if Britain were ever to entrench a bill of rights, accompanied by judicial review of primary legislation, the judges' recourse to political theory (and its application elsewhere) would become all the more obvious and necessary.

In neither country can public lawyers escape responsibility for seeking a coherent scheme of legal principle which can justify decisions defining the scope of rights and provide a legitimate counterweight, in appropriate contexts, to the outcome of ordinary politics and the exercise of political power. Our shared commitment to the rule of law imposes that responsibility. Political tradition no doubt significantly determines the nature and style of judicial review which each country would be willing to accept. But tradition affords no safe refuge from the controversial conclusions of 'abstract' theory. As the cases discussed reveal, the present Supreme Court is deeply divided about how the appropriate balance should be struck between theory and tradition. Conservatives, like Scalia, who favour the traditional scope of majoritarian power over considerations of personal liberty and autonomy drawn from the abstract clauses of the Constitution, are generally suspicious of the enlargement of judicial power. Such suspicions must be assuaged by convincing argument; but the appeal to tradition needs similar justification. Claims of tradition must themselves appeal to a conservative vision of the political order, in which individual autonomy in the areas we have studied gives way to a rival conception of the public good.

The appropriate role of judicial review must be found in the context of a theory of the rule of law and the nature of democracy. There are many versions of democracy and, accordingly, many views of the appropriate balance between legislative and judicial power. Rawls's view of the

Supreme Court as the exemplar of public reason—interpreting the Constitution in the light of an appropriate conception of justice—is allied to an ideal of democratic citizenship which itself appeals to public values which all citizens, whatever their religious or philosophical affiliations, can reasonably be expected to share.[101] Rawls questions even the common assumption that constitutional amendments, in the United States, must invariably be accepted; and there may be implications here for the theory of parliamentary sovereignty. Could the Court properly accept repeal of for the fundamental provisions of the First or Fourteenth Amendments as valid constitutional change?[102]

David Richards has argued that the American Bill of Rights serves to protect an inalienable right to freedom of conscience as the means of preserving the ultimate moral sovereignty of the people over the State or the political community. Drawing on Locke's arguments in favour of toleration and the idea of the social contract, in which basic human rights such as the right to conscience are placed beyond legitimate state interference, Richards explains that the sovereignty of the people depends on the subjection of government to each person's moral sovereignty—the 'independent control of the formation, expression, and revision of personal conscience'.[103] Acknowledgment of a 'background constitutional right' to moral independence provides the basis for an adequate interpretation of the rights of privacy and of freedom of speech and religion. The requirement of religious toleration, for example, is demanded by a contractarian political theory which expresses equal respect for persons' highest-order interests in the exercise of their moral powers of rationality and reasonableness.

Richards examines the development of Locke's ideas in the writings of Jefferson and Madison, which extend the principle of respect for conscience to include both the free exercise of religion and opposition to an established church. But Locke, of course, propounded a theory of government by consent of the people in the specific context of the British constitution, as reformulated by the events of 1688. His insistence on the inherent limits of political authority, and the existence of inalienable rights beyond the scope of the social contract, are fully as part of the British constitutional heritage as of the American.

British lawyers should join the debate which flourishes in the guise of constitutional interpretation in the USA since they are ultimately involved in the same endeavour—to fashion a form of government worthy of allegiance. And they should be as reluctant to contemplate the surrender

[101] *Political Liberalism,* Lecture VI. For discussion of Rawls's theory, and its implications for judicial review, see Craig *op. cit.*, chs. 8–9.

[102] Rawls *op. cit.* (1993), 238–9.

[103] *Op. cit.*, 99.

of fundamental rights of conscience and moral autonomy to majority vote, or an omnicompetent legislature, as the more persuasive of their American counterparts. Locke was clear that the obligation of obedience to law was destroyed by the assertion of 'absolute power over the lives, liberties, and estates of the people'.[104] He also observed that every man is ultimately judge for himself whether government has so abused its trust as to destroy its legitimate authority.[105] If, then, the idea of moral independence—with all its implications for freedoms of speech and conscience and personal morality—accords with our convictions about equality and justice, it should be defended as a principle of fundamental importance in both British and American public law.

[104] *Second Treatise of Government*, para. 222.

[105] *Id.*, paras. 240–2.

3

A Special Relationship? American Influences on Judicial Review in England

CAROL HARLOW*

ON the surface, our common legal heritage does seem to point to a 'special relationship' between British and American lawyers.[1] It has created a common vocabulary which permits us to communicate with each other in a way which frequently proves more difficult outside the boundaries of the common law.[2] We can instantly grasp the implications of concepts like 'substantive due process' or 'natural justice', even if the precise nuances may escape us.[3] Habeas corpus is a shared inheritance[4] and the term *locus standi* does not need translating, though we must be careful not to assume identity of meaning.[5] We can talk until well into the present century of a common corpus of authoritative writing. Blackstone's *Commentaries* were the settlers' legal Bible and many later texts were treated as a common legal resource. Austin's theory of sovereignty, however unsuited to the American context, was claimed by Gray as the basis of his own jurisprudential writing[6] and its influence may have penetrated further into American realism through the great Holmes.[7] Authors, academics, judges,

* I am particularly grateful to Neil Duxbury, David Feldman, Martin Loughlin, and Richard Rawlings for their help with this essay.

[1] For the origins of which, see R. Cosgrove, *Our Lady the Common Law: An Anglo–American Legal Community, 1870–1930* (New York, 1987), esp. ch. 1. See also, P. S. Atiyah & R. Summers, *Form and Substance in Anglo–American Law, A Comparative Study of Legal Reasoning, Legal Theory and Legal Institutions* (Oxford, 1987).

[2] Sir Otto Kahn-Freund, 'Common Law and Civil Law—Imaginary and Real Obstacles to Assimilation', in M. Cappelletti & M. Kohnstamm (eds.), *New Perspectives for a Common Law of Europe* (Leyden, 1978).

[3] See, B. Schwartz, 'Wade's New Edition and its Relevance for Americans' (1990) 42 Administrative LR 67, 69–73.

[4] M. Cantor, 'The Writ of Habeas Corpus: Early American Origins and Development', in H. Hyman & L. Levy (eds.), *Freedom and Reform. Essays in Honor of Henry Steele Commager* (New York, 1967).

[5] See Cane at 125–132 below. In continental legal systems, the term 'interest to sue' is more common, though the concepts are, of course, comparable.

[6] See, N. MacCormick, 'A Political Frontier of Jurisprudence: John Chipman Gray on the State' (1981) 66 *Cornell LR* 973. (I am grateful to Neil Duxbury for this point). MacCormick labels Gray as 'not a real "Realist" '.

[7] Cosgrove, *op. cit.*, 116–23, though he discerns in Holmes 'a distinct ambivalence about acknowledging a debt to Austin'.

and other senior members of the profession, knew, corresponded with, and visited each other. Indeed, Dicey, who lectured at and gloried in Harvard Law School, inaccurately if characteristically remarked both that 'America was essentially an English society' and that 'the laws of America were essentially those of England'.[8]

In the context of constitution and government, the same ease of communication was at first experienced. The American polity originated, after all, in British colonialism and the Constitution has its roots (though not exclusively) in the writings of British political philosophers.[9] Today, however, we must be careful not to read too much into this aspect of the 'special relationship', allowing the existence of a common language and linked history to delude us into imagining a greater commonality than in fact obtains. The federal American system of government has diverged greatly from our own unitary system. The separation of powers model adopted in the United States constitution renders it very much less possible for either Congress or state legislatures to resolve policy problems in the political arena.[10] The implication must be that our 'special' public law relationship is really with those Commonwealth countries with whom we share the common constitutional starting-point of a parliamentary or 'Westminster' system of government. This does not mean that we have nothing in common with or nothing to learn from America but only that our first point of contact is with Commonwealth legal systems such as Canada, Australia, and (especially, perhaps) New Zealand whose constitutional heritage and legal arrangements bear a much closer resemblance to our own. The cardinal rule of comparative law, as one of its greatest exponents tellingly warned,[11] is that legal transplants can succeed only in a compatible environment. If we are primarily interested in negative lessons—for example, general warnings about litigiousness in modern society—then there is probably sufficient similarity between our societies for the American experience to prove helpful.[12] If, on the other hand, we are more interested in legal transplants, then we need to consider more carefully how similar our legal and governmental systems really are. To continue my example, although a majority of western constitutions

[8] Cited in Cosgrove, *op. cit.*, 10.

[9] See, M. White, *The Philosophy of the American Revolution* (London, 1982); E. S. Corwin, 'The "Higher" Law Background of American Constitutional Law' (1928) 42 *Harvard LR* 149 (1928); and 'The Worship of the Constitution' 4 *Constitutional Review* 3 (1920), both reprinted in vol. I of R. Loss (ed.), *Corwin on the Constitution* (Ithaca, 1981).

[10] R. Dahl, *Dilemmas of Pluralist Democracy* (New Haven, 1982), 75–80.

[11] Sir O. Kahn-Freund, 'On Uses and Abuses of Comparative Law' [1974] 37 *MLR* 1.

[12] e.g., M. Galanter, 'Reading the Landscape of Disputes: What we Know and Don't Know (And Think we Know) About our Allegedly Contentious and Litigious Society' (1983) 31 *Univ. of Calif. LR* 225; and 'Law Abounding: Legalisation Around the North Atlantic' [1992] 55 MLR 1.

incorporate some variant of the separation of powers principle and a majority of their legal systems contain arrangements for some sort of judicial review, it does not follow that, even within the family of the common law, these arrangements are identical or, more relevant to my argument, share the same objectives. Take the single issue of review of the constitutionality of statute law, permitted by many constitutions including, since the landmark case of *Marbury* v. *Madison*,[13] the American. Classically, the British system did not permit review of statute and it was this tradition which was handed down to Commonwealth countries. Other writers in this collection have made reference to the use made by Australian courts of American precedents in changing tack.[14] For British courts to have done the same would clearly have been unthinkable without the impetus of the European Community and the rulings of its Court of Justice.[15] That the change will produce effects on the British legal systems is glaringly obvious; indeed, the effects have already been felt in the temerity with which the House of Lords subsequently demolished the Crown's ancient privilege against injunctive relief preserved by section 21 of the Crown Proceedings Act 1947.[16] How they will respond to their changed role is not readily predictable in terms of American experience. This is not to say, however, that America as well as Europe might not be able to offer prescriptive guidance as to how the British judiciary should exercise its new-found powers.[17]

The closer the parallels, the better the chance of successful legal transplant. To take our illustration further, there is a clear analogy between the staged move in Canada from the traditional common law position of 'negative rights' first to a non-binding Bill of Rights and then on to the Charter of Rights,[18] and our own slow and stubborn progression

[13] 5 US 60 (1803).

[14] *Nationwide News Party Ltd.* v. *Wills* (1992) 108 ALR 681. See Loveland, Barendt, and Ewing below.

[15] *R* v. *Secretary of State for Transport ex p. Factortame (No. 2)* [1990] 3 WLR 818 (remedies *pendente lite* must be provided for the protection of EC rights in national legal systems; statutory barriers must consequentially be disapplied). See, N. Gravells, 'Disapplying an Act of Parliament Pending a Preliminary Ruling: Constitutional Enormity or Community Law Right?' [1989] *PL* 568. See also R. Rawlings, 'Legal Politics: The United Kingdom and Ratification of the Treaty on European Union (Part Two)' [1994] *PL* 367 commenting on *R* v. *Foreign Secretary ex p Rees-Mogg* [1994] 1 All ER 457. And see *R* v. *Employment Secretary ex p Equal Opportunities Commission and Day* [1994] 2 WLR 409.

[16] *M* v. *Home Office* [1993] 3 WLR 433 (HL (E)).

[17] B. Markesinis, 'Comparative Law—A Subject in Search of an Audience' [1990] 53 *MLR* 1.

[18] For a concise historical account, see, D. Gibson, *The Law of the Charter: General Principles* (Toronto, 1986), 1–42; P. Hogg, 'A Comparison of the Canadian Charter of Rights and Freedoms with the American Bill of Rights', in W. S. Tarnopolsky and G. A. Beaudouin (eds.) *The Canadian Charter of Rights and Freedoms*, (Toronto, 1982). See also, R. Sheppard and M. Valpy, *The National Deal: The Fight for a Canadian Constitution* (Toronto, 1982).

towards convergence with the European Convention on Human Rights.[19] The very different tradition of the federal United States, with an entrenched Bill of Rights interpreted and policed for over two centuries by its federal Supreme Court, is much less congruous with that of the United Kingdom. The Canadian situation straddles the two, enabling Canadian courts to utilize the American experience. Yet, as Loveland notes in his introductory essay,[20] even this North American transfer has aroused fears that the 'communitarian political environment' may in this way be penetrated by brash American individualism. The sharp contrast between the pyramidal British constitutional structure and American federalism, the absence of any domestic Bill of Rights, and the very different constitutional ethos graphically described by Roger Cotterrell,[21] to my mind combine to make the Canadian model more helpful in the development of a 'rights jurisdiction' by British courts. Clearly, however, this raises wider questions about the comparative method. Lessons from Canada may ultimately prove to be lessons from America in diluted form. Again, identity of legal solution may in fact represent no more than the attempt of similar societies to resolve similar problems.

What has so far been said shows that an examination of American influences on British public law might range very widely—indeed, the essays in this book vividly illustrate this point. One approach might be historical, tracing the influence of American legal culture or of American public law on our own. A second approach would try to draw lessons from the American experience. This paper generally adopts the first approach, focusing on the narrow subject of judicial review.

Starting with the classic or formalist model broadly common to both countries at the start of the century, the paper traces the influence of two American models on modern English judicial review. Somewhat tentatively, since nomenclature is so often a source of controversy and confusion, I have labelled these respectively the 'Public Interest' model and the 'Legal Process' model. There are difficulties with both labels.[22] Public interest law is a term so well entrenched in the United States as to make it evocative. In England, however, it is advocates of the legal process model who tend to regard the concept of public interest as peculiarly their own.[23] As we shall see, public interest law has very different objectives to

[19] A. Lester, 'Fundamental Rights: the United Kingdom Isolated' [1984] PL 46; and 'English Judges as Lawmakers' [1993] PL 269.

[20] Above 18.

[21] Above 25–27.

[22] A fuller and more complex modelling analysis developed by J. Mashaw, *Due Process in the Administrative State* (New Haven, 1985) uses different terminology and my idea of the legal process model may not tally with his usage.

[23] See particularly, T. R. S. Allan, *Law, Liberty, and Justice, The Legal Foundations of British Constitutionalism* (Oxford, 1993); J. Jowell 'The Rule of Law Today' in J. Jowell & D. Oliver (eds.), *The Changing Constitution* (Oxford, 1994, 3rd ed.). There is an analogy here with the American civic republicans: see below.

this second, consensual model.[24] On the other hand, in the United States, precisely who is and is not a 'legal process' scholar is a matter of opinion complicated by a variety of views as to Ronald Dworkin's position on the positivist/realist spectrum.[25] To label Dworkin as a legal process scholar may thus be seen as idiosyncratic and a source of confusion.

Finally, in reading what follows, the reader should bear in mind that the very ease of communication and familiarity of the terminology leaves room for misunderstanding as well as understanding. The cherished 'special relationship' may be read as no more than part of a continuous traffic in ideas, variable from time to time in extent and direction. It may also prove as illusory on the legal as on the political plane.

JUDICIAL REVIEW: THE CLASSIC ENGLISH MODEL RE-ANIMATED

Let us take as a starting-point a period around the turn of the century when legal formalism was the prevalent common law orthodoxy. (I am not suggesting that it was the sole legal theory, only that it was accepted and comfortable[26]). Into this frame, a model of judicial review—I shall call this the classic model—which was both highly individualistic and conspicuously marked by judicial restraint, fitted easily in both countries;[27] judicial restraint is, though not necessarily confined to this theoretical school, a central tenet of legal positivism and formalism. To make this point differently, the dominance of a so-called 'private law' model of public law[28] on both sides of the Atlantic was an integral part of the common law inheritance and the tradition of legal thought in both countries. By 1954, however, coincidentally the year both of the Crichel Down scandal and the indubitably activist case of *Brown* v. *Board of Education*,[29] American commentators were suggesting a much greater boldness on the part of American judges. While it is not necessary here to delve too deeply into the reasons for this difference in approach, it is interesting to note those advanced by contemporary public law scholars. Street, for example, blamed attitudes induced by the Second World War for English timidity.[30]

[24] See for a definition, J. Cooper & R. Dhavan, *Public Interest Law* (Oxford, 1986), 5 and see further below.

[25] V. Wellman, 'Dworkin and the Legal Process Tradition, the Legacy of Hart and Sacks' (1987) 29 *Arizona LR* 413.

[26] A full account is contained in M. Loughlin, *Public Law and Political Theory* (Oxford, 1992), 139–164.

[27] J. Dickinson, *Administrative Justice and the Supremacy of the Law in the United States* (Cambridge, Mass., 1927), esp. 32–8.

[28] See further, A. Chayes, 'The Role of the Judge in Public Law Litigation' (1976) 89 *Harvard LR* 1281.

[29] (1954) 347 US 483.

[30] H. Street, 'Book Review' 59 *Yale LJ* 590 (1950). See also, B. Schwartz & H. W. R. Wade, *Legal Control of Government: Administrative Law in Britain and the United States* (Oxford, 1978), 4–5.

Jaffe, in his study of English and American judges, remarked that it had always been anticipated that the federal American judge would 'assume a role in the polity far greater than that played by his confrère in Britain'.[31] K. C. Davis, visiting England in 1961, saw English judicial review as restricted by an old-fashioned, positivist corset, 'astonishing to one with a background in the American legal system'. English judges strove to avoid consideration of the policy aspects of the issues they decided, an attitude which he saw as running deep in the legal profession. The typical lawyer:

responds with consternation to an inquiry into the soundness of the policies embodied in a judicial decision, and, if he persists, the inquirer is gently reminded that judges do not consider policy questions and that only Parliament can change the law; the task of the judge is wholly analytical—to discover the previously existing law, and to apply it logically to the case before the court.[32]

Two dates are commonly chosen as significant in the creation and establishment of a modern system of judicial review in England. The first is 1963, the date of the first of the 'trilogy of great cases' which mark a more activist approach on the part of the British judiciary.[33] The second is 1977, the date of the introduction of the reform of administrative procedure by amendments to Order 53 of the Rules of the Supreme Court.[34]

For Wade, writing in 1978, the turn around was home-grown and based in the main on the discovery 'that Britain had in the past developed much more administrative law than the legal profession understood'.[35] At the constitutional level, it was premised on a strong 'control theory' of administrative law. The prevalent judicial ideology is conveniently summarized in a contemporary passage from Wade himself:

The state has seized the initiative, and has put upon itself all kinds of new duties. Hand in hand with these new duties must go new powers. In order to carry out so many schemes of social service and control, powerful engines of authority have to

[31] L. Jaffe, *English and American Judges as Lawmakers* (Oxford, 1969), 83.

[32] 'The Future of Judge-Made Public Law in England: A Problem of Practical Jurisprudence' (1961) 61 *Columbia LR* 201, 202.

[33] These are generally said to be *Ridge* v. *Baldwin* [1964] AC 40 (application of the rules of natural justice to the dismissal of a chief officer of police); *Anisminic* v. *Foreign Compensation Commission* [1969] 2 AC 147 (no ouster of an administrative decision flawed by a breach of the principles of administrative law); *Padfield* v. *Minister of Agriculture* [1968] AC 997 (mandamus lies to enforce a discretionary decision of a Minister); to which some might wish to add *Conway* v. *Rimmer* [1968] AC 910 (the judge is the final arbiter of whether Crown immunity from disclosure of documents can be claimed). The word 'British' is significant, as Lord Reid was a Scot. On the role of Lord Reid in reactivating judicial review see, J. A. G. Griffith, *Judicial Politics since 1920* (Oxford, 1992), 79–107.

[34] SI 1977/1955. See now, s. 31 of the Supreme Court Act 1981 and SI 1980/2000.

[35] Schwartz & Wade, *op. cit.*, 321.

be set in motion. To prevent them running amok, there must be constant control, both political and legal.[36]

Thus, for Wade, whose writings were to prove by far the most important influence on the judiciary,[37] administrative law is 'the law relating to the control of governmental power'. Equally important, it is the law relating to the protection of *individual citizens*, whose 'ideas of liberty, fair dealing, and good administration' should form the yardstick of a good administrative system. To epitomize, judicial review had moved from a formalist or functional concept of separation of powers, in which the emphasis was on the impropriety of judicial interference in the executive function of policy making, to a 'checks and balances' version (the Diceyan 'balanced constitution' or 'model of law'[38]) in which government and administration is kept in check by courts and Parliament—in which order is not always clear!

The classic model of judicial review with which, in 1964, the courts moved into the new era was formalistic in two senses: the grounds for review were restricted[39] and a strict interpretation of the doctrine of precedent inhibited rapid changes of direction. The formalist model was, however, to prove thoroughly serviceable as a basis for an onslaught on discretionary power. Key elements in its make-up, many shared with the classic American model, are as follows:

1. There is no developed distinction between public and private law. In England, there was, until the reformulated Order 53 spurred the creation of an exclusivity rule by judicial action,[40] a single jurisdiction and rules of 'public law', such as the rules of natural justice, applied where appropriate to private and non-governmental bodies. The dramatic change inaugurated by judicial fiat borrows from European[41]

[36] H. W. R. Wade, *Administrative Law* (Oxford, 1961), 1. And see Loughlin, *op. cit.*, 184–90.

[37] This was partly due to the untimely death of Professor S. A. de Smith, whose classic treatise, *Judicial Review of Administrative Action* (London, 1959) was twice reprinted within three years. de Smith is less approving of judicial imperialism (see, e.g., his comments on *Conway* v. *Rimmer* at App. to 2nd. ed. 1968 and p. 40 of the 4th. ed. with comment by J. M. Evans at n. 57). de Smith's tacit position as a functionalist is hinted at in his celebrated description of judicial review as 'peripheral and sporadic' (1980 ed., 3). Since the last ed. of his work by J. M. Evans was in 1980, its influence has steadily diminished in the last decade, to be replaced by Wade.

[38] M. Vile, *Constitutionalism and the Separation of Powers* (Oxford, 1967), 230–6; Loughlin, *op. cit.*, 140–59.

[39] D. Oliver, 'Is *Ultra Vires* the Basis of Judicial Review?' [1987] *PL* 543.

[40] The change was wrought in *O'Reilly* v. *Mackman* [1983] 2 AC 237 and *Cocks* v. *Thanet District Council* [1983] 2 AC 286. For subsequent developments, see Law Com. No. 126, *Administrative Law: Judicial Review and Statutory Appeals* (London: HMSO), 1993, 11–20; Law Com. No. 226, *Administrative Law: Judicial Review and Statutory Appeals*, (London: HMSO) HC 669, 1994, 19–30 (recommending retention of the exclusivity rule subject to minor amendments).

[41] C. Harlow, ' "Public" and "Private" Law: Definition Without Distinction' [1980] 43 *MLR* 241.

rather than American or Commonwealth models, although the same is not necessarily true of the procedural reforms incorporated in Order 53. As is well-known, this reform by the Rules Committee of the Supreme Court implemented recommendations from the Law Commission.[42] In 1972, however, Lord Diplock, on return from a high level Anglo–American exchange, had written that: 'The simplicity of the procedure for applying for judicial review . . . heightened our realization of the urgent need to sweep away the technical differences in the procedures . . . This has been done with success in many of the United States'.[43]

2. It is interest-oriented. In neither the English nor the American systems, is administrative action reviewable merely because it is unlawful.[44] An instructive contrast can be drawn here with the classic system of French administrative law, which is administration-oriented in the sense that the main thrust of the system is to test the legality of an 'administrative act', a concept which in consequence forms the keystone of the French administrative law system.[45] In England, administrative acts are not necessarily reviewable if they cause no injury to an individual interest.

Traditionally also, one finds much emphasis in the case-law on the distinction between 'rights' and 'privileges'.[46] *Locus standi* in the classic model often depended on possession of a legal right[47] and the application of the rules of natural justice was also dependent on a distinction between 'right' and 'privilege', the former worthy of protection, the latter not.[48] It is noteworthy that English courts, in escaping from this dilemma, central to the protection of licences, welfare benefits, and other forms of administrative law interest, did not follow the path delineated by Charles Reich and adopted by the American courts, of creating a 'new property' in 'government largesse' or intangible rights like freedom of speech.[49] Instead, over a period of time, they virtually annihilated the distinction between judicial and administrative acts and between rights and privileges, excising the terminology from their repertoire.[50]

3. It is remedy-oriented, a point usually epitomized in the traditional maxim *ubi remedium, ibi ius*. In Dicey's formulation of the rule of law doctrine, however, the

[42] Law Com. No. 40, *Remedies in Administrative Law* (London, 1971) and Law Com. No. 73, *Report on Remedies in Administrative Law* (Cmnd. 6407, London, 1976).

[43] 'Introduction' to Schwartz & Wade, *op. cit.*, xiii.

[44] B. Schwartz, in Schwartz & Wade, *op. cit.*, 271–8 and (1990) *op. cit.* suggests that American law may be more restrictive in this respect.

[45] A concept elucidated for the English reader in L. Neville Brown & J. Bell, *French Administrative Law* (Oxford, 1992, 4th ed.), 1992), 152–7.

[46] de Smith, *op. cit.*, 171, 188–9, citing *Nakkuda Ali* v. *Jayaratne* [1951] AC 66. See also *Re H. K. (An Infant)* [1967] 2 QB 617.

[47] de Smith, *op. cit.*, 411–2. For classic cases, see *Boyce* v. *Paddington Corporation* [1903] Ch. 109; *Gregory* v. *Camden LBC* [1966] 1 WLR 899.

[48] de Smith, *op. cit.*, 171–2, 177. See also, *Nakkuda Ali* v. *Jayaratne* [1951] AC 66; *McInnes* v. *Onslow-Fane* [1978] 1 WLR 1520.

[49] C. Reich, 'The New Property' *73 Yale LJ* 733 (1964). On the second point, see E. Barendt, *Freedom of Speech* (Oxford, 1986).

[50] See *R* v. *Secretary of State for Foreign and Commonwealth Affairs ex p. Everett* [1989] QB 811. And see, *R* v. *Secretary of State for Home Affairs ex p. Bentley* [1994] 2 WLR 101 (judicial review of the Crown prerogative of mercy).

point wears a different emphasis.[51] A cardinal feature of common law systems of administrative law is the possession of mandatory orders which lie to government and administration, in particular the orders of habeas corpus and mandamus. This tradition has been recently affirmed by the House of Lords in the significant case of *M* v. *Home Office*,[52] in which it was held that, despite the terms of section 21 of the Crown Proceedings Act 1947, an interim injunction and other mandatory relief was available against the Crown and government ministers in judicial review proceedings. In addition, these orders were enforceable through proceedings for contempt of court. At the start of his speech, Lord Woolf spoke firmly of the advantage of a mandatory model of judicial review, defined in terms of coercion, in contrast to one based on 'trust and co-operation'. A distinction could again be drawn with the public law model of France, where the point of departure is a declaratory judgment, primarily enforceable through an award of damages.[53]

TWO AMERICAN MODELS OF ADJUDICATION

The public interest model

I have already described the courts in England as moving during the 1960s into a new and activist era with a classic model of judicial review. On this dominant model, I shall now suggest the influence of two American models, very different in style. The first is the public interest model. This crossed the Atlantic to penetrate academic circles via the seminal articles of Richard Stewart,[54] Abram Chayes,[55] and Duncan Kennedy[56] in the 1970s. These articles sought new objectives for public law adjudication, powering a procedural argument for separate treatment of public law issues in the judicial process inside a wider debate over the discrete nature of public law.[57] In the public interest model, courts consciously function as

[51] E. C. S. Wade, *Introduction to the Study of the Law of the Constitution* (London, 1939, 9th ed. 197.

[52] [1993] 3 WLR 445, 447.

[53] In France, the primary recourse was traditionally through an action in damages against the state, significantly termed *le recours de pleine juridiction*. The Conseil d'Etat had consciously deprived itself of the power to grant injunctive relief: *Ste Hotel du 'Vieux Beffroi'*, TC 17 Mar., D 1949.201 concl. Devolve. See further, C. Harlow, 'Remedies in French Administrative Law' [1977] *PL* 227. A law of 16 July 1980 did something to remedy this by adding the possibility of an *astreinte* or *per diem* financial penalty for unexecuted judgments: Brown & Bell, *op. cit.*, 113. A bill presently under consideration will allow all administrative tribunals to issue injunctions against the administration, a change considered by experts a transformation of French administrative law.

[54] R. Stewart, 'The Reformation of American Administrative Law' (1975) 88 *Harvard LR* 1667.

[55] Chayes *op. cit.*

[56] 'Form and Substance in Private Law Adjudication' (1976) 89 *Harvard LR* 1685.

[57] See the difference of opinion between Martin Loughlin and myself in Loughlin *op. cit.*, and C. Harlow, 'Changing the Mindset: The Place of Theory in English Administrative Law', (1994) 14 *OJLS* 419.

a surrogate political process. The courtroom is seen as a forum for debate of matters of public interest as well as a platform for 'public advocacy' of the cause of underprivileged groups.[58] Its characteristics include generous access to the courtroom, often by groups, through liberal standing and intervention rules, judicial activism, and innovation in remedies.

The new, pluralist, courtroom model naturally found favour with the burgeoning public interest law movement[59] because it enabled them to raise in courts issues which were blocked in the complex American political process. Indeed, although in recent years, the tradition has been overlaid by public choice theory, it is by no means dead: it remains central to the thinking of critical legal theory and in diluted form infuses the writing of the 'civic republican' school of American constitutional law.[60] Public interest law travelled to the United Kingdom during the 1970s, when law centre and social action lawyers, many of whom had personal experience of the civil rights or public interest law movement in the United States, returned to Britain anxious to develop public interest law and, more specifically, to put into operation in English courts the test case strategies which they had seen operated in American appellate courts.[61] Increasingly in recent years, English courts have been asked, under the influence of the public interest law movement, to rule in a multiplicity of 'hard cases', the solution to which seems often to lie outside the courtroom.[62]

The legal process model

Before we consider the implications of this development, it is necessary to turn to the very different American 'legal process' model of public law, so-called because it aims to control and structure discretion throughout the governmental and administrative system. The inevitable effect is legalization through the insertion of legal processes into the administrative process.[63] Thus we find great stress laid on rule making and formalized and

[58] R. Cortner, 'Strategies and Tactics of Litigants in Constitutional Cases' (1968) 17 *J. of Pub. Law* 287. But see M. Galanter, 'Why the "Haves" Come Out Ahead: Speculations on the Limits of Legal Change' (1974) 9 *Law and Society Review* 225.

[59] On which see, J. Handler, E. J. Hollingsworth, H. Erlanger, *Lawyers and the Pursuit of Legal Rights* (New York, 1978).

[60] C. Sunstein, 'Beyond the Republican Revival' (1988) 97 *Yale LJ* 1539; F. Michelman, 'Law's Republic' (1988) 97 *Yale LJ* 1493.

[61] C Harlow & R. Rawlings, *Pressure Through Law* (London, 1992), ch. 2; T. Prosser, *Test Cases for the Poor*, (London, 1983).

[62] C. Harlow, 'Public Interest Law: the State of the Art' in Cooper & Dhavan, *op. cit.* See also Rawlings at 101–106 below.

[63] D. Galligan, *Discretionary Powers, A Legal Study of Official Discretion* (Oxford, 1990); Mashaw, *op. cit.* For a critique of this general approach see, for England, G. Ganz, 'Allocation of Decision-Making Functions' [1972] *PL* 215, 299 and *Administrative Procedures* (London, 1974); for America, M. Shapiro, 'APA: Past, Present, Future' (1986) 72 *Virginia LR* 447.

participatory rule-making procedures as well as on formal administrative adjudication.[64] Seminal to understanding the place of rules in modern administration has been the work of K. C. Davis.[65] Under his tutelage, administrative lawyers on both sides of the Atlantic have recognized the role of rule making as a legal technique for the control of modern bureaucracy.[66] The American Administrative Procedures Act has also stimulated a yearning for judicialized rule-making procedures in Britain.[67]

A second hallmark of the legal process school is emphasis on 'reasoned elaboration' in adjudication. If Dworkin is the best known, he is by no means its sole proponent. The ideas of Lon Fuller[68] have also met with a warm reception on this side of the Atlantic and there has been further infiltration through the course materials used for many years at Harvard Law School by Hart and Sacks[69] and through Nonet and Selznick's theory of 'responsive law'.[70]

Here we need to disentangle several separate though interwoven strands of thought. Dworkin's theory of hard cases, with his prototype adjudicators, Herbert and Hercules, together with the crucial distinction drawn in his work between 'principle' and 'policy', form two strands in the argument. The third is the same author's description of 'rights as trumps'.[71] Because all three strands are knitted into Allan's reformulation of the Diceyan rule of law ideal, it seems fair to talk in terms of one rather than two distinct models. Not only does Allan describe Dworkin's account of the distinction between principle and policy as making 'a helpful contribution to the task of defining the nature and limits of public law' but he knots the two threads by arguing that administrative law 'may be helpfully interpreted as a system of public law rights' and also that 'the legitimate boundaries of judicial review may be found in the process of defining and enforcing those rights'.[72] Both statements are questionable when we consider the evolution

[64] J. Jowell, The Legal Control of Administrative Discretion' [1973] *PL* 178. For the United States, see F. Michelman, 'The Rule of Law as a Law of Rules' (1989) 56 *U. of Chicago LR* 1175.

[65] K. C. Davis, *Discretionary Justice* (Illinois, 1991, 2nd ed.).

[66] See, R. Baldwin & K. Hawkins, 'Discretionary Justice: Davis Reconsidered' [1984] *PL* 570; R. Baldwin, *Rules and Government* (Oxford, 1995).

[67] Schwartz & Wade, *op. cit.*, 84–106 (but see, H. W. R. Wade & C. Forsyth, *Administrative Law* (Oxford, 7th ed.), 895–897. See also, *Making the Law*, The Report of the Hansard Society Commission on the Legislative Process (London, 1993), esp. ch. 3.

[68] See, e.g., L. Fuller, 'The Forms and Limits of Adjudication' (1978) 92 *Harvard LR* 353; 'Reason and Fiat in Case Law' (1946) 54 *Harvard LR* 376.

[69] H. Hart & A. Sacks, *The Legal Process: Basic Problems in the Making and Application of Law* (Cambridge, Mass., 1958).

[70] P. Nonet & D. Selznick, *Law and Society in Transition: Toward Responsive Law* (California, 1978).

[71] Ronald Dworkin, *Taking Rights Seriously* (London, 1976) and *Law's Empire* (London, 1986).

[72] Allan, *op. cit.*, 7. (I owe the point which follows to David Feldman).

of the classic English model of judicial review and set it in its Diceyan constitutional context. In other words, the 'special relationship' seems here to have led to imposition on the classic English model of judicial review of a rights-oriented theory devised for use by the American Supreme Court in deciding constitutional cases.

Each of these models aims in its own way at legitimation of judicial power. The public interest law model presents an obvious analogy with the collective and pluralist political process.[73] Its primary objective is to disclose the policy-making process to public scrutiny and afford access to the decision-making process.[74] I have already called it a 'surrogate political process' in which the courtroom offers a platform to underprivileged groups.

In a period when democracy is equated with popular control and the paradigm of representative government has established pre-eminence over separation of powers in constitutional theory, the public interest model offers an explanation of judicial review consonant with democratic theory.[75] Yet despite its popular pedigree, the model has a hole at the heart. Paradoxically, it attracts heavy criticism from the orthodoxy on the ground that it imperils the independence of the judiciary by involving judges in politics, while at the same time it is rendered suspect in democratic terms by its non-elected judiciary. As Hutchinson has argued,[76] genuinely popular control of administration involves the abandonment of traditional, separation of powers perspectives. It substitutes repoliticization of bureaucracy and administration, and real empowerment of the citizenry, inevitably leading outside the judicial process. Perhaps this is why the major attempt to provide an explanation of judicial review in terms of democracy, that of John Hart Ely,[77] in which the judicial process is to operate as a buttress for democratic institutions, is best described as a legal process model, strongly rooted in formalism and the ideal of judicial neutrality.

In sharp contrast, the legal process model seeks its legitimacy within the classic formalist tradition of law. Like the formalism which it seeks to replace (or perhaps update), legal process lays great emphasis on the scientific, professional formation of law. Here again, we find ourselves involved in paradox. While Dworkin's political credentials are impeccably

[73] Chayes, *op. cit.*; Stewart, *op. cit.*

[74] A point made clearly by Galligan, *op. cit.*

[75] F. Michelman, 'Foreword: Traces of Self Government' (1986) 100 *Harvard LR* 17; C. Sunstein, *The Partial Constitution* (Cambridge, Mass., 1993).

[76] 'Mice Under a Chair: Democracy, Courts and the Administrative State' (1990) 50 *U. of Toronto* LJ 374.

[77] J. H. Ely, *Democracy and Distrust* (Cambridge, Mass., 1980). I owe this point to Martin Loughlin.

liberal, his legal theory verges on the conservative. This is not accidental: a main objective of legal process theory is to camouflage the political content of judicial review, while at the same time enlarging its ambit, a point explored by Eskridge and Peller:

> The legal process synthesis was a brilliant achievement, for it transcends the realist/formalist debate in a way that fit [*sic*] well with the relativist theory of democracy. The scholars were able to marginalize *Lochner*-style[78] constitutional law as impermissible value-imposition by unelected judges, while simultaneously moving mainstream American jurisprudence into the modern era by acknowledging and legitimating the inescapably political character of the common law, statutory interpretation, and administrative law. In short, legal process asserted the illegitimacy of activist judicial review while asserting activism in virtually all institutional settings.[79]

Can this subterfuge work? Sunstein argues that, for all its insistence on neutral principles of adjudication, the legal process model has not escaped political censure. The notion of neutrality is itself seen as political because of its inevitable association with an existing state of society which is neither impartial nor inherently equal and just.[80] To Michelman, the model lacks political credentials, or 'dialogue':[81]

> Dworkin's mythic judge is a loner. He is much too heroic. His narrative constructions are monologous. He converses with no one, except through books. He has no encounters. He meets no otherness. Nothing shakes him up. No interlocutor violates the inevitable insularity of his experience and outlook. He is just a man, after all. He is not a whole community. No one man or woman could be that.

In other words, a central weakness of the legal process model lies in the insularity and élitism used to promote political neutrality, a defect which, ironically, the pluralist public interest model does not easily avoid. The truth is that the political nature of public law adjudication can neither be easily escaped nor disguised. Neither model can resolve the central constitutional dilemma of judicial review.

CONCLUSION

Given the pluralistic nature of judicial and academic opinion, it is scarcely surprising to find traces of both American models in the current English

[78] The reference is to *Lochner* v. *New York* 198 US 45 (1905) (unconstitutionality of protective employment legislation by reason of the constitutional 'freedom of contract' doctrine).

[79] 'The New Public Law Movement: Modernism as a Postmodern Cultural Form' (1991) 89 *Michigan LR* 707, 723.

[80] *Op. cit.*, v.

[81] 'Foreword: Traces of Self Government' (1986) 100 *Harvard LR* 17, 76.

practice of judicial review. The impact of the public interest model has so far been felt most keenly at the access stage.[82] The drift towards a mid-Atlantic, public interest model of judicial review, in which widened rules of *locus standi* provide generous access to the courtroom, has been picked up in the recommendations of the judicially influenced Law Commission Report which proposes an addition to traditional, interest-based standing in 'public interest cases'—significantly, not defined—at the discretion of the presiding judge.[83] That this shift has taken place within the parameters of, and with the approval of, the dominant legal process school is ironic. But can the changes be contained within this model? Certainly both judiciary and Law Commission hope that they can. But for reasons spelled out by Rawlings,[84] it seems unlikely that such a powerful genie can be contained within the bottle of judicial discretion.[85]

To open the courtroom door to campaigning groups will inevitably introduce campaigning techniques to the courtroom. Departure from the classic *amicus curiae* model in particular opens courts to a form of political lobbying, closing the gap between the judicial and political process.[86] *Pepper* v. *Hart*[87] is a straw in the wind; another is the admission by the House of Lords in the *EOC* case[88] of economic evidence on the subject of gender discrimination in part-time work situations, a usage borrowed from the Eurpean Court of Justice. These moves inevitably create concern over the competence of the generalist judiciary to deal with scientific and political material (a point to which I shall return) together with the adequacy of legal procedure to handle it.[89] Little by little, as the gap between legal and political procedures closes, politicization of the judicial process moves closer. And as the argument from expertise shifts and translates into an argument from legitimacy, a renewal of disquiet over the composition and selection of the higher judiciary is likely.[90] (There is, of

[82] The case-law is covered by both Cane and Rawlings below.

[83] Law Com. No. 126, *Administrative Law: Judicial Review and Statutory Appeals*, (London: HMSO) 1993, 61–2; Law Com. No. 226, *Administrative Law: Judicial Review and Statutory Appeals* (London: HMSO) 1994, 41–4.

[84] Below 106–108.

[85] See Law Com. No. 226, 43–4. The Commission's Draft Bill will revise s. 31 (4) (b) of the Supreme Court Act 1981 to grant standing where *the High Court considers that it is in the public interest* for a non-affected applicant, which may include an unincorporated association, to apply. See also, Sir Thomas Bingham, 'Should Public Law Remedies be Discretionary?' [1991] *PL* 64.

[86] Harlow & Rawlings *op. cit.*, 191–9.

[87] [1993] AC 593.

[88] *R.* v. *Employment Secretary ex p. Equal Opportunities Commission and Day* [1994] 2 WLR 409.

[89] J. Griffith, 'Judicial Decision-Making in Public Law' [1985] *PL* 564; P. Schuck, 'The new ideology of tort law' (1988) 92 *The Public Interest* 93; R. Livock, 'Science, Law and Safety Standards: A Case Study of Industrial Disease', (1979) 6 *JLS* 172.

[90] J. Griffith, *The Politics of the Judiciary*, (London, 1991, 4th ed.).

course, an alternative lesson from America: a rapid retreat from public interest doctrines of standing![91])

As yet the more commanding influence is undoubtedly that of the legal process school, whose efforts have largely been concentrated on the rationalization of judicial reasoning. This has been variously characterized as casuistic, unscientific and, in the technical sense, unprincipled. If rational decision making remains the primary objective, then a change in the terminology of judicial review—from reasonableness to rationality—may augur the desired 'new direction'.[92] Here Craig, a leading exponent of rationality and reasoned decision making, has clearly absorbed the American lesson; his lengthy exposition of the subject is based largely on American case-law.[93]

English judges have also been charged with failing adequately to explicate their background values,[94] a criticism underpinning a call for a 'rights-based' model of judicial review. There has, however, been no obvious rush to plunder the American jurisprudence;[95] indeed, the focus has been on Europe, where the activism of the French Conseil d'Etat, the European Court of Justice, and the German administrative courts in developing 'principled' systems of judicial control offer attractive paradigms.[96] The most obvious base for a 'rights' jurisdiction in English courts is the European Convention on Human Rights. Even if the case-law does not so far give full recognition to this fact, there is no doubt that influential members of the judiciary are highly sympathetic.[97] And the rights-based approach seems to strike a chord in the public consciousness,

[91] Cane at 125–127 below; C. Sunstein, 'Standing and the Privatisation of Public Law' (1988) 88 *Columbia LR* 1432.

[92] Oliver, *op. cit.*; J. Jowell & D. Oliver (eds.), *New Directions in Judicial Review* (London, 1988).

[93] *Administrative Law*, (London, 1994, 3rd ed.), 375–80.

[94] J. Jowell & A. Lester, 'Beyond *Wednesbury*: Substantive Principles of Administrative Law' [1987] *PL* 368.

[95] Though in *Derbyshire CC* v. *Times Newspapers* [1993] 2 WLR 449, 460, Lord Keith treated the ECHR as persuasive rather than binding and referred with approval, (457) to *City of Chicago* v. *Tribune Co* (1923) 139 NE 86 and *New York Times* v. *Sullivan* (1964) 376 US 254 as based on 'public interest considerations . . . no less valid in this country'.

[96] See M. Beloff, 'Judicial Review 2001: a Prophetic Odyssey' [1995] 58 *MLR 144.* J. Schwarze, 'Developing principles of European administrative law' [1993] *PL* 229 argues that harmonization is inevitable.

[97] See, Sir Thomas Bingham, 'The European Convention on Human Rights—Time to Incorporate' (1993) 109 *LQR* 390; Sir N. Browne-Wilkinson, 'The Infiltration of a Bill of Rights' [1992] *PL* 397; Lord Lester, 'European Human Rights and the British Constitution', in J. Jowell & D. Oliver (eds.), *The Changing Constitution* (Oxford, 1994, 3rd ed.); Sir Stephen Sedley, 'The Sound of Silence: Constitutional Law without a Constitution' (1994) 110 *LQR* 270. But see for a persuasive counter-argument, C. Adjei, 'Human Rights Theory and the Bill of Rights Debate' [1995] 58 *MLR* 17. And see Sir John Laws, 'Is the High Court the Guardian of Fundamental Constitutional Rights?' [1993] *PL* 59.

drawing on interest in constitutionalism and constitutional reform, favoured by the main opposition parties and finding public expression in the Charter 88 movement.[98]

But how well does the legal process model really gear into the context of modern British administration? In the jargon of Osborne and Gaebler,[99] British government has been reinvented over the last decade—with the help of Friedrich Hayek, Milton Friedmann, the Adam Smith Institute, and other disciples of public choice economics. In America, administrative law has long been agency-oriented, in Britain, less so. Today, regulation and regulatory agencies proliferate. English administrative law has to adapt to take this development on board.[100] Both countries are currently in the grip of privatized, 'contracted out' models of public administration; where nationalization in Britain once transferred large swathes of private industry to the public sector, privatization has now reversed the process. The public service is hived off to 'Next Steps' agencies.[101] Ironically, we may have come full circle. Perhaps the classic Anglo-American 'private law' paradigm of public law is today best placed to cope with recent developments in public administration, where the emerging boundaries are complex and hard to discern.[102]

There is a superficial similarity between the rational decision making idealized in the legal process model and the audit emphasis of the new public administration, where policies find expression in targets and performance indicators.[103] Again, the key doctrine of 'proportionality', a central plank in rational decision making,[104] seemingly derives directly from techniques of cost-benefit analysis. Yet the resemblances are illusory. A profound clash of values is involved when the legal process model comes up against an administrative system which prioritizes economists' and accountants' values of economy, efficiency, and effectiveness.[105] As Baldwin indicates,[106] lawyers characteristically find the discipline of

[98] D. Oliver, 'Law, Politics and Public Accountability. The Search for a New Equilibrium' [1994] *PL* 238.

[99] *Reinventing Government*, (Reading, Mass., 1992).

[100] R. Baldwin & C. McCrudden (eds.), *Regulation and Public Law* (London, 1987); Craig, *Administrative Law* (London, 1994 3rd ed), 81–121, 211–42.

[101] *Improving Management in Government: The Next Steps* (The Ibbs Report) (London, 1988). And see, N. Lewis, 'The Citizen's Charter and Next Steps: A New Way of Governing?' (1993) *Political Quarterly* 316.

[102] Sir Gordon Borrie, 'The Regulation of Public and Private Power' [1989] *PL* 552. And see, J. Alder, 'Hunting the Chimera—the End of *O'Reilly* v. *Mackman*' (1993) 13 *Legal Studies* 183.

[103] M. Power, *The Audit Explosion* (London, 1994).

[104] Jowell & Lester, *op. cit.*; and 'Proportionality: Neither Novel nor Dangerous', in J. Jowell & D. Oliver (eds.), *New Directions in Judicial Review* (London, 1988).

[105] N. Luhmann also argues that legal reasoning differs inherently from criteria of efficiency: see, R. Cotterrell, 'Law's Community: Legal Theory and the Image of Legality' (1992) 19 JLS 405, 416.

[106] Baldwin, *op. cit.*, 201.

economics antipathetic, preferring 'the language of distributional rights and justice'. Argument based on economic criteria or cost/benefit equations is unpopular with judges and is likely to be dismissed as 'more appropriate to economists than lawyers'.[107] Judicial reasoning has not really kept pace with the thought processes of regulation and the prospect of a model of judicial review founded in economics[108] seems frankly surreal. The applauded leading case deals with a technical point of jurisdiction[109] and the judicial instinct is automatically to remit difficult technical issues to experts or, the next best thing, expert courts.[110] Across the Atlantic, science-blindness has led the Supreme Court to a sharp retraction—admittedly, politically led—of justiciablity, a course which exponents of legal process in this country would hardly relish.[111]

Dworkin's theory of reasoned adjudication suggests consonance with the growing use of rules as a technique of modern government. The truth is, however, that we have drifted a long way from Davis's metaphor of rule making as a 'miniature democratic process'. A technological revolution has landed us with a tangle of rules, codes of practice, guidelines, and other 'quasi-legislation', its legal status often as suspect as its democratic pedigree.[112] This network purports to govern every aspect of our public and private lives and it is far from clear that rationality rather than chaos will be the outcome.[113] Through its monopoly of every type of rule-making power, modern government has everywhere become the paramount law-making body. The sovereign Parliament is today the prisoner of the executive and the theory of parliamentary sovereignty invites critical scrutiny, 'not because it is too strong but because it is too weak'.[114]

Baldwin notes that regulatory rule making is becoming less popular;

[107] *Per* Forbes J in *Pickwell* v. *Camden LBC* [1983] 2 WLR 383.

[108] W. Bishop, 'A Theory of Administrative Law' (1990) 19 *J. of Legal Studies* 489. And see, S. Rose-Ackerman 'Progressive Law and Economics and the New Administrative Law' (1988) 98 *Yale LJ* 341.

[109] *R* v. *Panel on Take-Overs and Mergers ex p. Datafin plc* [1987] QB 815.

[110] *Mercury* v. *Oftel and Director General of Oftel*, *The Times*, 10 Feb. 1995, where the meaning of 'charge' was held justiciable in the Commercial Court. And see, *R* v. *Monopolies and Mergers Commission ex p Argyll Group plc* [1986] 1 WLR 763.

[111] *Chevron USA Inc* v. *Natural Resources Defense Council Inc.* 467 US 837 (1984). For comment, see T. Dyk, 'The Supreme Court's Role in Not Shaping Administrative Law' (1992) *Administrative LR* 429; C. Sunstein 'Law and Administration after *Chevron* (1990) 90 *Columbia LR* 2072; S. Shapiro & R. Glicksman, 'Congress, the Supreme Court and the Quiet Revolution in Administrative Law' (1988) *Duke LJ* 819.

[112] G. Ganz, *Quasi-Legislation* (London, 1986); Hansard Society, *op. cit.*

[113] R. Baldwin, 'Why Rules Don't Work' [1990] 53 *MLR* 321; H. Perritt Jr., 'The Electronic Agency and the Traditional Paradigms of Administrative Law' (1992) 44 *Administrative LR* 79.

[114] Sir John Laws, 'Judicial Remedies and the Constitution' (1994) 57 *MLR* 213, 223. See also, F. Mount, *The British Constitution Now* (London, 1992).

deregulation is high on the political agenda in both societies.[115] But the legal process model is essentially bureaucratic. The delays and costs of its procedural claims undermine effective administration to the extent that it has been described as 'simultaneously underprotective and over-intrusive.'[116] From a more theoretical angle, Cotterrell has explored the changing image of legality, arguing for an enhanced effort to discover reason and consistency in law.[117] Reasoned adjudication purports to provide the answer because it deals in principles and standards rather than rules. But principles and standards are replete with judicial discretion, reintroducing the argument over the democratic credentials of the judiciary.[118]

There are no easy American answers. Mashaw's 'dignitary model' is firmly founded on rules.[119] Theories of judicial review spawned by public choice theory are overtly political, underpinned by values which find no echo in the legalistic repertoire of English lawyers.[120] The 'republican' response, which sees the role of the judiciary as being to supply a 'public interest' dimension[121] is more in keeping but presents serious legitimacy problems.

Perhaps it is time to reinvent the classic model? Its elements are coherent and functional. The restricted standing rules serve to demarcate legal and political territory in the public mind; the two processes are seen, I believe correctly, as serving different purposes.[122] Because of its limited ambit, it is less intrusive. It is less bureaucratic and not afraid of judicial discretion. Its traditional terminology and conceptual vocabulary—natural justice, fairness, reasonableness—is accessible and helps to empower the public, exposing the mechanics of the rule of law to public gaze and comprehension.

So long as the 'political constitution' survives, judicial review is legitimated by the need for checks and balances.[123] Its role is to provide

[115] Baldwin (1995) *op. cit.*, 201. And see, A. Aman, 'Administrative Law in a Global Era: Progress, Deregulatory Change, and the Rise of Administrative Presidency' (1988) 73 *Cornell LR* 1101, 1191 ff. See now, the Deregulation and Contracting Out Act 1994.

[116] Mashaw, *op. cit.*, 41.

[117] (1992) *op. cit.*, 409.

[118] On the possible background values of the proponents of standards and balancing tests, see, K. Sullivan, 'Foreword: the Justices of Rules and Standards' (1992) 106 *Harvard LR* 56.

[119] *Op. cit.*, 267–71. See also, J. Mashaw, *Bureaucratic Justice* (New Haven, 1983).

[120] See, F. Easterbrook, 'The Supreme Court 1983, Foreword: The Court and the Economic System' (1984) 98 *Harvard LR* 4; B. Ackerman, 'Constitutional Politics, Constitutional Law' (1987) 99 *Yale LJ* 453 and 'Interpreting Statutes in the Regulatory State' (1989) 103 *Harvard LR* 407.

[121] Sunstein, *op. cit.*; Michelman, *op. cit.*

[122] J. Griffith, 'The Political Constitution' [1979] 42 *MLR* 1.

[123] e.g. *R* v. *Secretary of State for the Home Department ex p. Fire Brigades Union* [1995] 2 WLR 1.

constitutional reassurance. Absent a powerful judiciary armed with potent mandatory remedies, democracy might not survive. We do not want mice, eternally gnawing at the wires of government. Lions, on the other hand, should know their place. The throne rests on them but they can afford to rest under the throne.

4

Courts and Interests

RICHARD RAWLINGS

THE subject matter of this discussion is the role of courts as a forum for the pursuit of collective objectives. Within this broad rubric, particular attention will be paid to purposeful, strategic litigation in the sense of litigation designed to generate change in legal norms and/or in bureaucratic practice; or, less obviously, support for the status quo. The chapters by Peter Cane and Genevra Richardson in this collection develop this theme in rather more specific ways: this essay, in contrast, explores the issue in more general terms.

The topic is peculiarly appropriate in this volume of essays because the relevant forms of legal action are not only in America recognized as a familiar, significant, and long-standing phenomenon, but in this country have tended to be seen as distinctively American in character. Paradoxically, in an exercise in comparative method, a necessary first step is identification of an indigenous tradition of campaigning through courts in Britain.[1] Only then are we appropriately placed, first to consider what lessons could be drawn from American experience; and, second, in a field of activity which today in Britain is increasingly recognized as a pervasive feature of the legal environment, to appreciate the very great influence of American experience in modern times.

The term 'interests' is used advisedly, to draw attention not only to the collective aspect but also to the range of applicants involved. Strategic litigation is often associated with so-called 'social action litigation', the use of law on behalf of disadvantaged sections of society, as for example in this country by the Child Poverty Action Group, or most famously in America by the NAACP.[2] But in both jurisdictions even a cursory glance at some test cases indicates a much wider circle of interests. In turn, this may be said to entail the use of courts in a competitive struggle for law,

[1] A major theme of C. Harlow & R. Rawlings, *Pressure Through Law* (London, 1992).

[2] Thus one potent explanation of group behaviour is court action as an attempt to compensate for weakness or lack of 'voice' in the political process. See, e.g. R. Cortner, 'Strategies and Tactics of Litigants in Constitutional Cases' (1968) 17 *Journal of Public Law*

participants in which may comprise other types of cause group (perhaps explicitly conservative[3] or non-political in orientation); interest groups, such as professional organizations and trade unions;[4] and powerful, perhaps multinational, corporate interests.[5]

Naturally, inside a rubric of public law, a prime focus of this discussion is judicial review: all the more so, given an evident expansion in recent years of judicial review's frontiers, as also a sharp growth in the volume of cases.[6] Nevertheless, we should not lose sight of other avenues by which relevant litigation involving public authorities is carried on. At the cutting edge of doctrinal development are many cases with a European dimension (and which may or may not involve judicial review proceedings).[7] Again, special reference may be made to the mass disaster claim, the product of civil procedure, and in which important techniques of collective legal practice have been honed.[8] And of course there is significant potential for strategic litigation in the guise of defences to the enforcement or regulatory role of public authorities, as demonstrated recently across various tiers of the court system.[9]

Clearly, the topic of courts and interests is a vast topic and, further, a

287; T. Prosser, *Test Cases for the Poor* (London, 1983); and see on the NAACP, M. Tushnet, *The NAACP's Legal Strategy Against Segregated Education, 1925–50* (Chapel Hill, 1987).

[3] See in particular, L. Epstein, *Conservatives in Court* (Knoxville, 1985).

[4] A standard theme in the literature of labour law and industrial relations; see, e.g., Lord Wedderburn, *The Worker and the Law* (London, 1986, 3rd ed.).

[5] The Supreme Court as a forum for the business lobby is a notable theme of classical works in America on group theory and behaviour: see A. Bentley, *The Process of Government* (Chicago, 1908); D. Truman, *The Governmental Process* (New York, 1951). See also, on the role of lobbyists in Washington, J. Heinz, E. Laumann, R. Nelson & R. Salisbury, *The Hollow Core: Private Interests in National Policy Making* (Chicago, 1993).

[6] See M. Sunkin, L. Bridges & G. Mészaros, *Judicial Review in Perspective* (London, 1993); also Law Com. No. 226, *Administrative Law: Judicial Review and Statutory Appeals* (London, 1994), paras.2.12–2.20.

[7] On judicial review procedure as a vehicle for Community law, see *R* v. *Secretary of State for Employment ex p. The Equal Opportunities Commission and Day* [1994] 2 WLR 409. For present purposes, it suffices to underscore the broad implications of Britain's membership of the European Community and adherence to the European Convention on Human Rights for the national legal system. Clearly, at one level, it may be possible for applicants to 'trump' the outcomes of the domestic legal and political processes (see Harlow & Rawlings, *op. cit.*, ch. 6). At another, legal doctrines and modes of thought familiar in continental civil law systems are becoming, through the vehicle of European law, much more familiar in England. For discussion, see e.g. J. Levitsky, 'The Europeanization of the British Legal Style' (1994) 42 *Am. J. of Comp. Law* 347; A Lester, 'European Human Rights and the British Constitution' in J. Jowell & D. Oliver (eds.), *The Changing Constitution* (London, 1994, 3rd ed.). This argument is developed at greater length in the introductory chapter to this volume.

[8] For discussion see Harlow & Rawlings, *op.c it.* (1992), esp. chs. 3 & 4.

[9] In a vast public law litigation over Sunday trading, which notably took place almost entirely outside judicial review procedure. See for discussion P. Diamond, 'Dishonourable

topic which is usefully approached in a variety of ways. On this occasion I have chosen to address some contemporary issues in practice and procedure and in scholarship and theory.

The first section looks to developments in the English courts, which are seen to raise themes common to American experience and, further, the prospect of increased collective legal action in the sphere of judicial review. Section two pursues the matter with reference to a recent venture by the Law Commission into reform of judicial review proceedings. Here, use will be made of American materials, particularly as regards third party interventions, to put in issue the piecemeal character of the reform. In section three the emphasis changes, and I consider a contemporary debate in the American literature of relevance to future directions for research into collective legal action in this country. The final section addresses some recent controversy relating to the practice and study of collective legal action, set against general tendencies in the legal order.

SIGNPOSTS

A convenient starting point is provided by two judicial review decisions, handed down on consecutive days in November 1994, both of which caused the Government considerable embarrassment. The case of the criminal injuries compensation scheme involved a decision by Home Secretary Michael Howard to introduce a cheaper, tariff-based system.[10] His preferred method was to replace the existing non-statutory scheme (based on the royal prerogative) with another non-statutory scheme. The legal argument derived from sections of the Criminal Justice Act 1988 which provided for the existing rules to be placed on a statutory footing: provisions which the Home Office did not arrange to have implemented. The Court of Appeal held that even though the provisions were never brought into force, the Home Secretary could no longer bypass the legislative process. In effect, Parliament had provided a 'blueprint' for the legal form of the scheme which it was an abuse of the Home Secretary's powers to ignore.[11] The second case of the Pergau Dam involved a use of some £234 million from the Government's aid budget on an infrastructure

Defences: The Use of Injunctions and the EC Treaty—Case Study of the Shops Act 1950' [1991] 54 *MLR* 72; R. Rawlings, 'The Eurolaw Game: Some Deductions from a Saga' (1993) 20 *JLS* 309.

[10] *R* v. *Home Secretary ex. p. Fire Brigades Union and Others* [1995] 2 WLR 1.

[11] *Ibid.*, *per* Sir Thomas Bingham MR. Hobhouse LJ dissented. The Court of Appeal's decision was subsequently upheld (by a majority of 3–2) in the House of Lords: [1995] 2 All ER 244.

project in Malaysia. The relevant provision in the 1980 Overseas Cooperation and Development Act permits the payment of aid for the purpose of promoting the development of a country's economy. Foreign Secretary Douglas Hurd was held by the High Court to have acted unlawfully, on the basis that the project was so economically unsound as to fall outside the ambit of the legislation.[12]

The two cases can be used to illustrate several important themes bearing on the place of collective legal action in our system of public law. The first theme concerns judicial creativity, in particular associated with constitutional development. The two cases provide further evidence of what is now generally recognized as a more assertive mood among the English judiciary towards the executive in general, and ministers of the Crown in particular.[13] Notably, in the victims compensation case, the Master of the Rolls explicitly addressed the issue as one of constitutional *principle*, in this instance the overriding legislative role of Parliament as a representative assembly. To this end, one function of judicial review was to reinforce the legislative process.[14] Again, in the Pergau Dam Case, the judges showed no inclination to defer to the judgement in the matter of the Foreign Secretary, despite an express plea by counsel. Not only was it a question of law for the courts to determine, but (judicial tongue in cheek), if Parliament had intended to confer a power to disburse money for unsound developmental purposes, then 'it could have been expected to say so expressly'.[15]

A second theme concerns the explicit acknowledgment of collective participation in court process. The proceedings in the victims compensation case were instituted by the Fire Brigades Union and nine other trade unions whose members, such as prison officers, teachers, and nurses, risk violence at work, together with the Trades Union Congress. In the case of the Pergau Dam, the application was made by the World Development

[12] *R* v. *Secretary of State for Foreign Affairs ex p. The World Development Movement Ltd* [1995] 1 All ER 611. For discussion, see S. Grosz, 'Pergau Be Damned' (1994) 144 *NLJ* 1708. See for the background to the case, F. White, I. Harden & K. Donnelly, 'Audit, Accounting Officers and Accountability: The Pergau Dam Affair' [1994] *PL* 526.

[13] Best illustrated in *M* v. *Home Office* [1993] 3 WLR 433. Relevant extra-judicial writings include Sir Harry Woolf, *Protection of the Public—A New Challenge* (London, 1990); Sir Thomas Bingham, ' "There is a World Elsewhere": The Changing Perspectives of English Law' (1992) 41 *ICLQ* 513; Sir John Laws, 'Is The High Court the Guardian Of Fundamental Constitutional Rights?' [1993] *PL* 59; and Sir Stephen Sedley, 'The Sound Of Silence: Constitutional Law Without A Constitution' (1994) 110 *LQR* 270.

[14] In the sense of requiring the Home Secretary's decision-making power to be exercised through Parliament. In stark contrast, in the context of national acceptance of the Treaty on European Union, the relevant judges demonstrated no interest in this principle. See *R* v. *Foreign Secretary ex p. Rees Mogg* [1994] 1 All ER 457; R. Rawlings, 'Legal Politics: The United Kingdom and Ratification of the Treaty on European Union (Part Two)' [1994] PL 367.

[15] [1995] 1 All ER 611, 626 *per* Rose LJ.

Movement, a pressure group which campaigns on economic and development issues affecting the Third World, for example famine relief and international trade agreements.

The cases point to a diverse range of organizational structures and alliances. For example, the World Development Movement not only has several hundred supporting groups, but is closely allied to major charities such as Oxfam and Christian Aid, being established originally by reason of legal restrictions on the aid organizations' political activity.[16] Again, the arrangement of the trade unions typifies a 'litigation coalition', by which is meant a group of individuals and/or organizations each with an interest in the outcome of a particular case, which comes together for the purpose of litigation. In turn, the relevant coalition can be seen to represent a process of so-called 'plaintiff stacking': an attempt to enlist the sympathy of the court by demonstrating a wide spectrum of support for the litigation, as also the involvement of highly 'respectable' individuals or organizations.

To pursue the point, the litigation coalition is recognized today as a major instrument of collective action in the courts, in public as in private law.[17] In particular, it is the standard methodology of the mass disaster claim, previously mentioned, and notably for present purposes demonstrates there a direct American influence, in the shape of techniques of legal practice for the organization and pursuit of group claims pioneered in the United States.[18] It is also the case that as a strategem of collective action, plaintiff stacking is not a novel development in England,[19] but it is far more familiar to American eyes. Notably, by implying that claims to 'representativeness' typical in the political arena can with utility be pursued in the legal arena, the strategem signals a significant perception of instrumentality in the law and legal system.[20]

Further, the Pergau Dam Case highlights related developments in judicial doctrine, concerning the key issue of standing to sue.[21] The former restrictive approach of the English courts is familiarly associated with a 'private law' or 'individualist' model of adjudication, a model which, significantly for present purposes, has in the United States been subject to

[16] See The *Guardian*, 11 Nov. 1994.

[17] For official recognition, see J. Bowsher, *Guide For Use In Group Actions* (London, 1991).

[18] See above, n.8.

[19] A notable example is provided in *R* v. *Secretary of State for Social Services ex p. Child Poverty Action Group* [1990] 2 QB 540.

[20] We return to the issue of instrumentality later on. Evidence on whether the strategem actually 'works' is predicably elusive: see e.g. S. Olsen, 'The Political Evolution of Interest Group Litigation', in R. Gambitta, M. May & J. Foster (eds.), *Governing Through Courts* (Beverley Hills, 1981).

[21] Since this issue is the subject of Peter Cane's essay in this volume, the analysis which follows is confined to the bare essentials.

more sustained criticism and greater modification than in this country.[22] Elsewhere, I point to a dual role for such a model, operating not only to constrain collective legal action, but also and especially through standing requirements to render it less visible, in the sense that a collective entity must take proceedings through a named individual or 'front man'.[23] The Pergau Dam Case caps a line of cases in which, on the basis of a notably American-style test of standing introduced in 1977,[24] English courts have struggled towards a concept of representative standing, which implies an explicit acknowledgment of collective legal action in judicial review proceedings.

Unlike the victims compensation case, the case of the Pergau Dam did not involve a so-called 'associational plaintiff', as where an interest group claims to take action on behalf of its members.[25] But nor was it clearly a case of a 'surrogate plaintiff', where a cause group claims to represent the interests of others.[26] Although the World Development Movement has a considerable history of promoting aid to the Third World, it could not in the circumstances of the case directly claim to represent a client group affected by the Foreign Secretary's decision. Instead, the challenge was permitted because *inter alia* if the Movement could not take action, it was difficult to see who could.[27] Simultaneously then, the case demonstrates acceptance of a wider role for judicial review in controlling unlawful government action than in protection of the personal interests of litigants,[28] and sends a strong positive signal concerning collective forms of participation in the legal process.[29]

[22] Classic articles include R. Stewart, 'The Reformation of American Administrative Law' (1975) 88 *Harvard LR* 1667; A. Chayes, 'The Role of the Judge in Public Law Litigation' (1976) 89 *Harvard LR* 1281.

[23] See Harlow & Rawlings, *op.cit.* (1992), esp. 147–54.

[24] See Law Com. WP No. 40, *Remedies in Administrative Law* (London, 1971), paras.125–33.

[25] The leading case is *R* v. *Inland Revenue Commissioners ex p. National Federation of Self-Employed and Small Businesses Ltd.* [1982] AC 617. See further Cane in this volume.

[26] For judicial recognition of surrogacy claims on behalf of the poor and disadvantaged, see *R* v. *Secretary of State for Social Services ex p. CPAG and GLC* (1985) *The Times*, 16 Aug.; *R* v. *Secretary of State for Social Services ex p. CPAG* [1990] 2 QB 540.

[27] [1995] 1 All ER 611, 620 *per* Rose LJ. In this sense, the ruling represents a structured approach to standing to sue, of the kind discussed in Harlow & Rawlings, *op. cit.*, 313–14, drawing on work by P. Bryden, 'Public Interest Intervention in the Courts', (1987) 66 *Canadian Bar Review* 490. Rose LJ stressed further the seriousness of the allegation, the importance of the issue raised, and the importance of vindicating the rule of law.

[28] A familiar debate in the literature: for example, P. Cane, 'The Function of Standing Rules in Administrative Law' [1980] *PL* 303.

[29] See to similar effect in the environmental field, *R* v. *Inspectorate of Pollution ex p. Greenpeace Ltd. (No. 2)* [1994] 4 All ER 329, in which an earlier, contrasting approach in *R* v. *Secretary of State for the Environment ex p. Rose Theatre Trust Co.* [1991] All ER 754 was not followed. See also *R* v. *Secretary of State for Employment ex p. The Equal Opportunities Commission and Day* [1994] 2 WLR 409.

A third general theme which the cases underline concerns the partial and often highly contingent role of strategic litigation. For example, court action as a continuation of a larger political campaign is illustrated by the victims compensation case, which led on from a fierce Parliamentary struggle in which the Home Secretary was repeatedly warned of potential legal challenge.[30] Again, the World Development Movement was only able to penetrate the secrecy surrounding official decision making and so pinpoint a lack of developmental purpose by reason of prior investigations by two House of Commons committees which generated the relevant information.[31] Notably, the court itself adhered to a restrictive view of discovery and refused to order disclosure of the relevant documentation.[32]

Furthermore, in both cases the judgments were not decisive of the policy issues, but rather resources to be fought over and used.[33] Thus to buttress the legislative process is not to disable it: clearly a cheaper, tariff-based compensation scheme was still an option, if now more difficult to achieve[34] In the Pergau Dam case, the subsequent political question was not whether the project would receive £234 million from Britain, but by what means and with what consequences (if any) for the overseas aid budget.[35] Emphasis may also be placed on the potential and complex indirect effects of the litigation, for example on official approaches to decision taking,[36] as

[30] The proposed changes were at the centre of a House of Lords revolt led by the former Law Lord, Lord Ackner. See HL Deb. 16 June 1994, cols. 1828–51.

[31] The relevant committee reports are Foreign Affairs Committee, 'Public Expenditure: The Pergau Hydroelectric Project, Malaysia, The Aid and Trade Provision and Related Matters', HC 271-I, Session 1993/94; Public Accounts Committee, 'Pergau Hydro-Electric Project', HC 155, Session 1993/1994.

[32] [1995] 1 All ER 611, 622 *per* Rose LJ. Generally, on the authority of *R* v. *Secretary of State for the Environment ex p. Islington LBC and London Lesbian and Gay Centre* [1992] COD 67, a court can order disclosure of documents in judicial review proceedings only if it can otherwise be shown that the respondent's evidence is false or inaccurate. For discussion, see Law Com. No. 226, paras.7.4–7.12. See also the essay by Richardson in this volume.

[33] There is a paucity of 'impact' studies of judicial review in England, in sharp contrast to America. The exceptions include L. Bridges, C. Game, O. Lomas, J. McBride & S. Ranson, *Legality and Local Politics* (Birmingham, 1987); I. Loveland, 'Legal Rights and Political Realities: Governmental Responses to Homelessness in Britain' (1991) 16 *Law and Social Inquiry* 249; M. Sunkin & A. Le Sueur, 'Can Government Control Judicial Review?' (1991) CLP 161. For recent criticism, see R. Cranston, 'Reviewing Judicial Review', in G. Richardson & H. Genn (eds.), *Administrative Law and Government Action* (Oxford, 1994).

[34] In the event, the Government introduced a Criminal Injuries Compensation Bill containing proposals for higher compensation awards but retaining a tariff scheme. See *The Times*, 12 May 1995.

[35] The Foreign Secretary announced that he accepted the court's ruling, but that funding would continue from outside the overseas aid programme: HC Deb., 13 Dec. 1994, cols. 7[illegible]3–86. Also, Mr Hurd refused to restore £24m. of the aid budget already spent on the dam: in consequence, at the time of writing, the World Development Movement is threatening further legal action. See The *Guardian*, 23 Dec. 1994.

[36] The Pergau Dam case provoked a review of major aid projects, which identified three further instances of possible illegality. See *The Times*, 14 Dec. 1994.

also a transformative legacy of legal action for subsequent group development.

Enough has been said to demonstrate the uncertain prospect that is collective legal action. Elsewhere, however, I draw attention to a diverse range of factors operating to encourage an increased recourse by groups to litigation, for example a rise of new social movements, a decline in consensus politics, and changes in the ethos and culture of the legal profession.[37] In this context, and specifically in relation to public law litigation, it is I think appropriate to pay special heed to the role of contemporary judicial creativity as a catalyst for collective legal action; and, further, of collective legal action as a catalyst for such creativity.[38] Although from the viewpoint of protagonists there will inevitably be many eventual disappointments, this increasingly evident symbiosis holds out the prospect of a major and influential collective participation in public law litigation, at least in the foreseeable future.

PROCEDURAL REFORM AND THE CASE OF THE *AMICUS* BRIEF

It is also appropriate in this context to consider recent proposals by the Law Commission for further reform of judicial review procedure.[39] In several important respects, the Commission signals a greater accommodation of collective legal action; and, conversely, a drift away from a private law or individualistic model of adjudication. In turn, the proposals help to legitimize contemporary judicial developments of the kind previously explained, as well as indicating some future likely directions. However, the report also demonstrates a notable failure to pay heed to American experience, in circumstances where the relevant lessons were both appropriate and easy to comprehend.

First, as regards standing, a new twin-track procedure has been proposed. The first track would cover those personally adversely affected by a decision (a formulation sufficiently wide to cover some cases of associational plaintiffs). The second track, which would cover so-called 'public interest challenges', is clearly designed to underpin the 'liberal'

[37] Harlow & Rawlings, *op. cit.* (1992), 293–8.

[38] For a similar assessment by a leading practitioner, see M. Beloff, 'Judicial Review—2001. A Prophetic Odyssey' [1995] 58 *MLR* 144. Beloff identifies as a key condition of the 'judicial renewal' an increasing awareness of the potentialities of public law, in particular among pressure groups.

[39] Law Com. No. 226. The report stems from the Commission's decision in 1991 to review the workings of the judicial review machinery put in place in 1977, following Law Com. No. 73, *Remedies in Administrative Law* (London, 1976).

trend in the case-law, and thereby represents a further, explicit acknowledgement of group legal action.[40] It should be noted, however, that this track would be a discretionary track, and that the Law Commission rejected the idea of laying down relevant guidelines.[41]

A second major proposal concerns jurisdiction to make advisory declarations,[42] so that relevant actors 'know where they stand' when, for example, faced with the interpretation of complex statutes.[43] This clearly represents a departure from a classical dispute-oriented model of adjudication, and as such presents a novel window of opportunity most likely to be used, on the one hand by public authorities and, on the other, by powerful collectivities, perhaps in strategic litigation. Indeed, this type of procedural development could be anticipated to underpin further judicial creativity, allowing the courts to exercise 'abstract' or '*a priori*' judicial review free from the constraints of an ordinary law suit.[44] Finally, it is relevant to note that this proposal leaves much to be resolved, notably in relation to questions of *res judicata* and participation. Instead, the Law Commission anticipates that such proceedings will be permitted only in exceptional cases, where the court considers that the matter is one of general public importance.[45]

Thirdly, where there is a 'public interest challenge' or an advisory declaration is sought, it has been proposed that the costs rule be modified in favour of applicants. Briefly, the court deciding the case would have discretion to award costs from central funds, instead of from the losing party.[46] Clearly, this does not go so far as relevant groups would like, since exposure for their own costs would not be reduced, nor would the risk of an adverse order be removed at an early stage. Nevertheless, there is some

[40] Specifically, it is aimed against restrictive decisions, notably the *Rose Theatre Trust* case (see above, n. 29).

[41] The Commission's preferred test is if 'the High Court considers that it is in the public interest for an applicant to make the application': Law Com. No. 226, para. 5.22. Clearly, this formulation also covers relevant challenges by individuals, e.g. in relation to the European Community: *R* v. *HM Treasury ex p. Smedley* [1985] QB 657; *R* v. *Secretary of State for Foreign and Commonwealth Affairs ex p. Rees Mogg* [1994] 1 All ER 457. See further Cane in this volume.

[42] Arguably, such a course can already be followed by virtue of the courts' inherent jurisdiction: see *per* Laws J in *R* v. *Home Secretary ex p. Mehari* [1994] 2 WLR 349, 366.

[43] Law Com. No. 226, paras.8.9, 8.10.

[44] e.g. in constitutional cases. For discussion see Sir John Laws, 'Judicial Remedies and the Constitution' [1994] 57 *MLR* 213; R. Rawlings, 'Legal Politics: The United Kingdom and Ratification of the Treaty on European Union (Part 2)' (1994) *PL* 367, 376–7.

[45] Law Com. No. 226, paras. 8.13, 8.14.

[46] Law Com. No.226, para. 10.5. In this context, the Commission also made reference to an increasing practice in the courts not to award costs against a relevant applicant: see, e.g. *New Zealand Maori Council* v. *Attorney General of New Zealand* [1994] 2 WLR 254.

potential here for a relaxation of a costs regime widely recognized to inhibit recourse to strategic litigation by the less well-heeled.[47]

Enough has been said to show a clear intent to render judicial review more permeable, at the initial stage of access to court.[48] Yet this is predicated on high levels of judicial discretion, inside an already discretionary framework. At one level, this renders future development uncertain and contestable. At another, it helps mask a failure by the law reform agency to articulate clearly a view of the purposes and character of judicial review proceedings.[49] It is evidently the case that other potentially conflicting policy factors have been in play, notably case-management, speed and certainty in administrative decision taking, and pressures for European legal harmonization.[50] American experience is in this context particularly helpful in a consideration of the piecemeal character of contemporary English developments and of the problems thereby likely to arise.

Carol Harlow's essay in this collection makes extensive reference to the implications raised by Abram Chayes's famous article in the *Harvard Law Review*, 'The Role of the Judge in Public Law Litigation',[51] but they may also usefully be alluded to here. Chayes examined contemporary American developments by reference to two ideal typical models of adjudication: the familiar adversarial, bipolar private law model, and a much less rigid public law model which incorporated elements such as negotiation and judicial management, broad discovery and forward-looking remedies. For present purposes, the article teaches the utility of examining the relevant procedure in its entirety, and in particular the internal relation of the various component parts. Unfortunately, in this country the lesson appears to have been lost on the Law Commission.

Let us pursue the point. Elsewhere, I attempt to build on Chayes's work

[47] Notably in comparison with America: for discussion see Harlow & Rawlings, *op. cit.* (1992), 115–20. Conversely, the English approach has recently attracted considerable interest in America as a way of curtailing litigation: see e.g. President's Council on Competitiveness, *Agenda for Civil Justice Reform in America* (Washington, 1991), 24.

[48] To the proposals examined in the text may be added the following: a further weakening by reason of a transfer power of the principle of procedural exclusivity laid down in *O'Reilly* v. *Mackman* [1983] 2 AC 237; a modification of the legal aid scheme to allow 'the wider public interest' in having a case heard to be considered; and providing one form of collective-unincorporated associations—with a clear legal capacity to seek judicial review. See respectively, Law Com. No. 226, paras. 3.21, 10.9 & 5.41.

[49] For discussion in relation to the Law Commission's earlier consultation paper (No. 126, 1993), see M. Loughlin, 'The Limits of Judicial Review', in P. Birks (ed.), *Frontiers of Liability* (Oxford, Vol. 1 1994). For a notable defence of judicial discretion in this context see Woolf, *op. cit.* (1990); also 'Judicial Review: A Possible Programme for Reform' [1992] *PL* 221. The Law Commission was clearly greatly influenced by Lord Woolf's views.

[50] See in particular, Law Com. No. 226, Part 2, 'General Considerations'.

[51] *Op. cit.*

by postulating three ideal typical models of adjudication with which to examine the receptivity of English judicial review process to group legal action.[52] Briefly, the opening up of standing shows the courts moving towards a hybrid or 'funnel' model, as between the traditional restrictive English approach and a more flexible, open model of the kind visualized by Chayes.[53] As the metaphor implies, the litigation process is seen as increasingly permeable at the initial stage and yet restrictive later on, in terms not only of grounds of review and remedies, but also discovery and third party intervention. Two points require emphasis. First, although as American experience illustrates,[54] the English machinery is hardly unique in failing to satisfy the aspirations of many of those whom it encourages to participate, the shape of the model is peculiarly apt for this kind of consequence. Second, by operating to accommodate applicants and then to exclude a plurality of interests, the hybrid model creates difficulties of adequacy of representation, notably in a so-called 'public interest challenge' where the version of the 'public interest' put forward may be hotly contested.

We may deduce that the hybrid model, notably the product of piecemeal judicial development, is both internally incoherent and inherently unstable. Specifically, pressures are generated not only as indicated for a more vigorous application of extended grounds of review, but also, better to support the enterprise, for improvements to judicial information mechanisms widely held to be deficient.[55] Further, we now observe that the Law Commission's recommendations would exacerbate the problem, operating to ease further entry to court but failing to address the quality of evidence on which courts must ground decisions. Here it suffices to say, first, that the Commission treated the giving of reasons as beyond its remit;[56] second, adhered to the current restrictive rules on discovery;[57]

[52] See Harlow & Rawlings, *op. cit.* (1992), 310–17.

[53] It should be stressed that my competing models, the so-called 'drainpipe' and American 'freeway', are seen respectively as restrictive and permeable at successive stages of the litigation process.

[54] See further below.

[55] e.g., J. Griffith, 'Judicial Decision-Making in Public Law' [1985] PL 564; M. Purdue, 'The Scope of Fact-Finding in Judicial Review', in G. Hand & J. McBride (eds.), *Droit Sans Frontiers* (Birmingham, 1991); Woolf, *op. cit.* (1992). Here it is important to note the challenge presented by Community law, especially in cases where domestic legislation is required to be justified. See e.g., *R* v. *Secretary of State for Employment ex p. The Equal Opportunities Commission and Day* [1994] 2 WLR 409; and for discussion, A. Boyle, 'Sovereignty, Accountability, and the Reform of Administrative Law', in G. Richardson & Genn *op. cit.*

[56] On the basis that questions of substantive law were in the Law Commission's view best left to judicial development: Law Com. No. 226, paras. 1.3, 2.29. The leading case is now *R* v. *Secretary of State for the Home Department ex p. Doody* [1994] 1 AC 531.

[57] Despite making criticisms: see Law Com. No. 226, paras. 7.4–7.12. And see above, n. 32.

and, third, passed over the idea of a new information conduit in the shape of a Director of Civil Proceedings.[58] In this context, a failure by the Commission to take into account the single most relevant consideration of American legal procedure, the role of the *amicus* brief, may fairly be characterized as misguided.[59]

Some thirty years ago, Krislov demonstrated that in America the traditional role of *amicus curiae* or impartial 'friend of the court' was increasingly taken over by, and recast to the uses of, a variety of collective interests.[60] Subsequent accounts confirm the *amicus* brief as the commonest way for groups to participate in Supreme Court litigation.[61] Notably, it is seen as a prime instrument for repeat players, led by the Justice Department and states attornies, and encompassing, among 'unofficial' interests, large corporations, diverse lobby groups and, more recently, so-called 'public interest law firms'.[62]

Of particular relevance is a plurality of function and style. The *amicus* brief allows interested non-parties to penetrate the adversarial process, and, by virtue of the documentary or written procedure, to do so in relatively concise and economical fashion. At one level, characteristic of a more pluralist political culture, this helps to mitigate the problems of adequacy of representation, which we have seen a funnel model of process maximizes. To make the point differently, there is a proper recognition in America, unlike in this country, that standing and intervention are facets

[58] Put forward by H. Woolf, 'Public Law—Private Law: Why the Divide? A Personal View', [1986] *PL* 220; *op. cit.* (1992).

[59] At the time of writing, there is the curious spectacle of the Law Commission's work having to be done by a working party on third party intervention established by two unofficial groups, JUSTICE and the Public Law Project, chaired by a High Court judge, Sir John Laws.

[60] S. Krislov, 'The *Amicus Curiae* Brief: From Friendship to Advocacy' (1963) 72 *Yale LJ* 694. For a comparative perspective see J. Mclinden, *Amicus Curiae: an American Model for the New Zealand Court of Appeal* (*mimeo*, Auckland, 1992) 48; E. Angell, 'The *Amicus Curiae*: American Development of English Institutions' (1987) 16 *ICLQ* 1016.

[61] K. O'Connor & L. Epstein, '*Amicus Curiae* Participation in US Supreme Court Litigation: An Appraisal of Hakman's "Folklore" ' (1981) 16 *Law and Society* 311; G. Caldeira & J. Wright, 'Organized Interests and Agenda-Setting in the US Supreme Court' (1988) 82 *American Political Science Review* 1109; and '*Amici Curiae* Before the Supreme Court. Who Participates, When and How Much?' (1990) 52 *Journal of Politics* 782.

[62] A growth industry in the United States, of which leading examples are the American Legal Defense Fund, an offshoot of the NAACP, the Center for Law and Social Policy, and the conservative Pacific Legal Foundation. Public interest law firms are beginning to develop in this country, for example the Public Law Project. At Strasbourg, organizations like INTERIGHTS play a similar role, acquiring a semi-official status. See further, the Public Law Project, *The First Three Years* (London, 1994); E. Playfair, 'INTERIGHTS—An International Human Rights Law Centre' [1994] PL 573. See also, A. Lester, '*Amici Curiae*: Third-Party Interventions before the European Court of Human Rights', in F. Matscher & H. Petzold (eds.), *Protecting Human Rights: The European Dimension* (Berlin, 1990, 2nd ed.).

of the same problem of access and need to be considered in tandem.[63]

The *amicus* brief is also commonly recognized as a tolerably efficient judicial information mechanism, which thereby encourages judicial assertiveness and creativity.[64] Famously, this has entailed in America not only diverse sources of legal argument, but also, in the guise of the Brandeis Brief,[65] a blending of conventional legal material with socio-economic data and analysis of established patterns of behaviour and likely consequences of decisions. Lastly, and perhaps less well known in this country, the *amicus* brief is used as an instrument of court lobbying, in the sense akin to 'plaintiff stacking' of persuading a court of a wide spectrum of support.[66] In a context where other usages may tempt courts to take on broad, policy-making issues, this usage underscores the pressures which may be imposed by lobbyists on the boundary between legal and political processes.

Here we identify an important area of legal practice largely without parallel in England. The courts in this country have continued to adhere to a more classical model of the *amicus curiae*, in terms both of the source and quality of the contribution. Typically this involves the appointment of an *amicus* at the request of a court by a law officer of the Crown, with the express purpose of assisting the court with legal arguments which might otherwise not be put, perhaps because one party is not represented.[67] Notably, the model implies a high degree of official control and, further, as regards adversarial, bipolar process, a minimum corrective.

As the funnel model of process would suggest, strains in the existing system are increasingly in evidence. On the one hand, we find growing

[63] For discussion in the context of European Community litigation, see C. Harlow, 'Towards a Theory of Access for the European Court of Justice' (1993) 12 *Yearbook of European Law* 213. In this respect, perhaps one should not be too harsh on the Law Commission, since our leading textbooks on administrative law also fail to make the connection.

[64] For contemporary argument that in this country judicial review is unduly restricted by a lack of such information mechanisms, see D. Jabbari, 'Criticial Theory in Administrative Law' (1994) 14 *OJLS* 189; J. Allison, 'The Procedural Reason for Judicial Constraint' [1994] PL 452.

[65] After Louis Brandeis, the counsel who first presented this type of submission to the Supreme Court. See C. Vose, 'The National Consumers' League and the Brandeis Brief', (1957) 1 *Midwest Journal of Policial Studies* 267; N. Erickson, 'Historical Background of 'Protective' Labour Legislation: *Muller* v. *Oregon*' in D. Weisberg (ed.), *Women and the Law: The Social Historical Perspective* (Cambridge, Mass., Vol. 2 1982).

[66] This may entail either multiple briefs or briefs subscribed to by multiple organizations, and is a long-standing practice illustrated as early as *Morehead* v. *New York ex rel. Tipaldo* (1936) 298 US 587. In the 1950's, significant judicial efforts were made to curtail multiple briefs: see for discussion, N. Hakman, 'Lobbying the Supreme Court—An Appraisal of "Political Science Folklore" ' (1966) 35 *Fordham LR* 15.

[67] See J. Edwards, *The Attorney General, Politics and the Public Interest* (London, 1984), 153–8: see also Mclinden, *op. cit.*, 2–40.

acceptance of intervention by official or semi-official representative bodies. Predictably, this is most apparent in the difficult area of discrimination law, where the Equal Opportunities Commission and the Commission for Racial Equality have been allowed oral arguments concerning European law, or on procedural points relating to tribunals.[68] On the other hand, the most notable example of a non-official surrogate body trying to intervene arose in the *Gillick* case.[69] Briefly, whereas a challenge to contraceptive advice to young girls was permitted, although Mrs Gillick's own family was not affected, the Children's Legal Centre, which functions as an advocate for young people, was refused permission by the House of Lords to either make oral submissions or lodge a written brief. This approach, which would simply be incomprehensible in the United States, made blatant the inadequacy of representation. The parties involved in the bipolar process could hardly be said to have exhausted the possible range of interests involved in the case.[70]

Enough has been said to show that intervention is a considerable topic by itself. It raises, at one level, vital constitutional questions about the role of courts; and, at another, the role of judicial discretion and of procedural considerations such as notice, delay, and expense.[71] Set against the litigation process as a whole, it also demonstrates the difficulties of a piecemeal approach to procedural reform of the kind favoured by the Law Commission.

For present purposes, the position might be summarized as follows. First, contemporary judicial developments and specifically the Law Commission's report demonstrate a crossing of the Rubicon: there is today in judicial review no going back to an individualistic, private law model of adjudication. Second, the hybrid model is an imperfect model, as reference to American legal practice confirms. Third, and associated with evident

[68] Examples include *Shields* v. *E. Coomes (Holdings) Ltd.* [1978] 1 WLR 1408; *Science Research Council* v. *Nassé, Leyland Cars* v. *Vyas* [1979] 3 WLR 762. See also for an intervention by the United Nations High Commissioner for Refugees, *R* v. *Secretary of State for the Home Department ex p. Sivakumaran* [1988] AC 958.

[69] *Gillick* v. *West Norfolk and Wisbech Area Health Authority* [1985] 1 All ER 533; for critical analysis, see C. Harlow, '*Gillick*: A Comedy of Errors' [1986] 49 *MLR* 768. In contrast, in *Phoenix General Insurance Co. of Greece* v. *Administratia Asigurarilor de Stat* [1988] QB 216, the House of Lords expressed willingness to accept a Brandeis-type brief about the possible impact on the insurance market of validating insurance policies issued by unauthorized insurers.

[70] Very recently, in a judicial review case, *R* v. *Coventry City Council ex p. Pheonix Aviation*, (1995) 145 *NLJ* 559 the pressure group Compassion in World Farming was allowed to intervene. The case involved restrictions on the export of live animals for slaughter.

[71] Elsewhere I advocate a structured approach of the type propounded in Canada by Bryden, *op. cit.* See also J. Koch 'Making Room: New Directions in Third Party Intervention' (1990) 48 *Univ. of Toronto* LR 151.

pressures for a more dynamic regime of judicial review to enhance the accountability of government, pressures will multiply for improved information mechanisms and explicit rights of intervention: in other words, correctives to adversarial, bipolar procedure of which the American-style *amicus* brief is a leading example.[72] Finally, again drawing on American experience of the *amicus* brief, we might hypothesize that not only will judicial review proceedings tip further in the direction of collective legal action, but that increasingly they will be populated by a compendium of powerful repeat players—associational groups, surrogate groups, corporations as well as government agencies—concerned to ensure that relevant precedents do not cut across collective interests, and, further, to use litigation strategically in the development of long-term policy strategies.[73]

CONTEMPORARY PERSPECTIVES

Judicial creativity, explicit acknowledgment of collective legal action, a high degree of contingency: all this finds echoes in a voluminous American literature in recent decades on the contribution of collective, strategic litigation, in particular in relation to social reform. Most studies in the 1960s and early 1970s provided optimistic assessments commending the benefits of liberal activism by the courts.[74] Subsequently, however, critical legal scholarship has introduced a much more sceptical approach, with great stress on contingency and the limitations, institutional and ideological, of legal strategies for advancing social change.

Specifically, numerous neo-realist accounts emphasize how law tends to be an ineffective resource for reformers, owing to limited judicial capacities notably at the stage of monitoring and implementation.[75] Structuralist accounts emphasize further the adverse organizational costs of legal strategies that work to undermine movement advances: typically, a

[72] For a recent discussion of alternative options, including a shift towards inquisitorial procedure, see Allison, *op. cit.*

[73] This theme is pursued in the context of European Community litigation by F. Snyder, 'The Effectiveness of European Community Law: Institutions, Processes, Tools and Techniques' [1993] 56 *MLR* 19; Harlow (1992) *op. cit.*

[74] e.g., C. Vose, *Caucasians Only: The Supreme Court, the NAACP, and the Restrictive Covenant Cases* (Berkeley, 1959); J. Sax, *Defending the Environment: A Strategy for Citizen Action* (New York, 1971); and J. Denvir, 'Towards a Political Theory of Public Interest Law Litigation' (1976) 54 *University of North Carolina LR* 1133.

[75] See e.g., T. Becker & M. Feeley (eds.), *The Impact of Supreme Court Decisions* (London, 1973 2nd ed.); D. Horowitz, *Courts and Social Policy* (Washington, 1977); and J. Handler, E. Hollingsworth & H. Erlanger, *Lawyers and the Pursuit of Rights* (New York, 1978).

draining of resources or diversion of energies away from other more productive (and radical) tactics.[76]

Naturally, as in this country,[77] other accounts combine elements of both approaches. Here, I propose to single out Gerald Rosenberg's *The Hollow Hope: Can Courts Bring About Social Change?*[78] This leading work, and notably the critical response to it,[79] not only encompasses many of the central themes of contemporary American writing on the topic, but also, I shall suggest, contains some important lessons for the study and practice of collective legal action in this country.

One way of presenting the contemporary American debate is in terms of a methodological divide between top-down, court-centred approaches, and bottom-up, dispute-centred (or decentred) perspectives familiarly associated with studies of dispute resolution and legal mobilization.[80] *The Hollow Hope* exemplifies a court-centred approach and to this end postulates two ideal type positions regarding the capacity of courts to effect significant social change. The first is a constrained court model, wherein courts face a near insuperable set of institutional constraints. These constitute the limited nature of constitutional rights and binding quality of legal precedent, a lack of judicial autonomy from other branches of government and public opinion, and the courts' limited capacity for developing and in particular implementing effective social policies. In contrast, a dynamic court model is said to emphasize the accumulated moral authority of courts, their relative insularity and proven problem-solving capacities, and thereby identifies the judicial branch as effective producers of social change. Rosenberg's thesis is that significant social

[76] See e.g., S. Scheingold, *The Politics of Rights: Lawyers, Public Policy, and Political Change* (New Haven, 1974); J. Katz, *Poor People's Lawyers in Transition* (New Brunswick, 1982); and M. Kessler, *Legal Services for the Poor: A Comparative and Contemporary Analysis of Inter-organisational Politics* (Westport, 1987). For a useful historical introduction to the relevant jurisprudential approaches in this area, see H. Stumpf, *American Judicial Politics* (New York, 1988).

[77] See, e.g., C. Harlow, 'Public Interest Litigation in England: the State of the Art', in J. Cooper & R. Dhavan (eds.), *Public Interest Law* (Oxford, 1986).

[78] (Chicago, 1991).

[79] For the so-called McCann-Feeley-Rosenberg debate see M. McCann, 'Reform Litigation on Trial', (1992) 17 *Law and Social Inquiry* 715; M. Feeley, 'Hollow Hopes, Flypaper, and Metaphors', (1992) 17 *Law and Social Inquiry* 745; and G. Rosenberg, 'Hollow Hopes and Other Aspirations: A Reply to Feeley and McCann', (1992) 17 *Law and Social Inquiry* 761.

[80] Briefly, legal mobilization approaches emphasize an understanding of law as identifiable traditions of symbolic practice, which for present purposes both provide interests with malleable resources and impose constraints on manipulation. For an introduction, see F. Zemans, 'Legal Mobilisation: The Neglected Role of the Law in the Political System' (1983) 77 *American Political Science Review* 690; and M. Kessler, 'Legal Mobilisation and Social Reform: Power and the Politics of Agenda Setting' (1990) 24 *Law and Society Review* 121.

change is liable to occur only when the specified institutional constraints can be overcome. To this end, he identifies a number of favourable conditions: these include positive incentives or costs to induce compliance and the presence of officials willing to use court orders as a tool for action.[81]

A specification of constraints and conditions clearly implies a contingent view of judicial impact. Nevertheless, an enduring quality to constraint and an uncommon occurrence of favourable conditions point inexorably to Rosenberg's conclusion that a constrained court model 'more closely approximates the role of the courts in the American political system'.[82]

Detailed empirical evidence is adduced to the effect that a liberal pantheon of Supreme Court decisions had no or almost no significant independent direct or indirect effect in terms of social change.[83] Thus Rosenberg points to an empty promise or 'hollow hope' offered to social reform activists by litigation. Further, the metaphor of 'the fly-paper Court' is used to gild an argument that the Supreme Court attracts would-be reformers only to entrap them in a futile struggle.[84]

As indicated, *The Hollow Hope* reflects and reinforces some familiar themes in the American literature: to the extent of criticism that an easy target has been chosen in the shape of a dynamic court model, which existing accounts of law as an ineffective resource, even impediment for reformers, had already undermined.[85] Nevertheless, Rosenberg's specification of conditional factors in conjunction with the well-known institutional constraints provides a useful analytical framework for explaining when, and in what circumstances, courts can produce significant social reform.

Here, it is appropriate to identify some notable limitations to, and difficulties with Rosenberg's analysis, which possess a transatlantic resonance for studies of this kind. *The Hollow Hope* exhibits a familiar tendency to undervalue collective legal action by too narrow a focus on appeal cases and too high an expectation. There is for example an 'Aunt Sally' type quality to defining 'significant social reform' for these purposes as 'policy change with nationwide impact' in multiple bureaucratic and

[81] G. Rosenberg, *op. cit.*, 9–36.

[82] *Id.*, 35.

[83] *Brown* v. *Board of Education*, 347 US 483 (1954); *Roe* v. *Wade*, 410 US 113 (1973); *Mapp* v. *Ohio*, 367 US 643 (1961); *Miranda* v. *Arizona*, 377 US 201 (1966); *Baker* v. *Carr*, 369 US 186 (1962).

[84] Rosenberg, *op. cit.*, 336–43. (Similar criticism is provoked by a 'funnel' model of litigation: Harlow & Rawlings, *op. cit.* (1992), 312–13.) Throughout, Rosenberg places great emphasis on political efforts separate from the courts as effective stimulants of significant social reform.

[85] Feeley, *op. cit.*, 750–2. Critics rightly concede the telling way in which the case is made through reference to Supreme Court decisions often regarded as important sources of new policies: see Feeley, *op. cit.*, 746–7.

institutional settings.[86] Further, as the title implies, judicial impact is measured by reference to the hopes expressed by activists, perhaps in the heat of battle. It is therefore not surprising that Rosenberg should observe a considerable 'gap' with the reality of subsequent events. Conversely, the contrast is less between court rulings and subsequent behaviour, notably in those many circumstances in which a court ruling is more modest than is the rhetoric of reformers.[87]

Of particular note are limitations inherent in a court-centred approach. If Rosenberg's conceptual framework is recognized as generally useful for evaluating whether courts can 'produce' significant social change, the formulation itself may be criticized as less illuminating than Rosenberg suggests. Foremost among the critics is Michael McCann, whose recent work draws on some familiar insights of a dispute-centred approach to legal practice. These include recourse to judicial action as the exception not the rule, collective legal action as part of multidimensional conflict, non-judicial actors as practical legal agents (not simply reactors to judicial command), and the importance of indirect or 'radiating' effects of litigation.[88] The key feature for present purposes is a focus less on whether courts 'produce' intended change than on the diverse ways in which actors deploy legal resources in multiple venues outside the courts. This is typified in a closer look at the wider implications of legal action than a top-down approach suggests, notably for agenda setting, movement building, lobbying, and negotiation—in the classic phrase—'in the shadow of the law'.[89]

Enough has been said to indicate the rich diversity that characterizes recent American debate, as also to indicate some strengths and weaknesses of rival approaches. A court-centred approach of the Rosenberg kind certainly allows an opportunity to generalize more broadly, but paradoxically at the price of a panoramic perspective. Specifically, it may underplay the significance in terms of symbolism and resource of relevant forms of legal action. On the other hand, decentred approaches which are more sensitive to context and local explanation are also vulnerable to a charge of particularity.[90] Since, as Rosenberg and McCann properly

[86] See Rosenberg, *op. cit.*, 4. For a very different approach, premised on legal change as Supreme Court created shifts in legal doctrine, see L. Epstein & J. Kobylka, *The Supreme Court and Legal Change* (Chapel Hill, 1992).

[87] For criticism of Rosenberg's approach for paying insufficient attention to the substance of Supreme Court rulings, see McCann, *op. cit.*, 725–7; and Feeley, *op. cit.*, 752–6.

[88] See in addition to the sources cited in n. 80, M. McCann, *Rights at Work: Pay Equity Reform and the Politics of Legal Mobilisation* (Chicago, 1994); also M. Galanter, 'The Radiating Effects of Courts', in K. Boyum & L. Mather (eds.), *Empirical Theories of Courts* (New York, 1983). See to similar effect in this country, Prosser, *op. cit.*

[89] R. Mnookin & L. Kornhauser, 'Bargaining in the Shadow of the Law: the Case of Divorce' (1979) 88 *Yale Law Journal* 951.

[90] A main plank in Rosenberg's reply to McCann: Rosenberg, *op. cit.* (1992), 777–8.

concede, each approach has considerable merit, further studies in the United States will surely attempt the not inconsiderable task of combining more closely the diverse strands of explanation.

GENERAL TENDENCIES AND THE IMAGE OF LEGALITY

At this point especially, in seeking to absorb lessons from the United States, Kahn-Freund's famous warning about the misuses of comparative method, adverted to in the introductory chapter, must be borne in mind.[91] Elsewhere, I draw attention to a tendency in the British commentaries, on the one hand to idealize relevant American phenomena such as the class action, and, on the other, to underplay the continuity and vibrancy of indigenous British practices.[92] It is after all fairly easy to make the case that the constitutional setting in the United States has been considerably more favourable to collective, strategic litigation than in this country. Most obviously, the written constitution limits the competence of both state and federal legislatures, while the considerable obstacles to securing amendments to the constitution encourage a dependency on judicial interpretation of the text. Again, particular emphasis may be placed on a 'rights culture', underpinned by the Bill of Rights, which renders recourse to law an obvious strategem. Famously, Scheingold speaks of a 'myth of rights' in the sense of popular belief in judicially affirmed rights as self-implementing instruments of social justice. Of special relevance for bottom-up perspectives is Scheingold's insistence on American exceptionalism as regards the rhetoric of rights and the symbolic importance of this language in the American political process.[93]

Contemporary British and American debates naturally have much in common at the level of general tendencies in the legal order.[94] In this context, it is worth focussing on several arguments in the recent British literature, better to assess the role and place of collective legal action in our system of public law.

A relevant theme is a fragmentation of the form of law in contemporary society, and in particular increased emphasis on a range of non-judicial fora and techniques for pursuing legal disputes.[95] Alternative dispute

[91] 'On Uses and Misuses of Comparative Law' [1974] 37 *MLR* 1.

[92] See Harlow & Rawlings, *op. cit.*, 124–6 and 290–3. For a practical example, see G. Alderman, 'Book Review' [1993] PL 548.

[93] S. Scheingold, *op. cit.* See Further M. Glendon, *Rights Talks: The Impoverishment of Political Discourse* (New York, 1991); and the essay by Cotterell in this volume.

[94] A theme of Allan's essay in this volume.

[95] R. Cotterell, 'Law's Community: Legal Theory and the Image of Legality' (1992) 19 *JLS* 405, 409–10. See also M. Galanter, 'Law Abounding: Legalisation Around the North Atlantic' [1992] 55 *MLR* 1.

resolution is notably a movement far advanced in America, and many apparent advantages such as access, expertise, and limited disruption to long-term relationships can clearly be of particular value to particular groups, as well as to corporations.[96] In this context, it is hard to resist an argument that, as legal form mutates, it may do so in ways which are increasingly unlikely to involve collective resort to the courtroom.[97] However, as the American debate indicates, it is equally important that this argument be not allowed to prove too much.

At one level, the argument sits more easily with a decentred model of legal practice than a court-centred approach of the Rosenberg type. Yet, as we have seen, a bottom-up perspective not only confirms litigation as exceptional, but may also assign it a broadened significance. In this way, collective recourse to courts should not be too easily distinguished from, or opposed to, other forms of collective recourse to law. Further, it is relevant to note that as the form of law fragments, so—on both sides of the Atlantic—law abounds, in the sense of more legal regulation, more litigation, more legal actors, and so on.[98] Given this general tendency, any decrease in collective resort to courts is considerably less likely in absolute than in relative terms. Finally, an awareness of contextuality and segmentation is clearly appropriate, as already indicated in the present context of our system of public law. In Stanley de Smith's famous phrase, the 'sporadic and peripheral' quality of judicial review has long been recognized.[99] Yet the peculiar hold on the legal imagination of judicial review in our system of public law is hard to exaggerate.[100] We can now add that judicial review is not only becoming, but is increasingly being seen to be, rather less peripheral in this jurisdiction.

A second theme concerns an instrumentality to law—which recourse to courts for campaign purposes clearly assumes—in the sense of law as an instrument for realizing particular political objectives.[101] At one level, work on the phenomenon serves as a valuable corrective to narrow and élitist views concerning the reach of, and popular involvement with, the concepts (in this context) of public law. This is particularly so in the case of bottom-up perspectives focused on group motivation and strategy, and peculiarly so with the kind of analysis propounded in America by McCann.

[96] S. Goldberg, E. Green & F. Sander, *Dispute Resolution* (Boston 1992 2nd ed.); and, for a comparative perspective, M. Cappelletti, 'Alternative Dispute Resolution Processes Within The Framework Of the Worldwide Access To Justice Movement' [1993] 56 *MLR* 282.

[97] N. Walker, 'Law Under Pressure' [1994] 57 *MLR* 130, 148.

[98] M. Galanter, *op. cit.* (1992).

[99] S. de Smith, *Judicial Review of Administrative Action* (London, 1980 4th ed., 3.

[100] A point neatly made by P. Cane, *An Introduction to Administrative Law*, (Oxford, 1992 2nd ed.), 4–5.

[101] A point made explicit in the practice of 'plaintiff stacking' and in the use of the *amicus* brief as an instrument of court lobbying: see above.

Here, it is relevant to note that his type of focus on the many ways in which citizens act upon the disparate signals of official law and, specifically, on judicially articulated norms taking on a life of their own as they are deployed in practical social action, is closely associated with broader studies of local and popular 'legal consciousness', as represented in Austin Sarat's phrase 'the law is all over'.[102]

Of course, in this context we must bear in mind not only as regards 'a rights culture' Scheingold's warning of American exceptionalism, but also the particular British tendency to an exclusive 'club' style of government.[103] Nevertheless, the contrast implicit in recent work by Martin Loughlin concerning the nature of our public law is surely too stark. On the one hand, Loughlin views public law as a form of political discourse in which actors use concepts (sovereignty, rights, natural justice, proportionality, etc.) to help realize their political goals. On the other, he presents as relevant actors: lawyers, judges, politicians, and scholars.[104] The difficulty is not simply that a model of public law litigation which excludes applicants is impoverished. As in America, we can hardly ignore the role of wider publics and of popular legal consciousness which (expressed through concepts like proportionality and natural justice) is part of common experience. In his classic work *Whigs and Hunters*,[105] much referred to in the American literature,[106] E. P. Thompson draws attention to law as ideology in terms of a set of norms 'tenaciously transmitted through the community'.[107] As regards the contemporary British scene, Cotterrell observes that law's community of interpretation 'is not one but many', and—in decentred fashion—stresses the importance of examining the way in which legal interpretive communities (within legal professions and judiciaries, but also outside them) are established and maintained.[108]

[102] See A. Sarat, ' "The Law is all Over": Power, Resistance and the Legal Consciousness of the Welfare Poor' (1990) 2 *Yale J. of Law and Humanities* 343; also, S. Merry, *Getting Justice and Getting Even: Legal Consciousness Among Working Class Americans* (Chicago, 1990); and M. Minnow, *Making All The Difference: Inclusion, Exclusion and American Law* (Cornell, 1990).

[103] W. Bagehot, *The English Constitution* (London, 1963), 156. A style which still finds powerful echoes, as e.g. in the small cadre of 'nominated' judges on which the present system of judicial review is predicated.

[104] M. Loughlin, 'The Pathways of Public Law Scholarship', in G. Wilson (ed.), *Frontiers of Legal Knowledge* (Warwick, 1995). In contrast, Chayes sees judges in public law litigation as engaged in 'a continuous and rather tentative dialogue with other political elements—Congress and the executive, administrative agencies, the profession and the academics, the press and wider publics'; *op. cit.*, 1316.

[105] (London: Penguin edition, 1990).

[106] A good example of the two way transatlantic trade: see McCann, *op. cit.* (1994) for references.

[107] Thompson, *op. cit.*, 261.

[108] Cotterrell, *op. cit.*, 415. See also, R. Cotterrell, 'Judicial Review and Legal Theory', in Richardson & Genn *op. cit.*

At another level, by reason of the focus on a use of courts for explicitly instrumental purposes, scholarly enquiries into collective, strategic litigation are susceptible to a charge of undermining such basic beliefs as judicial neutrality and the rule of law: *in extremis*, of removing the essential supports which law requires to function effectively.[109] Conversely, however, as other American sources demonstrate, this kind of work can help to clarify not only the kinds of threat presented to the image of legality, but also, via the responses of legal institutions, an understanding of the processes by which that image is maintained. In this context, reference may be made to early work on the lobbying of courts by Nathan Hakman, which represents a political scientist's fierce defence of disinterested justice.[110] This influential study stands as a valuable corrective to cruder or more austere forms of socio-economic determinism and helps to underline the symbolic and cultural importance of the idea of law in social ordering and evolution. Again, it is permissible to single out a famous article by Resnik, which drew attention to the dangers posed by managerial judges (especially prevalent in collective litigation) for the legitimacy of the American legal system.[111] More recently, drawing in part on this work, Harlow and I examined the key function of the constitutional doctrine of judicial independence in a British context. We endeavoured, at one level, to identify the problems of 'fit' or friction which inevitably arise when more blatant forms of court lobbying are used; and, at another, to emphasize the ideological function which the doctrine serves in underpinning the legitimacy of the legal system. The threat posed here by certain forms of campaign litigation was, we thought, one which, far from being ignored, should not be taken lightly.[112]

Collective, strategic litigation, I have argued, is an increasingly evident phenomenon in our system of public law. It may also be seen as one element in an enhanced visibility of policy in law, relating, as with fragmentation in the forms of, and abounding of law, to a changed image of legality.[113] In this context, it has again been suggested that a drift away from courts is likely. So, the argument goes, in so far as the law acquires a more instrumental image, the ethos of disinterested justice on which the seductiveness of courts depends, will be undermined.[114] Once more, it is worth approaching domestic controversy with reference to American experience.

First, as regards campaign litigation, an ethos of disinterested justice is more aptly characterized in terms of a magnetic force, operating not only

[109] Loughlin, *op. cit.* (1995).
[110] Hakman, *op. cit.*
[111] J. Resnik, 'Managerial Judges' (1982) 96 *Harvard LR* 374.
[112] See on the concept of 'separate identity' of the judicial role, Harlow & Rawlings, *op. cit.* (1992), 156–8 & 192–9.
[113] See Cotterrell, *op. cit.*, 411–13.
[114] Walker, *op. cit.*, 147–8.

to attract as a source of symbolic capital, but also to repel in the sense of maintaining a distance between the courts and the political process. To the extent that the message is increasingly sent and received that courts are an available instrument, we could anticipate that more collectivities will choose, or feel compelled, to participate. In other words, the relevant argument can as well be stood on its head.

This aspect is neatly illustrated by a surge of conservative group litigation before the Supreme Court in the 1980s. In a classic study, Epstein reveals how these groups were increasingly motivated to offset the influence of liberal groups (attracted previously by the perceived radicalism of the Warren Court).[115] Initially at least, the balancing of countervailing interests was seen as a goal in and of itself.[116] Significantly, this required lobbying techniques like the *amicus* brief, which sat uneasily with the conservatives' preferred vision of a formalist, apolitical judicial function.[117] The inevitable consequence was a much increased competitive or oppositional involvement by groups in proceedings, exemplified in the abortion and death penalty cases.[118]

Second, around the Atlantic and beyond, many commentators have drawn attention to the capacity of law to withstand, in Galanter's phrase, 'large doses of realism'.[119] Studies in popular legal consciousness have notably stressed law's resilience as an authoritative expression of shared values, and, further, how this image coexists with the image of law as an instrument for the pursuit of particular, political objectives.[120] We may conclude, first, that a removal of the props of law is hardly imminent; and, second, that an ethos of disinterested justice endures in both nations despite evident threats from explicitly instrumental forms of litigation.

115 Epstein, *op. cit.*
116 For a discussion of 'balancing', see Epstein & Kobylka, *op. cit.*, 30–2.
117 Epstein, *op. cit.*, esp. 134–5.
118 For detailed analysis see Epstein & Kobylka, *op. cit.*, esp. apps. 1 & 2.
119 Galanter *op. cit.*, (1992), 22.
120 See e.g., Merry, *op. cit.*; also Post, 'On the Popular Image of the Lawyer: Reflections in a Dark Glass' (1987) 75 *California LR* 379; and T. Tyler, *Why People Obey the Law* (New Haven, 1990). The point is effectively conceded by Walker, *op. cit.*, 148.

5

Standing, Representation, and the Environment

PETER CANE

I HAVE chosen environmental law as the prime (although not the exclusive) focus of this essay for several reasons. One is that both in this country and in the United States, a significant number of the most important judicial decisions about the law of standing have concerned environmental matters. Another reason, which partly explains the first, is that environmental harms often affect many people; and although they often affect a smaller group much more than they affect the generality, large sections of the population can often claim to be directly or indirectly injured by conduct which degrades the environment.

The law of standing is, of course, concerned with the question of who can invoke the judicial process. Put in these terms, issues of standing arise not only in applications for judicial review but also in tort actions for damages or injunctions under the rubrics of public nuisance and breach of statutory duty. A person claiming an injunction or damages for public nuisance has to show that he or she was personally affected; and a plaintiff suing for breach of statutory duty will succeed only if the purpose of the statute was to protect people like the plaintiff from harm of the type suffered. Such focus on the individual is a feature of what we call 'private law', which is quintessentially concerned with the rights of natural persons and only recognizes collectivities if they assume the form of a corporation. There are a few contexts in which unincorporated groups can (indirectly, at least) claim the protection of the law of tort. For instance, a group of individuals may enlist the aid of the Attorney-General to seek an injunction on behalf of them all to restrain a public nuisance or a breach of statutory duty. On the whole, however, tort litigation by groups is handled by aggregating individual claims rather than by treating the group as different from the sum of its parts. The procedural device of the representative action[1] is, for all practical purposes, of no use to groups of tort litigants.

In the environmental context, the law of tort is primarily an avenue by

[1] RSC Ord. 15 r. 12.

which victims of environmental harms can obtain redress from those who inflict such harm. I am using the term 'environmental harm' in a very wide sense to cover any (alleged) degradation of the natural or built environment. For the sake of convenience I shall refer to environmental harm as 'pollution', its victims as 'pollutees', and its perpetrators as 'polluters'. My focus in this paper is not on the rights of pollutees against polluters but on the rights of citizens (whether natural persons or corporations) against government bodies in respect of decisions and actions affecting the environment; and more particularly, on judicial review[2] of decisions and actions of regulatory bodies charged with protection of the environment. For this reason I will not discuss private prosecutions in detail. But they are worth a mention because of the increased importance they have assumed in environmental law in recent years. To an individual or a group wishing to preserve good relations with a regulator, private prosecution of a polluter may seem preferable to judicial review as a way of making good official inaction against polluters;[3] and especially so since in relation to environmental offences, any person may institute and conduct criminal proceedings.[4]

For my purposes, citizens can be divided into objects of environmental regulation (polluters) and beneficiaries of regulation (pollutees). But it must be said immediately that so far as the law of standing is concerned, beneficiaries are much more interesting than objects because they are much less likely to be able to bring themselves within the terms of narrow standing rules; whereas regulation typically impinges on the proprietary, contractual, or financial interests of its objects. So what follows will deal mainly with the beneficiaries of environmental regulation.

I will discuss three issues: first, what interest must the applicant for judicial review have in order to possess standing? Secondly, under what circumstances may an applicant for judicial review claim standing to represent the interests of someone else? Thirdly, what environmental interests are sufficient to generate standing? The second of these issues is referred to in the US as the problem of 'third party standing' and I have elsewhere[5] referred to it by the term 'representative standing'. It is important in the environmental context because, both in the US and the UK, conservation groups have often seen the judicial process as a useful way of furthering their causes.

These three issues are, of course, related, but it is useful to distinguish

[2] This term refers to direct challenges to government decisions in the courts; it is not limited to applications for judicial review under RSC Ord. 53.

[3] See generally C. Harlow & R. Rawlings, *Pressure Through Law* (London, 1992), ch. 5.

[4] A. Geddes, '*Locus Standi* and EC Environmental Matters' (1992) 4 *J Env. L* 29, 36.

[5] *Introduction to Administrative Law* (Oxford, 1992 2nd ed.), 54–6.

the first two from one another if only because the US Supreme Court[6] treats the interest requirement, but not the rules governing third party standing, as a constitutional matter. The third deserves separate treatment because it is only by looking at how courts have applied the standing requirement in individual cases that one can properly assess the role of the courts in environmental matters.

THE BASIC RULES OF STANDING

The basic English rule of standing is, of course, that the applicant for judicial review must have a 'sufficient interest in the matter to which the application relates'.[7] The concept of 'sufficient interest' is a complex one requiring reference to previous case-law, relevant statutory provisions, the factual circumstances of the particular case, the substance of the applicant's claim, and the seriousness of the respondent's allegedly illegal action. The question of standing can arise at both the leave and the hearing stages. At the leave stage, the court should deny standing only in clear cases; but the respondent is free at the hearing stage to argue that despite the grant of leave, the applicant lacks standing.

The US rule[8] (as developed by the Supreme Court) has a core which is said to be of constitutional status. According such status to standing rules gives them (it is said) a role in securing the separation of powers embodied in the Constitution. Also, to the extent that standing rules have constitutional force, they are immunized from legislative abrogation.[9] The core rule is that the applicant must have suffered:

[6] I will deal only with US federal law.

[7] Supreme Court Act 1981, s. 3(3); RSC Ord. 53, r. 3(7). The Law Commission has proposed a new test: the court must be satisfied that the applicant 'has been or would be adversely affected' or must consider 'that it is in the public interest for an applicant to make the application' (Law Com. No. 226 (1994), 44). It is not proposed that this test should replace the term 'person aggrieved' when used in a statute in relation to a right of appeal (*ibid.*, 109). The Commission refers to the second limb of the proposed test as 'discretionary'. I believe that access to judicial review should not be a matter for judicial discretion but should be regulated by reasonably precise rules of law. The second limb is designed to cover all cases in which the applicant is not 'personally adversely affected', and it may also cover some cases in which the applicant is personally affected but does not have a 'sufficient interest' in challenging the decision (*ibid.*, 43 n. 38). The purpose of the proposed change is to make 'special provision in cases where the applicant is a representative or pressure group or in cases where no individual has standing but it can be demonstrated that there is a sufficient public interest in the matter being litigated' (*ibid.*, 43). The Commission has chosen a very cumbersome formula which resolves none of the issues of representative standing raised in this essay.

[8] I will deal only with standing in non-constitutional cases; that is, cases in which the plaintiff does not allege that government conduct breached the Constitution.

[9] In *Lujan* v. *Defenders of Wildlife* (1992) 112 S Ct. 2130 the Court held that a statutory provision granting standing to 'any citizen' was invalid. This aspect of the decision will be

'injury in fact'—an invasion of a legally-protected interest which is (a) concrete and particularized . . . and (b) actual or imminent, not conjectural or hypothetical . . . Second, there must be a causal connection between the injury and the conduct complained of . . . Third, it must be 'likely', as opposed to merely 'speculative', that the injury will be redressed by a favourable decision.[10]

This complex test has attracted considerable criticism since it was first introduced in the early 1970s. The main burden of such criticism until recently was that the test was so open-textured and manipulable that it enabled the Court to give effect to its own value judgements about the merits of the applicant's case and, more particularly, about whether the applicant's injury deserved redress, without articulating those value judgements.[11] This criticism hits its mark because despite the fact that 'injury in fact' is defined in terms of invasion of a legally protected interest, the Supreme Court has tended to focus on the factual underpinning of standing claims and to give little attention to elucidating the concept of 'legally protected interest'. In other words, the Court has been much more concerned to identify the harm allegedly suffered than to justify its decisions as to whether the suffering of particular harms should entitle the sufferer to invoke the judicial process in an attempt to redress them. Underlying such criticism was the simple point that the 'brute fact' that someone has suffered a consequence which we are prepared to classify as harm[12] does not, by itself, tell us whether the person should be entitled to complain of that harm before a court and be granted redress.

Critics of the Court also said that by elevating the injury-in-fact test to constitutional status, the Court had usurped the power of Congress to decide how complaints about governmental activity should be dealt with. In the last few years, commentators have made more of this second line of attack by arguing that standing should not be seen as a factual issue depending on whether the applicant has suffered some injury, but as a legal issue depending on whether the applicant is seeking to vindicate some common law or statutory right, or on whether Congress in the relevant statute has expressly or impliedly accorded standing to people in the applicant's position.[13] Critics who argue thus seek to strip standing of its

considered in more detail later. Congress can create 'statutory rights' which can provide a basis for findings of standing. Presumably, however, a statutory right, e.g., not to be subjected to the risk of environmental degradation, might fall foul of the 'injury-in-fact' requirement (considered below) if it was a right enjoyed by all citizens equally. For a different view see C. R. Sunstein, 'What's Standing After *Lujan*? Of Citizen Suits, "Injuries" and Article III' (1992) 91 *Michigan LR* 163, 234–5.

[10] *Lujan* v. *Defenders of Wildlife* (1992) 112 S Ct. 2130, 2136.

[11] See, e.g., G. R. Nichol, 'Rethinking Standing' (1984) 72 *California LR* 68.

[12] We may not, e.g., be prepared to classify as 'harm' an event which the sufferer perceives as adverse but which many others would not.

[13] e.g. Sunstein (1992) *op. cit.*

constitutional status and thereby accord to Congress the ultimate power to grant or deny standing. More particularly, they want to undermine the requirement of 'personal stake' which is said to be implicit in the injury-in-fact test, so as to leave Congress free to pass wide 'citizen standing' or 'private Attorney-General' provisions.[14] In the context of environmental law, the motivation behind this approach is to make it easier for beneficiaries of environmental regulation to challenge regulatory action (or inaction).

An important consequence of the injury-in-fact rule of standing is that issues of standing have become inextricably tied up with rules of pleading.[15] Distinctions are drawn between three different stages of proceedings: the motion to dismiss (strike out) stage, the summary judgment stage, and the final (trial) stage. In the pleadings the applicant must allege injury in fact caused by the challenged act and redressable by a favourable decision. Provided such allegations are 'something more than an ingenious academic exercise in the conceivable',[16] the respondent will not succeed on a motion to dismiss; but unless the applicant, by affidavits or other evidence, 'sets forth specific facts' showing injury in fact, there is a real risk that the respondent will be granted a motion for summary judgment; and at the trial stage the allegations must be 'supported adequately by the evidence'.[17]

In the environmental context the injury-in-fact test encourages a sharp distinction between the objects and the beneficiaries of regulation. The former, it is said, are much more likely to be able to establish the requisite injury in fact than are the latter. This distinction between objects and beneficiaries is not brought so close to the surface by the English concept of 'sufficient interest'. 'Liberal' critics of the Supreme Court argue that the recent introduction of the distinction between the objects and the beneficiaries of regulation is part of a shift to the 'right' amongst the justices, led by Justice Scalia.

There is another strand in the US case-law worth mentioning. When the injury-in-fact test was first introduced, the formula used was 'injury in fact within the zone of interests' sought to be protected by the statute under

[14] See also n. 9 above. Sunstein thinks that the **Court** should not have power to accord citizen standing. He believes that courts should only listen to litigants with a personal stake, and that causation and redressability requirements provide a suitable means of ensuring such stake. In his view, it is for the legislature to define the interests (and hence the harms) to which causation and redressability requirements apply, and the concept of 'protected interest' should be defined in terms of Congressional intention: 'Standing and the Privatisation of Public Law' (1988) 88 *Columbia LR* 1432, 1461 ff.

[15] D. M. Roberts, 'Notice Pleading and Standing' (1980) 65 *Cornell LR* 390.

[16] *United States* v. *Students Challenging Regulatory Agency Procedures* (1973) 412 US 669, 686–7.

[17] *Lujan* v. *Defenders of Wildlife* (1992) 112 S Ct. 2130, 2136–7.

which the challenged action was taken. The zone of interests test was derived from the Administrative Procedure Act which, in the absence of an express grant of standing under the relevant statute, conferred a right to judicial review on (*inter alia*) persons 'adversely affected or aggrieved by agency action within the meaning of a relevant statute'. The zone of interests test was criticized by both judges and commentators on two main grounds: first, that it was uncertain and introduced difficult questions of statutory interpretation; and secondly, that the question of whether the applicant's interest was statutorily protected was not relevant to whether the applicant had standing but to the subsequent question of whether relief ought to be granted. Standing, it was said, is a preliminary issue about whether the applicant is a suitable person to argue the case. If the applicant has suffered injury in fact, he or she is qualified to argue the case regardless of whether that injury is 'legally recognized'.

The zone-of-interests test was effectively ignored for many years by the US courts. But there are signs of its revival.[18] This development is, of course, welcomed by writers who argue that the injury-in-fact test pays insufficient attention to normative criteria of standing and to the role of the legislature in conferring standing.

The core constitutional requirement of injury in fact is supplemented by what are called 'prudential considerations', by which is meant principles of 'judicial self-restraint' designed to prevent the judiciary becoming involved in matters which are perceived by the judges to be, in some sense, beyond the competence of the courts.[19] These prudential considerations are somewhat difficult to pin down, but in a 1982 case[20] the Supreme Court cited three: that the applicant must assert his or her own rights and interests and not those of a third party;[21] that the court will not entertain widely held grievances more appropriately addressed in the representative branches of government; and that the applicant's interest must be one protected by the relevant statute. The last of these apparently imposes only a minimal requirement of statutory nexus, and anyway adds nothing to the zone-of-interests test discussed above. The second seems superfluous because Congress could not displace it by enacting 'citizen standing' provisions, which have been held to conflict with the (constitutional)

[18] See e.g. *Lujan* v. *National Wildlife Federation* (1990) 110 S Ct. 3177, 3186; Sunstein *op. cit.*, 185.

[19] The main purpose of the injury-in-fact requirement is usually said to be to ensure that the applicant has a personal stake in the outcome and that the case for relief will be presented effectively.

[20] *Valley Forge Christian College* v. *Americans United for Separation of Church and State* (1982) 102 S Ct. 752, 759.

[21] Because this consideration does not have constitutional status, it is open to Congress to provide for 'third-party standing'.

injury-in-fact requirement.[22] The first consideration will be central to the later discussion of representative standing. Prudential considerations are subsidiary to the constitutional core in two ways: first, the force to be given to them in particular cases is a matter for the discretion of the court; and secondly, even if an applicant's claim satisfies all of the prudential considerations, standing will only be granted if the applicant can pass the injury-in-fact test.

The secondary literature from the US on standing has been preoccupied with three main questions. First, what issues should the rules of standing be used to deal with? Secondly, should standing be treated as a preliminary matter concerned with entitlement to invoke the judicial process, or as integral to the ultimate question of whether and what relief ought to be given to the applicant? And thirdly, what should the respective role of the courts and the legislature be in laying down rules of standing?

As to the first question, at one extreme the courts have been willing (or so it has been alleged) to use the law of standing to focus not only on the qualifications of the applicant as a litigant but also on large constitutional and institutional issues about the separation of powers and the competences of the different branches of government. Various commentators have also seen standing as a legitimate mechanism for rationing scarce judicial resources[23] and for discouraging paternalism (that is, a concern for the interests of others on the part of someone with no personal stake).[24] Adopting a middle path, some writers have argued that standing should only concern the qualifications of the applicant as litigant. At the other extreme are those[25] who have argued that standing rules ought to be abolished and replaced with rules about the justiciability of disputes.

Attitudes to the second question of whether standing ought to be seen as a preliminary issue tend to be related to views about the function of standing rules. Those who see standing rules in narrow terms as concerned only with identifying suitable litigants might be expected also to see standing as preliminary to the 'substantive merits'. By contrast, those who see standing as having wider functions would naturally see it as central to the resolution of cases; and some have perceived a danger that if standing is treated as a preliminary issue, it will not receive the depth of consideration which it deserves. Some writers in the 1970s accused the

[22] See n. 9 above.

[23] K. E. Scott, 'Standing in the Supreme Court—a Functional Analysis' (1973) 86 *Harvard LR* 645.

[24] L. Brilmayer, 'The Jurisprudence of Article III: Perspectives on the "Case or Controversy Requirement" ' (1979) 93 *Harvard LR* 297.

[25] Especially L. A. Albert, 'Standing to Challenge Administration: an Inadequate Surrogate for Claims for Relief' (1974) 83 *Yale LJ* 425.

Supreme Court of giving effect in some cases to unreasoned hostility to the merits of the applicant's cause by summary dismissal of the action for want of standing.

Concerning the third question of who should make standing rules, the courts have given themselves a pivotal role in particular by elevating standing to constitutional level; whereas several commentators argue that the balance of power should rest with the legislature.

What lessons, if any, might be drawn from the US experience? The obvious first point to make is that the English law on standing lacks the constitutional dimension which is central to the US approach. In domestic law there is no impediment to Parliament conferring standing on parties who lack it according the judge-made rules; nor is Parliament prevented from denying standing to parties who would have it according to the common law, or even from entirely excluding judicial review by a suitably worded ouster provision. The position in EC law is different. We know that ouster provisions can fall foul of EC law,[26] and there may well be limits, derived from the requirement of effective protection of rights, to the power of Parliament (or the courts) to restrict access to the courts by means of narrow standing rules. It is much less clear whether EC law would object to a Member State adopting standing rules which were more generous than necessary to secure 'effective protection' and also wider than those adopted by other Member States.[27] This issue might be particularly important, for example, in the environmental context in relation to the standing of beneficiaries as opposed to objects of regulation. The constitutional aspects of the US law of standing are, then, of only limited relevance to the UK situation.

Secondly, I do not believe that we have much to learn (at least at the abstract level) from the US debate about the balance between factual and normative elements in the test for standing. It is, of course, important to understand that the facts of an applicant's situation must be made the subject of a value judgement before we can say whether the applicant has standing; but I do not think that English judges or writers have ever been in serious danger of making a mistake on this point. If anyone is in such danger, let them be warned!

What should we make of the debate about the function and nature of standing rules? Three points deserve to be made. First, it is useful to have a clear idea of what standing rules are for. I would say that they serve the function of focusing attention on the question of whether the particular applicant should be allowed access to the judicial process. Consider the

[26] *Johnston* v. *Chief Constable of the Royal Ulster Constabulary* [1987] QB 129.

[27] An analogy can be drawn with the impact of minimum Directives, as to which see J. Stapleton, 'Minimum Directives: Do Not Be Misled' (1994) 110 *LQR* 213.

Rose Theatre case, for example.[28] It might be argued that there were good reasons to deny standing to the applicants in that case because of who they were and because of what the relevant statute said about who was to be consulted. But the reasons which the judge gave for the denial of standing (namely, that judicial review of government decisions can cause financial and administrative inconvenience and have a chilling effect on executive action) had nothing to do with who the applicants were. Rather they addressed the question of which decisions should be subject to judicial review. If it is held that a particular decision should not be subject to judicial review, no question of standing can arise. We can only address the issue of whether a particular applicant should be allowed to challenge a decision when we have decided that the decision should be challengeable by someone. So in *Felixstowe Justices*,[29] the court clearly believed that the decision to suppress the names of the justices who heard the case in question and the general policy of suppression of names should both be challengeable by someone; the standing issue was whether the applicant journalist was to be allowed to challenge either or both of them.

Secondly, I think that there is no case for abolishing standing rules entirely. This move could only be justified if standing rules could be said to perform no distinctive function. The argument to this effect is usually based on the idea that standing rules really address issues of justiciability, that is questions about the proper scope of judicial review. Now it is clear that standing rules can be used in this way, as the second of the prudential considerations cited by the US Supreme Court in *Valley Forge* (discussed above) attests. But the real question to be answered is whether all so-called standing rules actually address justiciability concerns. To me it is clear that they do not. Consider the first of the *Valley Forge* prudential considerations: should A be allowed to seek judicial review on behalf of B even though B could seek it personally? This question seems to me to focus on the applicant and on the applicant's relationship with the directly affected party, and to be capable of being answered independently of considerations about the proper scope of judicial review.

Thirdly, should standing be treated as in some sense a preliminary matter or should it be treated in the same way as any other element of the applicant's case? In considering this question we must note the relationship between substantive rules of standing and procedural rules. In both the US and England the formal position is that at each stage of the proceedings, standing is entitled to the same consideration as any other element of the case receives at that stage. In practice, in England at least, the issue of

[28] *R* v. *Secretary of State for the Environment, ex p. Rose Theatre Trust Co Ltd* [1990] 1 QB 504; P. Cane, 'Statutes, Standing and Representation' [1990] *PL* 307.

[29] *R* v. *Felixstowe Justices, ex p. Leigh* [1987] QB 582.

standing is often passed over cursorily or in silence. This is obviously detrimental to the development of the law of standing, but is it cause for serious concern? It seems to me that so long as courts observe the distinction between issues which go to the question of whether *any* applicant would succeed on a particular claim and those which concern whether **the applicant before the court** should succeed, then no great harm will ensue if a court passes lightly over the latter issue in cases where it is clear that **no** applicant would succeed on the claim. One of the positive aspects of the decision in the *Fleet Street Casuals* case[30] was the insistence by the House of Lords that the issue of standing should not be considered in total isolation from the other issues in the case, and that standing should be denied at the leave stage only in very clear cases. It should be remembered, too, that an application for leave can be renewed and, in certain cases, refusal of leave can be appealed against.[31]

REPRESENTATIVE STANDING

It is important at the very beginning to distinguish several different types of situation which might be covered by the phrase 'representative standing':

1. Where an association[32] seeks standing to represent a group of interested parties. We might attach the label 'associational standing' to this type of case.

2. Where an individual or an association seeks standing to represent 'the public interest'. This type of case is usually referred to in terms of allowing 'citizen standing' or actions by 'private (or, as I will say, "unofficial")[33] Attorneys-General'.

[30] *R* v. *Inland Revenue Commissioners, ex p. National Federation of Self-Employed and Small Businesses Ltd* [1982] AC 617.

[31] Sir William Wade & C. F. Forsyth, *Administrative Law* (Oxford, 1994 7th ed.), 677.

[32] In *R* v. *Darlington BC, ex p. Darlington Taxi Owners' Association*, *The Times* 21 Jan 1994 Auld J held that as a general rule, an unincorporated association could not make an application for judicial review in its own name. This, his Lordship said, was not a rule of standing but of capacity to sue. He was worried about the enforceability of costs orders and cross-undertakings as to damages against unincorporated applicants. The Law Commission has recommended that this decision be reversed so that an application for judicial review could be made by an unincorporated association 'where the court is satisfied that the members of the applicant association have been or would be adversely affected or are raising an issue of public interest warranting judicial review, and that the members of the association are appropriate persons to bring that challenge' (Law Com. No. 226 (1994), 52). In form, such an application would be a representative action brought by a member or members of the association on its behalf. The recommendation seems to confuse capacity to sue with standing to sue, and glosses over the latter too lightly.

[33] 'Unofficial' is wider than 'private' because it is apt to cover public applicants other than the Attorney-General.

3. Where an individual or an association seeks standing, as a sort of 'guardian *ad litem*', to represent the interests of an individual (typically a natural person). This type of case we might refer to by the term 'surrogate standing'.

Associational standing

We have seen that in the US, as a matter of judicial self-restraint, the federal courts will not listen to a litigant who seeks to protect the interests of another. But the ban on representative standing is not absolute. The leading case on associational standing is *Hunt* v. *Washington State Apple Advertising Commission*.[34] The Commission challenged the constitutionality of a North Carolina statute which prohibited the display of Washington State (as opposed to Federal) apple grades on closed containers shipped into the state. It was argued that the Commission lacked standing because it was not itself engaged in the apple trade but only in advertising, and because the challenged statute did not interfere with its freedom to advertise. It was also argued that the Commission should not be allowed to represent apple growers because they could come forward themselves if they wished; and because the Commission was not a traditional voluntary membership organization such as a trade association.

The Supreme Court held that an association could be granted standing if three conditions were satisfied:

1. that the members of the association would have standing to sue in their own right;
2. that the interests which the association sought to protect were germane to its purposes; and
3. that neither the claim asserted nor the relief sought required the participation of individual members in the lawsuit.

Condition 1 is central to the idea of representative standing. The applicant seeks access to the court in order to represent some interest other than the applicant's own. It is a precondition of associational standing that the represented have a sufficient interest in the outcome of the litigation. As Schiemann J said in *Rose Theatre*, a group of uninterested persons cannot give themselves standing by forming an association or corporation to represent them.[35] But the interest of the person(s) represented does not provide the justification for allowing the representative to claim. The standing of the representative must be based on some good reason why the interest-bearer should not be expected to claim personally. It is, therefore, striking that the Court in *Hunt* did not lay it down as a condition of associational standing that it would be unreasonable to expect the

[34] (1977) 432 US 333.

[35] The fact that 2,500 supporters of Greenpeace lived in the Sellafield area was greatly important in *R* v. *Pollution Inspectorate, ex p. Greenpeace Ltd (No. 2)* [1994] 4 All ER 329.

represented parties to sue personally. Condition 3 requires that the participation of the represented parties should not be necessary. But we might also ask why, if those directly affected choose not to sue, anyone else should be allowed to sue on their behalf. It might be thought that representative standing requires some positive justification.

Two such justifications might be suggested. The first is procedural: when there are many similarly interested parties, it may be administratively and procedurally convenient and efficient to allow one party to claim on behalf of them all. The appeal to procedural simplicity is at its strongest in cases where all the relevant issues are common to the cases of all the interested parties, and where the relief sought will benefit them all, typically because it directs the respondent to act or to refrain from acting in a particular way. Procedural simplicity is least valuable in situations where the cases of the interested parties share no common elements and where the remedy sought (typically damages) relates to the position of each individual interested party rather than to the conduct of the respondent. As a general principle, procedural simplicity is only desirable to the extent that it does not lead to an oversimplification of the issues.

The second positive justification for representation is that it may facilitate access to justice. Especially where the impact of challenged conduct is diffuse, or small in any particular case but large in aggregate, or both, then the benefit to any particular interested party of engaging the judicial process may not match the costs. But the balance of the cost-benefit calculation might favour litigation if the benefits to all the affected parties were aggregated and the costs were spread amongst them. The benefits of aggregation for the purposes of litigation will be even greater for interested parties who are poor or politically unaware or unorganized.

A third consideration which may support associational standing, in some cases at least, is this. In private law contexts we generally take the view that other things being equal, settlement of litigation out of court is desirable and, indeed, essential for the smooth running of the court system. But in public law contexts it may be less clear that extra-curial settlement is a good thing if the result is that allegedly illegal government conduct is never exposed to public scrutiny. It is not unknown for test cases brought in the name of an individual claimant for the benefit of a group of similarly situated claimants, to evaporate when the individual is 'bought off' by an out-of-court settlement. An associational action will clearly reduce the risk of such a buy off for the benefit of some of the aggrieved group and the consequent risk that the government will never be called to account in court for what it has done or failed to do.[36] For individuals, an

[36] Cf. M. C. Jensen, W. H. Meckling, & C. G. Holderness, 'Analysis of Alternative Standing Doctrines' (1986) 6 *IRLE* 205, 212.

associational suit might offer the additional benefit of achieving a desired end without having to expose themselves to public gaze and possible retaliation; and for associations, an action brought in the association's own name might be an attractive way of generating more (legitimate) publicity and kudos than would one or a number of actions in the names of individuals, even if they were supported by the association.

There are, then, good reasons why courts should not be indiscriminately hostile to representative claimants in general and to associational claimants in particular.

It should be noted that condition 1 entails a requirement about the relationship between the representative and the represented, namely that the latter be 'members' of the former. The paradigm of the associational claimant adopted in *Hunt* is that of the voluntary membership assocation, typically a trade union or trade association. In fact, the Commission in *Hunt* was a state instrumentality, not a voluntary membership association. But the Court looked to the substance rather than the form and held that the relationship between it and the apple growers it represented possessed all the indicia of membership:[37] the apple growers alone financed the Commission (and the litigation) by paying levies; they alone elected the Commission's members and only they could be members. The fact that the apple growers were financially interested in the activities of the Commission and that the Commission was democratically chosen by its constituency gave it a strong claim to be a legitimate representative of the growers even though it was not a membership organization of apple growers.

Applying this condition, should we say that associational standing ought only to be granted to bodies which are financed and, in some sense, democratically controlled by those whom they purport to represent? This question leads us on to discussion of condition 2 laid down in *Hunt*, namely that the interests of the represented should be germane to the purposes of the associational claimant. This condition may impose a limitation on the sorts of litigation which an association can bring on behalf of its 'members'. But by itself, it does not require that the represented parties have either a financial or a democratic stake in the conduct of the representative. It only requires that those who constitute the association adopt as one of their aims the furthering of the interests of the represented group. So we must inquire whether financial and democratic control are so important that they should be made a precondition of associational standing.

The answer, I think, lies in condition 3, namely that the participation of

[37] Once the criterion is relaxed in this way, it may theoretically be possible for an individual representative to satisfy the requirements for associational standing if that individual was, for instance, chosen and financed by a group to represent it. But this is unlikely in practice and so I shall ignore it in the following discussion.

the represented should not be necessary. The implications of this condition are not spelled out in detail, but in my view we can at least say that the participation of the represented will not be unnecessary unless the court can be satisfied that the association properly represents those it purports to act for.[38] I would say that a financial stake is not necessary for proper representation,[39] but that a democratic stake is.[40] An association cannot properly represent the views and interests of others unless there is an effective mechanism for ascertaining what those views and interests are and for ensuring that the views put forward by the association are a fair reflection of the views of the represented. In the words of one US court, without some nexus of control between the association and those it purports to represent, the association may simply be expressing 'a well-informed point of view'.[41] It does not follow that the represented must all share the same views or equally support the litigation by the association, because notions of democracy allow that a person can properly represent those who did not vote for the views the representative espouses. Moreover, an individual who does not support the action may be allowed by the court to intervene to oppose the application.[42] But if the internal organization of the association is not democratic in some sense, it seems hard to argue that the association is properly representative of the individuals who constitute it.

Democratic stake, then, is a token of representativeness.[43] It provides reassurance that there is no serious conflict of interest between the representative and the represented.[44] But it is not a concept with a fixed meaning. In some cases, the very existence of an association may satisfy the requirement it imposes; as where a membership organization is set up specifically to launch the litigation in question. Also, where individuals have voluntarily associated themselves with the organization and can disengage from it at will without undue cost, a court may require less additional evidence of democratic stake than where joining the organization is effectively compulsory (for example, in order to carry on a trade or

[38] Cf. *Associated General Contractors* v. *Otter Tail Power Co* (1979) 611 F2d 684.

[39] Nor is it sufficient unless it carries with it control of the representative: *Health Research Group* v. *Kennedy* (1979) 82 FRD 21.

[40] Cf. *National Collegiate Athletic Association* v. *Califano* (1980) 622 F2d. 1382.

[41] *Health Research Group* v. *Kennedy* (1979) 82 FRD 21.

[42] RSC Ord. 53, r. 9(1) provides that 'on the hearing of any motion or summons . . . any person who desires to be heard in opposition to the motion or summons, and appears to the Court to be a proper person to be heard, shall be heard, notwithstanding that he has not been served with the notice of motion or summons'. It is not clear why this 'right of intervention' is limited to persons wishing to *oppose* an application for judicial review.

[43] D. Simone, 'Associational Standing and Due Process: the Need for Adequate Representation Scrutiny' (1981) 61 *Boston ULR* 174.

[44] *Calvin* v. *Conlisk* (1975) 520 F2d. 1.

profession) and where some serious detriment will flow from withdrawal. Again, the greater the likely impact of the court's decision on the represented individuals personally, the greater the control a court may require that they have over the representative association's actions.

Also important is whether the represented parties will be bound by the court's decision or only by the precedential force of the decision. If the court's decision will raise a cause of action estoppel (*res judicata*) against the members of a group, then the law should require that the group be 'strongly represented' in the sense that its members were not only entitled to receive notice of and information about the litigation[45] and to exercise a high degree of control over the representative, but also that they were free to opt out of the action, at least before it commenced. On the other hand if the decision will have only precedential force *vis-à-vis* a group, then perhaps the law need only require that it be 'weakly represented' in the sense that the case being put forward by the representative reflects the views of at least a majority of the group. Furthermore, whereas a decision could fairly bind the individuals in a group only if its membership was exhaustively defined in advance, there would be no need for such accuracy if only the representative would be bound.

It might be argued that it makes little sense to limit the binding effect of a decision to a representative who might have no personal interest in the outcome, and that the concept of representative standing serves no useful function unless any decision made in an action brought by the representative in that capacity also binds the represented parties. If this argument is accepted it provides grounds for holding interested parties bound by any decision made in an action brought by their representative as such, but only if they were strongly represented. On the other hand, it might be thought worthwhile (for the sake of reducing litigation and improving access to justice) for the law to grant standing even to 'weak representatives' even though any decision in such representative litigation would have only precedential force *vis-à-vis* the represented parties, on the ground that in practice group members would be unlikely to attempt to litigate afresh the issues canvassed in the representative action. If a represented party did attempt to relitigate issues raised in an earlier representative action, his or her interests could be protected by allowing the fresh action to proceed unless that person had been strongly represented in that earlier action.

The principle of democratic stake concerns the internal organization of associations and the accountability of the officers of associations to their constituency. As such, it may overlap with other legal rules about the

[45] Note that RSC Ord. 53, r. 5(3) provides that 'the notice of motion or summons must be served on all persons directly affected'. The phrase 'directly affected' seems narrower than the phrase 'sufficiently interested' and might not, e.g., cover a representative association.

internal affairs of companies or trade unions, for example.[46] But since these rules have not been designed specifically to ensure that officials efficiently and properly represent the views of their constituents in litigation, the principle of democratic stake should be used to supplement them in the present context.

The requirement of democratic stake is, from one point of view, an uncomfortable one because it would seem to rule out grants of standing to cause and issue groups such as the Child Poverty Action Group and Greenpeace. Moreover, the sorts of actions it is most likely to prevent are those which it might be thought most desirable to encourage, namely altruistic actions brought on behalf of the poor and unorganized—people to whom it might never occur to join, let alone to set up, a pressure group. Nor have English courts apparently imposed any such requirement. Standing has been conceded to voluntary non-membership groups (such as the Child Poverty Action Group and Greenpeace)[47] and to statutory agencies (such as the Equal Opportunities Commission (EOC))[48] regardless of whether the persons whose interests they purported to represent were either members of the organization or individually consulted by it about the litigation. We must, therefore, confront the question of whether democratic stake (as I have defined it) is the only proper basis for associational standing. With one qualification, I would answer this question positively. The qualification is that democratic stake should not be a precondition of associational standing if the representative is the beneficiary of a statutory grant of standing. A statutory grant of representative status provides the democratic legitimacy which self-appointed representatives may lack. This qualification explains why the EOC could properly be accorded standing without inquiry into the matter of democratic stake. An association which is not the beneficiary of a statutory grant of representative standing should not be allowed to represent the interests of others unless it can demonstrate its legitimacy as a representative in terms of its having ascertained the views and wishes of the represented. If such an association cannot do this, then it should be expected to put itself forward as an unofficial Attorney-General; that is, as

[46] See generally P. Birkinshaw, I. Harden, & N. Lewis, *Government by Moonlight* (London, 1990), ch. 6.

[47] *R* v. *Secretary of State for Social Services, ex p. Child Poverty Action Group* [1990] 2 QB 540 (on the nature of the CPAG see Harlow & Rawlings, *Pressure Through Law*, 150–1); *R* v. *Pollution Inspectorate, ex p. Greenpeace Ltd (No. 2)* [1994] 4 All ER 329.

[48] *R* v. *Secretary of State for Employment, ex p. Equal Opportunities Commission* [1995] 1 AC 1. The standing of the Commission was based on a statutory provision defining the powers of the Commission; but the provision was sufficiently general that a decision against standing would, as a matter of statutory interpretation, have been possible.

a representative of the 'public interest', not of the interests of identifiable individuals.[49]

It might be asked how it matters whether an association makes a claim to standing *qua* representative on the one hand or qua unofficial Attorney-General on the other. The importance of the basis of the claim to standing can be shown by observing the link between standing and remedy. In *Felixstowe Justices*[50] the applicant, a journalist, sought an order of mandamus to require the clerk to the justices to reveal the name of the magistrates who had sat on a particular case, and a declaration that the policy of the chair of the justices of withholding the names of magistrates in certain circumstances for security reasons was unlawful. A Divisional Court held that the applicant had standing to obtain the declaration as 'guardian of the public interest', but that he lacked standing for the order of mandamus because he did not have sufficient interest in knowing the identity of the magistrates who heard the case in question. This decision makes it clear that the nature of the applicant's interest is relevant not only to standing but also to remedy; and that the basis on which standing is granted may determine the sort of relief which will be available. The relief which the interests of a group of represented individuals might support may be different from the relief which the public interest will support.[51] In this important sense, standing to apply for judicial review is related to the substance of the applicant's case.

But even if the basis of a grant of standing will have no such ramifications for remedy, it may still dictate the sort of arguments which can be used in favour of the granting of relief of some sort. A group of individuals may have an interest in challenging a decision which it is not in the public interest to question; and conversely, there may be a public interest in challenging a decision which no affected individual or group of affected individuals wishes to question. So a litigant who purports to act on behalf of a group of individuals should be required to demonstrate that it has the consent of those individuals to, or at least their acquiescence in, the litigation.

The third condition for associational standing laid down in *Hunt* was that the participation of the represented individuals should not be necessary. I have already suggested that this condition cannot be met if the representative lacks a democratic mandate from the represented. It has also been suggested that this condition would rule out associational standing in a case

[49] The best explanation of the *CPAG* and *Greenpeace* cases may be that the applicant was granted standing as an unofficial Attorney-General.

[50] [1987] QB 582.

[51] Cf. *R* v. *Pollution Inspectorate, ex p. Greenpeace Ltd (No. 2)* [1994] 4 All ER 329, 351b–c.

where the remedy sought was damages,[52] because damages is an individualized remedy related to the position of the applicant.[53] By contrast, it is said, if the remedy sought relates to conduct of the respondent which affects all the represented individuals in the same way, the participation of those individuals would not be necessary. In other words, the participation of individuals will be necessary if, but only if, the desired or available remedial outcome varies from individual to individual. This explication of the condition does not really convince me. Although it may be necessary, in the 'variable remedy' type of case, for each affected individual to provide the court with the material necessary to enable it to fashion a remedy appropriate to each person, it does not seem necessary that each of the affected individuals should be parties to the action, as opposed to witnesses or beneficiaries. For example, it might be that the claims of a group of individuals share some common features but also that the claim of each affected individual has some unique aspects. Why, in such a case, should the applicant not be a representative who could argue the common features on behalf of all the represented, but also present the unique aspects of each claim in turn, the whole proceedings being terminated by a series of judgments in favour of each of the affected individuals? These are procedural matters which have little to do with the principle of representativeness. Putting the point differently, participation of affected individuals is not ruled out by representative presentation of the case to the court.

Finally, let us note that it is often suggested that representative standing should be granted only to an association which the court is satisfied will be a competent advocate for the represented in terms especially of funding and expertise.[54] But it seems to me that provided the requirement of democratic stake is taken seriously, there is no need to impose an additional and essentially paternalistic requirement of competence. Conversely, competence is an inadequate surrogate for democratic stake.[55]

Citizen standing

I have argued that an association ought to be entitled to standing to represent a group only if the association can claim democratic legitimacy

[52] Of course, a claim for damages can only be brought under RSC Ord. 53 as an adjunct to a claim for a prerogative order or a declaration or injunction.

[53] *Associated General Contractors of America Inc* v. *Kreps* (1978) 450 F Supp. 338, 346 n. 3; V. Lathers, 'Associational Third Party Standing and Federal Jurisdication under *Hunt*' 1978) *Iowa LR* 121., 132.

[54] e.g. Simone *op. cit.*, 196.

[55] But in *R* v. *Pollution Inspectorate, ex p. Greenpeace Ltd (No. 2)* [1994] 4 All ER 329 Otton J laid great emphasis on the respectability and competence of Greenpeace, even though he also stressed the fact that 2,500 of its supporters lived near Sellafield. The issue of democratic stake was not raised or discussed.

either because it is the beneficiary of a statutory grant of representative status or because it can demonstrate that it has a democratic mandate from those it purports to represent. The question which now arises is whether this requirement of democratic legitimacy also applies to associations (or individuals) which cannot satisfy the requirements for associational standing and who (I have argued) must seek to act as unofficial Attorneys-General on behalf of the public (or some section of it). In support of a positive answer to this question we could cite the traditional principle that the only permitted representative of the public interest is the Attorney-General. This rule can be seen as expressing just such a requirement of democratic legitimation. On this basis, it could be argued that unless an unofficial Attorney-General could point to a statutory grant to it of representative standing, it should be required at least to obtain the consent of the (real) Attorney-General to the litigation. It might be thought inconsistent for a court to entertain an application in the name of the public interest made without the consent of the Attorney-General when, if such consent had been sought and refused, such refusal would have been unchallengeable.[56]

A reply to such reasoning might be that the enactment of the phrase 'sufficient interest' indicates that Parliament intended to allow 'citizen actions' and actions by unofficial Attorneys-General even in the absence of either a statutory grant of representative status or the consent of the (real) Attorney-General. But that phrase is too vague to compel such a conclusion. Furthermore, it can be argued that to allow citizen actions is to turn the judicial process into a surrogate political process for the airing of grievances which would be better pursued through political channels. This is the basis on which the US Supreme Court has adopted standing rules which require applicants to show a 'personal stake' and on which it has held statutory provisions for citizen standing to be unconstitutional.[57]

It would be undesirable to allow any and every citizen to challenge any and every governmental action in the courts subject only to some doctrine of the non-justiciability of certain issues (such as national security). However it may be possible to construct a justification for limited citizen standing freed of the requirement of democratic legitimation by developing a theory of the judicial role in government which sees the judiciary as the guardians of certain (fundamental) interests which governments must respect and which (in the absence of a constitution permitting judicial review of legislation) the legislature can only encroach upon by express provision to that effect. In modern times, English judges have seen themselves as having a role to play in the protection of individual rights, and this role has

[56] *Gouriet* v. *Union of Post Office Workers* [1978] AC 435.
[57] See n. 9 above.

been made quite explicit in the increasing and creative use of the European Convention on Human Rights as a source of standards for governmental conduct. More generally, the assumption on which the supervisory jurisdiction is based is that there are certain limits to the proper use of governmental power which the courts should enforce for the sake of protecting the interests of individuals and minority groups which may be ignored or trampled upon in the political process. It is now widely accepted that the attribution of these limits to the intention of Parliament is often, or even usually, a fiction. Such limits are, in fact, a product of judicial activity.

By developing some theory of fundamental rights or interests, we might hope to carve out not only an area of legitimate activism for the courts but also a set of limits to the competence of the political process. The traditional conclusion of arguments based on the notion of (fundamental) rights is that the courts have a role to play in protecting the rights of **individuals** from undue encroachment by government.[58] From the point of view of standing, however, using the judicial process to enable individuals to vindicate their rights or interests is not problematic. What we are looking for is an argument which would justify allowing **the public**, in the guise of a representative of the public interest, access to the judicial process. By analogy with the argument about individual rights, we need to start with the proposition that the citizenry as a whole has certain interests which should be more or less immune from governmental curtailment or encroachment. I do not feel able to provide an exhaustive catalogue of such interests. But it is clear, for instance, that the public has a justiciable interest in the observance by government of basic constitutional principles such as 'no taxation or expenditure without Parliamentary approval'.[59] Again, the substantive basis of the decision in the applicant's favour in *Felixstowe Justices*[60] was that the administration of justice should be public

[58] T. R. S. Allan, *Law, Liberty and Justice* (Oxford, 1993), esp. 223–36.

[59] *R* v. *Her Majesty's Treasury, ex p. Smedley* [1985] QB 657; *R* v. *Secretary of State for Foreign and Commonwealth Affairs, ex p. World Development Movement Ltd* [1995] 1 WCR 386. The public also has a justiciable right that the power to ratify treaties (*R* v. *Secretary of State for Foreign and Commonwealth Affairs, ex p. Rees-Mogg* [1994] 2 WLR 115) or to set up a non-statutory compensation scheme (*R* v. *Secretary of State for the Home Department, ex p. Fire Brigades Union* [1995] 2 WLR 1) be exercised in accordance with law. In the *EOC* case ([1995] 1 AC 1) it was held that while the EOC had standing to claim a declaration that UK law was inconsistent with EC law, an individual did not because her grievance was justiciable before an industrial tribunal. The latter holding should be read as turning on the existence of an alternative remedy rather than on lack of sufficient interest. A person may have sufficient interest to make an application for judicial review, but may not be allowed to do so until alternative remedies have been exhausted.

[60] [1987] QB 852. *Query* whether it was relevant that the applicant was an investigative journalist? In *R* v. *Horsham JJ, ex p. Farquharson* [1982] QB 762 it was held that an order restraining publication of details of proceedings before the magistrates could be challenged both by a journalist on a local newspaper and by the National Union of Journalists.

and open; and this desideratum might be seen as an aspect of the public's wider interest in freedom of information.[61] The protection of the fundamental rights and interests of the citizenry against government can be seen as a proper job for the courts. So long as we do not adopt the view that whatever the government bodies do is, *ex hypothesi*, in the public interest, there may be situations in which the public as a whole has an interest in opposing something which such a body has done, even if the action is not without its supporters in the populace at large. In a system in which Parliament is under the effective control of the government, the courts have a role to play in protecting the interests of citizens against government.

The decision whether or not to activate the judicial process in order to vindicate or protect the fundamental interests of the citizenry against the government should ideally not be in the hands of an officer of the government. If certain rights and interests ought to be more or less immune from political encroachment in the name of the public interest, then it makes no sense to give to a politician (the Attorney-General) the final decision as to whether alleged encroachments should be challengeable in the courts on the ground that they constitute an illegitimate interference with the rights or interests of citizens. But this proposition, by itself, does not support the citizen action. We might, for example, create an office along the lines of Lord Woolf's proposed Director of Civil Proceedings.[62] The Director might be empowered, *inter alia*, to make judicial review applications at the instigation of citizens if the Director took the view that either the interests of the individual or some wider public interest was at stake and needed protection from encroachment by a government body. The essential characteristic of any officer with this power would be independence from government. But in the absence of such an officer and since, of all our public decision makers, the higher judiciary are the ones whose independence from government is most effectively guaranteed, there seems little reason not to allow the courts themselves to decide whether to entertain public interest challenges to government decisions and to decide the fate of such challenges.

It is often argued that to allow self-appointed representatives of the public interest access to the courts would be to risk an avalanche of unmeritorious, vexatious, and politically-motivated claims. It is exactly in this context that the requirement of leave for judicial review proves its worth as a mechanism for weeding out cases which should never have been started. An important function of the leave procedure is to prevent

[61] For an account of the law on access to environmental information see S. Ball & S. Bell, *Environmental Law* (London, 1994 2nd ed.), ch. 7.
[62] *Protection of the Public—A New Challenge* (London, 1990), 109–13.

complaints which should properly be pursued through political channels or which have no merit from becoming the subject of litigation.

My argument is, therefore, that the public as a whole has certain interests (such as freedom of information) which ought to be protected from encroachment by government and (to a lesser extent) the legislature, and that the protection of such interests is appropriately a task for the courts. I would also argue that the citizen action is a suitable medium for protecting such interests. I suggest that associations or other litigants who purport to represent groups but who lack 'democratic legitimacy' should be accorded standing, if at all, as unofficial Attorneys-General to represent the public interest.[63]

Three final points on citizen standing. First, it might be thought that to allow citizen standing is effectively to abolish standing rules altogether. This would be so only if any and every citizen was allowed to challenge any and every governmental action. My view is that citizens as such should be allowed to challenge governmental action in the courts only in order to protect fundamental public interests. Secondly, those[64] who object to the recent decision of the US Supreme Court that statutory citizen standing provisions are unconstitutional,[65] do not necessarily object to the common law rule that the applicant must have a personal stake. Rather they say that it should be open to Congress to grant citizen standing, but that the Court is right to allow access by its own rules only to those who are personally interested. However, it seems to me that in the Westminster system in which the government has effective control of the legislature, it is undesirable that citizen access to the courts should depend solely on a positive grant of standing. Thirdly, should unofficial Attorneys-General be required to meet some requirement of competence? Given the requirement of leave for applications for judicial review, I would argue that no such requirement is needed. If the court thinks that the applicant lacks the resources to mount an effective case with a *prima facie* chance of success, it can refuse leave. It would, of course, be open to some other more competent person to make an application.

Surrogate standing

Except in cases of incapacity (resulting from age, mental condition, or the

[63] The role of associations and groups with considerable resources is particularly important when no individual has a personal interest because the fact that the public has an interest is not, in itself, relevant to the grant of legal aid: S. Grosz, 'Pergau Be Damned' [1994] *New LJ* 1708.

[64] Such as Sunstein.

[65] See n. 9 above.

like)[66] there is no case for surrogate standing.[67] I say this because even if surrogates were allowed to bring actions on behalf of people who were capable of instituting an action themselves, surrogate actions should be allowed only with the consent of the represented. On this basis, since the substitution of one claimant for another offers no gain in procedural efficiency; and since there is, in the great majority of cases, no moral or legal objection to the funding of litigation by someone other than the claimant, surrogate standing does nothing to facilitate access to the judicial process. There may, however, sometimes be room for a citizen action to protect a fundamental public interest affected by a governmental decision about which no individual whose personal interests are affected wishes to complain.

Conclusion on representative standing

It should be clear from this discussion of representative standing that there is much to learn from the US experience, which is so much richer than our own. The chief importance of this mine of experience is that it alerts us to the issues and questions. The answers must be worked out by us in the context of our own constitutional and social traditions. I have made some proposals as to how this rich vein of material might be used in the UK, but on matters as complex as this the fire of experience is needed to purify and temper abstract principles.

WHAT IS A SUFFICIENT INTEREST IN THE ENVIRONMENT?

This question is actually shorthand. Applications for judicial review in this context will typically involve challenges to decisions either to regulate or not to regulate some activity which threatens pollution. So the question really is: when will a litigant have a sufficient interest in decisions concerned with the regulation of (potentially) polluting activities?[68]

In answering this question we must, I think, distinguish between two

66 For the famous suggestion that humans should be allowed to bring surrogate actions on behalf of specific natural features such as trees and lakes see C. Stone, 'Should Trees Have Standing?' (1972) 45 *So. Cal. LR* 450.

67 Cf. *R* v. *Legal Aid Board, ex p. Bateman* [1992] 1 WLR 711. Surrogate standing is sometimes allowed in the US to improve the protection of constitutional rights: R. A. Sedler, 'The Assertion of Constitutional *Jus Tertii*: a Substantive Approach' (1982) 70 *Cal. LR* 1308; *Note*, 'Standing to Assert *Jus Tertii*' (1974) *Harvard LR* 423; M. Rohr, 'Fighting for the Rights of Others: the Troubled Law of Third Party Standing and Mootness in the Federal Courts' (1981) 35 *U of Miami LR* 393.

68 On the US position see Sunstein (1992) *op. cit.*, 224–6.

types of litigant: private individuals (whether natural persons or corporations) and associations representing such individuals, on the one hand; and unofficial Attorneys-General on the other. So far as the first type of litigant is concerned, injury to one's person, health,[69] or property clearly generates a sufficient interest. So, too, does economic injury. Pollutees are more likely to allege injury of the former type than are polluters, while polluters are more likely to allege economic injury; although claims by pollutees that pollution will adversely affect their livelihood are, of course, not unknown. While it may be very difficult for a litigant in a particular case to prove such injuries or a causal link between injury and the relevant pollution, such forms of injury, if proved, can easily justify holdings of sufficient interest.

Difficulty, in relation to litigants of the first type, arises in respect of intangible injuries. What are we to say of a claim that a change in the environment would restrict a person's recreational opportunities, or offend his or her aesthetic sensibilities, or (even more problematically) result in psychological upset or anxiety caused by knowledge that the environment is being degraded? Courts have been ready to accord standing on the basis of allegations such as that the claimants' recreational use of a particular area or their recreational interest in a particular animal species was endangered;[70] and in relation to the built environment at least, aesthetic and amenity considerations would seem to provide a good cause for complaint.[71] On the other hand courts, especially in the US, have been much less receptive to individuals' claims to standing based on emotional or ideological concern for preservation of cultural heritage or natural environment or the diversity of animal species (for instance).[72]

Various explanations may be offered for such reluctance. One radical

[69] *R* v. *Pollution Inspectorate, ex p. Greenpeace Ltd (No. 2)* [1994] 4 All ER 329.

[70] The leading US case is *US* v. *Students Challenging Regulatory Agency Procedures* (1973) 412 US 669. See also *Japan Whaling Association* v. *American Cetacean Society* (1986) 106 S Ct. 2860, 2866 n. 4; *Lujan* v. *Defenders of Wildlife* (1992) 112 S Ct. 2130, 2137. The British Herpetological Society (BHS) was in a strong position in *R* v. *Poole BC, ex p. Beebee* [1991] COD 264 because BHS members had expended time, skill, and energy to preserve wildlife at a proposed development site. But the Worldwide Fund for Nature was denied standing even though it had funded the work of the BHS at the site for almost 20 years and so, as an organization, arguably had an institutional interest in the fate of the site. The *BHS* case is full of ironies: the nominal applicants were individuals representing the association (rather than vice-versa); but the judge considered the standing issue not in respect of the nominal plaintiffs but in respect of the BHS.

[71] *Covent Garden Community Association Ltd* v. *Greater London Council* [1981] *JPL* 183. *R* v. *Hammersmith and Fulham BC, ex p. People before Profit Ltd* [1981] JPL 869; *R* v. *Stroud DC, ex p. Goodenough* (1982) 43 P & CR 59. See further B. Hough, 'Standing in Planning Permission Appeals' [1992] JPL 319.

[72] e.g. *Lujan* v. *Defenders of Wildlife* (1992) 112 S Ct. 2130, 2139–40. Contrast, in a different context, *Gillick* v. *West Norfolk AHA* [1986] AC 112, discussed by Allan, *op. cit.*, 220–32.

opinion is that it is a result of viewing preservation of the environment as being solely for the benefit of human beings and not also for the benefit of the environment itself.[73] In the US context, it is arguably a product of the emphasis on personal stake: the courts deem that every citizen has (or, perhaps, wrongly assume that each has) an equal emotional or ideological interest in the environment and so lacks a **personal** stake in it. Another suggestion, consistent with what I have said above about the relationship between associational and citizen standing, would be that the courts consider that all citizens have an interest in the cultural heritage of their society and in biodiversity, and that in the absence of some injury to individuals over and above emotional or ideological concern, such interests are properly regarded as public interests and not as interests which individuals can use as a basis for claiming in their own right. Furthermore, the courts will allow individuals to represent the public interest before the courts only if the interest in question is so fundamental that it ought to be judicially protected against undue government encroachment except by express legislative provision. One might conclude from the unwillingness of the courts to recognize emotional or ideological concern for things such as cultural heritage and biodiversity, that they do not view the public's interest in such things as so fundamental (or so uncontroversial, perhaps) that it deserves such judicial protection.

In practical terms this means that if an individual or an association wants to vindicate an ideological or emotional interest in the environment, it must do so as an unofficial Attorney-General. For such an action to succeed, however, I contend that the the claimant should have to argue that some fundamental interest of the public has been unduly infringed by the decision maker.

This conclusion raises the question of whether the courts would ever recognize a public interest in the environment independently of a statutory provision for citizen standing. Does the public have any interest in the continued integrity of the environment which the courts will perceive as so fundamental that they should be prepared to intervene to protect it against undue interference except by express legislative provision? In attempting to answer this question we might note that the standing of a 'conservation group', Save Britain's Heritage, was not even raised as an issue when it sought to challenge a decision of the Secretary of State to allow demolition of a group of Grade II listed buildings on the ground that inadequate

[73] Stone *op. cit.* argues that people should be allowed to sue as guardians for living species and inanimate environmental features. *Note Bumper Development Corporation* v. *Metropolitan Police Commissioner*, *The Times* 14 Feb. 1991 in which, as a matter of private international law, a Hindu temple was allowed to bring a suit in an English court for the recovery of artifacts stolen from the temple.

reasons had been given for the decision.[74] This can be seen as supporting my argument if one interprets the right to a reasoned decision (where it exists) as not only one belonging to individuals affected by government decisions, but also as one belonging to the public (in appropriate cases), being an aspect of its right to information about government activities. On this interpretation, Save Britain's Heritage was not vindicating an ideological or aesthetic or emotional interest as such, but only indirectly by asserting the public's right to know.

On this basis, what are we to say of that *cause célèbre*, the *Rose Theatre* case?[75] Except for the fact that the Rose Theatre Trust Co was very recently formed to save one particular site, it was similar in its nature and aims to Save Britain's Heritage. There were, it seems to me, two important features of this case: first, that Rose Theatre Trust Co sought to challenge directly the substance of the Secretary of State's decision not to schedule the theatre remains; and secondly, that the Minister had consulted extensively with English Heritage before making the decision. We might interpret the decision of Schiemann J consistently with the argument of this paper by saying that Rose Theatre Trust Co was acting as an unofficial Attorney-General and was arguing, in effect, that the Rose Theatre should have been scheduled. But the public has no fundamental right that any particular item of the nation's cultural heritage should be saved. It might have a fundamental right that the decision whether to save particular cultural icons should be made only after proper consideration has been given to the public's interest in the matter; however, there was no argument in this case that the public interest had not been represented to and considered by the Minister, but only that he had given insufficient weight to the interest in preservation.

My suggestion that access to information about the environment is seen by the courts as a fundamental (although, of course, not an absolute) interest of citizens may be tested by considering the related issue of environmental assessment. Both in the US and the UK governments are often required by statute to consider in a structured and formal way the impact of proposed development on the environment, and to prepare 'environmental assessments' or 'environmental impact statements'. In the US there have been many cases in which applicants with a recognized interest (such as a recreational interest) in the environment have been allowed to challenge government decision making on the ground of failure

[74] *Save Britain's Heritage* v. *No. 1 Poultry Ltd* [1991] 1 WLR 153.

[75] [1990] 1 QB 504. Schiemann J seems to have been chiefly motivated by fear of a flood of litigation and its likely chilling effect on government activity. For the wider background of the case see M. Redman, 'Archaeology and Development' [1990] *JPL* 87.

to conduct an environmental assessment.[76] Courts have been less receptive to the argument that conservation groups might have 'informational standing' in their own right simply on the basis that dissemination of information is one of their functions.[77] The basic argument against such 'pure' informational standing is that every citizen has an interest in receiving information about the environment, and so no individual can demonstrate a personal stake in the sense required by Supreme Court jurisprudence. In the light of the *Felixstowe Justices* case, it may be that in this respect English law would be more generous to environmentalists than US law. There are at least two reported English cases in which conservation groups have challenged failure to conduct an environmental assessment, but in both the decision turned on whether an obligation to make such an assessment had arisen in the circumstances of the case; the issue of informational standing was neither raised nor discussed.[78]

CONCLUSION

Can we draw any positive guidance for the future development of English law from this discussion of American principles and practice? It is quite clear from the US cases that the line between sufficient and insufficient interests in the environment is drawn by reference to some notion of the proper role of the judiciary *vis-à-vis* the government and the legislature. Precisely where the line is drawn may well differ from one system to another, and I doubt that we should pay too much attention to the exact contours of the American law on this topic because they are inevitably a product of the power balance between the various institutions of **American** government. But what of the broad outline? The US courts are keen not to decide issues which they think would be more appropriately decided through the political process, or to protect interests which they believe ought to be the subject of political bargaining. The notion of 'personal stake' is the main conceptual tool used to this end. Indeed, we have seen that the Supreme Court has gone so far as to deny to Congress (on constitutional grounds) the power to confer standing on citizens generally.

[76] L. Gerschwer, 'Informational Standing under NEPA: Justiciability and the Environmental Decisionmaking Process', (1993) 93 *Col. LR* 996.

[77] See esp. *Foundation on Economic Trends* v. *Lyng* (1991) 943 F2d. 79, 84–5.

[78] See Ball & Bell, *op. cit.*, 239–40. The English law on environmental assessment is based on EC Directive 85/337. In this context, therefore, the EC law principle of effective protection may in future exert expansive pressure on standing rules. See Geddes *op. cit.*, 36–8. Ironically, however, individual access to the European Court is very restricted: T. C. Hartley, *Foundations of European Community Law* (Oxford, 1994 3rd ed.), ch. 12; for a theory as to why see H. Rasmussen, 'Why is Article 173 Interpreted Against Private Plaintiffs' (1980) 5 *ELR* 112 and C. Harding, 'Who Goes to Court in Europe? An Analysis of Litigation Against the EC' (1980) 5 *ELR* 354.

By contrast, English courts have been more willing to encourage unofficial Attorneys-General. This course obviously carries with it the danger of embroiling the courts in politically contentious and highly complicated ('polycentric') disputes. My argument in this paper has been that the public as a whole may well have interests which are sufficiently important that they deserve judicial protection against undue government interference unless such interference is explicitly authorized by statute. On that basis, I would favour an approach which allowed citizen standing in principle but which used it only to protect the most important of the public's interests. In this essay I have not directly or systematically tackled the question of how these interests are to be identified. At a descriptive level, we must look at the decisions of the courts to discover what values (such as openness or procedural propriety) the judges deem important enough to deserve their protection. At a normative level the task of identification would require a political (or perhaps an economic) theory from which could be derived standards of public decision making. Such a theory would also need to contain principles about the proper relationship between the judicial and the political processes which could be used to identify an acceptable sphere for judicial activism.

6

Contracts, Prisons, and Public Law

GENEVRA RICHARDSON

IN the second half of the 1980s correctional authorities in the United States began to contract out the management and daily running of prisons. Tennessee with its Private Prison Act 1986 was the first state to authorize the contracting out of an adult general purpose prison. In the early 1990s England and Wales followed suit. Contracting out was authorized by the Criminal Justice Act 1991 and the first private prison, a remand centre, opened at the Wolds in April 1992. From these beginnings the practice of contracting out has expanded on both sides of the Atlantic. To date the total number of adult prisoners held in private prisons remains small in both jurisdictions, but in both the proportion of private prisoners is due to rise significantly. In the US the prison population had grown to just over one million by 1991, whereas by the end of 1990 there were only 44 secure adult facilities operated by private firms in the US holding approximately 15,000 inmates.[1] At the time of writing there are three new privately run prisons operating in England and Wales, the Wolds, Blakenhurst, and Doncaster with a capacity of up to 1,639 between them, and the refurbished Strangeways with an ultimate capacity of 971, out of a total prison population of nearly 50,000.[2] This relative insignificance in quantitative terms should not, however, belie the importance of private prisons not only to prison policy but also more generally to public law.

The completion of a contract between a public authority and a private security firm for the running of a prison provides a clear example of the growing process of contractualization within government. Contractualization, or the pursuit of government through contract, can take a variety of forms in the UK including privatization, contracting out, and even restructuring within the public sector itself, as with the Next Steps programme in central government and the creation of an internal market in the NHS.[3] Whatever its objective merits contractualization raises

[1] *National Prison Project Jo.* (1991) 6/1 and D. McDonald 'Public Imprisonment by Private Means' (1994) 34 *Brit. Jo. Crimin.* 29: C. Logan, *Private Prisons* (New York, 1990), 20.

[2] Prison Service *Annual Report and Accounts April 1992–March 1993* (1993) HMSO Cm. 2385.

[3] See M. Freedland, 'Government by Contract and Private Law' [1994] *PL* 86 for an interesting discussion of contractualization, and see T. Daintith & M. Sah, 'Privatization and the Economic Neutrality of the Constitution' [1993] *PL* 465.

important questions for public law in relation both to the openness and the accountability of the contracting process and to the process for ensuring compliance with the contractual terms. I have argued elsewhere that we as citizens of a democracy are entitled to expect that any power which permits interference with the interests of individuals does so in the reflection and furtherance of the full public interest, and that each specific exercise of such a power is similarly reflective of the public interest.[4] According to such an argument it is immaterial whether the powers in question are exercised directly by the government or are contracted out to private concerns. In either case it is entirely appropriate that the public law should concern itself with the imposition of requirements designed to facilitate the proper formulation and exercise of those powers. The creation of privately run prisons offers a peculiarly stark example of the contractualization of the government process. The operation of public sector prisons in England and Wales already raises acute issues of legitimacy and accountability owing to the breadth of the discretion possessed by the prison authorities, the importance of the individual interests at stake, and the invisibility of much prison decision making. With the introduction of the private sector these problems have been compounded by the supposed requirements of commercial confidentiality, the extension and multiplication of lines of responsibility, and the possibility of conflicts of interest.

By considering the various mechanisms which are available to regulate the operation of this particular area of private enterprise, it is hoped that this essay will help to inform the more general debate concerning accountability, legitimacy and the process of contractualization. In making its analysis the essay will trawl the American experience to assess what principles, if any, we might usefully draw upont to structure policy and practice in this country. Although there is clearly a limit to the useful parallels that can be drawn between US and UK public law, in this specific context the American experience may be particularly revealing. In the first place, since the process of contracting out started earlier in the US than here, the Americans have been at it longer. Secondly American companies are becoming involved in the running of prisons here.[5] And finally, the prison privatization debate in the US is taking place against a far greater experience of judicial intervention in prison administration than exists in this country.

[4] This argument is developed in G. Richardson, *Law, Process and Custody* (London, 1993).

[5] The Corrections Corporation of America is involved in the company running Blakenhurst prison; Premier Prison Services Ltd, a joint venture company partly owned by Wackenhurst Corrections Corp., is operating Doncaster prison. On the international nature of the private prison business see J. Lilly & P. Knepper, 'An International Perspective on the Privatisation of Corrections' (1992) 31 *Howard J. of Criminal Justice* 174.

As suggested above, contractualization gives rise to problems of accountability and participation in relation both to the formulation of the contract and to the monitoring of compliance with its terms. The essay will examine each of these stages in turn, but first it is necessary to offer a very brief description of the statutory framework provided for the privatization of prisons in England and Wales.

THE STATUTORY FRAMEWORK

Section 84 of the Criminal Justice Act 1991 empowers the Secretary of State to contract out the running of individual prisons. In its original form it related only to new remand prisons but it did contain powers enabling the Secretary of State to amend the Act by way of statutory instrument in order to permit the privatization of other types of prison. In the course of the parliamentary debate concerning the introduction of these amendment powers Angela Rumbold, the minister of state at the Home Office, described them as enabling the Secretary of State to come back to the House for an extension of his privatization powers 'if, and only if, the remand centre contracting out proved to be a success'. Wolds remand centre, the first establishment to be privatized, opened in April 1992 and by July that year the Secretary of State had achieved the necessary statutory instrument to extend his contracting out powers to any type of new prison. By February 1993 his powers were again extended to cover existing prisons. The success of the Wolds, it seems, was very quickly proved. Finally, the Criminal Justice and Public Order Act 1994 has further extended the scope of privatization by allowing for the provision of prison buildings by private contractors.

According to section 84(1) of the 1991 Act a private prison must be run according to the Prison Act 1952 and the Prison Rules. Each private prison must have a director appointed by the contractor, who will perform most of the functions of a governor within the state sector, apart from those relating to disciplinary charges and hearings, the removal of a prisoner from association, and the use of temporary confinement or special control and restraint. Each prison must also have a controller, appointed by the Home Office, who will perform the functions listed above, report to the Secretary of State on the running of the prison, and investigate all inmate grievances relating to prison custody officers.

FORMULATING THE CONTRACT

The private prison contractor is empowered to exercise highly coercive powers over individuals and is paid to do so directly from public funds. The framework within which he or she is required to operate, therefore, becomes a matter of considerable public interest. In line with the argument alluded to above, the powers possessed by any custodial agency can only be justified if they reflect the public interest in the fullest sense.[6] In formal constitutional theory these powers will do so if they are expressly contained in primary legislation since they will then have passed through the 'democratic' process, and if there are adequate mechanisms to ensure that each exercise is itself reflective of the public interest. In practice, however, the formulation and application of prison policy falls far short of this ideal. In relation to policy formulation specifically, whatever the shortcomings of the parliamentary process, prison policy in the UK has been largely ignored by Parliament for over forty years. It has thus bypassed the formal mechanisms for democratic participation and has evolved instead through statutory instruments and administrative rules. While private prisons, operating as they do within the same statutory framework as their public sector counterparts, must inevitably be tarnished by the same democratic inadequacies, they at least might recoup some of that democratic deficit if the process of contract formulation were one of open and full participation. For a contracted out prison the terms of the contract perform a crucial role in defining the nature of the prison regime and in specifying the respective roles of the contractor and the public agency. They form the operational framework according to which custodial powers are exercized over individual prisoners. A contractual process which facilitates the full reflection of the public interest through wide publicity and consultation would therefore greatly enhance the legitimacy of contractualization in this context.

Legality and legitimacy: substantive considerations

With this in mind the structures adopted for the formulation of prison contracts both here and in the US will be considered. But before examining these structures it is necessary briefly to consider whether there are any constitutional or legal principles that might prohibit altogether the contracting out of prison management to a private company however exemplary the process. The question is of more obvious relevance to the US structure of government than to our own since, until the enactment of the Deregulation and Contracting Out Act 1994, there appeared to be few constraints, either legal or constitutional, imposed upon the UK government's power to contract out.[7] Indeed it has been suggested that it was only

[6] Richardson *op. cit.*

[7] Sections 69–71 of the 1994 Act are designed to facilitate contracting out by both central and local government. See, generally, Freedland, *op. cit.*, and Daintith & Sah *op. cit.*, 476, and for a brief discussion of the impact of the 1994 Act see P. Craig, *Administrative Law* (London, 1994 3rd ed.).

the need to amend the Prison Act 1952 that required the government to acquire parliamentary approval for its prison privatization programme.[8] Nevertheless the issues raised by the question in the US help to highlight the need to impose limits on the power of the contractor whatever the precise constitutional position.

In the US there has been some discussion as to whether the contracting out of prisons by either federal or state authorities could be in breach of the delegation doctrine springing from Article I of the Constitution.[9] The majority view seems to be that no breach will occur provided sufficient care is taken to ensure that any rule making power remains ultimately with the public agency and that disciplinary decisions are taken by an adjudicator who is independent of the contractor.[10] The concern with accountability (rule making) and conflict of interest (disciplinary adjudications) which appears to lie behind these two provisos should be as relevant on this side of the Atlantic as it is on the other irrespective of the strict constitutional position.[11] Indeed the general significance of adjudication and rule making is now recognized by the Deregulation and Contracting Out Act 1994 which excludes from contracting out both the exercise of 'the judicial power of the state' by courts and tribunals and the power to make subordinate legislation.[12] However, since the extent to which the legislative structure provided specifically for prison contracting in 1991 has been affected by the general provisions of the 1994 Act remains unclear, the discussion which follows will concentrate on the requirements of the earlier Act.

So far as disciplinary adjudications are concerned the structure provided by the 1991 Act for private prisons in this country would meet the US requirement of independence. Disciplinary charges are heard by the controller who is appointed by the Home Office rather than the contractor. Thus, in strictly formal terms, adjudication is not delegated. The question of rule making, however, is more troubling. In public sector prisons the main 'rules' are contained within the Prison Rules 1964, a statutory instrument, and their many amendments. Under the provisions of the 1991 Act section 84(1) these Rules are extended to apply to contracted out

[8] Freedland *op. cit.*

[9] The argument is most relevant in relation to contracts reached by federal authorities. See, Logan, *op. cit.*; I. Robbins 'The Legal Dimensions of Private Incarceration' (1989) 38 Am. Univ. LR 531, and D. Dunham, 'Inmates' Rights and the Privatization of Prisons' (1986) 86 Col LR 1475. The issue of delegation in the UK context is discussed by Freedland, *op. cit.*, 95–9.

[10] Logan, *op. cit.*, 57; and McDonald, *op. cit.*

[11] A modest example of the shared political heritage adverted to on a much wider scale by Allan in ch. 2.

[12] Section 71(1). Also excluded are powers which interfere with the liberty of any individual and powers of entry, search, or seizure.

prisons, and there is certainly no formal delegation of rule making powers to the contractor. However, only a small proportion of the rules applying within prison establishments are contained within the Prison Rules themselves. Standing Orders and Circular Instructions devised internally within the Prison Service and of which no mention is made in section 84 are used extensively to supplement the Rules. Within private prisons contractors must comply with the specifics of the contract but, provided they meet the requirements of the Prison Rules, it is up to them to decide how to do so. If they determine that compliance can best be achieved through the imposition of internally generated rules, either instead of or as a supplement to Circular Instructions and Standing Orders, they are presumably free to employ such rules provided there is nothing in the contract to stop them. Indeed the tender documents specifically refer to 'house rules'. While it might be argued that internal rules are inevitable and largely trivial, they still impose directly on the interests of individuals and thus require to be justified in the public interest. The inability of our public law to regulate the processes of administrative rule making is already well recognized, and the lack of accountability and openness surrounding the formulation of Circular Instructions and Standing Orders within public sector prisons has been extensively documented elsewhere,[13] but it is perhaps worth remarking that the problem does not go away just because a contract is employed. The 1991 Act may retain within the public sector the power to make delegated legislation but it does nothing to regulate and render accountable the less formal rule making processes.

Legality and legitimacy: questions of process

Having conceded that the contracting out of prison management is not of itself unconstitutional on either side of the Atlantic, it is necessary to return to the process of contract formulation. Any contract between a public authority and a private contractor for the operation of a prison must include terms relating to cost and regime quality, both of which will impinge directly on the interests of individuals. Thus according to what has been said above, the process of contract formulation should be such as to enable the fullest participation and consultation in order to encourage the agreement of terms which reflect the broadest public interest. In reality it seems the position in the United States is less remote from this ideal than is the practice of contracting in this country.

Although few general constitutional restrictions are imposed on the process of government contracting in the United States, some individual state legislatures have been more rigorous in their requirements. The

[13] For further discussion of policy formulation within state prisons see Richardson, *op. cit.*

constitutional due process protections attaching to 'new property' by virtue of *Goldberg* v. *Kelly*[14] do not apply to government procurement contracts. The government apparently has unrestricted power in procurement contracts to determine those with whom it will deal and to fix the terms of the contract.[15] Further the Administrative Procedure Act exempts contracts generally from the notice and comment requirements of rule making.[16] However, much of the contracting in relation to prison administration is conducted by state agencies and is governed by specific enabling legislation. This can provide an opportunity both to debate the principles to be reflected within the contracts and to regulate the process of contract negotiation itself. In some states the enabling legislation is very specific as to regime quality, thus retaining within the democratic process the power to set regime standards.[17] In others the legislation significantly constrains the freedom of the contracting agency by specifying the factors which either must or must not be taken into account in selecting the successful contractor.[18] Alternatively, as in Tennessee, the legislation can lay down detailed procedures for the tendering process requiring broad consultation. The Tennessee Private Prison Act of 1986 requires four separate committees to look both at the requests for proposals (tender documents) and at the proposed contracts themselves. McAfee suggests that such a deliberative and open process of contract negotiation should avoid the difficulties encountered in nineteenth century California where the adoption of 'secretive and hasty' procedures resulted in 'an immediately suspect contract'.[19]

The position in the UK is very different. Apart from the stipulation that private prisons be run in accordance with the Prison Act and Rules, the enabling legislation gives no guidance as to the contents of the contract thus restricting parliamentary debate to a minimum. It also fails to impose any procedural requirements on the process of negotiation and tendering. The tender documents on regime specifications etc., are published prior to the completion of contracts, but there has so far been little public debate as

[14] 310 US 254 (1970).

[15] M. Baram, *Alternatives to Regulation* (Lexington Mass, 1982), 115.

[16] Section 551, 5 USC 1976. For an introduction to the subject see, J. Whelan, 'An Introduction to the US Federal Government System of Contracting' [1992] *PPLR* 207.

[17] Some states, e.g., require adherence to the American Correctional Association standards, see Robbins, *op. cit*, 777–9, and D. Wecht, 'Breaking the Code of Deference: Judicial Review of Private Prisons' (1987) 96 *Yale LJ* 815.

[18] *Id*. Legislation in both Texas and Oklahoma requires that selection should not be made on grounds of cost alone.

[19] W. McAfee 'Tennessee's Private Prison Act of 1986: An Historical Perspective with Special Attention to California's Experience' (1987) 40 *Vanderbilt LR* 851, 853–4. Similarly rigorous requirements are imposed in relation to privatization in a different sphere by the Arizona Constitution, see Daintith & Sah, *op. cit.*, 480.

to their contents. In relation to the contract for the running of the Wolds it was only after the completion of the contract between the Home Office and Group 4 that details of the financial terms and the unsuccessful bids were revealed.[20] The secrecy which had surrounded the negotiations only served to increase public suspicion when it became apparent that Group 4's bid had not been the lowest and that a senior member of the remand contracts unit, which had been responsible for advising on the bids, had subsequently left the Home Office to take up a job with Group 4.[21]

Against such a background it becomes particularly important to consider the ability of the courts to provide some *ex post* accountability. Judicial oversight of the contracting process rather than the enforcement of the contractual terms themselves is, if anything, typically a matter for public law. Private rights have yet to be created. Unfortunately, here the UK law is confused and arguably inadequate in some significant respects.[22] Public law has an uneasy and somewhat ambiguous attitude to government contracting. In the first place it seems the mere presence of a contract will not of itself bar recourse to judicial review.[23] None the less, when it comes to the review of the contracting power itself the courts have been more willing to intervene in the case of local government contracts where there is typically a statutory base than central government contracts.[24] In *Hibbit and Saunders*, for example, the court refused judicial review because there was no sufficient element of public law in the tendering process employed between the Lord Chancellor's Department and the shorthand writers.[25] While the process for tendering for prison contracts might be more readily reviewable since the necessary public law element is provided by the statutory derivation of the power, the possibility of judicial review does not of itself guarantee adequate accountability. It is important to consider more closely the circumstances in which an application for judicial review might succeed. To date judicial review of the tendering process in fields outside prison management has typically been sought by disappointed

[20] National Audit Office, *Report on the Wolds Remand Prison* (1994) HC 309 1993–4 HMSO.

[21] See reports in the *Guardian* 10 & 13 Feb. 1995. The Public Accounts Committee has recommended that reasons be recorded whenever a contract is awarded to a bidder other than the lowest.

[22] For a recent discussion see S. Fredman & G. Morris, 'The Costs of Exclusivity: Public and Private Re-examined' [1994] *PL* 69.

[23] *R* v. *Secretary of State for Trade, ex p. Vardy* [1992] *The Times* 30 Dec.

[24] *R* v. *Lewisham LBC, ex p. Shell* [1988] 1 All ER 938. See also M. Taggart 'Corporatization, Contracting and the Courts' [1994] PL 351.

[25] *R* v. *Lord Chancellor, ex p. Hibbit and Saunders* [1993] *The Times* 12 Mar. S. Arrowsmith, 'Protecting the Interests of Bidders for Public Contracts' (1994) 53 *CLJ*, 104, argues that the court's decision regarding the public law element ignored earlier case-law where no such issue had been emphasized.

bidders.[26] In this form judicial intervention may help to ensure that the process is fair between the competitors but it does little to facilitate more general debate and participation. A fully effective mechanism for accountability must provide a means of ensuring both that the terms of the contract truly reflect the public interest and that the successful bidder has been selected according to proper criteria. If judicial review is to perform such a role in the context of prison privatization, it would have to be available to challenge the nature of the regime specifications in the tender document, or the financial provisions, or even to question the identification of the successful bidder. It would also have to be available at the suit of interested parties other than competitors for the contract: the rules on standing would require considerable liberalization.[27] While the courts might be reluctant to present themselves as a 'surrogate political process' by significantly enhancing their effectiveness as a mechanism for achieving *ex post* accountability in this way, there are strong arguments based on broad notions of democracy and the citizen's right to the authoritative exercise of public power that suggest they would be justified in so doing.[28]

Unfortunately a search through US material has yet to reveal any very useful lessons on these questions. There is a vast literature on public contracts but again the interest is focused on the disappointed bidder. In the specific context of prison privatization it would seem that the greatest legal interest has been generated in relation to the speculative building of prison establishments, something which may grow here following the 1994 Act. But again the main protagonists tend to be the contracting agencies and the disappointed speculators. One particularly bad tempered episode in Texas resulted in the indictment of the directors of the development company on charges of violating antitrust laws.[29]

Perhaps the most useful lesson we might import from the USA with regard to the formulation stage is to be derived not from the form of judicial intervention nor from principles derived from the Constitution, but from the legislative style adopted by individual states. Although we do not yet have minimum regime standards in this country which could be

[26] *Id.*

[27] In *R* v. *Hereford Corp, ex p. Harrower* [1970] 1 WLR 1425 a competitor was given standing to challenge the tender process not because he was a competitor but because he was a ratepayer. For a general discussion of standing see P. Cane in this volume.

[28] See Richardson *op. cit.* for an account of these arguments and for a discussion of the implications for the judicial role of the recognition of a citizen's right to authoritative government. As Peter Cane observes in chapter 5, it might now be suggested that within a democracy one of the most fundamental of all interests must be the citizen's interest in the authoritative exercise of power, and that the judiciary through the regulation of process have the potential to further and to protect that interest.

[29] *The Dallas Morning News* 3 Dec. 1991.

incorporated in the enabling legislation, our legislation could both include some essential quality specifications and make more rigorous demands on the tendering process along the lines of the Tennessee Act. A requirement of openness and broad consultation at the point when the tender documents are drawn up as well as at the selection of the contractor would do much to enhance the authority of the private regimes.[30] To an extent Europe might be forcing the pace on this with the Public Service Contracts Directive.[31] However, since the running of prisons is a 'non-priority service' under the Directive the tendering process is subject to only the most basic regulatory regime and much more is required if the public interest is really to be represented.[32]

MONITORING COMPLIANCE

Once the terms of the contract have been agreed it becomes important to ensure that the powers acquired by the private contractor are exercised in the public interest. If it is assumed, for the sake of the present argument, that the contractual terms represent the public interest then some effective mechanism is required to ensure compliance with those terms. It is important at the outset, however, to appreciate that such mechanisms can be either judicial or extrajudicial, and can be designed to monitor performance generally in the public interest, Her Majesty's Chief Inspector of Prisons for example, or specifically at the instigation of an aggrieved individual, the Prison Ombudsman for instance. In some cases a single mechanism such as the board of visitors or Members of Parliament can perform both functions. In relation to prison administration in England and Wales extrajudicial monitoring plays a very significant role, however due to time and space constraints this essay will concentrate on the role of the courts.[33]

England and and Wales—private law

In the UK the judicial enforcement of compliance with the terms of a contract is traditionally regarded as a matter for private law. It is a question

[30] But see Daintith & Sah, *op. cit.*, for further discussion of 'manner and form' requirements.

[31] 92/50/EEC, implemented July 1993.

[32] See P. Armin Trept, 'Extension of the EC Procurement Regime to Public Services Contracts: An Overview of the Services Directive' [1993] *PPLR* 1, and I Harden, 'Defining the Range of Application of the Public Sector Procurement Directives in the UK' [1992] *PPLR* 362.

[33] Questioning from members of the Public Accounts Committee, e.g., revealed that Group 4 is being paid £5.9 m. a year to run the Wolds instead of the £4.4 m. originally estimated when the contract was awarded, *The Times* 16 June 1994. For a general discussion of the various extra-judicial mechanisms see Richardson, *op. cit.*

for resolution between the parties alone. Arguably, however, once the subject matter of the contract involves the performance of a 'public' service the essentially private character of the transaction is lost. Interests beyond those of the immediate parties are at issue. In the case of private prisons these third party interests most obviously include prisoners, but reach further to include members of the public generally both as taxpayers and as the beneficiaries of imprisonment: we have it on ministerial authority that prison works, presumably to all our benefits. In English law the doctrine of privity operates to bar such third party beneficiaries from seeking to pursue any contractual remedy in the case of a breach. In certain circumstances tort might provide a remedy to the prisoner injured by a breach of the contractual terms if the courts were to accept the contract as evidence of the appropriate standard of care, but in the absence of such a claim in negligence, private law provides little protection to those affected by the non-compliance of either party to a contract for the operation of a private prison (see below).

England and Wales—public law

With regard to state run prisons, prisoners and possibly members of the public can seek to protect their interests through the public law mechanism of judicial review. It therefore becomes important to consider the extent to which the scope of judicial review is affected by the existence of a contact. The position of the contractor and the Secretary of State will be examined in turn.

The Contractor

Section 84 of the Criminal Justice Act 1991 stipulates that a contracted out prison shall be run 'subject to and in accordance with' the Prison Act and Rules, and section 85(2) specifically confers on the director powers derived from that legislation. Thus when Group 4 runs the Wolds it is exercising powers derived directly from statute. While, arguably, the existence of a contract should not insulate the exercise of statutory powers from the supervision of the reviewing courts, the relevant case law is sadly inconclusive and it is not yet clear whether the contractor/director would be susceptible to judicial review.[34] However, on the assumption that the private contractor is so susceptible, any contractual breach which also

[34] See, e.g., *R* v. *Panel on Takeovers and Mergers, ex p. Datafin* [1987] QB 847, *R* v. *Disciplinary Committee of the Jockey Club, ex p. Aga Khan* (1992) 143 NLJ 163, and *R* v. *Chief Rabbi, ex p. Watchmann* [1993] 2 All ER 249. See also D. Pannick, 'Who is Subject to Judicial Review and in Respect of What?' [1992] *PL* 1; and N. Bamforth, 'The Scope of Judicial Review: Still Uncertain' [1993] *PL* 239.

constituted a breach of statutory obligations should be remediable by way of judicial review at the suit of any party having sufficient interest in the matter, in just the same way as if the breach had occurred within a state prison.[35] Different issues arise when the contractor's contractual non-compliance does not of itself amount to a failure to fulfil public law obligations. To the extent that the contract is published, can it be said to give rise to legitimate expectations in prisoners? If, for example, the contract requires the contractor to provide a library for prisoners and the contractor fails to do so, the prisoners might argue that they have acquired a legitimate expectation that a library will be provided. Such an argument brings difficulties with it, however. In the first place the exercise of statutory powers is not so directly in issue so the availability of judicial review becomes less likely. Secondly, the courts might view the argument as an attempt to circumvent privity of contract and might be reluctant to allow the public law notion of legitimate expectation to be used in such a way. Finally it is not entirely clear what the prisoner would gain from establishing a legitimate expectation in this context: a library, or merely an explanation for the failure to provide one? As yet the notion of a legitimate expectation to a substantive benefit, rather than to some form of procedural protection, is poorly developed in English law.[36]

The Secretary of State

Section 4(2) of the Prison Act 1952 imposes a duty on the Secretary of State to ensure that the provisions of the Act and Rules are duly complied with, and the Court of Appeal has confirmed that such a duty is potentially enforceable by way of judicial review.[37] The fact that the Secretary of State chooses to contract out the management of certain prisons cannot relieve him of that ultimate duty. Thus if the Secretary of State fails to take enforcement action against any contractor whose contractual non-compliance amounts to a breach of statutory obligations, that failure could be susceptible to judicial review. In this way, if judicial review is denied against the private contractor on the grounds that it is not a public body for the purposes of Order 53, the Secretary of State becomes the obvious respondent. In relation to contractual non-compliance amounting to a breach of public law obligations, therefore, the inmate of a private prison has equivalent recourse to judicial review to that enjoyed by the state prisoner. Where the contractual non-compliance does not amount to a

[35] Presumably the courts would adopt their usual rules as to the requirements of standing; see Cane, above.

[36] There is a rapidly expanding literature on legitimate expectation, but see particularly, C. Forsyth 'The Provenance and Protection of Legitimate Expectations' (1988) 47 *CLJ*. 238 and P. Craig, 'Legitimate Expectations: A Conceptual Analysis' (1992) 108 *LQR* 79.

[37] *R* v. *Deputy Gov. of Camphill Prison, ex p. King* [1984] 3 All ER 897.

breach of public law obligations, however, more difficult questions arise. As was the case in relation to actions against the contractor, much turns on the notion of legitimate expectation. Prisoners in a private prison might claim a legitimate expectation that the Secretary of State take appropriate action under the contract to ensure compliance on the part of the contractor. However, the goverment chose to promote legislation which does not require the default and termination provisions of prison contracts to be made public, thus making it difficult for prisoners to identify the precise promise or undertaking required to establish a legitimate expectation.[38] None the less, prisoners might argue common practice suggests that some default action must be available to the parties under the contract and that they have a legitimate expectation that the Secretary of State will take advantage of it. However, even if they are successful in establishing such a legitimate expectation the prisoners are unlikely to gain more than a requirement that the Secretary of State explain his lack of enforcement action. In the case of any member of the public wishing to challenge the Secretary of State's efforts to encourage compliance with the financial terms of the contract, for example, these problems would be compounded by the need to establish standing.[39]

In sum, if this brief synopsis is not being overcautious, the courts in England and Wales would seem to possess a fairly limited ability to oversee compliance with the terms of prison contracts. The law of contract provides relief only to the immediate parties, while the ultimate impact of the public law remedies will turn on the willingness of the judiciary to develop the notion of legitimate expectation. Further, thanks to the doctrine of privity of contract and the requirements of standing at public law, the judicial mechanisms that are available are designed primarily for the redress of individual grievances, rather than for the provision of monitoring in the public interest. However, even with regard to individual grievances, the court's efficacy is significantly limited by its inability to award compensation for the breach of obligations in public law.

[38] The Prison Reform Trust had to obtain documents from the US Securities and Exchange Commission in order to discover details of the contract between Premier Prisons Services Ltd. and the Home Office for the running of Doncaster prison, NACRO *Criminal Justice Digest* (1994) 81, 11. This recourse was only available because of the involvement of the Corrections Corporation of America in Premier Prisons. The inability to gain access to the necessary information is a very obvious problem for any applicant seeking to raise the question of compliance, and that problem is unlikely to be eased through discovery if current judicial practice is followed; see Rawlings, above; and Law Com. Paper No.226 *Administrative Law: Judicial Review and Statutory Appeals* (1994: HMSO) HC 669 1994/5, Part VII.

[39] Would a member of the public have the necessary standing to challenge the additional cost of the Wolds revealed to the Public Accounts Committee, *supra*, n. 33, e.g., or to challenge the steps being taken by the Secretary of State to ensure that Premier Prisons Ltd complies with its contractual obligations, The *Guardian* 8 & 20 Sept. 1994? For a discussion of Representative Standing see ch. 5 in this volume.

The United States—contract

In the US the position is very different. In the first place no doctrine of privity of contract bars the prisoner or even a member of the public from suing for breach of contract as a third party beneficiary. If a prisoner or a member of the public can show either that the contracting parties intended to give them legally enforceable rights, or that there was a law requiring certain categories of people to be considered third party beneficiaries, they may in certain circumstances bring an action in relation to any injury suffered by them as a consequence of the breach.[40] While an intention to create third party rights does not have to be specifically expressed in the contract, government contracts tend to be more strictly interpreted than do contracts between private parties, since in the case of government contracts it would be possible to argue that the entire public is intended to benefit. Nevertheless in 1979 a federal prisoner housed in a county jail pursuant to a contract between the county and the US government brought an action as a third party beneficiary claiming that he had received an injury while he was in the custody of the county. The US Court of Appeals for the Second Circuit held that he had such a claim because of the presence in the contract of a policy statement: 'prisoners shall be placed in contract facilities which provide a secure, humane, and orderly environment, and in which adequate attention is given to the maintenance of each inmate's health, safety and general welfare'.[41] From this it would seem that third party beneficiary claims are available at the suit of prisoners, or possibly members of the public, against a prison contractor for damages attributable to a breach of the contract, provided third party rights are either expressly created or can be implied. Indeed the enabling legislation in some states specifically provides for third party rights and the American Bar Association's model contract expressly creates such rights.[42]

The United States—civil rights suits

In addition to any potential vulnerability to third party beneficiary suits, both private prison operators in the US and their contracting agencies are liable for any violation of the constitutional rights of inmates through the mechanism of a civil rights suit. Commentators on both sides of the private prisons debate are agreed that since contractors are acting 'under color of state law' when operating private prisons, the state action requirement will be met rendering them responsible under section 1983 of the Civil Rights

[40] See Robbins, *op. cit.*
[41] *Owens* v. *Haas* 601 F 2d. 1242 (2d. Cir) cert. denied 444 US 980 (1979).
[42] Robbins *op. cit.*

Act for any constitutional violations.[43] Remedies available under that section include injunctive and declaratory relief and damages.[44] There is also agreement that privatization will neither eliminate nor reduce the liability of the contracting agency.[45]

Since the 1970s, prisoners in the US have increasingly sought to challenge the actions of public prison authorities by reference to the Constitution. In 1991 prisoners filed 26,786 civil rights suits in the federal courts.[46] To the extent that the Constitution guarantees basic freedoms, such as expression, association, and religion, it provides direct protection for a prisoner's essential civil rights. But the Constitution's net spreads further. Through the Fifth and Fourteenth Amendments it guarantees 'due process of law' in the protection of life, liberty and property, and has thus enabled prisoners to assert due process rights in the context of prison discipline, for example, and parole.[47] Finally, the Eighth Amendment forbidding cruel and unusual punishment has been used by prisoners to challenge prison conditions more generally.

The use of the Eighth Amendment in US prison litigation has been complicated and controversial. Since the 1970s it has been used to challenge the use of excessive violence by prison staff,[48] specific aspects of the prison regime, such as the standard of medical care provided for inmates,[49] and prison conditions generally,[50] and it is in this last respect that its use has been most controversial. During the 1970s the federal courts were prepared to declare that the conditions in individual prisons and occasionally throughout entire state systems were in violation of the Eighth Amendment. Strangely perhaps few of these cases ever reached the Supreme Court, and accordingly no authoritative guidance was given as to the standard below which prison conditions must fall before they constitute cruel and unusual punishment. During the 1980s the initial enthusiasm for court intervention in prisons began to fade, due perhaps in part to the mixed impact of that intervention itself, and in part to a change in the political climate, but violations of the Eighth Amendment were still found. By 1992 the prison systems in 43 states were operating under some

[43] 42 USC s. 1983. See Logan, *op. cit.*; Robbins, *op. cit.*; and S. Kay, 'The Implications of Prison Privatization on the Conduct of Prisoner Litigation under 42 USC s. 1983' (1987) 40 *Vanderbilt LR* 867.

[44] On the position of federal government see Logan *op. cit.*, 182.

[45] Robbins, *op. cit.*; and see *West* v. *Atkins* 108 S. Crt. 2250 (1988).

[46] Note, 'Supreme Court: Leading Cases' (1992) 106 *Harvard LR* 163, 220. For a general discussion of collective legal action in the sphere of judicial review see Rawlings, 000–000 above.

[47] *Wolff* v. *McDonnell* 418 US 539 (1974).

[48] *Hudson* v. *McMillan* 112 S Crt. 995 (1992).

[49] *Estelle* v. *Gamble* 437 US 678 (1978) and *West* v. *Atkins*, supra, n. 45.

[50] *Wilson* v. *Seiter* 111 S Crt. 2321 (1991).

form of court order arising from allegations of cruel and unusual punishment.

In 1991 the case of *Wilson* v. *Seiter* came before the Supreme Court. Pearly Wilson was an inmate of Hocking Correctional Facility, Ohio and she brought an action against the warden and the director of corrections under section 1983 for violation of the Eighth Amendment.[51] Amongst other things Wilson alleged insanitary eating conditions; unhygienic lavatories; insect infestation; inadequate heating, cooling, and ventilation; excessive noise; and overcrowding. According to the Supreme Court the prisoner must establish two things in order to claim a violation of the Eighth Amendment. First, the conditions must be such as to deny 'the minimal civilized measure of life's necessities'. The Constitution does not mandate comfortable prisons, and a violation will only occur when the prisoners are deprived of an 'identifiable human need such as food, warmth and exercise'. Secondly, and more controversially, according to Justice Scalia punishment requires some form of intent and only those conditions which arise out of, at the least, 'deliberate indifference' on the part of prison officers can constitute cruel and unusual punishment. Thus a mental element has been introduced which may enable conditions which fall below the objective standard to evade sanction if, for example, the authorities can claim that they were doing the best they could within the resources at their disposal.[52]

Even if it is accepted that *Wilson* v. *Seiter* constitutes a restrictive interpretation of the Eighth Amendment as applied to prison conditions, it remains evident that the constitutional prohibition of cruel and unusual punishment provides federal judges in the US with an entrée into the world of prison conditions which their English peers either lack or are reluctant to reveal. Indeed the Constitution in general and the Eighth Amendment in particular provides prisoners in the US with a wide range of opportunities to challenge the actions of prison management, whether that management be in the hands of a private contractor or a public authority. In the absence of comparable constitutional guarantees prisoners in England and Wales have had to rely primarily upon the European Convention and the common law rules of natural justice in order to assert their basic civil and procedural rights. In certain areas, such as access to lawyers, the abolition of routine mail censorship, and the right to a fair disciplinary hearing, prisoners have met with considerable success in the

[51] Above. For a discussion of the case see Note, 'Supreme Court: Leading Cases' (1991) 105 *Harvard LR* 177, 235.

[52] This argument has occasionally been deployed in this country in relation to other areas of government activity, see *R* v. *Bristol Corporation, ex p. Hendy* [1974] 1 All ER 1047.

courts.[53] Admittedly the existing case-law relates to state run prisons but, as explained above, to the extent that the matters in issue remain ultimately the responsibility of the Secretary of State, the private prison inmate will enjoy the same protection by way of an action for judicial review against the Secretary of State as his or her state counterpart. In relation to general prison conditions, by contrast, prisoners in the UK have received virtually no judicial support. In public law, although the principle of unreasonableness can be applied to prison conditions, its threshold is too high to have any real impact.[54] While in private law recourse to both breach of statutory duty relating to the Prison Rules and false imprisonment has been denied,[55] a remedy in tort may be available to a prisoner injured by the excessive use of force on the part of a prison officer,[56] but in relation to conditions more generally the recognition of a very low standard of care has reduced the chances of a successful claim in negligence against a state run prison, at least insofar as the provision of medical treatment is concerned.[57] There remains the possibility of an action for breach of the prohibition against 'cruell and unusuall' punishment contained in the Bill of Rights 1688, but the issue has yet to be pursued to any conclusion.[58]

Civil Rights Suits and Institutional Reform

Although the above account indicates that the US prisoner, whether held in a private or a public jail, has far more opportunity to seek judicial redress than does his or her UK counterpart, it is necessary to look a little more closely at the American experience before deciding whether there is a case for the provision of a comparable range of opportunities in England and Wales.

Civil rights actions in the US can perform at least two distinct yet interrelated functions. In the first place they can provide damages for injuries sustained as a result of any violation of an inmate's constitutional

[53] For a discussion of this case-law see S. Livingstone & T. Owen, *Prison Law: Text and Materials* (Oxford, 1993) and G. Richardson, 'Prisoners and the Law: Beyond Rights', in C. McCrudden & G. Chambers (eds.), *Individual Rights and the Law in Britain* (Oxford, 1994).

[54] *R* v. *Deputy Gov. Parkhurst Prison, ex p. Hague* [1992] 1 AC 154.

[55] *Hague*, supra.

[56] *Racz* v. *Home Office* [1993] *The Times* 17 Dec.

[57] *Knight* v. *Home Office* [1990] 3 All ER 237 and *Egerton* v. *Home Office* [1978] Crim. LR 494.

[58] In *Williams* v. *Home Office (No. 2)* [1981] 1 All ER 1211, Tudor Evans J read 'cruell and unusuall' disjunctively, thus setting a very high threshold: even if the conditions are cruel they may not be unusual. However, in preliminary proceedings in *R* v. *Secretary of State for the Home Department, ex p. Herbage* [1987] QB 1077 the Court of Appeal did not rule out the possibility of an action for breach of the Bill of Rights. The issue never came to trial.

rights. Secondly they can be used more directly to remedy the cause of the violation, to encourage reform. It is in its performance of this second function that judicial intervention in prison affairs in the US has attracted the most criticism. As mentioned above a large number of successful suits were brought by prisoners during the 1970s alleging violation of their constitutional rights. Initially the federal courts reacted by issuing declarations and ordering the authorities to come into compliance with their constitutional obligations. When such tactics met with recalcitrance on the part of the state authorities the courts began to employ injunctions to order more detailed and sweeping changes. The increase in judicial involvement in prison management coincided with a similar increase in intervention in public schools[59] and mental hospitals, and gave rise to the phenomenon known as 'institutional reform' litigation. Unsurprisingly perhaps this involvement of the federal judiciary in institutional reform attracted considerable criticism.[60] Too close an involvement in the running of institutions, it is alleged, can lead the judiciary into areas that are more properly the preserve of the legislature or the administration. More specifically the judiciary are said to lack the necessary expertise to manage an effective reform programme, and doubts have been cast on the ultimate value of some of the more notorious examples of judicial intervention.[61]

Whatever the merit of such criticisms in the context of public prisons, their impact loses considerable force when they are applied to the private sector. If it is assumed that the terms of the contract between the provider and the public contracting agency will at the very least mandate compliance with all obligations imposed by the Constitution, then any civil rights action brought by an inmate alleging a Constitutional violation can be seen as requiring no more of the contractor than compliance with the original agreement. On this view a court seeking to remedy a violation of the Eighth amendment, for example, would be doing no more than enforcing the original agreement between the parties. In public prison reform litigation it has become common to make use of a procedural device known as a consent decree.[62] The consent decree is a hybrid of contract and injunction. The parties agree a prospective remedy and request the court to enter judgment on that agreement. The court then monitors compliance with the agreement. According to some commentators the consent decree

[59] As a belated result of *Brown* v. *Board of Education* 347 US 483 (1954).

[60] For a selection of the arguments see: J. DiIulio, *Courts, Corrections and the Constitution* (New York, 1990); S. Rhodes, 'Prison Reform and Prison Life' (1992) 26 *Law and Society Review* 189; S. Sturm 'Resolving the Remedial Dilemma: Strategies of Judicial Intervention in Prisons' (1990) 138 *U. of Penn. LR* 805; and A. Chayes, 'The Role of the Judge in Public Law Litigation' (1976) 89 *Harvard LR* 1281.

[61] DiIulio, *op. cit.*

[62] *Rufo* v. *Inmates of the Suffolk County Jail* 112 S Crt. 748 (1992).

has now been developed to the point where it ensures a proper allocation of function between the judiciary and the administration: the court concentrates on the interpretation of the Constitutional right while the administration decides how best to honour it.[63] Where a civil rights action is brought against a private contractor a similar allocation might readily occur. The court could define the Constitutional requirements and leave the parties to decide how best to honour them within the contract. Here the civil rights suit would merely provide a non-contractual mechanism through which a third party could seek to enforce those elements of the contract which affected his or her Constitutional rights. Such a device might prove particularly useful where the public contracting agency was for some reason reluctant to act.

CONCLUSIONS

Through civil rights suits and third party beneficiary claims private prison inmates in the US are better equipped to challenge the conditions of their imprisonment than are their UK counterparts. In England and Wales the private prison inmate might have a public law remedy in the case of any contractual non-compliance which also amounted to a breach of public law obligations, but in view of the court's reluctance to become involved in policing prison conditions generally, there is no direct equivalent to the Eighth Amendment in English law.[64] Thus, in the absence of either a parliamentary or a judicial willingness to fashion radically new remedies, a prisoner's only possible public law remedy in the face of deteriorating conditions flowing from contractual non-compliance would be via the doubtful assertion of a legitimate expectation. The more direct mechanism for policing a serious deterioration in conditions which is available to a private prisoner in the US, through a civil rights action for violation of the Eighth Amendment, undoubtedly provides a more effective form of judicial monitoring. In the first place, although the civil rights suit is strictly designed to provide a remedy for those personally suffering from an infringement of their constitutional rights, its use as a trigger for more general monitoring has not in practice been restricted by problems of 'standing'. In prison condition litigation it is not hard to identify a directly affected individual, and occasionally large numbers of inmates within a single institution have joined together to bring class actions. Whatever the

[63] M. Fiemeger, 'Consent Decrees in Prison and Jail Reform' (1993) 83 *J. of Criminal Law and Crimininology* 1024.

[64] The European Convention does little to fill the domestic gap with regard to prison conditions, Livingstone & Owen, *op. cit.*, 134.

ultimate merit of such institutional reform litigation, however, in the absence of either a written constitution or the incorporation of the European Convention, the adoption by the UK of any equivalent to the civil rights action would seem highly unlikely.

Civil rights actions and third party beneficiary claims in the US also serve to remedy individual grievances through the award of damages, a role which is performed here by the private law. While it has been suggested that the level of monetary damages and settlements in prisoner cases in the US tend to be fairly low,[65] it is none the less thought necessary to stress in the contracts the obligation on the part of the contractor to provide adequate insurance cover and to indemnify the contracting agency for all liability in tort, contract, and civil rights actions.

Unless an action for breach of the Bill of Rights finally succeeds, the only realistic source of damages available to the private prisoner in England and Wales is likely to be through a claim in negligence. Here the private prisoner might be in a better position than the state prisoner, particularly if the courts are prepared to view the contract as a guide to the appropriate standard of care. In the absence of negligence, however, the injured prisoner in the UK will be unlikely to obtain damages against the private contractor. No action in contract is available and the breach of a public law obligation does not of itself give rise to damages. Thus, once again the UK inmate is in a worse position than his or her American counterpart. One possible solution, the introduction of a general right to compensation for damage flowing from unlawful public action, raises issues beyond the scope of this essay and will not be pursued further. However, there might be virtue in exploring the provision of a 'contractual-cum-statutory' remedy to private prisoners.[66]

The enabling legislation establishing the power to contract out the management of prisons in this country could (and, arguably, should) provide for third party actions on the part of prisoners. The relevant statute could stipulate certain basic standards to be incorporated in the contract, so many hours out of cell for example, and could provide for actions on the part of prisoners if 'prolonged' breach of these standards occurred. Such a device, which would effectively create a breach of statutory duty action linked to the contractual terms, would provide a mechanism for monitoring compliance with the essentials of the contract which was independent of both the contractor and the Home Office. It would also provide a much needed opportunity for parliamentary

[65] Logan, *op. cit.*, 189.

[66] The Law Commission has after all canvassed the idea of third party rights, see Law Com. Consultation Paper No. 121, *Privity of Contract: Contracts for the Benefit of Third Parties* (London, 1991).

involvement in the formulation of the contractual terms. To an extent, of course, it would place the private prisoner at an advantage over the inmate of a state establishment whose recourse to breach of statutory duty is extremely limited, but this is no argument against the proposal. The solution for the public sector prisoner must lie in an equivalent increase in statutory rigour, not in a denial of rights to the private inmate.

Admittedly the above proposal is unlikely to find approval within a Home Office which remains reluctant even to publish the existing contracts, but as lessons from America go, the lessons of third party beneficiary actions and of consent decrees seem to this public lawyer, at least, to be lessons worth considering and adapting to our domestic climate. A statutorily created third party action based on fundamental standards within the contract would reflect valuable aspects of the American experience, and would both provide a means of redress for those most directly affected by the operation of the contract and encourage some public debate as to the nature of the standards contained within it.

7

Jurisdiction, Judicial Control, and Agency Autonomy

PAUL CRAIG

THE scope of the courts' powers to control jurisdictional error by tribunals, agencies, and the like has recently been the subject of two important decisions by the House of Lords in *Page* v. *Hull University Visitor*[1] and in *R* v. *Monopolies and Mergers Commission, ex p. South Yorkshire Transport Ltd.*[2] These two decisions raise once again the important question as to the relative powers of courts and agencies concerning jurisdictional issues.

The present essay has two objectives. The first is to analyse these decisions in order to assess where the present law on this topic now stands. The second is to consider how the same problem is addressed in the jurisprudence of the US courts, paying particular attention to the recent decisions of the American courts in this area.

THE DOMESTIC PERSPECTIVE

The *Page* case

The decision of the House of Lords in *Page* v. *Hull University Visitor*[3] is the more general of the two latest pronouncements upon this issue. Page was a lecturer at Hull University who was made redundant. He argued that the terms of his appointment did not allow termination of his employment on this ground. The University Visitor, who was the ultimate authority within the University hierarchy on such matters, dismissed the argument, and Page then sought judicial review of the Visitor's decision. Much of the case turned upon particular issues concerning the nature of the Visitor's powers, and the extent to which these were susceptible to review. However, there are also more general observations concerning the scope of jurisdictional review. These observations can be summarized in the following manner.

[1] [1993] 1 All ER 97. [2] [1993] 1 All ER 289. [3] *Supra.*

Firstly, Lord Browne-Wilkinson, who gave the leading judgment, held that *Anisminic*,[4] combined with Lord Diplock's dictum in *O'Reilly*,[5] had indeed rendered obsolete the distinction between errors of law on the face of the record and other errors of law, and had done so by extending the *ultra vires* doctrine. Thenceforward, it was to be taken 'that Parliament had only conferred the decision making power on the basis that it was to be exercised on the correct legal basis: a misdirection in law in making the decision therefore rendered the decision *ultra vires*'.[6] In general therefore, 'any error of law made by an administrative tribunal or inferior court in reaching its decision can be quashed for error of law.'[7]

Secondly, the constitutional foundation for the court's power was, said his Lordship, the *ultra vires* doctrine. This was so for the following reason. In an ordinary case,[8] the law applicable to a decision made by such a body was the general law of the land. A tribunal or inferior court would, therefore, be acting *ultra vires* if it reached a decision which was erroneous under the general law.[9]

Thirdly, it was, however, only *relevant* errors of law which would lead to the decision being quashed or declared null. The error had to be one which affected the actual making of the decision and affected the decision itself. The mere existence of an error of law at some earlier stage of the proceedings would not vitiate the decision itself.[10]

Finally, the case is unclear as to whether varying presumptions still exist for administrative bodies on the one hand, and for inferior courts on the other. In previous case-law some judges had posited a distinction between the review of general administrative authorities and review of inferior courts:[11] in the case of the former the general presumption was that Parliament had not intended these bodies to make legal decisions in respect of which the reviewing court could not substitute its own judgment; in the case of the latter it was felt that no such general presumption should operate in relation to such inferior courts. A distinction of this nature does still appear to exist. Lord Browne-Wilkinson cited the relevant dicta from Lord Diplock in the *Racal* case, and then reasoned on the assumption that

[4] [1969] 2 AC 147.

[5] [1983] 2 AC 237.

[6] [1993] 1 All ER 97, 107. Lord Slynn and Lord Mustill dissented in relation to certain aspects of the case concerning the Visitor. However, on the general point concerning the scope of review for error of law they were of the same view as the majority; *id.*, 111.

[7] *Loc. cit.*

[8] The Visitor was regarded as being in a special position in this respect, since he was not applying the general law, but a special domestic legal regime; *id.*, 108.

[9] *Id.*, 108.

[10] *Id.*, 107–8, explaining *R.* v. *Independent Television Commission, ex p. TSW Broadcasting Ltd* (1992) *The Independent* 27 Mar.

[11] *Re Racal Communications Ltd.* [1981] AC 374, 381–4 *per* Lord Diplock.

differing presumptions did still exist in the two situations.[12] It was indeed this differing presumption as to legislative intent which provided part of the foundation for the argument that the powers of the Visitor could be treated differently from those of general administrative authorities. Thus Lord Browne-Wilkinson, having cited the relevant dicta from *Racal*, stated that if there had been a statutory provision to the effect that the decision of the Visitor was final and conclusive then the courts would have had no jurisdiction to review for an error of law made by the Visitor within his jurisdiction in the narrow sense. Given that this was so his Lordship could see no meaningful distinction between the situation where a statute has conferred final and conclusive jurisdiction and the case where the common law has 'for 300 years recognized that the Visitor's decision on questions of fact and law are conclusive and are not to be reviewed by the courts.'[13] Moreover, the reasoning of Lord Griffiths also appears to be based upon the continued vitality of the distinction between the scope of review of general administrative authorities and inferior courts.[14]

The *South Yorkshire Transport* case

The facts of *R* v. *Monopolies and Mergers Commission, ex p. South Yorkshire Transport Ltd.*[15] were as follows. The Secretary of State has power under the Fair Trading Act 1973, section 64(1)(a), to refer a merger to the Monopolies and Mergers Commission where it appears to him that the two or more enterprises have ceased to be distinct and that as a result the supply of over 25% of the services of any description 'in a substantial part of the United Kingdom' would be carried on by one person. The Monopolies and Mergers Commission investigated a merger between two companies which operated bus services within an area which was 1.65% of the total UK area, and which contained only 3.2% of the total population of the UK. The companies claimed that the investigation should be set aside because the jurisdictional condition relating to a 'substantial part of the UK' had not been fulfilled. Lord Mustill gave judgment for the Monopolies and Mergers Commission. He reasoned as follows.

His Lordship acknowledged that the term 'substantial' was open to a spectrum of possible meanings, ranging from 'not trifling' to 'nearly complete'. In between these two senses of the term there were many others which drew colour from the statutory context in which they were found.[16] Counsel for the applicants contended that it was for the court to determine

[12] *Id.*, 108–9. Cf. *R.* v. *Greater Manchester Coroner, ex p. Tal* [1985] QB 67, 82–3, where Goff LJ assumed that differential tests for review would not operate depending upon the nature of the decision maker.

[13] [1993] 1 All ER 97, 109.

[14] *Id.*, 100.

[15] [1993] 1 All ER 289.

[16] *Id.*, 294–5.

the meaning which the disputed term should bear, that this was a hard-edged question in the sense that there was one correct meaning which the term should have. Lord Mustill agreed, but only in part.

He accepted that it was for the court to decide where along the 'spectrum of possible meanings'[17] the term was to be placed:

> Once the criterion for a judgment has been properly understood, the fact that it was formerly part of a range of possible criteria from which it was difficult to choose and on which opinions might legitimately differ becomes simply a matter of history. The judgment now proceeds unequivocally on the basis of the criterion as ascertained. So far no room for controversy.[18]

However, the criterion which was chosen might itself be so imprecise that different decision makers, each acting rationally, might reach different conclusions when applying it to the facts of a given case:

> In such a case the court is entitled to substitute its opinion for that of the person to whom the decision has been entrusted only if the decision is so aberrant that it cannot be classed as rational: *Edwards* v. *Bairstow* . . . The present is such a case. Even after eliminating inappropriate senses of 'substantial' one is still left with a meaning broad enough to call for the exercise of judgment rather than an exact quantitative measurement.[19]

What emerges from the *South Yorkshire Transport* case can be presented in the following manner. A statutory jurisdictional term may be open to a spectrum of possible meanings and it will be for the court to determine which of these interpretations is to prevail. However the application of that particular interpretation may be contestable because the chosen meaning might itself be open to a range of possible constructions which call for the 'exercise of judgment rather than an exact quantitative measurement'.[20] This is rather like focusing in upon the chosen interpretation and then blowing this up to reveal a further spectrum of choices. In such a case the reviewing court will only intervene if the decision is irrational in the above sense.

Summary

The present law may be summarized as follows. The courts will exercise review over any error of law, and will, in general, no longer employ distinctions between jurisdictional and non-jurisdictional error. When an error has been made the court will normally substitute its view for that of the body subject to review. There appear to be three qualifications to this basic proposition.

17 [1993] 1 All ER 296.
18 *Id.*, 298.
19 *Loc. cit.*
20 [1993] 1 All ER 296, 298.

Firstly, the error of law must be relevant in the sense discussed above. Secondly, the varying presumption as to legislative intent does still appear to operate depending upon the type of institution being reviewed. If the institution being reviewed is a tribunal or other administrative body, then the presumption will be that Parliament did not intend that body to be the final arbiter on issues of law. If, however, the institution subject to review is an inferior court then there is no presumption that Parliament did not intend questions of law to be left to that court.[21] Thirdly, the court will not necessarily substitute its judgment for that of the agency in circumstances like those in the *South Yorkshire Transport* case. In such a case the reviewing court will define the actual meaning that the statutory term is to have, but where that particular meaning is itself inherently imprecise the court will only intervene if the application of the term is so aberrant as to be irrational.

THE PRESENT LAW: AN ASSESSMENT

Several related comments upon the present law are warranted. We can begin with the **formal demise of the collateral fact doctrine**. The *quietus* given to this doctrine in the *Page* case is to be welcomed, subject to a qualification to be mentioned below. The collateral fact doctrine never produced any real measure of predictability as to which issues would be deemed to be collateral or jurisdictional, nor could any *ex post facto* rationality be distilled from juxtaposing decided cases in order to work out why one case had been characterized in one way and another case had been treated differently. The root cause of these difficulties resided in the very nature of the test itself. The distinction between matters which went to the **scope** of the findings which the agency could make, which were treated as jurisdictional, and those matters which related only to the **statutory situation** which the agency had to determine, which were regarded as non-jurisdictional, was impossible to draw precisely because the two matters were inextricably interwoven.[22]

The force of the reasoning in *Anisminic* was against the continued viability of this traditional test, and this was so notwithstanding the fact that their Lordships attested to the continued existence of the doctrine. The persistent pressure to discard the collateral fact doctrine which is apparent in cases such as *Racal*,[23] *Pearlman*,[24] and *O'Reilly*[25] is indicative of the disjunction between the thrust of the actual reasoning in *Anisminic*,

[21] However, even in this latter instance it appears to be the case that, e.g., a legislative finality clause, which purports to render a decision of an inferior court final and conclusive, will only be interpreted to protect that body from errors of law within jurisdiction; [1993] 1 All ER 97, 109.

[22] P. Craig, *Administrative Law* (London, 1989 2nd ed.), 242–4.

[23] [1981] AC 374.

[24] [1979] QB 56.

[25] [1983] 2 AC 237.

which inclined towards the rejection of the collateral fact approach, and the formal reaffirmation in that case that the distinction between jurisdictional and non-jurisdictional errors still existed. This disjunction had to be resolved at some stage, and given the difficulties with the collateral fact doctrine, it is not surprising that it should be resolved in the manner finally settled by the *Page* case: the discarding of that doctrine.

Few then will shed any tears at the passing of a doctrine which has proven to be so problematic. Let me, however, advert to the point hinted at above when indicating that there was a qualification to be made to the general satisfaction at the demise of the old order. It is this. The critique of the collateral fact doctrine is often premised, explicitly or implicitly, upon the assumption that the courts which employed that test were simply missing an essential and elementary truth concerning the unworkability of this criterion; that we now have discovered this truth; and that in line with the commonly repeated theme that we should regard as suspect cases decided from a bygone era of administrative law we can now proceed to the new, improved order, basing review upon error of law.

This comforting picture of modern superiority contrasted with dated formalism is misleading in that it misses a vital element in the story. The courts which employed the discredited doctrine did so because they believed that it represented **some form of balance between agency autonomy and judicial oversight**. Administrative authorities should not be able to adjudicate upon issues which were really outside their remit, and in that sense they should not be able to exercise uncontrolled power over the meaning of the conditions of their jurisdiction. Yet at the same time the courts felt that they themselves should not substitute their judgment on all the issues which had been assigned to the agency by Parliament, including in this respect some of the conditions stipulating the issues which the agency had to determine. The collateral fact doctrine was an attempt to steer a course between unconstrained agency power and something approximating to complete judicial substitution of judgment on any issue of statutory interpretation. Now to be sure this attempt was flawed for the reasons which have been set out above. There is none the less a danger that disapproval of the mechanism will cause us to forget the rationale for its initial adoption. It is all too easy to reason from the unworkability of the collateral fact doctrine to the unquestioning acceptance of the idea that it is right and proper for the ordinary courts to substitute their judgment on any issue of law, and to give the word law a broad meaning with the result that any matter of statutory interpretation will signal judicial intervention. The proper balance of power between court and agency is still the central issue. The nature of this balance should be openly faced in its own terms, and the answer should not be assumed merely because one previous attempt to draw the balance has proven to be defective.

The nature of the point which has just been addressed leads naturally on to the second comment concerning the courts' recent jurisprudence in this area: **the change in the meaning of the *ultra vires* principle**. We have already seen that Lord Browne-Wilkinson based judicial intervention in the *Page* case upon the *ultra vires* principle. This should not, however, serve to conceal the fact that the principle is being used in a different manner than hitherto. When that principle was invoked as the basis for intervention, for example under the collateral fact doctrine, the assumption was that there was a distinction to be drawn between jurisdictional and non-jurisdictional errors. Only the former would result in the decision being regarded as *ultra vires* and void, because the tribunal had acted **outside** its jurisdiction. The latter were errors **within** jurisdiction and would only be open to attack if the error was one of law on the face of the record, and then the decision would only be regarded as voidable. Thus the *ultra vires* concept was previously used to demarcate errors which were jurisdictional from those which were not on the basis of statutory interpretation, the idea being that the courts were delineating the boundaries of Parliamentary intent. However, the *ultra vires* principle as used in *Page* bears a different meaning. Any error of law may lead to the decision being regarded as *ultra vires*, because the tribunal has reached its conclusion on a basis which is erroneous under the general law: *ultra vires* now becomes synonymous with the existence of an error of law.

It has been argued by Sir John Laws that once the distinction between jurisdictional and non-jurisdictional errors is discarded, as it has now been, there is no longer any need or purpose for the *ultra vires* principle as such, since the courts are in reality simply intervening to correct errors of law.[26] So why do the courts persist, as in *Page*, in employing the principle? On one view it provides a legitimating device for the exercise of the courts' power. Rather intervene by saying that the tribunal has acted *ultra vires*, than on the simple ground of error of law *per se*. Sir John Laws captures this idea:

> '*Ultra vires*' is, in truth, a fig-leaf; it has enabled the courts to intervene in decisions without an assertion of judicial power which too nakedly confronts the established authority of the Executive or other public bodies . . . The fig-leaf was very important in *Anisminic*; but fig-leaf it was. And it has produced the historical irony that *Anisminic*, with all its emphasis on nullity, nevertheless erected the legal milestone which pointed towards a public law jurisprudence in which the concept of voidness and the *ultra vires* doctrine have become redundant.'[27]

[26] 'Illegality: The Problem of Jurisdiction', in D. Supperstone & J. Goudie (eds.), *Judicial Review* (London, 1992).

[27] *Id.*, 67.

The third comment flows naturally from the second, as the second did from the first. What are the implications of the idea that all errors of law are open to scrutiny? What is the message concerning the relationship between courts and agencies which emerges from this recent jurisprudence? How much autonomy will agencies have under this new order? Much of course depends upon the interpretation which is accorded to the *Page* reasoning in later cases. **If** that reasoning is taken to mean that when **any** of the conditions describing an agency's sphere of authority involves **any** element of law the court will substitute its view for that of the tribunal on that issue, then review will indeed become extensive with a corresponding diminution of agency autonomy. For some this may be the desirable balance between courts and agencies. There are, however, both practical and conceptual problems with this view.

In **practical** terms it will embroil the courts in the minutiae of disputed interpretations as to what many, or all, of the conditions describing an agency's sphere of authority mean in any particular context. Problems of this nature have been recognized by the judiciary and have been a factor convincing some judges either that review should be cast in less extensive terms, or that the logical implications of review based upon error of law should somehow not be followed through. Lord Morris of Borth-y-Gest's dissenting judgment in *Anisminic*[28] provides an example of the former. His Lordship pointed out that the relevant Order in that case bristled with words which required statutory interpretation, and he was unwilling to accept that misconstruction of any of these terms would involve a jurisdictional error. Goff LJ's judgment in *Tal*[29] furnishes an example of the latter strategy. The decision, which predated *Page*, attacked the distinction between jurisdictional and non-jurisdictional error, posited review based upon error of law, but then emphasized that the court should not intervene merely because some error of law had been committed during an inquest. Future courts might well draw upon the analogous idea in the *Page* case that the error of law must be relevant. Whether devices of this kind really do serve to dispel the pragmatic difficulties created by review based upon errors of law remains to be seen.

The **conceptual** problem is that such an approach is based upon the presumption that the courts' particular interpretation of phrases such as 'employee', 'course of employment', 'boat', or 'resources' is necessarily to be preferred to that of the agency; **and** that such substitution of judgment is the only way to exercise control over such agency interpretations. Neither of these assumptions is well-founded. The courts' particular interpretation of such terms may not necessarily be better than that of the agency, **and**

[28] [1969] 2 AC 147, 182–90.

[28] *R* v. *Greater Manchester Coroner, ex p. Tal* [1985] QB 67, 82–3.

adequate control may be maintained through a different standard of review.

THE US JURISPRUDENCE

The *Chevron* Case

The issue as to the appropriate balance between courts and agencies has, not surprisingly, generated a considerable amount of jurisprudence in the US legal system. US courts discarded the collateral fact doctrine earlier this century for reasons similar to those outlined above: the test encapsulated in that doctrine provided no sound guide as to what should be regarded as collateral or jurisdictional issues. Although courts in the United States shed this approach some time ago the issue as to the appropriate degree of judicial control over the scope of agency findings which relate to the conditions of jurisdiction remains a live one. Put more specifically the central question has been the extent to which the ordinary courts should substitute their findings on all such conditions, or whether some less intensive test of review would better balance the respective powers of agencies and courts.

The seminal modern case on this topic is *Chevron, USA, Inc.* v. *Natural Resources Defense Council, Inc.*[30] The case concerned the legality of regulations made pursuant to the clean air legislation. The Clean Air Act Amendments of 1977 imposed certain requirements on states which had not met the national air quality standards established by the Environmental Protection Agency. The requirements included an obligation on such states to establish regulatory regimes under which permits would be issued relating to 'new or modified major stationary sources' of air pollution. A permit could not be issued unless stringent conditions had been met. The Environmental Protection Agency promulgated regulations designed to implement the permit requirement and these regulations allowed a state to adopt a plant-wide definition of stationary source. The effect of this was that an existing plant which had a number of pollution emitting devices could install or modify one piece of equipment without

[30] 467 US 837 (1984). For differing views on the case, see C. Farina, 'Statutory Interpretation and the Balance of Power in the Administrative State' (1989) 89 *Col LR* 452; A. Aman, 'Administrative Law in a Global Era: Progress, Deregulatory Change and the Rise of the Administrative Presidency' (1988) 73 *Cornell LR* 1101; C. Sunstein, 'Constitutionalism after the New Deal' (1988) 101 *Harvard LR* 421; A. Scalia, 'Judicial Deference to Administrative Interpretations of Law' (1989) *Duke LJ* 511; R. Pierce, '*Chevron* and Its Aftermath: Judicial Review of Agency Interpretation of Statutory Provisions' (1988) 41 *Vanderbilt LR* 301.

meeting the permit conditions, provided that the alteration did not increase the total emissions from the plant. The state was, therefore, allowed to treat all the pollution emitting devices within the same industrial grouping as though they were encased in a 'bubble'. It was this construction of the enabling legislation which was challenged by the National Resources Defense Council, the argument being that this interpretation was too generous to industrial users. Justice Stevens gave the judgment of the Supreme Court. The following passage identifies the court's approach:

> When a court reviews an agency's construction of the statute which it administers, it is confronted with two questions. First, always, is the question whether Congress has directly spoken to the precise question in issue. If the intent of Congress is clear, that is the end of the matter; for the court, as well as the agency, must give effect to the unambiguously expressed intent of Congress. If, however, the court determines Congress has not directly addressed the precise question at issue, the court does not simply impose its own construction on the statute, as would be necessary in the absence of an administrative interpretation. Rather, if the statute is silent or ambiguous with respect to the specific issue, the question for the court is whether the agency's answer is based on a permissible construction of the statute.[31]

What then more specifically did the court mean when it spoke of the agency making a finding which was based 'on a permissible construction of the statute'. Guidance on this crucial issue is to be found in the court's judgment:

> If Congress has explicitly left a gap for the agency to fill, there is an express delegation of authority to the agency to elucidate a specific provision of the statute by regulation. Such legislative regulations are given controlling weight unless they are arbitrary, capricious or manifestly contrary to the statute. Sometimes the legislative delegation to the agency is implicit rather than explicit. In such a case, a court may not substitute its own construction of a statutory provision for a reasonable interpretation made by the administrator of an agency.[32]

Justice Stevens continued in the same vein to emphasize that 'considerable weight' should be given to agency interpretations, and that the court should defer to the agency's construction whenever a decision as to the meaning or reach of a statute involved the reconciliation of conflicting policies, in circumstances where the agency had particular expertise in the matters subjected to its regulatory remit.[33]

Applying these principles the court then upheld the contested agency interpretation. It found that Congress did not have any specific intention with regard to the applicability of the bubble concept to the permit programme. Given that this was so the question was not whether the

[31] 467 US 837 (1984), 842–3. [32] *Id.*, 843–4. [33] *Id.*, 844.

reviewing court believed that the bubble concept was a good thing within the general context of a scheme designed to improve air quality, but whether the agency's view that the bubble concept was appropriate within this scheme was a reasonable one.[34] Looked at in the light of the objectives of the legislation in this area the court found that it was a reasonable interpretation which sought to balance the needs of the environment and those of business. The National Resources Defense Council was, said Justice Stevens, seeking to wage a battle over policy in the courts on an issue which Congress had not specifically addressed, having lost that battle in the agency itself: these policy arguments should more properly be addressed to the legislators or administrators rather than the judges.[35]

The case-law since the *Chevron* decision is itself of considerable interest as later cases have sought to test the metes and bounds of the principles set out above. Two lines of cases can be identified. On the one hand, there are those which give latitude to agency interpretations. On the other hand, there are decisions where the court comes closer to substitution of judgment, drawing upon that part of the argument in the *Chevron* case which asserts the primacy of Congressional intent where that can be identified. These will be examined in turn.

Cases applying a rational basis or reasonableness test

The decision of the Supreme Court in *National Labor Relations Board* v. *United Food and Commercial Workers Union, Local 23, AFL-CIO*[36] provides a good example of the application of the rational basis component of the *Chevron* test. The case concerned the scope of the powers of the National Labor Relations Board, which is the agency given power over labour relations, and also of the General Counsel of the Board, who is charged with the responsibility of bringing prosecutions under the legislation. The General Counsel investigated a complaint about unfair labour practices, but then reached an informal settlement of the issue which the union refused to join. The essence of the question before the court was as to the legality of certain regulations which permitted the General Counsel to determine a post-complaint informal settlement, without any recourse for an appeal to the Board. The answer to this question depended upon whether such authority constituted an infringement of the division of power between the agency itself, which is the adjudicator under the legislation, and the general Counsel, who exercises the prosecutorial powers.

The Supreme Court adopted the dichotomy laid down in *Chevron*, asking first whether Congress had given an unequivocal answer on this

[34] *Id.*, 845. [35] *Id.*, 864. [36] 484 US 112 (1987).

specific issue; if Congress had spoken to the issue then the regulations must be fully consonant with Congressional intent. Where, however, Congress was silent then the court would defer to the Board, provided that its interpretation of the primary legislation was rational and consistent with it.

The court then applied this test to the facts of the case. It reviewed the history of the relevant legislation and found a clear Congressional intent to divide authority between the Board which would adjudicate, and the General Counsel who would prosecute. The legislation did not, however, address this specific issue. While many cases would fall clearly into adjudication or prosecution the present situation did not fall obviously into one category rather than another. Given that Congress had not spoken on this specific matter, then the court's task under *Chevron* 'was not to categorize each agency determination, but rather to decide whether the agency's regulatory placement is permissible.'[37] The court concluded that it was a reasonable construction of the empowering Act to find that until a hearing begins settlement or dismissal determinations are prosecutorial.[38]

Sullivan v. *Everhart*[39] exemplifies the same approach within the context of more technical social security legislation. The question before the court was as to the construction of the Secretary of Health's powers under social security legislation, which entitled him to make the 'proper adjustment or recovery' where he determined that a beneficiary had received 'more or less than the correct amount of payment' under the legislation. The Secretary of Health had adopted certain 'netting' regulations, the purpose of which was to treat overpayments and underpayments in subsequent months cumulatively, and then to settle with beneficiaries. This was challenged on the ground that this method of calculation rendered it impossible for claimants to have overpayments and underpayments treated separately, with the corollary that they could not argue, in the case of overpayments, that there were reasons as to why they should not have to repay any excess which had been received.

Justice Scalia who gave the majority opinion of the court cited[40] the two part test from the *Chevron* case and then proceeded to consider whether Congress had spoken on this specific issue. He reviewed the parent legislation and found that it provided no certain guide as to how the key statutory phrases should be interpreted.[41] Given that Congressional intent was not clear, and given also that the Secretary's interpretation was reasonable, the netting technique was upheld.

It is unsurprising that cases of this nature should provoke disagreements amongst the members of the court as to whether Congress really has determined the issue which is the subject matter of the litigation. If it has

[37] 484 US 112 (1989), 125. [38] *Id.*, 125–6. [39] 484 US 83 (1990).
[40] 494 US 83 (1990), 89. [41] *Id.*, 90–3.

then there is, as we have seen, no room for reasonable agency determinations. In the *Sullivan* case the minority did disagree on this point, and expressed the force of their dissent by stating that 'the kingly power to rewrite history has not been delegated to the Secretary of Health and Human Services.'[42] We will return to the relevance of these disagreements at a later stage.

The decision of the Supreme Court in *Pension Benefit Guaranty Corporation* v. *LTV Corporation*[43] furnishes an interesting example of the way in which the court interprets the two parts of the *Chevron* test. The case concerned pension plans as covered by the Employee Retirement Income Security Act 1974 section 4047. The Act was designed to protect the pension plans of employees through the existence of a mandatory government insurance programme. The Pension Benefit Guaranty Corporation (PBGC) administered the programme the object of which was to ensure that employees were not deprived of their pensions by the termination of the pension plans before sufficient funds had been accumulated under the plans. If a fund terminated before sufficient funds were available then the PBGC became trustee of the fund, taking over the fund's assets and liabilities. The cost of PBGC insurance was borne primarily by employers who maintained pension plans, but Congress had found it necessary to supplement these payments in order to meet the PBGC's liabilities. The PBGC could terminate a pension plan upon a number of grounds including, *inter alia*, that the possible long run losses to the PBGC by the continuation of the plan might be expected to increase unreasonably if the plan were not terminated. However, this termination of the fund could be undone under section 4047 if the PBGC determined that such action was appropriate and consistent with its duties under the Act. The PBGC sought to invoke this power in the present case. It had intervened to terminate a pension plan made by LTV; LTV then sought to renegotiate the pension plan with their workers, devising what is known as a follow-on plan; and the PBGC then sought to use section 4047 on the ground that the restructured pension plan would have the effect of transferring LTV's pension responsibilities on to the PBGC. LTV challenged this decision, arguing that the PBGC had misconstrued its powers under section 4047, on the ground that Congress had not intended section 4047 to be used as a basis for restoring a pension plan merely because a follow-on plan had been made.

Justice Blackmun who gave the opinion of the Court cited the holding from *Chevron* and then began by asking whether there was any clear Congressional intent to avoid restoration of pension plans based upon the existence of successive plans. He observed that the text of section 4047 was

[42] *Id.*, 96. [43] 496 US 633 (1990).

broad, that there was no explicit limit of the kind which LTV were proposing, and that the use of the section in this manner was consistent with the general duties of the PBGC under the Employee Retirement Income Security Act.[44] Lower courts which had found for LTV had drawn upon Congressional history, reasoning that because Congress had not spoken of follow-on plans as a basis for the restoration of the earlier pension plan, therefore it could be concluded that this could not be a reason to justify the reimposition of the original plan. Justice Blackmun disagreed: broad statutory language was not to be regarded as modified by examples which were apparent from the legislative history, more particularly when those examples were not intended to be exhaustive of the statute's scope.[45] The Supreme Court also rejected the conclusion drawn by the Court of Appeals concerning the subsequent legislative history of the area. The lower court had relied on the fact that a provision which would have given the PBGC the explicit power to order restoration in the context of follow-on plans had not been passed in 1987. Justice Blackmun was unconvinced by this reasoning: Congressional inaction was not a sure guide to legislative intent because several equally tenable inferences could be drawn from such inaction, including the inference that the existing legislation already covered the situation.[46] Given that Congress had not specifically addressed the matter, the Supreme Court then went on to apply the rational basis test and found that the PBGC's interpretation of section 4047 could be sustained on this criterion.

The subject matter to which the rational basis test can be applied is brought out clearly by the separate opinion of Justice Scalia in *Mississippi Power & Light Co.* v. *Moore*.[47] The rule of deference to agency interpretations applied to an agency's interpretation of a statute designed to confine its authority, including in this respect an agency's interpretation of its own statutory authority or jurisdiction:

> it is plain that giving deference to an administrative interpretation of its statutory jurisdiction is both necessary and appropriate. It is necessary because there is no discernible line between an agency exceeding its authority and an agency's exceeding authorized application of its policy. To exceed authorized application is to exceed authority. Virtually any administrative action can be described as either one or the other, depending upon how generally one wishes to describe 'authority' . . . And deference is appropriate because it is consistent with the general rationale for deference: Congress would naturally expect that the agency would be responsible, within broad limits, for resolving ambiguities in its statutory authority or jurisdiction . . . Congress would neither anticipate nor desire that

44 496 US 633 (1990), 648. 45 *Id.*, 649. 46 *Id.*, 650.
47 487 US 354 (1988).

every ambiguity in statutory authority would be addressed, *de novo*, by the courts.[48]

Cases in which the courts deem Congress to have spoken to the issue

It should not, however, be thought that the courts always apply the rational basis part of the *Chevron* test. There are many instances in which they deem Congress to have spoken to the issue and in these cases the courts then apply this interpretation of the statutory words.

Etsi Pipeline Project v. *Missouri*[49] is one such case. The case turned upon whether the Secretary of the Interior had exceeded his authority under the Flood Control Act 1944 by authorizing a contract to remove water from a lake for industrial uses without the prior approval of the Secretary of the Army. The Supreme Court reviewed the history, purpose and wording of the legislation and concluded that the language of the statute was 'plain in every respect': if the Interior Secretary wished to remove water from the dam for any purpose the approval of the Army Secretary had to be secured. In these circumstances there was no room for deference to agency interpretation.[50]

In *Pittston Coal Group* v. *Sebben*[51] the Supreme Court had to consider the meaning of certain legislation concerning workers disabilities. The Black Lung Benefits Reform Act 1977 provided that, pending the issuance of regulations by the Secretary of Labor, cases which were filed or pending should be decided under 'criteria . . . not . . . more restrictive than the criteria applicable to a claim filed on June 30, 1973'. As of that date miners could establish a presumptive entitlement to benefits if they submitted medical evidence showing pneumoconiosis, plus either evidence of ten years of mining service, or evidence that the impairment arose out of coal mining employment. Under the Black Lung Benefit Reform Act, the Secretary of Labor made an interim regulation which accorded entitlement to benefit only where miners could show ten years of mining experience.

Justice Scalia gave the judgment for the majority of the Court. As we have already seen Justice Scalia is a prominent advocate of agency autonomy and deference to agency interpretation. Notwithstanding this doctrinal stance he found in favour of the applicant miners. He held that the Secretary of Labor's criteria were more restrictive than those which had previously existed because they limited benefits to those who had been employed for ten years, and made no mention of the second criteria for

[48] *Id.*, 381, citing *Japan Whaling Assn.* v. *American Cetacean Society* 478 US 221 (1986), 226 & 233; *Chemical Manufacturers Assn.* v. *Natural Resources Defense Council, Inc.* 470 US 116 (1985), 123 & 125–6; *Commodity Futures Trading Comm'n* v. *Schor* 478 US 833, (1986), 844–5; *NLRB* v. *City Disposal Systems, Inc.* 465 US 822 (1984), 830; *City of New York* v. *FCC* 486 US 57 (1988).

[49] 484 US 495 (1988).

[50] 484 US 495 (1988), 504 & 517.

[51] 488 US 105 (1988).

claiming which had existed hitherto. The Secretary of Labor had tried to defend his position by relying on an ambiguity in the word 'criteria' and then contending that the interpretation of this word should be subject to the rational basis test from *Chevron*. Justice Scalia disagreed, stating that the term would simply not bear the construction sought to be placed upon it.[52]

The line between the two parts of the *Chevron* test

The cases considered in the preceding discussion illustrate the use which has been made of the *Chevron* test by US courts. It is clear that judges possess considerable discretion as to how to characterize a particular case, in the sense of whether it comes within part one or part two of the *Chevron* formula. This is inevitable. What is less readily apparent is that there has been real disagreement among the judiciary as to the meaning which should be ascribed to the two parts of test, especially part one. This is particularly important as can be appreciated by considering two contrasting views on this issue.

In *Immigration and Naturalization Service* v. *Cardozo-Fonseca*[53] the Supreme Court decided that the meaning of a particular statutory term was clear within the first limb of the *Chevron* test because the Court could divine its meaning through the normal tools of statutory construction. This provoked a powerful separate opinion from Justice Scalia. He felt that the approach of the majority would radically undermine the purpose of the *Chevron* formula, given that a Court could always then hold that the meaning of a statutory term was clear through the use of 'normal tools of statutory construction'.

The approach in the *Cardozo-Fonseca* case can be contrasted with that in *Rust* v. *Sullivan*[54] where Chief Justice Rehnquist gave the leading judgment of the Court. His interpretation of the first limb of *Chevron* was markedly different. On his view a case would only fall under the first limb of the test if the Congressional meaning of the term really was evident on the face of the statute. If this was not so then the matter would fall to be determined under the rationality part of the formula. This then provoked a sharp dissent from Justice Stevens who argued that the majority was construing part one of the test too narrowly.

CONCLUSION

It is clear from the preceding analysis that judges in the Supreme Court take differing views as to how the two parts of the *Chevron* formula ought

[52] 488 US 105 (1988), 113–14.
[53] 480 US 421 (1986).
[54] 111 S Ct. 1759 (1991).

to be interpreted. The crucial issue is the meaning to be given to part one of the test, since this will then have direct implications for the ambit within which the more deferential approach of part two can operate.

Notwithstanding this diversity of view, we in the UK can still learn much from the US experience in the following sense. The range of options for dealing with the problem of jurisdictional error are finite. We have rightly discarded the collateral fact doctrine. Given this decision we are then faced with a choice. One option is to go down the road of judicial substitution of judgment on all issues of statutory interpretation. On this view any question of law which comes before the ordinary courts in a review action would see the courts simply substituting their view for that of the agency. The practical and conceptual problems with this approach have been considered above. These difficulties will be exacerbated if the word 'law' is interpreted in an analytical sense to mean any conclusion drawn from primary facts when construing the meaning of statutory terms such as 'employee', 'successor in title', etc.

The other option is to proceed in a manner analogous to that in the US jurisprudence. On some issues the courts would substitute judgment for that of the agency; on others they would still maintain some control through the medium of the rational basis or reasonableness test. While there are bound to be some disagreements as to which of these tests should be applied in any particular case the nature of these should not be overstated. Substitution of judgment is suitable either where the legislature really has spoken to the issue, or where the challenged decision involves an issue on which the agency does not have any special expertise. In other instances the rationality test would be applied, particularly in relation to those matters of statutory interpretation which do fall within the agency's sphere of competence. It should not moreover be forgotten that agency determinations can be struck down even under this latter standard of review.

The choice between the two options outlined above will have important implications for the more general relationship between agencies and courts. At base the issue is whether agencies are to have any autonomy over the meaning to be ascribed to their empowering legislation. Under option one the answer is essentially 'no'. Under option two the answer is a qualified 'yes'. It is clear that different commentators will have differing views as to which of these options is to be preferred, but at least the US jurisprudence enables us to see that there are ways of maintaining control over agency choices short of substituting judgment on each and every occasion.

8

The Constitution of The Excluded—Indians and Others[1]

PETER FITZPATRICK

> The origin of the supreme power, for all practical purposes, is *not discoverable* by the people who are subject to it. In other words, the subject *ought* not to indulge in *speculations* about its origin with a view to acting upon them, as if its right to be obeyed were open to doubt (*ius controversum*). . . . Whether in fact an actual contract originally preceded their submission to the state's authority (*pactum subiectionis civilis*), whether the power came first and the law only appeared after it, or whether they ought to have followed this order—these are completely futile arguments for a people which is already subject to civil law, and they constitute a menace to the state.
>
> (Kant, *The Metaphysics of Morals*)[2]

> 350. It is the absolute right of the Idea to step into existence in clear-cut laws and objective institutions, beginning with marriage and agriculture, whether this right be actualized in the form of divine legislation and favour, or in the form of force and wrong. This right is the right of heroes to found states.
>
> (Hegel, *Philosophy of Right*)[3]

> Nothing could be more central to American reality than the relationships between Americans and American Indians, yet those relationships are of course the most invisible and the most lied about. The lies are not simply a denial; they constitute a new world, the world in which American culture is located.
>
> (Durham, *A Certain Lack of Coherence*)[4]

[1] I greatly appreciate the help and revelation provided by Tony Carty and David Taylor when working on the parts dealing with international law. Thanks also to Robert Post for guiding me to the Insular Cases. David Goldberg offered acute and careful comments on a late draft. Fresh dimensions were added to my initial efforts when the paper was discussed at the Faculty of Law seminar series for 1994 at Queen Mary and Westfield College. Ian Loveland followed that up with a generous endowment of references and material.

[2] I. Kant, *Kant's Political Writings* (H. Reiss ed.), (Cambridge, 1970), 143 (original emphasis).

[3] G. Hegel, *Philosophy of Right* (Oxford, 1952), 219.

[4] J. Durham, *A Certain Lack of Coherence: Writings on Art and Cultural Politics* (J. Fisher ed.) (London, 1993), 138.

THE COHERENCE OF CONSTITUTIONS

THE constitution of the United States is a productively ambivalent instrument. As Roger Cotterrell's chapter in this collection so vividly reveals, that constitution resonates with an intense particularity.[5] It not only symbolizes the identity of a nation and a people but it is commonly taken as creating that very identity. What is more, the constitution is elevated in the performance of these functions to a 'sacred' and 'transcendent' realm. All of which, rather obviously, sustains the authority of the constitution, both its own intrinsic authority and the authority of the law derived from it. But the constitution of the United States is about more than particular identity. It also comprehends, perhaps more conspicuously than any other constitution, a certain necessary universality.

Constitutions are creatures of modernity. What Foucault called the 'age of codes and constitutions', or Poggi the 'constitutional state' provided, from the late eighteenth century, new origins of authority and legitimacy within occidental political society.[6] In accommodating the 'principle of the people as constituent power' in revolutionary France, Palmer finds that 'national sovereignty, equality of rights, and universality of free citizenship were the most prominent features of the new design'.[7] The thwarting of France's ambition to be the first 'universal nation' left a contradiction within the design between the particularity of the nation and the universality of the now sovereign subject from which the authority of the constitution was supposed to derive—that new subject freed from the burdens of ascribed identity, or indeed from any limited identity whatsoever. The resolution of this contradiction involved the elevation of the design itself as universal, with certain nations and their people becoming its repository and vanguard.[8] The United States has rarely shrunk from the burden of a certain pre-eminence in all this.[9] In Corwin's elegant history of origins, the constitution of the United States is revealed

[5] Ch. 1, *supra*.

[6] M. Foucault, *The History of Sexuality Vol. 1: An Introduction* (Harmondsworth, 1981), 89: G. Poggi, *The Development of the Modern State: A Sociological Introduction* (London, 1978) ch. 5.

[7] R. Palmer, *The Age of the Democratic Revolution: A Political History of Europe and America, 1760–1800* (Princeton, New Jersey, 1959), 500.

[8] The point is extensively developed in my chapter ' "We Know What It Is When You Do Not Ask Us": Nationalism as Racism', in P. Fitzpatrick (ed.), *Nationalism, Racism and the Rule of Law* (Aldershot, 1995).

[9] See e.g. H. Commager, *The Empire of Reason: How Europe Imagined and America Realized the Enlightenment* (New York, 1977).

as a fusion of the sovereignty of a particular people with their embodying universal rights enshrined in a transcendent legality.[10]

The blunt argument of my essay is that this kind of resolution is made possible only through the formation of modern, occidental identity in a process not just of universal or comprehensive inclusion but also one of invidious and persistent exclusion.[11] With its disavowal of any source of identity external to itself, modernity elevates its putative universality as the new transcendent. As universal, identity can now have no positive limits and would, without more, lack coherence. It can no longer take identity through some mythic sameness with a transcendent model outside of itself. Rather, identity and its limits are generated from within, as it were, by constituting identity as universal in opposition to what is exceptional to its universality. What is 'other' to the universal can only be absolutely, irredeemably other. It must remain in a distinct region, quite 'outside' the realm of the universal, and remain as a point of constant opposition to it. This dynamic inevitably results in the 'failure' of identity as universal. Identity must exclude the other, and so be non-universal, in order to be universal. Identity then, to borrow from Karl Miller's account of the double, is characterized by 'an innate dissociability'.[12] It cannot be encompassed in an original correspondence to some thing(s) which would tell us what it positively 'is'. On the contrary, identity as universal, formed in relation to the excluded other, is identity formed in terms of what it is not. In short, those characters which are contrary to an identity's positive, or posited, being are attributed to the excluded and the identity takes coherence in opposition to them.

The truly impossible identity ultimately becomes that of the excluded. Not only is the 'innate dissociability' of identity itself attributed to the excluded, but the resulting incoherence of the excluded typifies all that as yet detracts from the completed perfection of identity. The excluded, the carriers of difference, have thence to be exhorted and worked on constantly to become the same, to enter the realm of the universal. But if the excluded were to cross the primal divide and become included and the same, an occidental identity dependent on exclusion and difference would disintegrate. So, as well as becoming the same, the excluded are required to be utterly exceptional. In all, the excluded are required to achieve what they never can achieve, to be what they never can be. As exceptional and absolutely different, the excluded cannot change and be other than what

[10] E. Corwin, 'The "Higher Law" Background of American Constitutional Law Parts I and II' (1928) 42 *Harvard LR* 149 and 365.

[11] More detail can be found in Fitzpatrick (1995) *op. cit.*; and P. Fitzpatrick, *The Mythology of Modern Law* (London, 1992).

[12] K. Miller, *Doubles: Studies in Literary History* (Oxford, 1987), 24.

they are. In opposing the ability of occidental identity to change and progress, the excluded are afflicted by stasis and stagnation, by iron rule and inflexible order. The enlightened order and disciplined stability of an elect identity is, in turn, set against the excluded as chaotic, fickle and merely spontaneous. To accommodate such contradiction, the excluded become intrinsically incoherent and diverse—and conveniently opaque and mysterious.

In its ambiguity, the title of my essay—'The Constitution of the Excluded'—is meant to encapsulate this process of forming identity and to relate the process to the constitution of the United States. It thus deals, in a rather different vein, with the issue of the equal protection of minority groups discussed by Trevor Allan in chapter two. The constitution is a mode of constituting the excluded whilst itself being a construct that is of the excluded because its identity is dependent on them. This line of argument will be elaborated in two historical tranches. The first and most extensive considers 'the Indian' as a point and figure of exclusion. It focuses mainly on a formative period in the early nineteenth century when the Supreme Court created what became known as Indian law. Indian law, as we shall see, is about more than Indians. Despite its oft-asserted marginality, Indian law proves to be central to the whole constitutional and legal order. There follows a coda, providing support for that analysis, on the 'Insular Cases' of the late nineteenth and early twentieth centuries, cases generated by the perplexities of colonial acquisition under a professedly democratic and liberal constitution.

As for lessons, there are several and they will simply be previewed here. In a general and obvious way, there will be lessons for constitutional and legal theory. The claims to British or English exceptionalism in this area would be denied. As the incantations of the standard textbooks would still have it, the identity and authority of the British constitution are grounded in assumptions about its continuity. These assumptions have sustained a hierarchic authority and blunted the popular and egalitarian dimensions of the English revolutions of the seventeenth century, at least as far as domestic constitutional consumption is concerned. But as Corwin shows so vividly, in making a point reiterated by many of the contributors to this volume, it was these subordinated aspects of the British constitution that had such a large impact in the formation of its counterpart in the United States; the constitutional ideals exported there were those of the revolutionary constitution of Coke and Locke and, he could have added, Milton.[13] So, my intention is to engage with a general dynamic of exclusion in the formation of occidental constitutions, to engage with what has to be separated out or purified so as to constitute unity in division, order in

[13] Corwin *op. cit.* And see Loveland's introductory chapter above.

violence, and coherence in dissociation. It may be thought that there are more immediate lessons to be derived from the relation between the included and the excluded, lessons about effective rights to equal treatment or about measures of reform to overcome discrimination. There are such lessons, as we shall see, but in my account they are greatly complicated by the foundational nature of exclusion. The effects of exclusion are not those of some passing defect, some minor incompleteness, in an otherwise integral instrument or project. The constitution is fractured in exclusion and persistently ambivalent. To borrow from Foley's not dissimilar concerns, we are here dealing not with a constitutional settlement but with 'constitutional unsettlement'.[14]

THE CONSTRUCTION OF 'THE INDIAN'

The Indian as a construct has, especially in its North American setting, been a formative figure in creating the identity of the Occident and of its law. This is something explored elsewhere.[15] The story is resumed here in its relation to the constitution of the United States as foundational of a legal order. That may not seem a propitious beginning since the Indian was and is little mentioned in the constitution and, in marked contrast to the slave, was not conspicuously present in Convention debates. Furthermore, much of the law that regulates Indian people is extra-constitutional and uncertain in its legal origins. But in my argument this is saying something significant about the constitution and about the legal system that it supposedly founds. The Indian is a mode of exclusion and division through which the constitutional and legal system acquires identity.

In terms of legal regulation, the Indian appears explicitly once and briefly in the constitution.[16] This is in the commerce clause giving Congress the power 'to regulate commerce with foreign nations, and among the several States, and with the Indian tribes'.[17] The inclusion of 'Indian tribes' was almost incidental.[18] The commerce power was used to support intrusive regulation of Indian affairs, covering the sale of liquor for example.[19] That part of the commerce power relating to Indian tribes provided some support for an unbounded regulatory ethos since it was taken to be 'as broad and free from restrictions as that to regulate

[14] M. Foley, *The Silence of Constitutions: Gaps, 'Abeyances' and Political Temperament in the Maintenance of Government* (London, 1989) ch. 5.

[15] Fitzpatrick (1992) *op. cit.*, 76–91; R. Williams, *The American Indian in Western Legal Thought: The Discourses of Conquest* (New York, 1990).

[16] Provision is also made for the electoral apportionment of representatives 'excluding Indians not taxed' in Art. 1 s. 2 and Amendment 14 s. 2.

[17] Art. I, s. 8, cl. 3.

[18] See E. Dumbauld *The Constitution of The United States* (Norman, Oklahoma, 1964), 111.

[19] *United States* v. *Forty-Three Gallons of Whiskey* (1876) 93 US 188.

commerce with foreign nations'.[20] But this power could not support the pervasive controls, extending well beyond commerce, which were eventually assumed over Indian people. Nor could the only other constitutional source adduced to found relations with Indian people, the treaty clause. This gave the President 'power, by and with the advice and consent of the Senate, to make treaties'.[21] Indian 'tribes' were accorded a sovereign status for the purpose of entering into such treaties. They were, however, kept within range of regulation. The commerce clause was taken to justify distinguishing 'Indian tribes' from 'foreign nations' and the distinction was refined, and Indian people reduced to 'domestic dependent nations', in *Cherokee Nation* v. *Georgia*.[22]

In this case the Cherokee nation sought redress against a depredatory State of Georgia. To gain access to the national legal system they sought to rely on the constitutional provision whereby the original jurisdiction of the Federal Courts extends 'to controversies . . . between a State, or the citizens thereof, and foreign states, citizens or subjects'.[23] Indian tribes were held not to be 'foreign states' within that clause and the Cherokee were thus denied relief on jurisdictional grounds. Although, in the words of Chief Justice Marshall, the Cherokee tribe was 'capable of managing its own affairs and governing itself' the tribe also 'looked to our government for protection' as would a 'ward' or someone in a 'state of pupillage':

> They and their country are considered by foreign nations, as well as by ourselves, as being so completely under the sovereignty and dominion of the United States, that any attempt to acquire their lands, or to form a political connection with them, would be considered by all as an invasion of our territory, and an act of hostility.[24]

The Indian was thus excluded from the constitutional and legal realm as a distinct sovereign entity yet included as a 'domestic, dependent nation', or as a 'ward'.

The Supreme Court found support for this strange and ambivalent constitutional status in some supposed doctrines of a supposedly international law. This was an immensely convenient international law which at the same time as the foundational 'Indian cases' in the Supreme Court, the early nineteenth century, 'started contracting into a regional (purely European) legal system, abandoning its centuries-old tradition of universality based on the natural law doctrine. . . . International law shrank to regional dimensions though it still carried the label of universality'.[25] This thesis of radical discontinuity is now often advanced

20 *United States* v. *Forty-Three Gallons of Whiskey* (1876) 93 US 194.

21 Art. II, s. 2, cl. 2.

22 (1831) 30 US (5 Pet.) 1.

23 Art. III, s. 2, cl. 1.

24 *Cherokee op. cit.*., 16–18.

25 C. Alexandrowicz, *An Introduction to the History of the Law of Nations in the East Indies* (Oxford, 1967), 2.

but it is also somewhat overdrawn.[26] It sets the 'natural universality of the law of nations' against a straightened universality arrogated to itself by Europe and confirmed in its claims by the 'writers of the positivist school in the nineteenth century'.[27] Without subscribing to the potted genealogies of the trade, which would trace an unbroken line of development in international law from beyond ancient Greece until now, there are, for our purposes, significant continuities into the modern period. Ancestor figures such Vitoria and Grotius are readily relied on to support the universal range of the law of nations, but closer observation shows this to be a qualified resort. The law of nations did not extend confidently beyond those taken to have the attributes of civilization. Where the civilization was heathen or barbarian, it was considered to be inadequate and much in need of conversion to standards typified by Europe.[28] The supposedly universal law of nations reflected, supported, and found explicit justification in the imperial practices of occidental powers. The parallels between all this and an imperial international law of the nineteenth century are obvious yet they also provoke some observation of differences. The standards of civilization in the nineteenth century were confined to virtues of an explicitly European kind.[29] The range of included 'nations' was thence bluntly reduced. True, peoples now rejected did retain the beatific prospect of conversion, of becoming the same as the elect nations, but they were also and at the same time fundamentally excluded. There is no longer an encompassing natural law within which all find a place. Only the included now have a rightful place and it is their actions or their usages, rather than a gregarious natural law, which produce the self-serving requirements of international law. Inclusiveness now becomes exclusiveness and the excluded become definitively so.

In the setting of the United States, the departure from natural law is attenuated in a way that comes to figure significantly in the so-called Indian cases. The demiurge here is Locke who, so Corwin finds, 'having transmuted the law of nature into the rights of men, . . . next converts them into the rights of ownership'.[30] Being natural rights they should of course inhere in all 'men'. Necessary distinctions had to be drawn, however. Such rights could for Locke only be fully enjoyed by those who enter into political society, the 'Civiliz'd part of Mankind'.[31] It is the entry

[26] The thesis now appears even in some of the textbooks: see M. Shaw *International Law* (Cambridge: 1986), 26.

[27] Alexandrowicz *op. cit.*, 57.

[28] See F. de Vitoria, *De Indis* Sect. III paras. 6 & 10 (xxxix & xli), the app. to J. B. Scott, *The Spanish Origin of International Law: Francisco de Vitoria and His Law of Nations* (Oxford, 1934) and H. Grotius *De Jure Belli ac Pacis I* (Sijthoff, 1919), 28.

[29] See G. Gong *The Standard of 'Civilization' in International Society* (Oxford, 1984), 46.

[30] Corwin *op. cit.*, 391.

[31] J. Locke *The Second Treatise on Government* (1690) paras. 30 & 87.

into political society which secures ownership: 'The great and *chief end* therefore, of Mens uniting into Commonwealths, and putting themselves under Government, *is the Preservation of their Property*'.[32] This blessed state was constitutively contrasted with the condition of those in the state of Nature who had an inadequately engaged relation to land:

> For I aske whether in the wild woods and uncultivated waste of America left to Nature, without any improvement, tillage or husbandry, a thousand acres will yield the needy and wretched inhabitants as many conveniences of life as ten acres of equally fertile land doe in Devonshire where they are well cultivated?[33]

Those who lacked as cultivators were, for Locke, lacking in reason also, and since reason was a necessary attribute of being 'men', the sufficiency of the Indian on that score had also to be doubted.[34]

We can begin to relate this baneful scene to the constitution and to Indian law through invoking the enigmatic figure of Vitoria. As well as providing a paternal origin of the discipline in standard accounts of international law, Vitoria is often taken as the source of Indian law.[35] This must be because decisions of the Supreme Court accord with his views rather than because of explicit judicial reliance on them. The presence yet absence of Vitoria points to an incongruence at the core of the enterprise of settlement. The main point of retrospective origin and legal validation of that enterprise is to be found in the judgments of Chief Justice Marshall in a series of 'Indian cases' in the early nineteenth century. In these he propounded a doctrine of discovery derived from international law so as to justify the imperious European occupation of the land. I will look firstly and briefly at that doctrine in the Supreme Court before considering the uses and abuses of Vitoria.

The Indian cases

From the practices of imperial states, Marshall derived a notion that Indian people were 'excluded . . . from intercourse with any other European potentate than the first discoverer of the coast of the particular region claimed'.[36] This so-called doctrine of discovery was also viewed by

[32] Locke, para. 124 (original emphasis).

[33] *Id.*, para. 37.

[34] See P. Hulme 'The Spontaneous Hand of Nature: Savagery, Colonialism and the Enlightenment' in P. Hulme and L. Jordanova (eds.), *The Enlightenment and its Shadows* (London, 1990), 30. The 'nature' of natural rights which attach to all 'men' and that 'nature' which insidiously excludes the Indian can perhaps only be reconciled in racism: cf. H. Bracken, 'Philosophy and Racism' (1978) 8 *Philosophia* 241.

[35] See F. Cohen, *The Legal Conscience: Selected Papers of Felix S. Cohen* (New Haven, 1960), 230–52: P. Shattuck & J. Norgren, *Partial Justice: Federal Indian Law in a Liberal Constitutional System* (Providence, 1991), 26. For Vitoria see n. 28 above.

[36] *Worcester* v. *Georgia* (1832) 31 US (6 Pet.) 515, 559.

Marshall as one which 'gave to the nation making the discovery the sole right of acquiring the soil from natives and establishing settlements upon it'.[37] He extended that right to accommodate 'absolute appropriation' and 'annexation'.[38] He also interpreted it so as to prevent the 'sovereign' Indian groups from entering into relations directly with foreign nations and to derogate from their sovereignty by denying 'their power to dispose of the soil at their will'.[39] In short 'discovery gave exclusive title to those who made it' leaving Indian people with at best a subordinate and fragile 'Indian title of occupancy'.[40] Yet Marshall also came to see Indian people as retaining 'their original natural rights' to the land.[41]

This is not the last contradiction we will find in the Court's judgments but, for present purposes, it is the most significant, and it is one that the resort to Vitoria illuminates. It has to be remarked at the outset that for contradiction thus to survive the ministrations of international law is an achievement. The right of exclusive relation to Indian people which this doctrine of discovery gave to the settlers was precipitately derived from the 'usage' of the imperial powers in acting that way, not excluding in this the usage of the United States itself.[42] If this distinctly self-serving scheme were not sufficient, there is usually adequate variety in international law and its sustaining usages to justify imperial appropriation. So whilst it could be argued that Marshall's doctrine of discovery was contrary to some versions of international law, there was also an abundance of available authority supporting even more draconic versions of discovery, ones that would deny Indian rights completely.[43]

Vitoria silently provides a necessary humanity for Marshall's less draconic doctrine, a humanity asserted in Vitoria's opposition to the more predatory and more resolutely genocidal among the Spanish colonists of Central and South America. In distinguishing Spanish settlement from other forms of acquisition—including acquisition by conquest and the full ownership bestowed by the law of nations on the first occupant of deserted regions—Vitoria found that 'the Indies' had not been 'without an owner': the Indians had rights of dominion over the land and, furthermore, they were basically human beings even if ones with considerable, but remediable, shortcomings.[44] These rights had, however, to adjust to the rights of

[37] *Johnson* v. *M'Intosh* (1823) 21 US (8 Wheat.) 543, 573.

[38] *Cherokee op. cit.*, 22.

[39] *Johnson op. cit.*, 574.

[40] *Id.*, 574 & 587.

[41] *Worcester op. cit.*, 599.

[42] As to the United States see J. Wunder *'Retained By The People': A History of American Indians and the Bill of Rights* (Oxford, 1994), 19 & 22.

[43] L. Green 'Claims to Territory in Colonial America' in L. Green & O. Dickason (eds.), *The Law of Nations and the New World* (Alberta, 1988).

[44] Vitoria *op. cit.* n. 27 Sect. I, para. 24 (xiii–iv). For an absorbing account of Vitoria on these things see A. Pagden, *European Encounters with the New World* (New Haven and London, 1993) ch. 4.

all people, including the Spanish, to travel, trade and, in the cause of Christianity, to proselytize.[45] Such rights could not be aggressively asserted unless they were aggressively resisted by the Indians.[46] There were, however, limits to the uses of Vitoria. He provided no warrant for an inexorable imperialism. And in recognizing Indian dominion over their lands, he recognized too much for the purposes of the European settlers of North America. What is more, the rights of the *barbari* were grounded in the law of nations as natural law. All of which may explain the muted nature of his reception.

No less than this natural law, however, the Lockean natural rights of ownership, so seminal in the formation and development of the constitution, intrinsically extended to all 'men'. But in this expanse, such rights would negative the imperial settlement of the land. There was an alternative, not uncommonly resorted to elsewhere, of denying that the natives were within the ambit of humanity and hence had no rights of ownership. This alternative was, however, not available here because Indian people had to have rights and some humanity thrust upon them so as to give effect to the transfers of land and to the treaties they had transacted with the governments of the settlers. Without this, the basis of settlement would be undermined. There was a further complication. Because of a 'political compromise agreed on by the Founders for the good of the new nation' the natural rights of Indians to transfer their land was confined to a transfer to the government of the United States.[47]

Ultimately, Marshall could not reconcile all this. He comments on the denial of the Indians' right to transfer 'the absolute title . . . of their lands to others' in this way:

> However this restriction may be opposed to natural right, and to the usages of civilized nations, yet, if it be indispensable to the system under which the country has been settled, and be adapted to the actual conditions of the two people, it may perhaps be supported by reason, and certainly cannot be rejected by courts of justice.[48]

I will return to the sheer expediency of this resolution later and simply note for now that the incoherence of the doctrine of discovery and of the foundational terms of settlement comes inevitably to reside in the Indians themselves. Their 'actual condition' is a degraded and recalcitrant one—'the condition of a people with whom it was impossible to mix, and who could not be governed as a distinct entity'.[49] It was the Indians' own irresolute condition that required the ambivalent and truncated rendition

[45] Vitoria *op. cit.* Sect. III, paras. 3, 4, 9 & 10 (xxvii–viii & xli–ii).
[46] *Id.*, Sect. III, paras. 6 & 12 (xxxix & xlii).
[47] Williams *op. cit.*, 231.
[48] *Johnson op. cit.*, 591–2.
[49] *Id.*, 590.

of their rights to land. They could not be 'mixed' with, could not become the same and have the same rights as everyone else, but neither could they remain as distinct and different and retain their own natural and integral rights to land.

There were other and alternative means of acquiring title in international law—the settlement of a putative wilderness and conquest—which were judicially invoked either in substitution for discovery or, contradictorily, in support of it. This flexibility was made possible because even the oracle Marshall was not always consistent and because there were other judges on the Supreme Court even if their existence is now little remarked. Thus Marshall found that the impossible Indians could neither be mixed with nor governed as a distinct entity because they were 'fierce savages . . . whose subsistence was drawn chiefly from the forest' and to 'leave them in possession of their country, was to leave the country a wilderness'.[50] In that spirit, Chief Justice Taney applied an unqualified doctrine of *terra nullius*:

> The native tribes who were found on this continent at the time of its discovery have never been acknowledged or treated as independent nations by the European governments,nor regarded as the owners of the territories they respectively occupied. On the contrary, the whole continent was divided and parcelled out, and granted by the governments of Europe as if it had been vacant and unoccupied land, and the Indians continually held to be, and treated as, subject to their dominion and control.[51]

In a refinement of the doctrine of *terra nullius*, the grievous inability of Indian people to cover the land with furrow and fence was often used judicially to suggest or assert that their rights to land were less than resolved and hence inferior to the rights of the settlers or of their governments. Indian people were repeatedly and, for what it may be worth, inaccurately described as mere hunters who left the land 'a wilderness', and who would inevitably have to give way before agriculture and industriousness.[52] In terms of the ancestor figures of international law, Vattel was much relied on judicially to support this refinement: for him, it was not simply a matter of when 'a nation finds a country uninhabited and without an owner, it may lawfully take possession of it'; a nation may also occupy a territory 'in which are to be found only wandering tribes whose small numbers cannot populate the whole country' since 'their uncertain occupancy of these vast regions cannot be held as a real and lawful taking of possession'; 'merely . . . hunting, fishing and gathering wild fruits' was a profligate use of land and 'savages' indulging in such means of subsistence

[50] *Id.*
[51] *United States* v. *Rogers* (1846) 45 US (4 How.) 567, 572.
[52] *Cherokee op. cit.*, 23 and *Forty-Three Gallons op. cit.*, 196.

can justly be restricted 'within narrower bounds'.[53] Indeed, such arguments were used to justify legislation for the 'removal' of Indian people from their land.[54]

Settlement was also justified by amplifying the claims of conquest. Again, Marshall becomes the carrier of a revealing incompatibility: to 'convert' discovery into conquest 'may appear . . . extravagant', but if that is done, and the settlers hold their 'property' on that basis, 'it becomes the law of the land, and cannot be questioned'; 'conquest is a title which the courts of the conqueror cannot deny'.[55] But elsewhere, when expounding on the aptness of the doctrine of discovery, Marshall found that there had been no conquest by the European nations to whose rights the United States succeeded.[56] For Marshall's scheme of things, the distinction between discovery and conquest had to be maintained since, with conquest, the outcome is that 'the conquered inhabitants can be blended with the conquerors or safely governed as a distinct people'.[57] But, as we have just seen, Marshall could allow of neither consummation. Since Marshall recognized, as we have also just seen, that the rights asserted by the settlers were those of conquest, the settlement and its ensuing law assumed legitimate existence only in fictive terms. More robust rights were discovered by other justices: the United States was the successor to the British who had simply been 'conquerors' and had assumed full 'sovereignty'.[58] It must then remain a puzzle as to what the epic 'Indian wars' of the United States' first century were all about. The corresponding denial of the rights of Indian people was perceived as placing them in that condition of wardship and pupillage we considered earlier: no longer having adequate rights, 'they look to our government for protection; rely upon its kindness and its power'.[59] The duty of protection required in turn the regulation of what land remained to Indian people and the erection of colonial-style restrictions on their engaging in the wider economy.[60]

In the first half of the nineteenth century a legal *mélange* of rights and restrictions had been put together to support the exercise of a control and 'guardianship' the scope of which was to increase enormously in the second half, until it was indistinguishable from that all-encompassing responsible trusteeship exercised by more forthright contemporary colonial powers. Like the ravages of those powers, trusteeship was used to justify what would otherwise have resembled fraud and theft less

[53] As quoted in Green *op. cit.*, 74.
[54] Shattuck & Norgren *op. cit.*, 54–5 & 129–30.
[55] *Johnson op. cit.*, 588 & 591.
[56] *Worcester op. cit.*, 544–5.
[57] *Johnson op. cit.*, 589–90.
[58] See Johnson J in *Cherokee op. cit.*, 23–6.
[59] *Id.*, 17.
[60] Shattuck & Norgren *op. cit.*, 54–5 & 129–30.

equivocally. Amongst the types of controls the United States found necessary to protect its charges, the disposition of land was of some importance. In a considerable feat of legerdemain, the federal government as trustee—a trustee not held by the courts to the exacting standards of its private law counterparts—could and did readily dispose of Indian land as the act of the Indian people themselves.[61] This outcome was indicative of a sovereignty that had become compatible with its antithesis. There was little restraining the trustee in the relationship since the courts assumed a sufficient protection in that 'the United States would be governed by such considerations of justice as would control a Christian people in their treatment of an ignorant and dependent race'.[62] This corresponded to an influential view in international law at the time that any rights of the colonized are best left to the benign dispensations of the colonist.[63]

Towards the end of the nineteenth century, there was also an ostensible shift more from the exclusion to the inclusion of the Indian with the advent of professedly humane 'reform' aimed at 'assimilation', including 'bringing law to the Indian'.[64] The measure which now tends to be seen as synonymous with reform was the General Allotment Act of 1887 (The Dawes Act). This provided a method for individualizing title to Indian land as well as for conferring citizenship of the United States on the holders of such title and on Indian people who 'assimilated'. Yet, because of the burgeoning responsibilities of trusteeship, a trusteeship compatible with Indian people losing under this Act the bulk of their remaining lands, the legislation as amended made such title and citizenship subject to lengthy periods of restriction. This combined inclusion and exclusion of Indian people is compactly illustrated by another prominent measure of reform and assimilation, the Major Crimes Act of 1885. It 'brought law to the Indian' by taking certain major crimes out of the tribal arena and bringing them within the national jurisdiction. A provision in the Bill extending civil law in this way was, however, withdrawn, leaving Indian people in the classic position of the colonized—subject to the criminal law of the colonists but, in the name of protection, denied access to their civil law and to the subversive opportunities it provided for engaging in the colonial economy. The only reason officially given for maintaining the duality of inclusion and exclusion was the inadequacy of the Indian, still tied to a primordial existence and incapable of wholly attaining a civilized state.[65]

Although more adequacy has since been allowed Indian people, the duality persists. The bestowal of citizenship on them in 1924 and the Indian

[61] *Id.*, 115–21.

[62] *Beecher* v. *Wetherby* (1877) 95 US 517, 525–6.

[63] J. Westlake, 'John Westlake on the Title to Sovereignty', in P. Curtin (ed.), *Imperialism* (London, 1971), 47 & 50–1.

[64] See Shattuck & Norgren *op. cit.*, 86 & 82–102.

[65] *Id.*, 90–1.

Civil Rights Act of 1968 can be seen as belated extensions of constitutional rights and safeguards, or of something roughly equivalent to them. But these measures of inclusion remain typically inhibited, leaving an extant element of exclusion. For example, the Supreme Court has decided that the Act of 1968, although extending some guarantees of the Bill of Rights to Indian people, has left it to tribal governments rather than the federal courts to determine questions of adherence to rights and safeguards.[66] Nor has the assumption of greater adequacy eliminated extensive control of 'Indian affairs', including Indian lands.[67] And Congress still maintains, only marginally less free of constitutional restraint, the plenary power over Indian people assumed through imperial nineteenth century precedents.

The formative 'Indian cases' are still often and readily resorted to as foundation authority but now only briefly.[68] There is unease when it comes to talking of the sources of 'Indian law'.[69] There are doubtless proprieties to be observed here, limits to an explicit recognition of imperial underpinnings. But it may also be that there is too much of law's lost origins beneath the legal patina that would challenge its now 'whitened' identity.[70] I will next bring together and summarize the relation between the constitution and the Indian around this theme of lost origins.

The 'Indian cases' mark the consolidation of a law that is now positive but fused inseparably with a national and imperial identity, all of which was brought about to the accompaniment of orders perceptibly passing. Chief Justice Marshall, the received hero in all this, in mapping out his approach in a crucial case saw that it would be necessary to examine not only 'those principles of abstract justice, which the Creator of all things has impressed on the mind of his creature man, and which are admitted to regulate, in a great degree, the rights of civilized nations . . . but those principles also which our own government has adopted in the particular case, and given us as the rule for our decision'.[71] The deific invocation was but a tribute absence pays to presence. This was 'nature's God', in terms of the Declaration of Independence, and the rights of nature extended to all humanity. The commitment of a putative United States to natural rights was especially intense since natural rights were taken to have impelled the revolutionary struggle and to have been incorporated, at least 'in a great degree', within the constitution. But to have extended those rights to Indians, beyond Marshall's vaguely evoked limits of the 'civilized', would

[66] *Santa Clara Pueblo* v. *Martinez* (1978) 436 US 49.

[67] See Shattuck & Norgren *op. cit.*, 132–3.

[68] *Santa Clara op. cit.*, 72; *Merrion* v. *Jicarilla Apache Tribe* (1982) 455 US 10, 155.

[69] See M. Ball, 'Constitutions, Courts, Indian Tribes' (1987) 1 *American Bar Foundation Research Journal* 3, 50.

[70] Cf. J. Derrida, 'White Mythology: Metaphor and Text in History', in J. Derrida, *Margins of Philosophy* (Chicago, 1982).

[71] *Johnson op. cit.*, 572.

have ruptured what could be called the national settlement—both the settlement of the land and the settlement between the states and the national government.[72] These were inextricably linked. In particular, Indian people had 'natural rights' in their land and these had impeccable precedents in natural law and the law of nations.[73] In one judicial strategy, such rights were adroitly neutralized by recourse to nature herself. This involved following a line which connected ideas of progress or improvement from the eighteenth century with ideas of evolutionary development from the nineteenth. Indian people were typically seen to be in the 'hunter state' (hunting for many of them was more a consequence of being expelled from their agricultural land) and thus would have to give way before an 'advance' to the agricultural state; that 'would have a tendency to impair' their natural right 'and ultimately to destroy it altogether'.[74] That outcome was, without more, inadequate because the Indian could still respond to the call of a universal humanity and advance, acquiring full(er) rights to their land and thus undermine the national settlement. Johnson J came close to the whole truth of it when he remarked that the Indians were 'a race of hunters' and 'it is not easy to see how their advancement beyond that state of society could ever have been promoted, or, perhaps, permitted, consistently with the unquestioned rights of the States or United States, over the territory within their limits'.[75] Wise and benign attempts to advance the Indians beyond the hunter state had been 'altogether baffled' by 'their inveterate habits and deep seated enmity'.[76] The judgments thence, are replete with the inadequacy of the Indians, their wildness, lawlessness, cruelty, stupidity, and so, considerably, on—the usual catalogue.

In all—the bottom line—the Indians had to be included so that their lands could be acquired and controlled by the settler governments. They had to be excluded as different and savage so as not themselves to have or be able to acquire rights which would counteract that scheme of things. The resulting ambivalence and impossibility of their position, its lack of any clear or enduring content, is strongly indicated by the constant resort to the courts to this day for determinations of what that content may be in particular situations.

That impossible position was ultimately sustained in the judicial assertion of two positivisms. One of them was of the legal variety. The Supreme Court elevated a law which, in its solitary sufficiency, could stand against and override not just Lockean natural right but also that general

[72] Williams *op. cit.*, 306–8.
[73] See *Johnson op. cit.*, 563 and Williams *op. cit.*, 322–3 n. 132.
[74] Johnson J in *Cherokee op. cit.*, 23.
[75] *Id.*
[76] *Id.*, 24.

natural law basic to constitutional origins in the United States.[77] The subordination and dispossession of Indian people and the spurning of any restraining natural right was judicially perceived as the outcome, sometimes unfortunate but always unavoidable, of the law itself. It was certainly not an understatement for Marshall to say of the plight of the Indian people revealed in *Cherokee Nation* v. *Georgia* that 'if the courts were permitted to indulge their sympathies, a case better calculated to excite them can scarcely be imagined'.[78] A people 'sinking beneath our superior policy, our arts and our arms' are left with but a 'remnant' of their land.[79] That remnant was now to be taken from them through a massive violence and fraudulently enacted law of the State of Georgia. But to assume jurisdiction over this matter would, as we have seen, require the Cherokee to be either citizens or foreign states in terms of the Constitution and they were neither. They were both included and excluded in some other, necessarily impalpable terms. (It is never possible 'to come to terms' with the settler, to know where one 'stands'.[80]) To do anything about all this, according to Marshall, 'savours too much of the exercise of political power to be within the proper province of the judicial department'; 'this is not the tribunal which can redress the past or prevent the future'.[81] 'With the morality of the case', professed Johnson, 'I have no concern; I am called upon to consider it as a legal question'.[82] In the end it becomes solely the 'government' which has 'given us . . . the rule for our decision'.[83]

The judicial fiat elevating a legal positivism was complemented by a further variety. Whatever lay beyond law and its rule was intractable fact. Law would have to adjust to what Marshall called 'the actual state of things'.[84] That realism accompanied Marshall's recognition that the uses made of the doctrine of discovery, the conversion of its limited effects to those of conquest, may have been 'extravagant'. This did not vitiate the whole process but called for 'some new and different rule, better adapted to the actual state of things'.[85] This, as we saw, inevitably included being 'adapted to the condition of a people with whom it was impossible to mix, and who could not be governed as a distinct society'.[86] Such a condition and the apt imperial/legal response could be readily garnered out of Marshall's sweeping rendition of 'the history of America, from its discovery to the present day' and from the remarkable consistency of the

[77] e.g. the part of such natural law in the Declaration of Independence: C. Becker, *The Declaration of Independence: A Study in the History of Political Ideas* (New York, n.d.), 24–7.

[78] *Cherokee op. cit.*, 15.

[79] *Id.*

[80] One raises here, on a somewhat larger scale, the question of *locus standi* to which Peter Cane directs attention in a rather different context in ch. 5.

[81] *Cherokee op. cit.*, 20.

[82] *Id.*

[83] Marshall CJ in *Johnson op. cit.*, 572.

[84] *Id.*, 591.

[85] *Id.*

[86] *Id.*, 590.

claims of its various colonists.[87] For Johnson J, 'it cannot be questioned that the right of sovereignty, as well as soil, was notoriously asserted and exercised by the European discoverers. From that source we derive our rights . . .'.[88] That 'the Indian Territory is admitted to compose part of the United States' has to become simply manifest: 'in all our maps, geographical treaties, histories and laws, it is so considered'.[89] Such a mode of ascertaining the position of the Indian persists to this day.

This encompassing factuality was given some legal effect as international law, a variety of law which still managed the pre-modern feat of fusing law and fact. This international law now took positive identity in terms of its civilized opposition to those who were excluded in those same terms. The extraversion of the several sovereignties of a group of nation states—the bearers of civilization—became the foundation of international law and its content was provided by the 'usages' of those states and by the 'effectiveness' of their actions.[90] This closure, this wrapping up of the world, itself creates the position of the excluded as an inherently and enduringly deviant one. To secure this outcome, the Supreme Court could resort to all the vastness of European imperial history to contain the wildness of the Indian and to put the Indian in a colonized place. Then a scrupulous 'legal' formalism prevented its taking account of, say, the political savagery of the State of Georgia. There was, however, an ultimate element of factuality beyond even the indulgent expanse of international law. To refer again but summarily to Marshall's views, 'however extravagant' the departure from international law may be, and no matter whether the treatment of Indian people is 'opposed to natural right and to the usages of civilized nations', if the nation and its land have been settled on that contrary basis, then law cannot but unquestioningly accept that 'actual state of things'.[91]

The division of the world between law and fact, between the included and the excluded, between the lawful and the lawless was a division founded finally in force. The rights resulting from the actual state of things, said Marshall, 'have been maintained and established . . . by the sword', and 'it is not for the courts of this country to question the validity of this title, or to sustain one which is incompatible with it'.[92] And 'power, war, conquest, give rights which, after possession, are conceded by the world; and which can never be controverted by those on whom they descend'.[93]

[87] *Id.*, 575. [88] *Cherokee op. cit.*, 22. [89] *Id.*, 17.

[90] A. Carty, *The Decay of International Law?: A Reappraisal of the Limits of Legal Imagination in International Affairs* (Manchester, 1986) ch. 4.

[91] *Johnson op. cit.*, 591–2. [92] *Id.*, 588–9.

[93] *Worcester op. cit.*, 543. This is the most direct echo of Kant's point in the introductory quotation to this chapter. Marshall's formulation implies that this violence is preserved foundationally prior to the constitutional limitation of power.

The 'private and speculative opinions of individuals . . . respecting the original justice of the claim' are irrelevant.[94] Johnson J found the situation presented by the *Cherokee* case apt for an 'appeal . . . to the sword and to Almighty justice, and not to courts of law or equity. In the exercise of sovereign right, the sovereign is sole arbiter of his own justice. The penalty of wrong is war and subjugation'.[95] The law of the land, to borrow a phrase, could not question the 'momentous' national settlement which gave it being; that outcome 'is not now to be disturbed'.[96] Hence 'the right of society', conceived of as 'the nation', 'to prescribe those rules by which property may be acquired and preserved is not, and cannot be drawn into question'.[97] So, perhaps it may not be too 'extravagant' to discern in all this not only pioneering pronouncements of a positivist jurisprudence but also intimations of a 'sociology of law' or a 'politics of law' that would subordinate law instrumentally to the demands of society and nation.

THE INSULAR CASES

Imperial attitudes and origins were both challenged and confirmed in the so-called Insular Cases in the early part of the twentieth century.[98] The name 'Insular' seems to be derived from various islands which the United States came to rule—the Philippines, Puerto Rico and Hawaii—but it could just as accurately describe the attitudes of majorities on the Supreme Court as they delineated a national identity for the United States which for the most part could not extend to its new charges, who had thence to be essentially different and as such in need of subordination and guidance. The cases covered a complexity of issues but the central one was simple enough: could the island territories and their inhabitants be considered part of the United States. The reasons for posing the issue were also simple enough, the one of most relevance for my argument being whether these inhabitants came within the ambit of constitutional rights and safeguards. (I will also draw on cases dealing with other reasons, such as whether customs duty was to be levied on imports from territories.) The outcomes of the cases can be satisfyingly summarized as fitting my argument: the inhabitants were sometimes included and more often excluded, sometimes the same and more often different. My immediate concern with the Insular Cases, however, is the grounds for exclusion and

[94] Marshall CJ in *Johnson op. cit.*, 588.
[95] *Cherokee op. cit.*, 29.
[96] Marshall CJ in *Fletcher* v. *Peck* (1810) 10 US (6 Cranch) 87, 142.
[97] Marshall CJ in *Johnson op. cit.*, 572.
[98] See generally the excellent account in E. Rivera-Ramos, *The Legal Construction of American Colonialism: An Enquiry into the Constitutive Force of Law* (Ph.D. Dissertation, University College London, 1993) ch. 3.

the light these can throw on the rich jurisprudence of the cases affecting Indian people. With the exclusion of Indian people there were the pretexts of sovereign distinctness under the constitution and some difference extracted from certain nostrums of an imperial international law. Neither rationale was available, or at least relied on, for the colonizations involved in the Insular Cases. There appeared to be no reason why certain universal and self-evident truths should stop short in their application to the inhabitants of these territories, nor why constitutional rights and safeguards should not apply to them. The constitution, in the so-called territorial clause, empowered Congress 'to dispose of and make all needful rules and regulations respecting the territory or other property belonging to the United States'.[99] This, however, said nothing about the denial of rights and safeguards. Surely, for such a fundamental derogation, clear and explicit provision would be needed. It was not. As with Indian people, the Insular Cases gave Congress a power over the territories largely unrestrained by constitutional rights and safeguards.[100] In an impassioned dissent, Harlan J spelled out the immense implications of this: it meant that 'the will of Congress not the Constitution is the supreme law of the land . . . for certain peoples' now 'existing outside of the written Constitution by virtue of an unwritten law to be declared from time to time by Congress, which is itself a creature of that instrument'; the country had thus 'left the old ways of the fathers as defined by a written Constitution, and entered upon a new way', embracing 'a colonial system entirely foreign to the genius of and abhorrent to the principles that underlie and pervade the Constitution'.[101]

Majorities in these cases, however, purported to find other principles that underlie the constitution. The decisions relied on international law but of a somewhat different kind to that employed in the 'Indian cases'. The United States, as a national sovereign power, was taken to have the right to acquire territory and to determine what its relations with that territory would be.[102] Without such an unrestrained power, the United States could neither operate effectively in competition with other sovereign nations, nor effectively administer territories acquired in the international game.[103] Harlan J again provided a resounding response:

It was said that the United States is to become what is called a 'world power', and that if this Government intends to keep abreast of the times and be equal to the

[99] Art. III, s. 3, cl. 2.

[100] The culminating assertion of this power in the 'Indian cases' was *United States* v. *Kagama* (1885) 118 US 375.

[101] *Hawaii* v. *Mankichi* (1903) 190 US 197, 239–40.

[102] See the influential argument to that effect of White J in *Downes* v. *Bidwell* (1901) 182 US 244, 301–4.

[103] See *Dooley* v. *United States* (1901) 182 US 222, 232–3.

great destiny that awaits the American people, it must be allowed to exert all the power that other nations are accustomed to exercise. My answer is that the fathers never intended that the authority and influence of this nation should be exerted otherwise than in accordance with the Constitution.[104]

The Insular Cases, like their 'Indian' equivalents, attribute the necessity for all this to the lamentable condition of the subject people themselves. Such people could be 'utterly unfit for American citizenship' and often were; they were incapable of assuming 'the rights which peculiarly belong to the citizens of the United States'.[105] So, denial of the right to trial by jury, to take an example, had nothing to do with the challenge this procedure would pose to an authoritarian colonial rule and everything to do with the colonized being 'wholly unfitted to exercise the right'.[106] Congress had to act differently in the territories because the colonized themselves were different in 'race, habits, laws and custom'.[107] To the extent that this left people without constitutional rights and safeguards, a reassurance and substitute was provided by 'certain principles of natural justice inherent in the Anglo–Saxon character which need no expression in constitutions or statutes to give them effect or to secure dependencies against legislation manifestly hostile to their real interests'.[108] In sum, constitutional rights and safeguards are revealed as endowments of a racially inclusive community through their being rendered inapplicable to the racially excluded.

CONCLUSION

As we have seen, Indian people were excluded in terms similar to those found in the Insular Cases and rendered, as Harlan J put it in an 'Indian case', as 'a despised and rejected class of persons . . . not entitled to any of the rights, privileges, or immunities of citizens of the United States'.[109] Exclusion takes place at the defining edge of the whole constitutional and legal system. This darkened region may be glimpsed, and my general argument can be evoked, in two features commonly attributed to that 'Indian law' which is the legal creation and regulation of the Indian. One feature is the persistent incoherence of that law. There has been constant

[104] *Downes op. cit.*, 386. [105] *Id.*, 311 & 324.
[106] *Dorr* v. *United States* (1904) 195 US 138, 145. [107] *Downes op. cit.*, 282.
[108] *Id.*, 280. For an almost similar sentiment from the 'Indian cases' see n.61 above and the text accompanying it. There may be unwelcome resonances between such views and debates whether there is an 'unwritten constitution' or principles of constitutional interpretation 'so rooted in the traditions and conscience of our people as to be ranked as fundamental' to take a formulation from *Snyder v. Massachusetts* (1934) 291 US 97, 105.
[109] *Elk* v. *Wilkins* (1884) 112 US 94, 122–3.

lamentation about its inconsistency and intractable obscurity.[110] Such an Indian law seems to be capable of sustaining complete reversals of content and 'frequent wholesale restructuring' whilst accommodating these within the 'original principles' derived from the cases considered in this chapter.[111] Those original principles are themselves foundationally ambivalent. They call for the Indian to be included and the same yet, because of the coeval imperative of exclusion, such a consummation cannot be achieved. The resulting liminal state of the Indian is incapable of resolution and the law generated out of it cannot be anything but incoherent.

In occupying this position, the Indian was, as we saw, a carrier of the incoherence and ambivalence of the whole constitutional and legal system; this ascription may be perversely discerned in the second feature commonly attributed to Indian law, its insignificance. As Wunder remarks, the 'dominant society' often classifies 'Indian disputes as obscure and inconsequential'.[112] And Frickey has assembled a catalogue of epithets directed at 'federal Indian law cases by Justices themselves'; these cases are found to be 'crud' and 'peewee' cases, and worse.[113] All of which, in my argument, attests to the power of insignificance. As Douglas has shown, the 'purity' of ordering social classifications and identities can only be preserved in the face of 'danger'; the border areas of these classifications and identities are perilous and people placed there are perceived as dangerous.[114] That danger becomes most acute when such marginal people respond to the demand to be the same, or simply demonstrate the capacity to do so, and thereby challenge the integrity of identities founded on their being excluded. Hence there is the hysterical repression that meets the *évolue* in the colonial situation, or the denial of authenticity to the *évolue* who is allowed only a mimetic ability.[115] Or there is the infinitely disproportionate sense of threat induced by the migrations of people from the Third World to a Europe where they become 'dangerously similar', or where the terms of the difference attributed to them are contradicted or obfuscated.[116] For present purposes, a focal instance of this dangerous similarity can be extracted from the painstaking dissent of Thompson J in

[110] Wunder *op. cit.*, 3–4; P. Frickey, 'Marshalling Past and Present: Colonialism, Constitutionalism, and Interpretation in Federal Indian Law' (1994) 107 *Harvard LR* 381, 418 & 423; S. Harring, *Crow Dog's Case: American Indian Sovereignty, Tribal Law, and United States Law in the Nineteenth Century* (New York, 1994), 4.

[111] Shattuck & Norgren *op. cit.*, 23–4; Wunder *op. cit.*, 3.

[112] *Id.*

[113] Frickey *op. cit.*, 383.

[114] M. Douglas, *Purity and Danger: An Analysis of Concepts of Pollution and Taboo* (Harmondsworth, 1970) ch. 6.

[115] H. Bhabba, *The Location of Culture* (London, 1994) ch. 4.

Cherokee Nation v. *Georgia*.[117] He found 'that the Cherokees compose a foreign State within the sense and meaning of the Constitution, and constitute a competent party to maintain a suit against the State of Georgia'.[118] His main reason for so holding was that 'civilization and the establishment of a regular government' had 'been accomplished' by the Cherokee people.[119] And, indeed, constitutionally and legally, the Cherokee people had successfully adopted a model close to that of the United States itself. The offending laws of the State of Georgia were explicitly directed against that 'accomplishment': 'the laws of Georgia set out in the bill, if carried fully into operation, go the length of abrogating all of the laws of the Cherokees, abolishing their government, and entirely subverting their national character'.[120]

[116] J. Baudrillard, *The Transparency of Evil: Essays on Extreme Phenomena* (London, 1993), 129.
[117] *Cherokee op. cit.*, 50–80.
[118] *Id.*, 80.
[119] *Id.*, 72.
[120] *Id.*, 75.

9

The Importation of United States Free Speech Jurisprudence?*

ERIC BARENDT

IN the recent *Derbyshire* libel case,[1] perhaps the most important free speech decision in English legal history, the Court of Appeal and House of Lords relied significantly on United States' decisions. There were extensive references in the Court of Appeal judgements to the landmark ruling of the Supreme Court in *New York Times* v. *Sullivan,*[2] while Lord Keith in the Lords (like Balcombe LJ in the court below) quoted at length from a much earlier Illinois case outlawing libel actions by public authorities.[3] The courts here have now accepted that libel actions, and their threat, exercise a 'chilling effect' on freedom of speech and of the press, a principle long recognized on the other side of the Atlantic.[4] It is, however, premature to predict whether the law in England will follow the path trod by the US Supreme Court and outlaw, or at least discourage, libel actions by all public officials and figures.

What can be said is that the courts, and even more law reformers and pressure groups, will on occasion look to First Amendment jurisprudence to provide arguments how the common law principle of freedom of speech, discovered by the Lords in the *Derbyshire* case, should be developed. The United States case-law provides a standard by which we can examine not only our law of libel, but also the desirability of, say, provisions of our public order legislation, including those provisions criminalizing incitement to racial hatred,[5] or the wisdom of introducing a right of privacy. Indeed, some English judges may already be influenced by their awareness of US jurisprudence, for example, in exhibiting growing hostility in some

* This chapter is based on an article already published in *16 Sydney L. Rev* 149 [1994]. The author would like to thank the editors of the Review for permitting publication of this chapter.

[1] *Derbyshire County Council* v. *Times Newspapers Ltd.* [1993] AC 534, discussed by Eric Barendt, 'Libel and Freedom of Speech in English Law' [1993] *PL* 449.

[2] 376 US 254 (1964).

[3] *City of Chicago* v. *Tribune Co.* 139 NE 86 (1923).

[4] For an introduction to the different treatment of libel law in relation to free speech in England and US law, see F. Schauer, 'Social Foundations of the Law of Defamation' (1980) 1 *Jo. of Media Law and Practice* 3.

[5] Which is the subject of 11 in this volume.

contexts to prior restraints, and in their willingness to give freedom of the press increasing weight when applying the contempt of court 'strict liability' rule.[6] (The indirect influence of US law was also evident in the *Spycatcher* case.[7] Under the First Amendment it would have been impossible for the UK government to have prevented publication of Peter Wright's book in the United States, and the consequent availability of imported copies in this country made it impossible to sustain the argument that there was still a confidence to be preserved.)

English lawyers are not the only group likely to turn to the USA for ideas in this context. The Australian High Court in two decisions at the end of 1992 has 'found' a right to freedom of speech implicit in its Constitution.[8] In the remarkable *Political Ads* case it struck down legislation prohibiting political parties and candidates from advertising at election time on radio and television, while making some compensating provision for free time. The High Court made extensive reference to the leading US case, *Buckley* v. *Valeo*,[9] which had held limits on candidates' election expenditure incompatible with the First Amendment. Indeed, McHugh J went out of his way to find the US constitutional experience a better guide for Australia than the comparable laws in European countries, which generally look more favourably on such advertising regulation. As Ian Loveland has noted in the introductory chapter to this volume, the High Court's recent decision in *Theophanous* has embraced explicitly the *Sullivan* principle.[10]

It may be that the US decisions provide appropriate precedents for the Australian High Court to follow. There are significant similarities between the histories and culture of these two new world societies, which make it natural for Australia to adopt to some extent the institutions and legal principles of the USA. The principal argument of this essay is that it would be ill-advised for the courts and political branches of the UK **always** to follow this course in the context of freedom of speech and related freedoms. One obvious reason why a rigorous adherence to US law is most improbable is that legally we will be much more influenced, indeed controlled, by the very different jurisprudence of the European Court of

[6] See e.g. the judgments of Lord Denning MR and Lord Scarman in *AG* v. *BBC* [1981] AC 303 (arguing against the grant of an injunction to prevent the broadcast of a programme which might have prejudiced a claim for rating relief) and of Lord Taylor CJ. in *Ex p. Telegraph* [1993] 1 WLR 980 (refusing to uphold order postponing reporting of trial, on ground that no justification on facts for limiting open justice principle).

[7] *A-G* v. *Guardian Newspapers Ltd. (No. 2)* [1990] AC 109.

[8] *Nationwide News Pty. Ltd.* v. *Wills* (1992) 66 ALJR 658; *Australian Capital Television Pty Ltd.* v. *The Commonwealth* (1992) 66 ALJR 695 (subsequently referred to as the *Political Ads* case).

[9] 424 US 1 (1976), the case is discussed further below.

[10] See 22–23 above.

Human Rights in Strasbourg. The Lords in the *Derbyshire* case, in contrast to the Court of Appeal, admittedly placed much more weight on the American arguments than it did on the European Human Rights Convention. But that preference is atypical. In the *Spycatcher* case, and in recent cases on such diverse matters as the level of damages in libel[11] and restrictions on the reporting of ward placements,[12] the courts referred to the Convention, and not US law, as a standard by which to assess the common law. Such comparisons are made for the straightforward reason that otherwise there would be a risk of yet another application to the Human Rights institutions in Strasbourg.

There are, however, other reasons for approaching First Amendment jurisprudence with some caution when answers are required to novel free speech questions in English law. The divergences in the constitutional cultures of the UK and the USA on which Roger Cotterrel dwelt in chapter one have particular resonance in respect of the First Amendment, for in some respects US free speech law rests on a number of assumptions and arguments which are not widely shared or accepted either in this country or by our European partners. There are strong differences of perspective between the USA and the European approach to many free speech issues: consequently, there may be arguments of principle, as well as the practical point made in the previous paragraph, for preferring the latter.

This is not to contend, however, that we should ignore US free speech jurisprudence. It is without doubt the single most fertile source from which to draw ideas and inspiration in this area.[13] The Supreme Court in Washington and other (mostly federal) courts have considered virtually every conceivable free speech issue which can be litigated. In the era of the global village, exporting the First Amendment may be the most significant contribution the United States makes to international legal culture towards the end of the twentieth century.

Another preliminary, and cautionary, point should be made. There is no uniform approach to free speech issues among the American judicial and academic communities. Indeed, on many questions there is a fierce split. For example, as Ian Loveland makes clear in chapter eleven, there are strong divisions of opinion on such questions as the appropriateness (and constitutionality) of hate speech laws. The control of party political finance is also, as Keith Ewing stresses in chapter ten, a bitterly contested issue within both the judiciary and the academy. Similarly, the regulation of

[11] *Rantzen* v. *Mirror Group Newspapers (1986) Ltd.* [1993] 3 WLR 953 (CA).

[12] *In re W (A Minor)(Wardship: Restrictions on Publication)* [1992] 1 WLR 100 (CA).

[13] 'American thinking on freedom of speech is relevant to the rest of the world because our experience in wrestling with free speech conflicts and communications policy is unusually rich. American society may not have the best answers, but it has thought about the problems more': R. Smolla, *Free Speech in an Open Society* (New York; Knopf, 1992), 347.

broadcasting standards and other governmental attempts to promote the quality of speech are questions on which the debate as to constitutionality, still less as to desirability, is by no means closed. But on these (and many other) questions there is a general or majority view, reflected in the rulings of the Supreme Court. Thus, hate speech laws are against the First Amendment because they proscribe a particular type of speech on the basis of its contents,[14] while broadcasting regulation is suspect because it amounts to government interference with the market-place.

There is then a prevailing USA approach to free speech issues, and it is this which is set out in the second part of this essay. In the third part I explore some of the principles and cultural values underlying this jurisprudence. European free speech law provides a strong contrast with the American experience, largely, it is suggested, because the two systems are based on different values: these are explored in the fourth part. The paper concludes with a brief elaboration of some of these general points in the context of two areas of free speech law: the financing of political campaigns and broadcasting regulation.

UNITED STATES FREE SPEECH LAW—THE BASIC PRINCIPLES

It is impossible in the course of a few pages to provide an exhaustive summary of United States free speech law. Chapter eleven goes into slightly greater depth on those background principles of First Amendment jurisprudence which pertain directly to the question of hate speech, and chapter ten addresses in more detail the impact of the First Amendment on the regulation of electoral campaigning. In a more general vein, all that is offered in the next few pages is a survey of some of the major characteristics of that jurisprudence over the last thirty years. These have primarily been achievements of the liberal Warren Court, and have been largely unaffected by the Burger and Rehnquist Courts. Others were more firmly established under Burger CJ, with reservations expressed by the surviving Warren liberals, notably Brennan and Marshall JJ. To some extent this account follows that of Cass Sunstein, a dissenter from the standard perspective of United States commentators. But I do not think his description of the trends, as distinct from his commentary on their wisdom, is particularly controversial.[15]

The first characteristic is the coverage by the First Amendment of types

[14] This position is most recently illustrated by *RAV Petitioner* v. *City of St. Paul, Minnesota* 112 S Ct. 2538 (1992), discussed in ch. 11 below.

[15] C. Sunstein, 'Free Speech Now' in *The Bill of Rights in the Modern State* ed. by G. Stone, R. Epstein & C. Sunstein (Chicago, 1992), 259–60.

of speech which at one time were regarded as falling outside the principle altogether. (Speech which is 'covered' falls within the First Amendment; it does not mean that on the facts of the case it is protected.[16]) In *Chaplinsky* v. *New Hampshire* in 1942 the Court said:[17]

There are certain well-defined and narrowly limited classes of speech, the prevention and punishment of which have never been thought to raise any Constitutional problem. These include the lewd and obscene, the profane, the libelous, and the insulting or 'fighting' words—those which by their very utterance inflict injury or tend to incite an immediate breach of the peace.

Although the case has never been formally overruled, and, as suggested in chapter eleven, has latterly been deployed in a somewhat unconventional way,[18] the quoted proposition is now very misleading. Libel is covered by the First Amendment, though the scope of its protection varies depending on whether the plaintiff is a public official or figure on the one hand, or a private individual on the other.[19] The concept of 'obscenity' has been redefined, so that it refers in effect only to hard-core pictorial pornography.[20] Emotive lewd epithets are also immune from legislative restriction.[21] Finally, the 'fighting words' category, at issue in the *Chaplinsky* case itself, has been reduced to vanishing point: only inflammatory speech intended to bring about imminent violence falls wholly outside the First Amendment.[22]

From the mid-1970s commercial speech has usually been treated as covered by the First Amendment, though restrictions on its dissemination are more likely to be upheld than comparable restraints on the distribution of political speech.[23] (A substantial state interest, typically in consumer protection, will often justify a restriction on professional or commercial advertising.[24]) The First Amendment has also been interpreted to cover

[16] See F. Schauer, *Free Speech: A Philosophical Enquiry* (Cambridge, 1982) 89–92 for the coverage-protection distinction.

[17] 315 US 568 (1942). The unanimous judgment was given by Murphy J, one of the most liberal members of the Court.

[18] See 268–269 below.

[19] The leading decisions are *New York Times* v. *Sullivan* 376 US 254 (1964) and *Gertz* v. *Robert Welch* 418 US 323 (1974). The latter decision constitutionalized the whole law of libel, even where the plaintiff is a private citizen.

[20] See *Roth* v. *United States* 354 US 476 (1957) and *Miller* v. *California* 413 US 15 (1973).

[21] See *Cohen* v. *California* 403 US 15 (1971), holding the expression 'Fuck the Draft' protected.

[22] For the latest, highly controversial narrowing of the fighting words doctrine see Loveland's critique of Scalia J's majority opinion in *RAV* v. *St. Paul*, in ch. 11 below.

[23] The leading case extending coverage is *Virginia State Board of Pharmacy* v. *Virginia Citizens Consumer Council* 425 US 748 (1976).

[24] See, e.g., *Zauderer* v. *Office of Disciplinary Counsel* 471 US 626 (1985), upholding disclosure requirements to protect the public.

instances of so-called 'symbolic speech', for example, the wearing of armbands in protest against the Vietnam war[25] or flag burning.[26] Admittedly, some types of 'speech', in the dictionary sense of that word, remain wholly outside the Amendment. Perjury, blackmail, and contractual misrepresentations have never raised constitutional arguments; but overall this class of excluded 'speech' is much smaller than it used to be.

A second characteristic, in some ways associated with this development, is that the courts are particularly mistrustful of laws outlawing or restricting speech on the basis of its *content.* This principle of content-neutrality explains, I think, the tolerance of 'hate speech' or racialist propaganda, which is unique to the USA among western democracies. To allow a state or local community to proscribe, say, the marches of Nazi-type political parties would be to accept that government may outlaw speech of which it strongly disapproves.[27] This reasoning may also determine whether a 'time, place, and manner' regulation is acceptable. A community is free to ban all hoardings or leafleting on the grounds that they are unsightly or create litter; but it must not allow, say, charities to advertise in this way, while it proscribes political or commercial displays or leafleting.

Content neutrality appears ostensibly to be a benign organizing principle, but it has sometimes been applied to outlaw what might be regarded as sensible regulation. For example, a provision in the federal Public Broadcasting Act 1967 forbidding public broadcasters from editorializing was held contrary to the First Amendment as a content-based restriction on their speech.[28] The Supreme Court has also sometimes been reluctant to countenance restrictions on the siting of sex shops, cinemas, and comparable premises.[29] It is certainly right for constitutional courts to treat with great suspicion rules enabling government to choose which views may be expressed. It would clearly be wrong, for instance, to permit speech by Conservatives or Republicans, but forbid that of members of the Labour or Democrat party. On the other hand, one might expect courts sometimes to be more tolerant of broad classifications with regard to the *types* of speech which are permitted or regulated. The US Supreme Court

[25] *Tinker* v. *Des Moines School District* 393 US 503 (1974).

[26] See *Texas* v.*Johnson* 491 US 397 (1989); *United States* v. *Eichman* 496 US 310 (1990).

[27] See the decision of the Court of Appeals for the Seventh Circuit in the famous Skokie case, *Collin* v. *Smith* 578 F 2d. 1197 (1978), where the Court refused to ban a Nazi march through a Jewish suburb.

[28] *FCC* v. *League of Women Voters of California* 468 US 384 (1984).

[29] Thus in *Schad* v. *Mount Ephraim Borough* 452 US 61 (1981) the Court struck down a community's total ban on places of live entertainment which included nude dancing, while it had earlier upheld a zoning ordinance regulating 'adult theatres': *Young* v. *American Mini Theatres* 427 US 50 (1976).

is, however, generally hostile to both viewpoint and content discriminatory rules.

The third fundamental tenet of US free speech jurisprudence is more controversial. The courts are unsympathetic to arguments that a commitment to freedom of speech entails recognition of equal rights to, or opportunities for access to, expression. Thus, they have rejected an access right to the broadcasting media,[30] a right to leave unstamped mail in letterboxes,[31] and a right to put notices on local authority lampposts.[32] They are equally critical of legislative provisions intended to promote the opportunities of (minority) groups for speech, insofar as these rules would limit the freedom of those who currently enjoy such opportunities. This is illustrated first by *Miami Herald* v. *Tornillo,*[33] in which the Court held unconstitutional a Florida statutory right of reply, on the ground that it infringed a newspaper editor's free speech and free press rights.[34] Secondly, in *Buckley* v. *Valeo* the Supreme Court invalidated provisions of a federal statute limiting expenditure by and for political candidates, provisions which were designed to bring about greater fairness in the conduct of election campaigns.[35]

All these decisions can be defended with good arguments. The first three cases indicate that the First Amendment does not (usually) institute access or positive rights to free speech, beyond the cases of access to the traditional 'public fora' (rights to protest on the streets and in parks) recognized by the courts. Moreover, the regulations in question were content-neutral, a feature which would certainly have disposed the Court in their favour.

The explanation for the right of reply and campaign financing cases is that the Supreme Court is very reluctant to uphold legislation **promoting speech**. Put briefly, the First Amendment is usually interpreted as hostile to all government regulation. It is immaterial that the regulation was intended to increase the range of opinions circulating in society, or that its overall effects would probably be to produce a greater variety of available speech. In particular, it is irrelevant that the government has acted to limit the effects of what it considers to be a harmful *private* concentration of power, for example, in the ownership of the press or broadcasting media.

[30] *CBS* v. *Democratic National Committee* 412 US 94 (1973).

[31] *US Postal Service* v. *Council of Greenburgh Civic Association* 453 US 114 (1981).

[32] *City Council for Los Angeles* v. *Vincent* 104 S Ct. 2118 (1984).

[33] 418 US 241 (1974).

[34] Such rights are common in European press laws; for an overview see Barendt (1987) *Freedom of Speech* (Oxford: 1987) ch. 3.

[35] 424 US 1 (1976): see ch. 10 below for further discussion of this case. Again, such rules feature in the laws of some European countries, though there are no controls in the UK on the *national* expenditure of political parties; see ch. 10 below.

By and large, the First Amendment confers a freedom against *the government*, but not rights to control private media oligopolies.[36] One doctrinal manifestation of this is, of course, the 'state action' requirement, that is, that freedom of speech (and other freedoms in the Bill of Rights) is only at issue when there is some element of state (or public) action involved in the restriction.

THE INTELLECTUAL AND CULTURAL CONTEXTS

All these observations will be familiar to any student of the First Amendment. What has been less fully explored is how far these developments are explicable in terms of an understanding of free speech principles rooted in the intellectual history and traditions of the USA and so particular to that country. However, these themes have been touched on in recent American commentary, partly by scholars concerned to defend its distinctive tradition, partly (and more substantially, it seems to me) by critics uneasy with certain of its features.[37]

One major theme of American writing on free speech is that government cannot be trusted to determine truth or the limits of permissible political and social debate. Indeed, this has been regarded as a vital element in the justification for the free speech principle:

> Freedom of speech is based in large part on a distrust of the ability of government to make the necessary distinctions, a distrust of governmental determinations of truth and falsity, an appreciation of the fallibility of political leaders, and a somewhat deeper distrust of governmental power in a more general sense.[38]

To be coherent, this rationale for freedom of speech must, it seems to me, be linked to Mill's famous truth argument or to those arguments which base freedom of expression on the right of individuals to decide for themselves the good life.[39] We need only be particularly suspicious of government (or for that matter private) regulation of speech, if we have

[36] One qualification to this position was approved in the *Red Lion* case (395 US 367 (1969)), upholding a right of reply to personal attacks on the broadcasting media.

[37] Examples of works sympathetic to the principal lines of development sketched in this section are L. A. Powe, *American Broadcasting and the First Amendment* (California, 1987) and *The Fourth Estate and the Constitution* (California, 1991) and R. A. Smolla (1992) *op. cit.* For articles critical of the American Tradition, see O. M. Fiss, 'Free Speech and Social Structure' (1986) 71 *Iowa L. Rev.* 1405 and 'Why the State?' (1987) 100 *Harv. L. Rev.* 781; and Sunstein, (1992) *op. cit.*

[38] Schauer, (1982) *op. cit.*, 86.

[39] See the arguments, e.g., of T. M. Scanlon, 'A Theory of Freedom of Expression' (1972) 1 *Phil. and Public Affairs* 204, and of C. Fried, 'The New First Amendment Jurisprudence: A Threat to Liberty', in Stone, Epstein & Sunstein *op. cit.*

first shown that there is something special about speech, in comparison, say, with business activity. Otherwise we might be as (relatively) tolerant of government mistakes when it decides to proscribe speech, as we are when it pursues an erroneous economic policy.

If we do assume that freedom of speech is worthy of special (constitutional) protection, it is important to ask whether restrictions on speech imposed by the state differ fundamentally from those imposed by private people and institutions. Charles Fried argues that they do, because the state controls or in some sense is the law; private restrictions in contrast are imposed by the private person's own exercise of liberty, a right to privacy or a property right.[40] On the other hand, the *effects* of private restrictions on speech may be just as significant as those imposed by the state. Consider, for example, the impact on political debate, if all newspapers and broadcasting companies were controlled by one or two magnates, sympathetic to right-wing political parties. Also imagine that this happened in a society which had no public broadcasting system and which, moreover, imposed no positive programme requirements on broadcasters, let alone the press, because they were regarded as content-based restrictions.

Another important aspect of the 'distrust of government' perspective so characteristic of US jurisprudence is the famous 'slippery slope' argument. If government is allowed to outlaw an admittedly dangerous type of speech or something on the margins of 'speech', for example, explicit pornography, then inevitably it will slide down the slope and start to ban some types of harmless speech. This argument has exercised an enormous influence on US free speech jurisprudence, dictating, for example, the narrow definition of 'obscenity' which allows for the unhindered publication of much indecent and pretty revolting material. It also constitutes one of the most important arguments for the unique US tolerance of 'hate speech': if legislatures or universities were allowed to ban racialist insults, they would next start to police the quality of political debate. The slippery slope argument provides a major reason for the hostility to content-based restrictions on speech, to which I have drawn attention in Part II of this essay.

What is odd about this argument is that it reveals doubts about the capacity of the courts themselves to draw the right lines, as well as a mistrust of the legislature. Let us suppose that the Supreme Court upheld as constitutional a tightly-drawn 'hate speech' ordinance, criminalizing insulting remarks or literature disseminated directly to members of the insulted group. That would only lead to a slide down the notorious slippery slope, if first, a state legislature were to enact broader prohibitions and

[40] Fried, *op. cit.*, 236–7.

secondly, state courts failed to distinguish the constitutionality of this later legislation from that of the earlier narrowly-drawn ordinance. Of course, until the correct decision (invalidating the second statute) were taken, some speech which ought to be permitted might be the subject of criminal proceedings and other prospective publishers might be deterred from speaking. Surely these temporary effects, however unattractive, do not provide a decisive argument against the drawing of lines between permissible and impermissible speech?

The American suspicion of government assumes more paranoid proportions, when it is directed against legislative measures (actual or potential) designed to promote or enhance speech. Access rights to the media and political financing rules, for example, are regarded as suspect because government might police them in a discriminatory way. A government arbiter determining access to a public forum could not, it is claimed, be content-neutral.[41] There may be some warrant for this scepticism in recent United States history. Members of administrative agencies, such as the Federal Communications Commission, are appointed exclusively by the President, and have generally been chosen to implement his political ideology. There has been great controversy about the award of funds by the National Endowment for the Arts to support arguably 'indecent' art exhibitions; inevitably the allocation of limited resources in this context will create administrative and perhaps constitutional problems.[42]

But regulatory authorities for the press and broadcasting media, for the oversight of elections, and for the allocation of government funds, can be constituted in such a way as to be independent of government. Indeed, the balanced composition of the bodies regulating public and private broadcasting is regarded in Germany as one of the principal attributes of the broadcasting freedom guaranteed in the Basic Law.[43] Positive rules to promote speech can be administered in a neutral manner and in a way which increases the range of opinions discussed in a particular society, with minimal risk of government control. There is, in short, a distinction between state control of speech, which is 'bad', and its regulation in some contexts by an independent public authority, which may be beneficial.

Another idea running through United States free speech theory is that truth should be determined in the 'market-place'. The idea goes back to Holmes J's famous judgment in *Abrams*: 'the best test of truth is the power of the thought to get itself accepted in the competition of the market'.[44]

[41] Fried, *op. cit.*, 251.

[42] For a discussion of the controversy arising from the funding of exhibitions of Mapplethorpe's work, see O. M. Fiss, 'State Activism and State Censorship' (1991) 100 *Yale LJ* 2087.

[43] See E. Barendt, *Broadcasting Law* (Oxford, 1993), 41 & 60–3.

[44] 250 US 616, 630–1 (1919).

This remark really amounts to a denial of the notion of objective truth. As Tom Campbell has argued, success in the market of ideas of a particular belief does not provide any proof of its truth.[45] It shows its attractiveness to the public, a different matter altogether.

Notwithstanding its incoherence, the 'market-place' theory has exercised a significant influence on the development of free speech law, reinforcing the distrust of government, which, as already emphasized, is another peculiar feature of the US approach to freedom of speech. It has played a part in the extension of the First Amendment to cover much commercial speech, in the deregulation of programme standards and the removal of broadcast advertising limits (even for a time for children's programmes), and in justifying the absence of restraints on the spending of political parties. In all these situations, it is argued, individual choice in the free market provides the best control. For example, if advertisements flatter the services and products they promote or unregulated television offers poor quality programmes, a self-correcting market mechanism will operate.

To be fair, there are many critics of this ideology in the United States itself.[46] Equally it has some adherents in Europe, particularly in the United Kingdom. But I doubt whether it has exercised any great influence on free speech law outside the USA. Certainly anyone considering the import, whether selective or wholesale, of US free speech jurisprudence should reflect on the coherence of the market-place theory and examine its underlying assumptions. Among these is the belief that existing distributions in the market are broadly just and that it is right to protect them through the law, even to the extent of giving them constitutional protection. For example, the guarantee of a newspaper editor or owner's free speech and press rights against claimed rights of reply and access would seem to rest on that assumption—although it is arguable that recognition of reply and access rights would increase the range of views available for public discussion and that the newspaper is really claiming a disguised property right. Another awkward question for proponents of the theory is whether in practice the self-correcting market mechanism works; for instance, in the absence of programme standards, can or do advertisers and viewers successfully press for better quality material on television?

Finally, these features of US free speech theory are obviously connected with United States' history and political traditions. Americans have always been distrustful of government, an attitude rooted in the origins of the country—the gaining of its independence from a remote and ineffective

[45] See his paper, 'Rationales for Freedom of Communication', paper given at conference in Canberra in Aug. 1993 (to be published).

[46] See especially Sunstein (1992) *op. cit.*, 285–9.

British regime—and later the pioneering spirit of the nineteenth century. Equally, socialist and egalitarian political theory has exercised relatively little influence on American thinking about fundamental rights.

As far as freedom of speech and media freedom are concerned, a few points are particularly striking. One is that the USA was geographically and psychologically far removed from experience of the totalitarian regimes in Europe of the late 1920s and 1930s. That was the time when the Supreme Court first began to take the free speech limb of the First Amendment seriously, applying it to strike down state legislation. It is perhaps then not surprising that US politicians and courts have usually shown a greater tolerance of racialist and other extremist speech than their European contemporaries. In contrast, during the First World War and its immediate aftermath, and again during the early years of the Cold War, the courts were more hesitant to strike down restrictions on freedom of speech, particularly when they were incorporated in Acts of Congress. Secondly, in contrast to the position in Europe and Australia there was until recently no public broadcasting in the USA. Even now it plays a very minor role compared to the networks and private cable systems. As a result programme controls have always been much laxer in the USA than in other countries, where the 'public service' model has influenced to some extent the regulation of private radio and television. A third point is that the Presidential and gubernatorial system of government has probably contributed to the blurring of political and personal questions, and the constitutionalizing of libel and privacy actions to the particular advantage of the institutional press.[47]

BETTER LESSONS? EUROPEAN PERSPECTIVES

Postwar European constitutions cover freedom of speech among the other fundamental rights guaranteed to individuals. The German Basic Law, originally drawn up for West Germany and now governing the united country, has provided a particularly rich jurisprudence fully worthy of comparison with that of the United States courts.[48] Article 5(1) provides that everyone has the right to disseminate his opinions and the right to receive information from generally accessible sources. Press and broadcasting freedom are guaranteed by the same Article, which also explicitly

[47] See the article by Schauer (1980) *op, cit.*, which draws a strong contrast between US and UK law in this context.

[48] See Donald P. Kommers, *The Constitutional Jurisprudence of the Federal Republic of Germany* (Durham, North Carolina, 1989) for a valuable collection of cases and some comparative commentary.

forbids censorship. These rights may be limited by general laws, by provisions to protect youth, and by 'the right to inviolability of personal honour'.[49]

Freedom of expression (*Meinungsfreiheit*) is interpreted by the German Constitutional Court in the context of the other rights guaranteed by the Basic Law. The most important of these is the inviolable dignity of man guaranteed by Article 1. This provision, one of the few which cannot be amended,[50] states that '[t]he German people acknowledge inviolable and inalienable rights as the basis of' the community. What is most striking from the text of the Basic Law itself is its emphasis on freedom of expression and other basic rights as fundamental *human rights*, a perspective also evidenced in the Universal Declaration of Human Rights and the European Convention, both legacies of the Second World War. The German Constitutional Court has similarly stressed the importance of free speech to the development of the human personality, as well as its essential contribution to the formation of public opinion on social and political issues.[51]

On the other hand, it is hard to find either in the Court's jurisprudence or in academic writing any echo of arguments frequently made in the United States to justify the free speech guarantee: the market-place of ideas rationale, and the distrust of government or of the courts' ability to draw appropriate lines.

This distinctive perspective has important consequences. If freedom of speech is regarded as a fundamental **human** right, it becomes difficult to justify its application to commercial speech and advertising, or the extension of the principle to corporate speech, as has happened in the United States.[52] The German Constitutional Court has ruled a number of times on party and election financing laws, in particular on the constitutionality of provisions for tax deductions in respect of individual and corporate contributions. In none of these cases was Article 5 seriously put in issue. The Court has similarly been unwilling to extend it to cover commercial advertising. (The European Court of Human Rights has, however, held in a case brought from Germany that the provision of information by a vet is covered by Article 10 of the European Convention on Human Rights,[53] but refused to hold that it protected disparaging advertising of mail-order firms published in a trade magazine.[54])

[49] Art. 5(2). [50] Basic Law, Art. 79(3).

[51] See the famous *Lüth* case, 7 BVerfGE 198 (1958) and 54 BVerfGE 129, 136–7 (1980).

[52] See H. Goerlich, 'Fundamental Constitutional Rights: Content, Meaning and General Doctrines', in U.Karpen (ed.) *The Constitution of the Federal Republic of Germany* (Baden-Baden, 1988) 45, 56–7.

[53] *Barthold* v. *Germany* [1985] 7 EHRR 385.

[54] *Markt Intern* v. *Germany* (1990) 12 EHRR 161.

Another feature of German jurisprudence, particularly evident in libel cases, is the Constitutional Court's insistence on the detailed balancing of relevant constitutional and other interests by the lower civil and administrative courts.[55] What concerns it is that proper consideration has been given to relevant constitutional values. That is a radically different approach from that of the US Supreme Court, though not dissimilar to that of the European Court of Human Rights in determining whether the limits (permitted by Article 10(2)) on freedom of expression are 'necessary in a democratic society'. In libel and other contexts, the Washington Court is more inclined to formulate general rules, which must then be observed by lower federal and state courts. The American commentator Melville Nimmer characterized this difference as that between *ad hoc* and definitional balancing.[56] In his view the latter had the advantages of greater predictability of decision and a wider scope for free speech. Under definitional balancing a rule is formulated to allow a margin of error in favour of speech: so the famous *New York Times* absolute malice rule allows some inaccurate defamatory allegations to be published, as that is preferable to a case-by-case weighing of speech and reputation interests, which would sometimes lead to liability for (and the chilling of) true speech.

Another example of the difference between the two jurisdictions is shown by their distinctive approaches to hate speech. Not surprisingly Germany has strict group libel and racial hatred laws. These limit freedom of expression; if challenged under Article 5, they would certainly be upheld as general laws which properly limit *Meinungsfreiheit* or as laws protecting personal honour. One crucial factor would be that any balancing of freedom of expression against the general laws or against reputation rights would have to take account of the dignity of man guaranteed by Article 1 of the Basic Law.[57] That is a more fundamental right even than freedom of speech, giving the balancing process a dimension entirely absent from United States argument in this context. It should be added that France, Britain, and other European countries all have laws on their statute-books proscribing incitement to racial, and in some cases religious, hatred.[58] In contrast US law, as already mentioned, uniquely sets its face against hate speech laws, largely because if they were countenanced there would (it is

[55] For a brief discussion, see Barendt, (1987) *op. cit.*, 150, 171–2, 184–7.

[56] 'The Right to Speak from *Times* to *Time*: First Amendment Theory Applied to Libel and Misapplied to Privacy', (1968) 56 *Calif. L. Rev.* 935.

[57] See the *Mephisto* case, 30 BVerfGE 173 (1971).

[58] For a vigorous defence of the strong French laws in this area, see R. Errera, 'In Defence of Civility: Racial Incitement and Group Libel in French Law', in S. Coliver (ed.), *Striking a Balance* (London, 1992).

feared) be a slide down the slippery slope to the suppression of acceptable political speech.[59]

A further characteristic of the continental European approach, again connected with its human rights perspective, is the doctrine of abuse of rights. In Germany this may lead to forfeiture of certain basic constitutional rights, including freedom of speech and freedom of the press, though only after a decision of the Constitutional Court.[60] There is a similar provision in the European Convention, which has been invoked to hold inadmissible an application by Dutch right-wing extremists (convicted for possession of hate literature).[61] There is no equivalent provision in the US Constitution, and it is virtually inconceivable that the Supreme Court would develop such a doctrine.

But of more interest than these differences, partly explicable in terms of the constitutional texts, is the fact that the German Court (and some other continental jurisdictions) are much more willing than the United States Supreme Court to countenance legislation promoting freedom of speech. In other words, at least in some contexts, freedom of speech is not solely a negative freedom, guaranteed merely against interference by government. In its early decisions the Court took the view that the rights set out in the first Part of the Basic Law were primarily instituted to protect the citizen against the state. Later it formulated the doctrine that the provisions 'establish a value order that represents a fundamental constitutional decision in all areas of law'.[62] In the case from which this statement is taken the Court required state legislatures to reformulate their university admissions rules in the light of the constitutional right to choose an occupation, profession and place of training, and of the basic right of equality, guaranteed by Articles 12 and 3 respectively.

The general principle formulated in the *University Admission* case has had two significant consequences for freedom of speech law in Germany. One is that there is little difficulty in applying the freedom to purely private disputes; the law of libel and privacy, for example, must be developed in light of the freedom of expression guaranteed by Article 5, though account must also be taken by the ordinary civil courts of Article 2 (right to the development of the personality) and Article 1 (human dignity). Secondly, the Court requires the legislature to promote the values of freedom of speech in the way, for example, it frames broadcasting legislation. In that context freedom of expression is not merely a defensive right. Thus, the

[59] Although as Loveland suggests in ch. 11, some American States have found legal mechanisms which may deal with the most egregious manifestations of racist expression in a manner consistent with First Amendment freedoms.

[60] Art. 18 of the Basic Law, and see Art. 17 of the ECHR.

[61] *Glimmerveen* v. *Netherlands* 18 D & R 187.

[62] *Numerus Clausus* case, 33 BVerfGE 303, 330 (1972).

Court requires both public and private broadcasting legislation to provide for supervisory authorities representative of all significant interest groups, and to lay down minimum programme standards in the interests of listeners and viewers.[63] In short, the law not only may, but must, promote freedom of expression. The Court has tried to meet anxiety about the dangers of regulation and of administrative discretion by its insistence that the most important rules are set out in primary legislation.

This approach is shared in the context of broadcasting and press regulation by the French Constitutional Council and by the Italian Constitutional Court. The former has developed the constitutional principle of pluralism of voices in the media as an attribute of the freedom of speech guaranteed by Article 11 of the Declaration of the Rights of Man. Thus, press legislation should effectively prevent the development of concentrations of press power; although the Council arguably weakened this principle when it invalidated retrospective application of the market share ceilings.[64] The principle was applied to broadcasting legislation in 1986, when the Council struck down the competition provisions of the Chirac Bill as inadequate to limit, for example, the growth of multi-media oligopolies.[65]

So in France and other European jurisdictions freedom of speech is not regarded purely as a limit on what government may do, but as a value which may require it to act to break up concentrations and to promote pluralism of voices. This approach goes further than any the Supreme Court would be prepared to take. The Court has admittedly upheld the application of antitrust legislation to the press,[66] but it is virtually inconceivable that it would compel Congress (or the Federal Communications Commission) to introduce tighter antitrust rules because the First Amendment required that step.

PROTECTING SPECIFIC FORMS OF 'SPEECH': A COMPARATIVE CRITIQUE

This chapter ends with a brief discussion of two important areas where the traditional US approaches seem particularly problematic. Certainly they contrast with the general European perspective. Indeed, in the case of political campaign financing most European lawyers would even deny that

[63] There have been six major decisions of the Court on broadcasting legislation: perhaps the most important rulings are the *First Television* case, 12 BVerfGE 205 (1961) and the *Fourth Television* case, 76 BVerfGE 118 (1986).

[64] See Decision 84–181 of 11 Oct. 1984 and Decision 86–210 of 29 July 1986.

[65] Decision 86–217 of 18 Sept. 1986.

[66] *Associated Press* v. *US* 326 US 1 (1945). Also see *FCC* v. *National Citizens' Committee for Broadcasting* 436 US 775 (1978).

there are significant free speech interests, a scepticism shared by some, albeit a minority of, US commentators.

Campaign Financing

In *Buckley* v. *Valeo*[67] the Supreme Court invalidated limits on expenditures which could be incurred by or on behalf of election candidates, while upholding limits on contributions to party or candidate funds. (In later cases ceilings on the level of contributions to local referendum committees[68] and on expenditure by political action committees[69] have equally been held incompatible with the First Amendment.) All these restrictions were regarded as tantamount to restrictions on speech and, therefore, were subject to strict scrutiny. However, the Court was prepared to uphold provisions necessary to prevent corruption; this was the basis for ruling the contribution limits valid in the *Buckley* case. But the Court in that case summarily rejected the argument that the government could legitimately restrict the speech (or expenditure) of the wealthy in order to give more opportunity for poorer people and groups to contribute to political debate.

One might raise several doubts as to both the political desirability and legal defensibility of these decisions. First, was it right for the Court to treat the expenditure of money as equivalent to the dissemination of speech? Granted that the effective dissemination of most speech in a mass media society is dependent on money, does it follow that a restraint on expenditure should be treated in the same way—that is subject to the same careful scrutiny as a restriction on the substance of the speech itself would be? As dissenting judgments have pointed out, the ability to make effective speech is also dependent on the receipt of a good education and a living wage, but financial or other limits on the enjoyment of these goods are not subject to strict scrutiny (unless they contain some element of racial or perhaps sexual discrimination). The Supreme Court found implicit in the First Amendment an individual's right to use her money or property for the dissemination of effective speech. Secondly, expenditure limits do not discriminate on the basis of the contents or viewpoints of the speech. It was not as if, either on their face or in their application, they would necessarily discriminate against, say, Republicans or Democrats. The same point is also true of limits on corporate speech, which until recently the Court has been reluctant to countenance.[70]

[67] 424 US 1 (1976).

[68] *Citizens against Rent Control* v. *Berkeley* 102 S Ct. 434 (1982).

[69] *FEC* v. *National Conservative Political Action Committee* 105 S Ct. 1459 (1989).

[70] See however the recent decision in *Austin* v. *Michigan Chamber of Commerce* 110 S Ct. 1391 (1990), upholding the prohibition of campaign expenditure by the Chamber of

The most problematic aspect of the *Buckley* decision is the Court's opposition to legislation designed to equalize opportunities for speech at elections. It thought this aim wholly contrary to the First Amendment, which (citing the *New York Times* libel case) in its view was designed to guarantee the widest possible dissemination of ideas from a variety of sources. But from that perspective the legislation should have been upheld. The effect of the ruling is to allow a handful of the super-rich to dominate national election campaigns, as evidenced in 1992 by Ross Perot's campaign. There are no limits on the amount candidates may spend on newspaper and television adverts and this inevitably favours rich Republican and other candidates to the prejudice of the generally poorer Democrats. If the Court had taken into account the probable impact of the Federal Election Campaign Act, it would surely have concluded that more ideas, particularly those of minority candidates, would have reached the voters had its provisions been upheld. Moreover, it is misleading to suggest that the Federal Election Campaign Act interfered with the free market of ideas.[71] Rather it attempted to redress economic inequalities and to mitigate their damaging consequences for democracy.

Broadcasting Regulation

There is a marked contrast between the US and European approaches to broadcasting regulation, to some extent shaped by constitutional arguments. Although the famous *Red Lion* case[72] upheld the Fairness Doctrine and the right of reply to personal attacks, most programme standards have been abolished in the last decade. The federal courts have almost always been sympathetic to this development, abandoning their previous view that in the context of radio and television the rights of viewers and listeners were at least as important as those of the broadcasters. So public as well as private broadcasters are free to editorialize,[73] while the DC Circuit of Appeals has approved the repeal of the Fairness Doctrine. It held in the latter case that television and radio stations need no longer be required to present programmes on controversial matters or to observe balance in this context.[74] Starr J even considered the Doctrine unconstitutional in view of its interference with the freedom of broadcasters; with the greater number of available frequencies the

Commerce from its general funds. The Court majority did recognize the state had a compelling interest in preventing distortion of political campaigns by massive corporate expenditure.

71 Smolla, *op. cit.*, 221–6.

72 *Red Lion Broadcasting* v. *FCC* 395 US 567 (1969).

73 *FCC* v. *League of Women Voters* 468 US 364 (1984).

74 *Syracuse Peace Council* v. *FCC* 867 F 2d. 654 (1989).

communications market-place was able to provide for a variety of programmes and voices.[75]

Apart from the ban on cigarette commercials, there are now virtually no broadcast advertising restrictions in the United States, and indeed for a time they were even removed for children's programmes. When Congress in 1990 passed a Bill imposing a limit of twelve minutes advertising an hour during children's weekday programmes, President Bush argued that the 'First Amendment does not contemplate that government will dictate the quality or quantity of what Americans should hear—rather, it leaves this to be decided by free media responding to the free choices of individual consumers'.[76] That broadly was the philosophy of the Federal Communications Commission, when it repealed the Fairness Doctrine and most other programme standards during the 1980s. There is, however, little evidence to warrant the belief that the market produces the serious news and other quality programmes that some people want. Broadcast programmes are, Sunstein has argued, a 'public good', like clean air, a good railway system, or an effective police or defence force. Nobody as an individual is prepared to pay enough for such goods, bearing in mind that if they are provided, everyone can take advantage of them without having to pay (much) for the benefit. In short, people are tempted to be 'free riders'.[77]

But quite apart from this economic argument, the constitutional free speech case against broadcast regulation is relatively weak. When we ascribe free speech rights in this context, are we referring to the rights of station owners, channel controllers, programme editors, producers, or journalists? Do listeners and viewers have any rights, or at least legally protected interests? I have discussed these complicated issues at some length elsewhere.[78] Put simply, the USA perspective assumes that only broadcasting licensees (and their appointees) enjoy free speech rights on radio and television. Moreover, after the demise of the Fairness Doctrine, they are entitled entirely to exclude from their schedules programmes of interest to minority groups, as well as denying those groups and their members access to the air waves. Broadcasting may be as partial and biased as the press often is. That is a tenable perspective, though not in my

[75] The Supreme Court has, however, upheld the FCC minority ownership policies, partly on the ground that they encourage diversity of programmes: *Metro Broadcasting, Inc.* v. *FCC* 497 US 547 (1990). It is not clear it would uphold rules requiring programmes sympathetic to minorities, etc.

[76] Quoted by Sunstein (1992) *op. cit.*, 258. The President did not however veto the Bill.

[77] *Id.*, 285–7. It is possible that the spread of subscription television may weaken this argument, but it seems to work for advertising financed broadcasting. It also distinguishes broadcasting from the press and publishing markets.

[78] 'Press and Broadcasting Freedom: Does Anyone Have Any Rights to Free Speech?', [1993] *CLP* 63; (1993) *op. cit.*, ch. 2.

view an attractive one, for it allows too few people an effective opportunity to speak. What it is important to realize is that such limited access to media outlets is not inevitable. It reflects an administrative and judicial choice which is as much influenced by background social views as it is by legal reasoning. The different approach of German and other European systems shows that media freedom can be understood in another way.

CONCLUSION

This paper has been somewhat critical of American free speech jurisprudence. But there is much in it which is worthy of (almost) unqualified admiration: in particular, the Supreme Court's opposition to prior restraints, the principle of the *New York Times* libel case, and the protection of speakers in the face of hostile audiences. In these and some other areas, courts and commentators in the United States show a profound concern for freedom of expression which other jurisdictions should emulate. It should also be emphasized again that the most vigorous criticism of the 'Free Speech Tradition', as it has been termed, comes from within the USA itself.[79] There is indeed, in addition to the mainstream perspective outlined in this essay, a dissenting tradition, which has something in common with the approach to free speech issues found in continental Europe.

But this intellectual struggle within the United States' legal community only underlines the principal point of this chapter and the two which immediately follow it. When one legal system contemplates adopting concepts and perspectives from another, it should be aware that these ideas are very likely to be contested in their home jurisdiction. Moreover, whatever political philosophers may say, the interpretation of freedom of speech as a constitutional right is as much dependent on historical and underlying social factors as it is on legal precedent and abstract argument. English judges and legislators should always examine what the Supreme Court says about freedom of speech, but should also see what other approaches are possible before its jurisprudence is imported. As the two following chapters suggest, there may be subdivisions of free speech law in the uniquely British context in which the importation of American ideas could produce alternately immensely valuable and intensely damaging results.

[79] The term 'Free Speech Tradition' was coined by Harry Kalven: see O. M. Fiss, 'Free Speech and Social Structure', 71 *Iowa LR* 1405 (1986).

10

Legal Control of Party Political Finance

KEITH EWING

IN many respects the United States is not obviously a suitable jurisdiction to which one would look for lessons about how to deal with the question of campaign finance reform. Important historical, constitutional, and political differences suggest that a more fruitful line of enquiry would be with countries such as Canada which not only inherited (perhaps surprisingly) the British constitutional principle of parliamentary sovereignty but also developed a system of strong party government, albeit without the pivotal involvement historically of the organized labour movement, and albeit one with limitations which were exposed by the federal election in 1993. But this is not to suggest that the American experience is completely irrelevant or wholly without interest, or that there are no lessons whatsoever to be drawn from the attempts at legal regulation in that country. At a time when the issue of party funding is exercising keen interest in Britain, closing our minds to the United States' experience would betray an astonishing insularity, particularly as the Americans have the experience of almost ninety years of legislating in the field, and particularly as they have been grappling with principles and policies which might equally inform legislation here and elsewhere, notwithstanding our different historical, constitutional and political legacies.

Compared to the United States, Britain is a country in which election campaigns are largely unregulated by law.[1] Unlike many liberal democracies, political parties are not required to publish their accounts or to identify those who make large donations. There are no direct restrictions on the sources of party finance, though trade unions are restricted indirectly from donating to political parties by the requirement that any such contributions may be made only by those trade unions with political funds which have satisfied a number of rigorous statutory criteria.[2] Nor are there any restrictions on political party expenditure in a campaign, though

[1] For an account of the law in Britain, see H. F. Rawlings, *Law and the Electoral Process* (London, 1988) chs. 5–8.

[2] Trade Union and Labour Relations (Consolidation) Act 1992, ss. 71–96 (previously Trade Union Act 1913). See now Trade Union Reform and Employment Rights Act 1993, s. 3.

candidates have been restricted by a statutory ceiling which has operated since 1883[3] and the parties are controlled—crucially—by the prohibition on political advertising on radio and television.[4] Otherwise the political parties are free to spend as much as they can raise, as is anyone else or any interest group wishing to participate in the electoral process.[5] This free-for-all has not, however, always been fully accepted and questions have been raised from time to time about political donations buying improper influence on the one hand, and about unrestrained expenditure giving some parties an unfair advantage on the other.

These concerns were expressed with a renewed sense of urgency in the summer of 1993, when claims were made that the Conservative Party had received substantial gifts from overseas businessmen, including the disgraced tycoon and head of the Polly Peck Empire, Mr Asil Nadir, who was rumoured to have donated as much as £440,000.[6] The summer of 1993 in fact gave rise to a feverish degree of activity in this area, with the matter being the subject of investigation by the House of Commons Home Affairs Committee. Evidence was taken from the political parties and others,[7] private members' bills were introduced in the House,[8] and most recently a lively and authoritative booklet was produced by the Institute for Public Policy Research.[9] Although the report of the Home Affairs Committee was eagerly awaited,[9a] to a large extent it was overshadowed by the activity which it has generated. There are now many proposals in circulation for the reform of British election campaign finance laws, including the mandatory disclosure of income and expenditure; restrictions on the source (with particular reference to those from overseas) and size of donations; restrictions on election expenditures by the political parties (with a statutory ceiling such as that which applies to the candidates); the introduction of various additional measures of public funding for the parties; and the creation of a new Election Commission which would supervize and enforce the legislation. At a time when so much activity is taking place, it is particularly appropriate to look closely at developments in other jurisdictions—wherever they may be—to identify any problems

[3] Corrupt and Illegal Practices Act 1883, s. 8.

[4] Broadcasting Act 1990 s. 9. For background, see Rawlings, *op. cit.*

[5] A classic example being the campaign of the iron and steel industry in 1959, campaigning against nationalization and the election of a Labour government.

[6] Martin Linton, *Money and Votes* (London, 1994), 66.

[7] Home Affairs Committee, Funding of Political Parties, Minutes of Evidence HC 726 (1992–3).

[8] See HC Debs, 16 June 1993, cols. 867–9.

[9] Linton, *op. cit.*

[9a] Home Affairs Committee, Funding of Political Parties HC 301 (1993–1994)—a rather damp squib.

which may accompany the process of reform, as well as any pitfalls which are to be avoided.

THE EMERGENCE OF PRINCIPLE

The first US federal legislation on campaign financing was passed in the Tillman Act of 1907 when Congress enacted that 'it shall be unlawful for any national bank, or any corporation organized by authority of any laws of Congress, to make a money contribution in connection with any election to any political office'.[10] This was later said to be 'merely the first concrete manifestation of a congressional concern for elections free from the power of money'[11] and reflected an anxiety, not confined to the United States, about the growing influence of money and economic power in the electoral process. In Canada, the Dominion Elections Act 1908 sought to prohibit corporations from contributing to candidates and political parties,[12] while even in Britain a motion was debated in the Commons in 1908 regretting 'the secrecy under which political funds are accumulated and administered'.[13] Also in 1908, W. V. Osborne began his historic journey to the House of Lords, where in holding trade union political expenditure to be unlawful, at least one of their lordships (Lord Shaw of Dunfermline) expressed alarm about the growing political dependence on economic power.[14] Unlike in the United States, however, where there has been a sustained and continuous attempt to regulate, the concerns in both Canada and the United Kingdom were short-lived. The Canadian legislation of 1908 was repealed in 1930, unused and unlamented,[15] while nothing came of the parliamentary concerns in Britain which washed over a complacent government. Indeed, paradoxically perhaps, the only legislation of the time was the Trade Union Act 1913 which removed the restrictions on trade unions which had been imposed by the House of Lords three years earlier.

In the United States, in contrast, the Tillman Act of 1907 was followed by further legislation three years later, adding to the ban on corporate (but not at this stage trade union) contributions with a requirement of 'publicity of contributions made for the purpose of influencing elections at which

[10] Act of 26 Jan. 1907.

[11] *US* v. *International Union, UAW* 352 US 567 (1957), 575.

[12] See K. D. Ewing, *Money, Politics and Law. A Study of Electoral Campaign Finance Reform in Canada* (Oxford, 1992), 9–10.

[13] HC Debs, 19 Feb. 1908, cols. 899–939.

[14] *Amalgamated Society of Railway Servants* v. *Osborne* [1910] AC 87.

[15] See *Report of the Committee on Election Expenses* (Chairman: A Barbeau) (1966), 18–22.

Representatives in Congress are elected'.[16] The provisions of the 1910 Act, translating into law 'popular demand for further curbs upon the political power of wealth',[17] were in fact rather far-reaching, and there are proponents of campaign finance reform in this country who would be not unhappy to adopt something similar here, albeit some eighty-five years later. Political parties were required to keep accurate financial records and to report to the Clerk of the House of Representatives a detailed statement of accounts within thirty days after a Congressional election. The report was to contain the name and address of each contributor of $100 or more, as well as the total income of and expenditure by the party. The information reported in this way was open to public inspection for a period of fifteen months. There was also a duty of disclosure on third parties; that is to say those who incur expenditure in a campaign independently of the political parties and candidates. So every person, firm, association, or committee (other than a political committee) was required to report and disclose expenditure of $50 or more at a federal election. Amendments in the following year extended the duty to report and disclose campaign funds from the political parties to the candidates and also introduced a requirement of pre-election as well as post-election reporting and disclosure of income and expenditure.[18]

These measures promoted two different though related objectives. The reporting and disclosure requirements promoted openness and transparency in the electoral process, though they may also have helped to restrain those who wished to make or receive compromising contributions. The ban on corporate contributions sought to do directly what the reporting and disclosure requirements may do indirectly—namely to restrict the malignant influence of accumulated corporate power. There is, however, a third dimension to campaign finance reform. This is the principle of fairness between rival candidates for office, to be achieved principally by restrictions on the amounts of money which candidates or parties may spend in a campaign to secure their election to office. Regulation of this type also helps to reduce the influence of private power because it eliminates the need to raise unlimited sums of money. It is perhaps this function of expenditure limits which led Parliament in this country to enact limits on candidates' election expenses in 1883.[19] Yet whatever the reason, spending limits were introduced in the United States in 1911, and, as was the case in Britain at the time, those restrictions appear to have been confined to candidates only, and did not appear to

[16] Act of 25 June 1910.
[17] *US* v. *International Union, UAW* 352 US 567 (1957), 575.
[18] Act of 19 Aug. 1911.
[19] Corrupt and Illegal Practices Act 1883, s. 8.

apply to the political parties or their committees. Complementary measures to restrict independent expenditures in favour of candidates were introduced by legislation in 1940, as were a number of other reforms, including the imposition of a ceiling of $3 million on the amount of money which the political committees of political parties could (receive and) spend in a year.[20]

THE ROLE OF THE COURTS

So by the beginning of the First World War the United States had in place a framework of campaign finance regulation which, with the benefit of hindsight, might be said to have promoted three principles in relation to the electoral process. These measures were later consolidated and refined by the Federal Corrupt Practices Act of 1925 which (with further refinements in 1940, 1943, and 1947) was the foundation text until the amending legislation of the 1970s. Yet despite the importance of this legislation and the principles it embraced, these were not the only principles at play in the American system. So while Congress embraced openness, the Constitution requires the protection of privacy.[21] And while Congress chose electoral equality, the Constitution requires (at least on its face) political liberty, particularly liberty of expression as guaranteed by the First Amendment. It is true that First Amendment jurisprudence was relatively undeveloped during much of the life of the 1925 Act and its predecessors. Constitutional issues were raised in a number of cases, but the Court managed to avoid having to reach these larger questions by adopting very narrow interpretations of the legislation, thereby contributing to the spirit of laxity which accompanied the operation in practice of the principles of campaign finance reform. Apart from a very early decision in 1916 to uphold the ban on corporate contributions against a First Amendment challenge,[22] the role of the courts was generally subversive rather than supportive.

Alexander has written that for many years the 'enforcement of the federal prohibitions was marked by frank failure to press for indictment or to convict those under indictment'.[23] There had been only eighteen convictions of corporations, mostly since 1969. Although there were also a few indictments brought against labour unions, 'no conviction has been

[20] Act of 19 July 1940.
[21] See *NAACP* v. *Alabama*, 357 US 449 (1958).
[22] *US* v. *United States Brewers' Association* 239 Fed Rep. 163 (1916).
[23] H. Alexander, *Money in Politics* (Washington DC, 1972), 165.

upheld upon appeal'.[24] In the first of these cases,[25] which made its way to the Supreme Court, the Congress of Industrial Organisations (CIO) and its president were charged with violating the 1925 Act (as amended by the Taft–Hartley Act of 1947 which extended the ban on corporate contributions and expenditures to trade unions) in connection with an article in *CIO News*, a weekly journal published by the CIO. The issue in question carried a front page statement by the president urging all eligible CIO members to vote for a named candidate for Congress in Maryland. Although the lower courts were prepared to rule against the Act on constitutional grounds, the Supreme Court studiously avoided the constitutional question (to the disappointment of the union) by holding that as a matter of statutory interpretation, the terms of the Act had not in any event been violated. Thus the Court distinguished between a 'trade journal, a house organ or a newspaper, published by a corporation, . . . expressing views on candidates or political proposals in the regular course of its publication', and a 'periodical financed by a corporation or labor union for the purpose of advocating legislation advantageous to the sponsor or supporting candidates'.[26] Explicit words would be required to convince the Court that Congress had intended to prohibit the former type of activity, in which case the 'gravest doubt' would have arisen as to its constitutionality.[27]

The *CIO* case appears thus to endorse the practice of direct political advocacy by a union on behalf of its members.[28] This could be carried to extraordinary lengths, as in one case where the union used general funds to place political advocacy advertisements in a daily newspaper of general circulation and to pay for the cost of a political broadcast on a local radio station.[29] A number of other practices were also condoned by the courts (including the use of union labour for campaign purposes),[30] but of these perhaps the most significant was the tolerance shown by the Supreme Court to the political action committee as a means by which both labour and capital could avoid the statutory prohibitions on corporate and union political donations and expenditures. The first 'political action committee' had been set up by the CIO in 1943, financed by the voluntary donations of trade union members. A second labour political action committee was formed by the American Federation of Labor in 1947, and the two political

[24] Alexander, 165.

[25] *US* v. *CIO* 335 US 106 (1948).

[26] *Id.*, 123 (Mr Justice Reed).

[27] *Id.*, 121.

[28] See also *US* v. *International Union, UAW* 352 US 567 (1957).

[29] *US* v. *Painters' Local Union No 481* 172 F 2d. 854 (1949). Also *US* v. *Anchorage Central Labor Council* 193 F Supp. 504 (1961).

[30] *US* v. *Construction and General Laborers' Union No 264* 101 F Supp. 869 (1951).

action committees merged with the merger of the American Federation of Labor and the CIO in 1955, the new body becoming known as the Committee on Political Education.[31] These political action committees became the means by which unions could expend money directly for political campaigns and indeed the success of the labour movement in this area led to other special interests to follow suit. In 1963 the National Association of Manufacturers made an untied grant for a new organization, The Business—Industry Political Action Committee, the purpose of which was 'to provide financial support to Congressional candidates who support the principles of constitutional government'. Just as the labour political action committees were funded by the voluntary donations of individual union members, so the business committees were financed by the voluntary contributions of individual businessmen.[32]

It appears that large sums of money were spent by these committees on direct political campaigning. The Committee on Political Education, for example, reported expenditure of just over $1 million in 1968 and just under in 1970.[33] It appears also that the numbers of such funds were growing, and this practice was eventually challenged as violating the requirements of the 1925 Act in *Pipefitters' Local Union No 562* v. *US*.[34] The case provides a useful insight into the nature of the political action committee phenomenon. The indictment charged that the union had from 1963 to 1968 established and maintained a fund that would receive regular and systematic payments from union members. The fund was separate from the union, though it was administered by union personnel. It has been suggested that 'A strong union may . . . use means, not the least of which is simple social pressure, to persuade members to volunteer',[35] and there is certainly some evidence in *Pipefitters* to cast doubt on the truly 'voluntary' character of the fund in that case, though there was also evidence that donations to the fund were not in fact a condition of employment or union membership. The money raised by these small contributions of members was then used for a variety of purposes which included contributions to candidates in federal elections. But again demonstrating a remarkably high level of tolerance to political campaign-ing by economic interests, the Supreme Court held that these facts did not reveal a conspiracy to violate the Federal Corrupt Practices Act of 1925.

The Court took the view that the Act did not prohibit a union from making, through the medium of a political fund organized by it, contributions or expenditures in connection with federal elections, so long as the money spent is in some way volunteered by those who are asked to

[31] A Heard, *The Costs of Democracy* (Chapel Hill, North Carolina, 1960) ch. 7.
[32] Alexander, *op. cit.*, 175. [33] *Id.*, 170. [34] 407 US 385 (1973).
[35] Alexander, *op. cit.*, 170.

contribute. This was in fact conceded by the government and is a point which had been conceded in some of the earlier cases in this area. The prosecution case, however, related to the nature of the fund through which individual union members could lawfully contribute. Thus, it was argued that the fund must be separate from the sponsoring union and may not be its '*alter ego*' in the sense of being dominated by it and serving its purposes. But this narrow approach was rejected by the Court which preferred the view that a fund must be separate from the sponsoring union only in the sense that there must be strict segregation of its monies from union dues and assessments. There was no requirement that the political organization be formally or functionally independent of union control or that union officials be barred from soliciting contributions or even precluded from determining how the money will be spent. The only condition imposed by the Court was that any solicitation should be conducted under circumstances plainly indicating that donations are for a political purpose and that those solicited may decline to contribute without loss of job, union membership, or any other reprisal within the union's institutional power.[36]

A FRESH START: CAMPAIGN FINANCE REFORM REFORMED

As Frank Sorauf has pointed out, the 1925 Act thus 'scarcely impeded the flow of campaign money'.[37] A combination of inadequate drafting (the legislation appeared to be passed with the 'loopholes tailored in'),[38] an unwilling judiciary (with the First Amendment lurking in the background), and inadequate enforcement machinery (by the Justice Department) all conspired to ensure that the fine principles embodied in the statute were never fully realized in practice. On the contrary 'the regulation of the financing of American elections had a long history of futility and the cynicism that futility breeds'.[39] Further pressure for reform—induced in part by the rising costs of campaigns on the one hand and the financial embarrassment of the Democrats on the other—led eventually, however, to the Federal Election Campaign Act of 1971. This introduced a number of fresh controls, aimed principally at extending disclosure and keeping down campaign costs by imposing a ceiling on candidates' permitted media expenditures. Congressional candidates were permitted to spend $50,000 or 10 cents per voting age resident, thus permitting senatorial candidates in California to spend up to $1.4 million! But although the 1971 Act 'stands as

36 407 US 385 (1973), 414.
37 F. Sorauf, *Inside Campaign Finance. Myths and Realities* (New Haven, 1992), 6.
38 *Id.*, 6.
39 *Id.*, 6.

evidence that the reasons for reform ran earlier and deeper than the traumatic events of Watergate',[40] there is no doubt that it was the latter which (together with the continuing increase in the cost of campaigns) was primarily responsible for the 'comprehensive corrective measures'[41] introduced in 1974.

Among the many issues raised by Watergate were 'the gamy stories of illegal campaign money: political money laundered to conceal its illegal corporate or foreign origin, secret and unreported funds, and funds raised in exchange for favourable government action'.[42] In the same vein, Sabato has written that:

> The 1972 re-election effort for President Richard Nixon included practices bordering on extortion, in which corporations and their executives were, in essence, 'shaken down' for cash donations. Up to $30 million was legally and illegally contributed by the business sector to Nixon in 1972.[43]

The 'public outrage and humiliation' which 'followed the revelations' led to a 'remarkable flowering of legislation designed to improve American political ethics'.[44] This included the Federal Election Campaign Act Amendments Act of 1974 which maintained a sense of continuity with the past but also introduced a number of important new measures. The scope of the legislation was comprehensive and without parallel. Apart from the reporting and disclosure requirements, tight contribution and expenditure limits were imposed on candidates, parties and others, and a new federal agency—the Federal Election Commission—was established to administer and enforce the legislation. Before looking at those measures in some detail it is to be noted that the effects of Watergate were not confined to the United States. It also gave great impetus to the reform movement in Canada which led eventually to the enactment of the Election Expenses Act 1974. This legislation introduced a requirement of annual disclosure by political parties, a ceiling on candidate and party permitted campaign expenditures, and the reimbursement from public funds of certain election expenses incurred by candidates and the parties.[45]

The three major areas covered by the US legislation as amended in 1974 (apart from the introduction of public funding for presidential campaigns introduced by the Presidential Election Campaign Fund Act) were contributions and expenditures; reporting and disclosure; and enforcement

[40] *Id.*, 7.

[41] *Buckley* v. *Valeo* 519 F 2d. 821 (1975), 837.

[42] Sorauf, *op. cit.*, 7.

[43] L. Sabato, *PAC Power: Inside the World of Political Action Committees* (New York, 985), 5.

[44] Sorauf, *op. cit.*, 7.

[45] See F. L. Seidle & K. Z. Seidle, 'Party Finance, the Election Expenses Act, and Campaign Spending in 1979 and 1980, in H Penniman (ed.), *Canada at the Polls in 1979 and 980: A Study of the General Elections* (Washington DC, 1981), 232.

and administration. So far as the first is concerned, the limits were set very low so that an individual could contribute up to $1,000 to a candidate for federal office and could incur expenditure of up to $1,000 'relative to a clearly identified candidate', advocating the election or defeat of such a candidate. The purpose of this latter measure (which is less restrictive than the parallel provisions of the Representation of the People Act 1983) was to prevent 'would-be contributors from avoiding the contribution limitations by the simple expedient of paying directly by media advertisements or for other parts of the candidate's campaign activities'.[46] Apart from the limits on individuals, restrictions were also imposed on political committees, though these were slightly higher in the case of contributions. No political committee (including a political committee of a party) could donate more than $5,000 and no political committee could incur expenditure of more than $1,000 relative to a clearly identified candidate (but there appears to be no limit on the number of candidates who may be supported by a particular political action committee). Congress was not content, however, simply to limit the flow of money into party funds, nor was it content simply to control expenditure on behalf of candidates and parties. Important restrictions were also imposed on the expenditures of candidates and political parties in federal elections, whether they be for the Presidency or Congress. Candidates for the House of Representatives, for example, were limited to $70,000.[47]

Moving from contributions and expenditures to reporting and disclosure, the new legislation also required the filing of quarterly reports by candidates and political committees. In addition pre-election and post-election reports were to be filed in an election year. As to the content of the reports, they were to include the following:

- cash in hand at the beginning of the reporting period;
- the total sum of contributions in the reporting period of $100 or less;
- the name and address of any political committee from which the reporting committee or candidate received funds;
- the names, occupations and principal places of business of any donors of more than $100;
- the details of any loans to or from any person, in excess of $100;
- the total amount of money raised from fund-raising events;
- details of expenditures, including the identity of any person to whom an expenditure of $100 (in aggregate) was made.

The legislation also required records to be kept of all persons contributing

[46] *Buckley* v. *Valeo* 424 US 1 (1976), 46.

[47] Senate candidates could spend $100,000 or 8 cents times the voting age population of the state.

more than $10, and although there was no need to report this information, the records were subject to audit by the Federal Election Commission.

Turning finally to enforcement and administration, as already suggested the main initiative here was the creation of the Federal Election Commission of eight members. The Secretary of the Senate and the Clerk of the House of Representatives are ex-officio non-voting members of the Commission, with the remaining six members being appointed by the Senate, the House, and the President. The two appointees of each of these three bodies must not be members of the same political party, and all appointees are subject to confirmation by both Houses of Congress. The Commission was given wide powers under the Act to fulfil its duties of administration and enforcement. These include 'rulemaking, subpoena, a power to require submission of written reports, a power to conduct investigations and hearings, a power to initiate civil actions to enforce FECA, a power to request the Attorney-General to institute civil actions to ensure compliance with FECA and certain election law criminal provisions, and a power to issue advisory opinions'.[48] Although enforcement by an independent specialist agency was an advance on enforcement by the Justice Department ('whose traditions and budgets had not prepared it for riding herd on candidate spending'),[49] it has been suggested that the opportunity for supervision and enforcement in this way has not been fully realized. According to Sorauf: 'Underfunded by the Congress and kept on a short leash for 15 years, the FEC had never been able to establish its independence as a regulator; its even division between three Democrats and three Republicans has additionally made it difficult for the Commission to deal with problems that are inevitably partisan'.[50]

THE RULE OF THE COURTS

The 1974 amendments had been scarcely enacted when a constitutional challenge was mounted to the legislation. This had been brewing ever since the Supreme Court decisions in the *CIO*[51] and *UAW*[52] cases in 1948 and 1957 respectively. In both cases the Court had managed to avoid confronting the thorny constitutional issues, but in both a sufficiently significant minority had indicated that there were stormy waters ahead. It might have been thought that these waters would have been calmed by Watergate and its revelations; there is certainly some reason to believe that

[48] *Buckley* v. *Valeo* 519 F 2d. 821 (1975), 888–9.
[49] Sorauf, *op. cit.*, 6.
[50] *Ibid.*, 185.
[51] *US* v. *CIO* 335 US 106 (1948).
[52] *US* v. *International Union, UAW* 352 US 567 (1957).

Watergate had a powerful effect on the Court of Appeals which upheld the legislation in face of the challenge mounted in the landmark decision in *Buckley* v. *Valeo*.[53] Like the Court of Appeals below the Supreme Court upheld the contribution limits of the 1971–74 Acts, the reporting and disclosure requirements (despite their alleged violation of privacy), and the public financing of presidential campaigns. But the Supreme Court took issue with the lower court on the question of spending controls, holding that they violated the First Amendment. According to the Court, a restriction on the amount of money a person or group can spend on political communications during a campaign necessarily reduces the number of issues discussed, the depth of their exploration, and the size of the audience reached.[54]

So far as the reporting and disclosure provisions are concerned, the Court accepted that 'compelled disclosure, in itself, can seriously infringe on privacy of association and belief guaranteed by the First Amendment'.[55] In this case, however, it was also accepted that these interests were subordinate to a number of compelling, countervailing public interests, which are as relevant to the debate for the introduction of compulsory disclosure in Britain as they were or are in the United States. The first of these is to promote more information about the candidates for public office, to enable electors to make more fully informed decisions at the ballot box. So disclosure 'allows the voters to place each candidate in the political spectrum more precisely than is often possible solely on the basis of party labels and campaign speeches' and also helps to 'alert the voter to the interests to which a candidate is more likely to be responsive and thus facilitate predictions of future performance in office'.[56] Additionally, it was held that disclosure helps to deter corruption by exposing large contributions and expenditures to the light of publicity.[57] The view was also expressed that quite apart from the merits of disclosure as a method of control, it was important as a necessary adjunct to other methods of regulation which had been introduced in the Act. So there would be no point in having contribution (or expenditure) limits without the machinery of disclosure to gather the data necessary to detect violations of these limits.[58]

In taking a similarly benevolent view of the contribution limits, the Court rejected the claim that they violated the First Amendment's protection of free speech, and concluded that:

[53] 424 US 1 (1976). [54] 424 US 1 (1976), 64.
[55] 424 US 1 (1976), 64. See also *Brown* v. *Socialist Workers '74 Campaign Committee (Ohio)* 459 US 87 (1982). [56] 424 US 1 (1976), 67. [57] *Id*
[58] *Id.*, 68.

> a limitation in the amount of money a person may give to a candidate or campaign organisation . . . involves little direct restraint on his political communication, for it permits the symbolic expression of support induced by a contribution but does not in any way infringe the contributor's freedom to discuss candidates and issues.[59]

But as already indicated, the position was different with regard to the spending limits. In striking down the limits on campaign expenditures by candidates, the Court held that the 'major evil associated with rapidly increasing campaign expenditures is the danger of candidate dependence on large contributions', but that this interest was 'adequately served by the Act's contribution limitations and disclosure provisions'.[60] In the same vein, the $1,000 ceiling on independent expenditures ('relative to a clearly identified candidate') was thought to exclude all citizens and groups except candidates, political parties, and the institutional press from any significant use of the most effective modes of communication. It would, for example, have been a federal criminal offence 'for a person or association to place a single one-quarter page advertisement 'relative to a clearly identified candidate' in a major metropolitan newspaper'.[61]

But what about the argument that spending limits are necessary in order to promote electoral equality in the sense that those who compete for political office should have a broadly equal chance of reaching and persuading the voters, and in the sense that those who have amassed great personal fortunes should not be permitted to employ this to disproportionate effect in election campaigns?[62] In what is perhaps the most important feature of this case the Court rejected the argument that promoting political equality is a compelling restraint on First Amendment freedoms. In the case of independent expenditures, it held that:

> the concept that government may restrict the speech of some elements of our society in order to enhance the relative voice of others is wholly foreign to the First Amendment, which was designed to secure the widest possible dissemination of information from diverse and antagonistic sources and to assure unfettered interchange of ideas for the bringing about of political and social changes desired by the people.[63]

The Court went on to say that: 'The First Amendment's protection against governmental abridgement of free expression cannot properly be made to depend on a person's financial ability to engage in public discussion'.[64] People should be free to spend as much as they can raise or as much as they

[59] *Id.*, 21. [60] *Id.*, 55. [61] *Id.*, 49.

[62] For a discussion of this issue see R. Dworkin, 'What is Equality? Part 3: The Place of Liberty' (1987) 73 *Iowa LR* 1. Also interesting from a different perspective is J. Fleishman, 'Freedom of Speech and Equality of Political Opportunity: The Constitutionality of the Federal Election Campaign Act 1971' (1973) 51 *North Carolina LR* 389.

[63] 424 US 1 (1976), 48–9. [64] *Id.*

want. If that means that some people will not be heard because they cannot shout loudly enough, then too bad. That is neither the business of Congress nor the concern of the Court.

Predictably, this last aspect of the decision in *Buckley* unleashed a torrent of criticism. Some of this came from influential sources, including Judge Skelly Wright who had delivered the judgment in the court below. A blistering attack in 1976[65] was followed by another in the 1982 *Columbia Law Review*[66] in which he referred to the decision as being 'tragically misguided', as having 'gutted vital portions of the legislation', and as having denied the political system some of its most powerful defences against electoral inequalities. The Supreme Court, however, appeared undaunted by the charge that it had placed 'serious obstacles in the path of our society's advancement toward political equality through law'[67] and continued in the years after *Buckley*[68] to deconstruct other key provisions of the legislation,[69] though with much less devastating effect.[70] Many vain attempts have been made since 1976 to retrieve the principles of political equality, though these have all come to grief, and it is by no means clear whether any such legislation would withstand close scrutiny.[71] A recent proposal is for voluntary limits, with the rivals of candidates who exceed these limits being eligible for public funding for their campaign in the form of vouchers to be used for media advertising.[72] But even this measure—which seems calculated to inflate rather than curtail campaign costs—is likely to be challenged if passed, with one Kentucky Senator promising to be the 'Jim Buckley of 1993'.[73] This led one (not unsympathetic) commentator to remind today's reformers' that 'the effort to alter election law ends not in the legislative arena but in the courts, where judges have jealously guarded the First Amendment values threatened by regulation of the political process'.[74]

[65] J. Skelly Wright, 'Politics and the Constitution: Is Money Speech?' (1976) 85 *Yale LJ* 1001. See also B. Clagett & J. Bolton, '*Buckley* v. *Valeo*, Its Aftermath and Its Prospects: The Constitutionality of Government Restraints on Political Campaign Financing' (1976) 29 *Vanderbilt LR* 1327.

[66] J. Skelly Wright, 'Money and the Pollution of Politics: Is the First Amendment an Obstacle to Political Equality?' (1982) 82 *Columbia LR* 609.

[67] *Id.*, 611.

[68] 424 US 1 (1976).

[69] See *Federal Election Commission* v. *National Conservative PAC* 470 US 480 (1985); *Federal Election Commission* v. *Massachusetts' Citizens for Life, Inc.* 93 L Ed. 2d. 539 (1986).

[70] These cases are fully discussed in L. Tribe, *American Constitutional Law* (Mineola, NY, 1988, 2nd ed.), 1132–53.

[71] See K. Levit, 'Campaign Finance Reform and the Return of *Buckley v. Valeo*' (1993) 103 *Yale LJ* 469. See more recently, J. B. Raskin 'Challenging the "Wealth Primary" ' *The Nation*, 21 November 1994 and T. S. Purdum 'Trying a constitutional tack to curb campaign spending' *New York Times*, 21 October 1994.

[72] Levit, *id.*

[73] *Id.*

[74] *Id.*

LESSONS FROM THE UNITED STATES

Politicians and policy makers in the United States are engaged in a renewed attempt at campaign finance law reform in an attempt to reduce campaign costs and to retrieve in some way the principles of 1974. Their task is not made any easier by more sober assessments which are beginning to challenge the strong resistance to *Buckley* v. *Valeo*. There are those who are prepared to argue that strict review by the courts is perfectly justifiable,[75] that campaign costs are in fact not too high,[76] and that the interests of electors (rather than candidates or parties) demand that there should be little, if any, campaign finance regulation.[77] But regardless of what happens in the United States and regardless of how the movement for reform eventually unfolds, there is much to learn in this country from the American experience. The starting point is the lesson of principle which the American experience teaches: in terms of the need for openness and transparency of campaign finance; in terms of the need to eliminate the risk of or scope for undue and improper influence over elected officials; and in terms of the need to promote equality of electoral opportunity amongst those who compete for political office. Some of these principles are already recognized by the British system—we have disclosure and spending limits for candidates[78]—but these have not been developed and maintained to keep pace with the dynamic and changing nature of the electoral system.

So far as the first of these principles is concerned, there is renewed interest in mandatory disclosure of campaign contributions and expenditures. Many of those who gave evidence to the Home Affairs Committee argued in favour of such an initiative, and only the Conservative Party seems to be opposed.[79] The American experience suggests, however, that such measures while admirable in principle are not so easy to execute in practice. At the one extreme, before 1971 the reporting and disclosure requirements appear to have been easily evaded,[80] partly because of the absence of an enforcement agency and partly because of the tight restrictions on access to the information by journalists and academics.[81]

[75] L. BeVier, 'Money and Politics: A Perspective on the First Amendment and Campaign Finance Reform' (1985) 73 *Calif LR* 1045.

[76] Sorauf, *op. cit.*

[77] S. Gottlieb, 'The Dilemma of Election Campaign Finance Reform' (1989) 18 *Hofstra LR* 301.

[78] Representation of the People Act 1983, ss. 75, 76, 81, 82, Sch. 3.

[79] See Home Affairs Committee, Funding of Political Parties, Minutes of Evidence HC 726 (1992–3).

[80] See Heard, *op. cit.*, 359–70.

[81] See D. Adamany & G. Agree, *Political Money: A Strategy for Campaign Financing in America* (Baltimore, 1975), 87.

Since 1974, there is probably too much information. 'The sheer detail of the candidate, PAC, and party reports under the FECA', it is said, 'has become a wonder of the democratic political world.'[82] If it is thought desirable to encourage small donations from large numbers of people, there seems no reason why the duty to report and disclose should be fixed as low as $100, a figure first set in 1910. Apart from creating an oversupply of unnecessary information, such a requirement is arguably also an unnecessary invasion of personal privacy. This is not to reject the case for transparency first established in the United States in 1910. But it is to suggest that there is both a practical and a principled case for a more relaxed approach.[83]

The second principle established early in the American legislation—the elimination of undue and improper influence over elected officials—also strikes a chord here, though again it is open to question whether it is capable of implementation in the form adopted in the United States. The political parties in Britain rely heavily on corporate and trade union support, while the Conservatives in particular appear to have benefited from a number of large personal donations. It is not altogether clear precisely what influence this money buys, any more than it is in the United States.[84] But at the very least it does cause unease and may also buy access to elected officials—access of a type which voters normally will not have.[85] It is a matter of some difficulty knowing how to deal with this. A recognition of the need to eliminate undue and improper influence over elected officials might dictate following the American example of prohibiting corporate and trade union contributions, though this would fail to recognize the role of special interests in the American system through political action committees. We might alternatively or also wish to restrict to say £5,000 the total contributions from any source (whether it be a company, a trade union or an individual) to a political party in any one year. The difficulty with the introduction of a measure of this kind, however, is that in the absence of a massive injection of state aid for the political parties, it would cause severe financial embarrassment and would operate to the disproportionate disadvantage of one party in particular. There are many more companies than trade unions, all the more so as the number of unions continues to decline as the process of amalgamation increases.

[82] Sorauf, *op. cit.*, 229.

[83] See also *Brown* v. *Socialist Workers '74 Campaign Committee (Ohio)* 459 US 87 (1982) suggesting the need to qualify the obligation to disclose in respect of donors to small parties who may be subject to harassment, in this case by the FBI and others.

[84] But see Linton, *op. cit.*, 67–79.

[85] See M. Nicholson, 'Campaign Financing and Equal Protection' (1974) 26 *Stanford LR* 815, 820.

The lesson from the United States then is that while we might wish enthusiastically to embrace the need to eliminate undue and improper influence over elected officials, we may not be so enthusiastic about embracing the particular American method for its implementation. Just as Eric Barendt has shown in chapter nine that the reception of First Amendment jurisprudence must take account of the political soil in which it has grown, so the reception of other political principles must take account of the political soil into which they are to be transplanted. The American legislation has not in any event been effective in stopping the influence of big money, whether from special interests or other sources. This was to be expected with the lax enforcement regime of the pre-Watergate era. But even since then special interests have been key players in the American political process, both expressly facilitated by the legislation and well capable of exploiting its loopholes.[86] The application of principle must be adapted to the structural realities of our own political system, and in this particular case to the historical and cultural traditions of working-class representation. We cannot prohibit company political donations without prohibiting trade union affiliation fees and donations. Nor can we restrict the size of company donations, without at the same time restricting the size of trade union affiliation fees. And we cannot do that without destroying the organizational structure of the Labour Party. It may be that the structure will change, but campaign finance law should respond to rather than drive that change. The most we can do in the short term may be to require full and frank disclosure of contributions, inadequate though that may seem.

The third principle established in the American legislation—the principle of equality of electoral opportunity—is also relevant in this country. Indeed the principle is already recognized in the Representation of the People Act 1983 which imposes limits on candidates' spending. There are, however, no limits on the political parties even though the national campaign conducted by the parties is much more significant in determining the outcome of the election. This compares with the United States where there are now spending limits on the parties, but not on the candidates, the latter having been struck down in 1976. There is some support in Britain for extending spending limits to the parties, and this in fact was done in Canada in 1974 so that for federal elections in that country there are both spending limits on candidates and their parties.[87] The American experience does, however, invite caution before going down this road and before fully embracing the principle of political equality. The $3 million limit on

[86] For a good summary of the work of the PACS, see L. Epstein, *Political Parties in the American Mold* (Madison, Wis., 1986), 284–309.

[87] See Ewing, *op. cit.*, esp. ch. 4.

the national committees of political parties introduced in 1940 was not an unequivocal success. It appears to be accepted that the legislation may have contributed to (though it is unclear whether it in fact caused) a 'dispersion in the financial management of campaigns'.[88] The evidence tends to suggest that more money was spent by committees other than the national committees of the parties in support of party candidates and that more money was held or spent at the state level because of the ceiling than would otherwise have been the case. The evidence suggests then that rather than restrict campaign expenditures the effect of spending limits may be simply to re-route the money which will still be spent on broadly the same cause.

The problem of money being diverted to other sources and the related though separate problem of independent expenditures on behalf of a party or candidate invites consideration of the question whether it is enough to impose limits on political parties and candidates without also imposing controls on other third parties who may engage in an election campaign.[89] The problem is perhaps graphically illustrated by the $1.1 million spent by the National Conservative Political Action Committee to challenge six liberal Democratic senators running for re-election in 1980.[90] It may be thought inappropriate to impose tight limits on what the parties may spend if others are free to spend money with impunity in order to influence the outcome of the election. There are already indications that this could be a problem in this country with a number of interest groups having engaged in political advertising during the 1992 campaign, these including NALGO, the Institute of Directors and the International Fund for Animal Welfare.[91] The day has long passed when it would be possible to contemplate the effective banning of such advertising in order to maintain the integrity of the limits on the parties, as was done in 1918 in respect of the limits on candidates' expenditures.[92] Nevertheless it is not an issue which can be ignored, given the potential damage which it brings in its wake. One possibility would be the introduction of a limit on the permitted independent expenditures of groups and individuals in support of a political party, though this could be undermined by the proliferation and fragmentation of these groups. But it may be that the problem is largely

[88] Heard, *op. cit.*, 355.
[89] See also Linton, *op. cit.*, 93–7.
[90] See Sorauf, *op. cit.*, 180.
[91] See Linton, *op. cit.*, 96.
[92] For background, see K. Ewing, *The Funding of Political Parties in Britain* (Cambridge, 1987), 80–90. Evidence of the vulnerability of these measures is provided by the complaint by the Society for the Protection of Unborn Children that s. 76 of the Representation of the People Act 1983 violates Art. 10 of the ECHR. The complaint was referred to Strasbourg in Sept. 1993. See also the perceptive analysis by C. R. Sunstein 'Political Equality and Unintended Consequences' (1994) 94 Columbia LR 1390.

resolved in this country by the extraordinarily fortuitous ban on political advertising on radio or television.

CONCLUSION

There is thus much to commend in the underlying principles which can be teased out of the campaign finance legislation of the United States. These could be usefully adopted for implementation here, bearing in mind the need for a strong and independent agency to deal with problems of implementation, and bearing in mind also the need for a continuing commitment to reform to overcome and respond to the iron law of unintended consequences,[93] used by some as a reason for doing nothing. On a more negative note, perhaps, we have much to fear from the history of judicial intervention in the United States. We have seen how the courts have been reluctant to give effect to election spending limits, initially interpreted very narrowly and then struck down—at least so far as they applied to candidates and third parties. Neither the concern to reduce escalating campaign costs nor the desire to promote equality of electoral opportunity between those competing for political office were enough to persuade the Supreme Court of the merits of the legislation. If a similar approach were to be adopted in Britain—and we already had a taster in the *Tronoh Mines*[94] case,—not only could this lead to future reforms being called into question, it could also threaten those campaign finance measures which we already have in this country and which contribute greatly to the keeping down of costs.

These measures currently include sections 75 and 76 of the Representation of the People Act 1983 which impose limits on the expenditure not only of parliamentary candidates but also of those who campaign on their behalf. This is precisely the type of expenditure struck down in *Buckley* v. *Valeo* (indeed the British legislation is if anything more restrictive than the offending provisions of the Federal Election Campaign Act). Equally important are the provisions of the Broadcasting Act 1990 which prohibit political advertising on television. It is unlikely that such a ban would withstand constitutional scrutiny in the United States and it is already the case that the High Court of Australia has struck down detailed political

[93] See the discussion by D. Lowenstein 'On Campaign Finance Reform: The Root of all Evil is Deeply Rooted' (1989) 18 *Hofstra LR* 301. This also seems to be the approach the present government is adopting in relation to the issue of racially motivated crimes; see ch. 11 below.

[94] [1952] 1 All ER 697.

broadcasting legislation which included restrictions on political advertising.[95] This was done after the Court had first created a new implied constitutional restraint on government power which prohibited the federal government from unjustifiably restricting freedom of expression. This was then applied by the Court to strike down the legislation, in the case of one of its members after adopting the reasoning of the Supreme Court in *Buckley*. A similar approach in Britain would be disastrous, for in a country where there are no general restraints on national campaign expenditure and no restraints on national campaign expenditure by interest groups, the broadcasting restrictions, whatever their impact on freedom of expression, are an effective way of restraining campaign costs and of restraining the political influence of the economically powerful.

Such an approach by the courts would also call into question possible future reforms such as general spending limits on the parties and the attendant restrictions on interest group campaigns, with the result that current proposals of this kind currently on the agenda could be stillborn. It is already the case that the national campaign expenditures introduced in Canada in 1974 were thrown into disarray by the unreflective adoption of *Buckley* v. *Valeo* by the Alberta Court of Queen's Bench in 1984 and again in 1993.[96] Those with an interest in campaign finance reform are thus quite properly concerned by the spectre of a domestic Bill of Rights which is currently haunting Britain. The principle of political equality which campaign finance legislation often seeks to embrace has been comprehensively rejected by the landmark decision of the Supreme Court in the United States which, in a spirit of forensic imperialism has now been extended to Australia and Canada. It may well be that these decisions are theoretically unsound and that equality is after all a constitutional principle (though whose equality: the candidates', the parties', or the electors'?). This may be intellectually satisfying, and a convenient way of contending what ought to be done by institutions which conspire to destroy democratic self-government. But it is of little practical relevance if the principle of political equality is one which our courts would subsequently prove too ready to sacrifice on the altar of unrestrained political liberty.

[95] *National Citizens' Coalition, Inc* v. *Attorney General for Canada* (1985) 11 DLR (4th) 481; *Sommerville* v. *Attorney General of Canada*, 30 June 1993.

[96] *Australian Capital Television Pty.* v. *Commonwealth of Australia* (1992) 66 ALJR 695.

11

The Criminalization of Racist Violence?

IAN LOVELAND[1]

RACIST violence appears to be a growing problem in modern Britain. The Qaddus Ali case is perhaps the best known, but by no means only example of an already significant and apparently intensifying social malaise.[2] The assault on Qaddus Ali has added extra urgency to an ongoing debate about the desirability of making racist violence a distinct criminal offence, to which we should attach penalties over and above those imposed for similar actions undertaken for non-racist motives.[3]

An increase in racist attacks is not a uniquely British phenomenon. We are all familiar with the revival of Nazism in the unified Germany, and of sporadic inter-ethnic violence, in forms ranging from isolated incidents to civil war, in many East European nations.[4] Such difficulties are also evident in the United States. By 1991, thirty-five States had responded to a rising incidence of apparently racially motivated offences by introducing so-called 'hate crimes' legislation, directed primarily (but not exclusively) at hatred founded on racial or ethnic hostility.[5] This legislation takes one of two forms. It either creates free-standing race hate offences, or it permits a sentencing court to increase the penalty attached to existing crimes if the perpetrator was motivated by racial hatred. Initiatives of this nature are a primary example of what Eric Barendt in chapter nine[6] termed the 'fierce split' which often divides the American legislative, judicial, and academic communities in respect of social policy reform. Moreover, as far as hate crimes are concerned, that split operates in the spheres both of desirability and of constitutionality.

The American hate crimes statutes are defended by their supporters on

[1] My thanks to Carol Vincent and Genevra Richardson for commenting on this essay at various stages of its development.

[2] D. Pallister & V. Chaudhary, 'Killer attacks detective at Old Bailey', *The Guardian* 19 Nov. 1993: Home Office, *Racially Motivated Crime: a British Crime Survey Analysis* (London, 1994): D. Rose, 'Racist Wave Sweeps East End', *The Observer* 13 Feb. 1994.

[3] See e.g. Geoffrey Bindman's article, 'Bringing Race Bigots to Book', *The Guardian* 30 Oct. 1993.

[4] L. Doyle, 'Racism: West Europe's Mounting Death Toll', *The Independent* 13 Jan. 1994.

[5] See S. Gellman, 'Sticks and Stones Can Put You in Jail, but Can Words Increase Your Sentence?' (1991) 39 *UCLA LR* 333.

[6] At 215.

the essentially public policy ground that such offences must attract greater punishment because they inflict greater damage on the victim and on society itself than similar conduct carried out for non-racist motives.[7] In part, this added harm arises from the fear of more general public order problems, as victims may be collectively driven towards vigilante style self-defence or preventive measures which are themselves criminal. A more substantial concern arises from the likelihood that other members of the victim's racial group may feel at greater risk of attack, and are thereby deterred from going about their normal everyday activities, or live in a state of ever present anxiety. This explicit harm shades into the more amorphous, but no less important problem that race hate crimes denigrate the societal status of the victim group: in Patricia Williams's graphic phrase, a society in which racist violence against minority groups is commonplace is in effect engaging in a process of 'spirit-murdering' sections of its population.[8] More broadly still, the prevalence of racist violence can be seen as undermining the values of pluralism and tolerance on which a democratic political order must rest.

Hate crimes legislation is then designed to have both practical and symbolic effects. In addition to its (it is hoped) punitive and deterrent impact on individual racists, the legislation is seen as a powerful and explicit expression of societal distaste for racist values.

There have however been dissenting voices in the USA, all be they raised against the means rather than the desired ends of such intitiatives. Critics of hate crimes legislation argue that it has adverse public policy implications. It may, for example, have the undesirable effect of stigmatizing the victim group by suggesting that they are less able than the majority population to fend for themselves. Secondly, penal legislation may divert attention and resources away from educational and social policy initiatives which might more successfully eliminate the problem. In effect a hate crime law could be simply an exercise in 'symbolic reassurance'. Indeed, such legislation could be counter-productive even at the symbolic level, insofar as infrequent use of the measure, or acquittals of those charged under it, may suggest to public opinion that there is no 'real' problem to be addressed.

The British government apparently sees no need to promote similar legislation here. This may be due in part to a perception that the present law (which will be discussed below) deals adequately with the problem. In

[7] See Gelman *op. cit.*: Note, 'Hate is not Speech: a Constitutional Defence of Penalty Enhancement for Hate Crimes' (1993) 106 *Harvard LR* 1315: M. Matsuda, 'Public Response to Racist Speech: Considering the Victim's Story' (1989) *Michigan LR* 2320.

[8] 'Spirit-Murdering the Messenger: the Discourse of Fingerpointing as the Law's Response to Racism' (1987) 42 *U. Miami LR* 127.

addition, the Home Secretary (Michael Howard QC) has announced his personal opposition to hate crime laws, on the grounds that racist motive would be so difficult to prove that one might produce the undesirable situation that perpetrators of violent crimes would be convicted of nothing at all.[9] However, the Commons Home Affairs Select Committee has recently been holding hearings on racial violence, and it would not seem improbable that MPs will recommend enactment of further race hate legislation.

This essay asks whether they would be well-advised to do so. The controversy over hate crimes in the USA has recently been heightened by a shift in the terms of debate. Attention has moved from discussing the wisdom of such legislation to questioning its constitutionality. There is now a burgeoning body of Supreme Court judgments addressing the compatibility of hate crimes statutes with the First Amendment. Clearly, our Parliament's law-making powers are not legally constrained by such considerations. However, I will suggest that Parliament should pay close attention to the American debate, because lessons drawn from that experience offer valuable guidance as to how we might maximize the legitimacy of what would necessarily be a controversial innovation with substantial civil liberties implications.

This argument will be fleshed out in the following pages, but it may be helpful to outline its skeletal form here. The presumption is that the legitimacy of any new legislation targeted at racist violence will be contingent not only on its effectiveness in reducing such violence, but also on its containing no scope for racist criminals to claim that they are being 'martyred' because their civil right to free expression is being infringed. The notion that the 'free-born Englishman' has a 'fundamental right' to be racist is a powerful icon in far right ideology,[10] and it is an argument that may acquire added force from the apparently strengthening predilection of some of our judges to find in the common law 'fundamental' civil liberties, including freedom of expression, which cannot be infringed by anything but the most explicit of statutory provisions.[11] Given that the United States has perhaps extended the right to be racist further than any other western democracy,[12] a British initiative which passed constitutional muster if measured against a First Amendment yardstick would enable Parliament plausibly to argue that regulating racial hatred need not impinge upon anyone's civil liberties.

[9] A. Travis, 'Howard Fears "BNP Martyrs" ', *The Guardian* 14 Oct. 1993.

[10] See e.g. the (obviously unsuccessful) defence raised in *Jordan* v. *Burgoyne* [1963] 2 QB 744.

[11] Lord Browne-Wilkinson, 'The Infiltration of a Bill of Rights' [1992] *PL* 397: Sir John Laws, 'Is the High Court the Guardian of Fundamental Constitutional Rights' [1993] *PL* 59.

[12] See e.g. *Terminiello* v. *Chicago* (1949) 337 US 1: *Brandenburg* v. *Ohio* (1969) 395 US 444: *National Socialist Party of America* v. *Village of Skokie* (1977) 432 US 43.

The method adopted in this chapter is as follows. Section I sketches the extent to which the First Amendment has traditionally protected the freedom of expression of purveyors of Nazi and racist opinion. Section II assesses the current British law in relation to race hate crimes, and suggests that little of it would be considered constitutional if it had been enacted in the USA. The third section then considers the recent Supreme Court decisions addressing the compatibility of hate crimes legislation with the First Amendment. In its concluding pages, the chapter suggests that Parliament adopts one type of US legislation, but suggests also that even while such a measure would be substantively 'legitimate' in principle, one would face many difficult choices when trying to turn that principle into practice.

RACE HATE AND THE FIRST AMENDMENT

The paucity of litigation concerning the scope of the First Amendment prior to the First World War is perhaps one of the great mysteries of American constitutional history. It may be explained by the 1833 decision in *Barron* v. *Baltimore*,[13] which concluded, contrary to Madison's original wishes, that the Bill of Rights did not apply to the States. That conclusion was not reversed in respect of the First Amendment until 1925 in *Gitlow* v. *New York*.[14]

The First Amendment had however been invoked in the immediate aftermath of World War I to challenge the constitutionality of convictions under Congressional anti-subversion legislation. The litigation in that era, built upon the celebrated 'clear and present danger' test formulated by Holmes J in *Schenk* v. *United States*,[15] suggested that lawful regulation of speech was contingent upon the Court concluding that communication of the speaker's ideas would lead to some violent public disorder, be it in the form of defeat in war,[16] a general strike,[17] or a non-electoral overthrow of existing constitutional government.[18] In crude terms, the First Amendment did not prevent Congress punishing speech that comprised a general or targeted invitation to engage in criminal behaviour.

'Clear and present danger' is an imprecise test, based on judicial notions of proximity and risk. Holmes rapidly found himself in a minority in interpreting his own criteria. The majority on the Court equated clear and present danger with a 'bad tendency' or 'incipiency' test, namely that the

[13] (1833) 8 L Ed. 672. [14] (1925) 268 US 652. [15] (1919) 249 US 47.
[16] *Schenk* v. *US* (1919) 249 US 47: *Abrams* v. *US* (1919) 250 US 616.
[17] *Gitlow* v. *New York* (1925) 268 US 652.
[18] *Whitney* v. *California* (1927) 274 US 357.

speech might lead at some distant time and place to a regulable threat to the public interest.[19] Holmes in contrast required some evidence that the threat posed a danger in the short term; under this variant of the test, the most ardent of anarchists would find his speech entirely unregulated if his message was one by which no one would be persuaded to unlawful action.[20] Holmes was more prosaic in describing his dissenting judgment in *Gitlow* to friends, referring to it as 'a page of slack on the right of an ass to drool upon proletarian dictatorship'.[21]

The Court quickly established that regulation of speech to prevent 'substantive evils' had to be content neutral, or devoid of viewpoint discrimination. Thus legislators could punish speech directed towards the violent overthrow of elected governments, but could not single out specific ideologies for legal control. A statute which punished the speech solely of communist revolutionaries, while ignoring that of fascist, Nazi, or anarchist groups directed towards the same evil ends would be inconsistent with First Amendment protection. Rather greater difficulties arise in respect of the selective enforcement of a statute which is not discriminatory on its face, but which may become so according to the way it is construed by a trial court.[22]

One can discern similarly blurred edges to the so-called 'fighting words' justification for regulation of speech offered by Murphy J in *Chaplinsky* v. *New Hampshire*.[23] Paraphrasing a segment of Zechariah Chaffee's 1941 book *Free Speech in the United States*, Murphy J concluded that 'fighting words'—'those which by their very utterance tend to inflict injury or tend to incite an imminent breach of the peace'—were to be bracketed with the obscene, the libellous and the profane as meriting no First Amendment protection. Such words were: 'no essential part of any exposition of ideas, and are of such slight social value as a step to truth that any benefit that may be derived from them is clearly outweighed by the social interest in order and morality.'[24]

In subsequent case-law, the libellous, the profane, and the obscene have all been accorded sometimes substantial First Amendment safeguards.[25] The fighting words doctrine continues to be authoritative; the difficulty is deciding what it is authoritative for. Murphy J's much quoted phrase lends

[19] *Frohwerk* v. *United States* (1919) 294 US 204: *Debs* v. *United States* (1919) 249 US 211: *Gitlow* v. *New York* (1925) 268 US 652.

[20] Cf. *Abrams* v. *United States* (1919) 250 US 616.

[21] Quoted in L. Baker, *Holmes and Brandeis: a Dual Biography* (New York, 1986), 250.

[22] See the discussion of *Terminiello* at n. 38 below and accompanying text.

[23] *Chaplinsky* v. *New Hampshire* (1942) 315 US 568.

[24] *Id.*, 572.

[25] *Roth* v. *US* (1957) 354 US 476: *Stanley* v. *Georgia* (1969) 394 US 557: *New York Times* v. *Sullivan* (1964) 376 US 254.

itself to many interpretations. Does it cover for example speech whose substance is intrinsically injurious, irrespective of how and to whom it is delivered? Or can it embrace speech which is entirely innocuous in content but delivered in a particularly spiteful or provocative way? Or does the test depend on whether the speaker's audience is atypically prone either to be injured by the speech, or to respond to it with violence that creates public order problems? Or must one consider a combination of any two or more of these factors? This is a point to which we will return below.

The Court has accepted that expressive acts or so-called 'symbolic speech' may also attract First Amendment protection, albeit to a lesser extent than 'pure speech'.[26] Actions such as wearing a black armband to denote opposition to the Vietnam war[27] and burning a US flag to protest against the first Reagan administration's foreign and military policies[28] have been so protected. The leading case on the issue remains *United States* v. *O'Brien*,[29] in which the majority held that governmental regulation of expressive conduct was defensible if 'it furthers an important or substantial governmental interest; if the governmental interest is unrelated to the suppression of free expression; and if the incidental restriction on First Amendment freedom is no greater than is essential to furtherance of that interest'.[30]

That final point in *O'Brien* indicates quite cogently that the notion of proportionality is well entrenched in First Amendment case-law. A more conventional label for this idea is the so-called 'overbreadth' doctrine. The nub of the doctrine is that in regulating speech to effect permissible ends, government must choose a means which does not impact adversely on legitimate individual or group interests. Murphy J's explanation of overbreadth in *Thornhill* v. *Alabama*[31] is perhaps the most helpful. In *Thornhill*, the Court struck down a statute which simply forbade all kinds of picketing in the vicinity of an industrial dispute. Murphy J condemned the statute because it:

> does not aim specifically at evils within the allowable sphere of state control [but] sweeps within its ambit other activities that in ordinary circumstances constitute an exercise of freedom of speech or of the press. The existence of such a statute . . . results in a continuous and pervasive restraint on all freedom of discussion that might reasonably be regarded as within its purview.[32]

This restraint on future belief, speech, and conduct might also be labelled as a 'chilling effect', so-called because it is presumed that such statutes

[26] For an overview of a complicated body of case-law see M. Nimmer, 'The Meaning of Symbolic Speech Under the First Amendment' (1969) 17 *UCLA LR* 29: K. Greenwalt, 'O'er the Land of the Free: Flag Burning as Speech' (1991) 38 *UCLA LR* 925.

[27] *Tinker* v. *Des Moines* (1969) 393 US 503.

[28] *Texas* v. *Johnson* (1989) 109 S Ct. 2533.

[29] (1968) 391 US 367.

[30] *Id.*, 372.

[31] (1940) 310 US 88.

[32] *Id.*, 102.

would deter individuals from expressing intrinsically lawful beliefs or opinons.

Overbreadth may often merge with the equally fatal flaw of 'vagueness'. A statute will be invalid if its text is so ambiguous or uncertain in its meaning that people of ordinary intelligence could not reasonably understand its scope, or if enforcement agencies or juries lack sufficiently clear guidelines to preclude the possibility of arbitrary arrest or conviction.[33]

This has been necessarily a very cursory overview of First Amendment principles. For the purposes of this essay, it may be helpful to narrow the focus a little, and examine briefly two of the leading cases on protection of racist expresssion, these being respectively *Terminiello* v. *Chicago*[34] and *Brandenburg* v. *Ohio*.[35]

Fascism and racism—protected speech and conduct

One of the more bizarre features of the McCarthy era is recalled by Justice William Douglas in his *Court Years* autobiography. During the 1950s, the periodical *US News and World Report*, which had a circulation of over two million, used to run a league table which analysed Supreme Court judgments to determine how 'communist' the various judges were. Even the conservative Chief Justice Fred Vinson was apparently 27% communist. Douglas, the 'most communist' member, generally scored 90%, and records that he was much aggrieved to find that one month he was pipped to the post by former Ku Klux Klan member Hugo Black, who managed a 91% score.[36]

Such barometers of public opinion presumably discounted Douglas's support for the free speech rights of virulent anti-communists, such as his opinion for a 5–4 majority in *Terminiello* v. *Chicago*. Terminiello was a Catholic priest, who had made a name for himself in fascist circles in the late 1940s as a purveyor of anti-communist, anti-semitic, and anti-black propaganda. He had been convicted under a Chicago ordinance which forbade the making of any 'improper noise, riot, disturbance, breach of the peace or diversion tending to a breach of the peace'. This ordinance had been interpreted by the trial court as encompassing any speech which, *inter alia*, 'stirs the public to anger' or 'invites dispute'.

Douglas J's majority opinion observed that the very purpose of free speech was to invite dispute, and dispute could often stir people to anger. Such argument was an essential characteristic of American society. It could

[33] See *Papachristou* v. *Jacksonville* (1972) 405 US 156: *Smith* v. *Goguen* (1974) 451 US 566: and the discussion of the issue in W. Lockhart, Y. Kamisar, & J. Choper, *Constitutional Law* (Minnesota, 1975 5th ed), 815–40.

[34] (1949) 337 US 1.

[35] (1969) 395 US 444.

[36] W. Douglas, *The Court Years* (New York, 1980), 209–11.

not in itself be a substantive evil which either a federal, state, or municipal legislature was entitled to prevent. Regulation was permissible only when such dispute comprised a clear and present danger of adverse public consequences 'far above inconvenience, annoyance or unrest'.

The majority did not hold the statute as void on its face, and suggested that had its construction by State courts been limited to fighting words Terminiello's conviction would have been upheld. The problem facing the majority was that it could not tell on what basis Terminiello was found guilty: 'For all anyone knows, he was convicted under the parts of the ordinance (as construed) which, for example, make it an offence merely to invite dispute'.[37] The trial court's instructions to the jury were therefore overbroad. Not only could they reach perfectly lawful expression, but they could also exert a chilling effect on the future communication of as yet unspoken thought. Citizens should not be at risk of prosecution simply for challenging, changing, or reinforcing the way their audience thought.

An example of more modern vintage is provided by the 1969 decision in *Brandenburg* v. *Ohio,*[38] (incidentally one of Douglas's final cases).[39] Brandenburg and a dozen like-minded citizens were Ku Klux Klan members who staged a cross burning ceremony, during which they advocated violent action to preserve the interests of whites. Brandenburg was convicted under Ohio's 1919 criminal syndicalism statute of 'advocating the duty, necessity or propriety of crime, sabotage or unlawful methods of terrorism as a means of accomplishing industrial or political reform'.

This statute was obviously more tightly drawn than the ordinance in *Terminiello*, and convictions of leftist agitators under virtually identical Federal and State legislation had regularly been upheld by the Supreme Court since the 1920s.[40] Brandenburg's conviction was however reversed. The Court overruled earlier case-law to hold that advocacy could be regulated only if it was intended and likely to produce **imminent** lawless action. Neither the statute itself, nor interpretive Ohio case-law, nor the trial judge's instruction to the jury, had distinguished between 'mere advocacy' and incitement to immediate criminality. The speech and cross burning in this case had been staged in a remote field, to which Brandenburg had invited a local television station's film crew in the expectation that the event would subsequently receive widespread publicity. Whatever adverse consequences such activities might have in the

[37] 337 US 1, 6.

[38] (1969) 395 US 444.

[39] He delivered a concurring judgment, in which he suggested that the clear and present danger test was too flexible a tool to be left in the hands of a Court which had in the past proved itself insuficently alert to the need to protect fundamental rights of expression against the transient whims of an oppressive majority.

[40] *Whitney* v. *California* (1927) 274 US 357: *Dennis* v. *US* (1951) 341 US 494.

long term, they presented no imminent threat of illegality. Any statute which swept such lawful activities within its reach would be facially invalid.

There is little doubt that analysts drawn to Patricia Williams's critique of racism in contemporary American society would construe the constitution's tolerance of the viewpoints and behaviour of whites like Terminiello and Brandenburg as a major contribution to the spirit-murder of minority communities. Whether more recent case-law has empowered State governments to produce some kind of effective response to the sentiments of racist whites which sustain that process is the question addressed in section III. For the moment, attention returns to the British context, in which the difficulties posed by a supra-legislative right to freedom of expression are something by which Parliament need not feel constrained.

THE EXISTING BRITISH LAW—RACE HATE CRIMES *PER SE* AND SENTENCE ENHANCEMENT

In Britain, the criminalization of incitement to racial hatred *per se* dates back to 1965,[41] although occasional prosecutions were instituted against such behaviour under the common law offences of seditious libel and public mischief, as well as under the Public Order Act 1936 section 5 when the incitement was contained in 'threatening, abusive or insulting speech' which was intended or likely to provoke a breach of the peace. These various provisions seemed to be little used in practice. In theory, they were directed not at thought or speech itself, but at expression coupled with consequent public disorder. If one was seeking a US analogy, one might say that all these offences were on their face examples of a clear and present danger test, and not necessarily inconsistent with First Amendment principles. A rather different theoretical basis can be discerned in the offence of 'incitement to racial hatred' created in 1965.

The 1965 legislation

The Race Relations Act 1965 section 6 seemingly detached race hate speech from public order issues. A disseminator committed the section 6 offence if her/his message was 'threatening, abusive, or insulting' and intended and likely to stir up racial hatred. The offence was triable either way, carrying a maximum sentence of two years imprisonment and/or a £1,000 fine. What was meant by 'hatred' was not defined. Section 6 itself made no express reference to public order. However it lay under a

[41] See D. Williams, 'Racial Incitement and Public Order', *Crim. LR* 320: P. Leopold, 'Incitement to Hatred—the History of a Controversial Offence' [1977] *PL* 389.

subheading to that effect, which might indicate that public unrest was an implied component of the crime. This presumption is reinforced when one considers that the 'threatening, abusive, or insulting' formula was lifted from the 1936 Act. On the other hand, in the 1936 Act 'threatening, abusive, or insulting' was expressly coupled with a consequential breach of the peace, which suggests that to threaten, to abuse, or to insult did not *per se* constitute public disorder. Further support for the argument that section 6 was not a public order matter is provided when one recalls that the 1965 Act was primarily concerned with civil law and educative initiatives against race discrimination. Moreover, section 6 prosecutions required the consent of the Attorney-General, which suggested that the offence had delicate public policy ramifications above and beyond public disorder. Prosecutions for riot, affray and breach of the peace do not generally have such a filter.

The 1965 Bill attracted strong opposition on civil liberties grounds, primarily because it was alleged to criminalize the holding of certain opinions. That analysis is not quite accurate. The inciter is not being prosecuted for his/her belief, but for expressing and/or acting upon that belief. The thought of the accused *per se* was therefore not made a crime. However, the 'thought crime' argument can be pursued in a slightly more tangential way. Section 6 did appear to make it a crime to disseminate information that might change the opinions people held, even if that change did not in fact take place, even if any such change was never expressed in any way at all, and even though the changed opinions were not in themselves criminal.

The conceptual basis for the criminalization of incitement seems to be that the situation the inciter seeks to create is in itself proscribed by the criminal law, whether it be robbery, assault, murder, or public disorder: if the incitee does as the inciter wishes, the incitee has herself committed a crime.[42] But in 1965 it manifestly was not a crime simply to hold hateful thoughts, to form a vehemently adverse opinion of an individual or a group, if one's hatred never leaves one's head. Clearly, Parliament could have made hateful thought motivated by racial bigotry a crime in itself. However it did not do so. Section 6 therefore seems to make a crime out of seeking to effect non-criminal ends. Thus construed, section 6 came very close to the outright criminalization of racist thought; one committed a crime if one sought to persuade someone else to subscribe to instrinsically lawful opinions.

Writing in the 1966 *Criminal Law Review*, David Williams suggested that section 6 was merely the latest in a line of statutory incitement

[42] Cf. Holems JA in *Nkosiyana*, 1966 (4) SA 655, 658; an inciter 'is one who reaches and seeks to influence the mind of another to the commission of a crime'; quoted in J. Smith & B. Hogan *Criminal law* (London, 1992 7th ed.), 265.

offences which had impinged on free speech without requiring consequential public disorder; the crimes he had in mind were incitement to mutiny, and incitement to disaffection in the armed services and the police.[43] Given these precedents, Williams suggested the 1965 Act did not represent a radical or illegitimate extension of criminal liability.

One might wonder if Williams was asking the right question. Mutiny is itself a crime, and it seems quite clear that the 'disaffection' identified in respect of the military and police forces would require speech or action by the disaffectee which amounted to a breach of military or police discipline.[44] For a soldier to feel mutinous, or for a police officer to feel less enthusiastic about performing her duties, is not in itself either a criminal or disciplinary offence, as long as that feeling is not expressed in any way. Unlike section 6, these statutes are therefore not envisaging that the inciter may be punished simply for changing the incitee's point of view.[45]

That section 6 did not in practice create a thought crime owed more to procedural than substantive factors. Section 6 prosecutions could be brought only with the consent of the Attorney-General, who had informed Parliament that the Act would be used only against the ringleaders and organizers of racial hatred. Although potentially far-reaching, the Act produced little litigation. Prosecutions were rarely brought, the courts tended to interpret the legislation rather restrictively, and on the few occasions that prosecutions were successful, the defendant seemed as likely to be black as white.[46]

The Act's efficacy was also compromised by judicial interpretation of its provisions. In *R* v. *John Kingsley Reid*,[47] the defendant, at a public meeting, had greeted the murder of an Asian youth in Southall with the comment 'one down, a million to go', and sprinkled his speech with references to 'niggers, wogs and coons'. The trial judge, Neil McKinnon QC, evidently praised Reid for standing up for what he believed in,

[43] *Op. cit.*, 326–7.

[44] See *R* v. *Arrowsmith* [1975] 1 All ER 463, in which the court suggested the offence could stretch as far as persuading a solider not to have his hair cut in accordance with army regulations. That consequence, while no doubt petty, would of course require action on the soldier's behalf, and moreover action which challenged military discipline.

[45] There is some South African case-law (*R* v. *Mailianga* (1963) 4 SA 229) dealing with similarly phrased legislation which suggests that mere thought could amount to disaffection. However, given the fundamentally anti-democratic basis of South African society during the post-war era it would be quite inappropriate to attach any weight to such judgments. See also *Burns* v. *Ransley* [1949] ALR 817. My thanks to Victor Tunkel for bringing these cases to my attention.

[46] M. Partington 'Race Relations Act 1965: a Too Restricted View' [1967] *Crim. LR* 497: A. Dickey, 'Prosecutions under the Race Relations Act 1965 s.6' [1968] *Crim. LR* 489.

[47] 6 Jan. 1978, Central Criminal Court; unreported, but noted in G. Bindman, 'Incitement to Racial Hatred' (1982) *NLJ* 299.

advising the jury in his summing up that: 'You have got to allow toleration and freedom to the individual otherwise we are all caught in a vice of dictatorship, repression and slavery'.[48] Reid was acquitted.

The 1976 legislation

In his report on the 1974 Red Lion Square disorder, Scarman LJ described section 6 as 'an embarrassment', which could not be enforced.[49] Scarman recommended radical reform to the offence, including a relaxation of the required *mens rea*.[50] The changes subsequently introduced by the last Wilson government made only faltering steps in that direction.

The 1976 Race Relations Act lifted an amended section 6 out of the race relations legisation and inserted it as a new section 5A in the Public Order Act 1936. However section 5A has no express requirement that public disorder be occasioned or even made likely by the speech. The forbidden consequence remained the legislatively undefined concept of 'hatred'.[51] Furthermore, it was no longer necessary that the disseminator intended to foster such a reaction; its mere likelihood now sufficed to create the offence. This was intended to facilitate conviction,[52] but it did nothing to address the conceptual difficulty that the offence made it a crime to incite what might be entirely lawful consequences. Race hate *per se* was still not made a crime.

The inference that the offence remained somehow distinct from other public order offences continued however, since the Attorney-General's consent was required to any prosecution. Despite Scarman LJ's criticisms, enforcement of the 1976 measure seemed no less problematic than had been the case with section 6. Writing in 1982, Bindman recorded there had been only thirteen prosecutions since 1976, just six of which had resulted in convictions.[53] This reluctance to prosecute was attributed to a government fear that an acquittal would be more damaging to race

[48] (1982) *NLJ* 301.

[49] Because, to adopt an American criterion, its scope was too vaguely defined.

[50] (1975) *Report on the Red Lion Square Disorders of June 15 1974* (Cmnd. 5919) at para. 125.

[51] Resort to Hansard is of little assistance here. Roy Jenkins stated quite clearly that the Act was intended to address not simply questions of violence or economic discrimination, but also the problems of 'cultural alienness' and 'low status' which minority communities suffered as a result of discrimination by whites; (HCD, 4 Mar. 1976 c. 1548–60). However, Jenkins equally clearly rejected criminalization of discriminatory belief itself as undesirably coercive and ultimately ineffective (*id*. c. 1566).

[52] Whether it did so in practice is a moot point; see R. Cotterrell, 'Prosecuting Incitement to Racial Hatred' [1982] *PL* 378. On the background to the change see A. Smith, *Offences Against Public Order* (London, 1986), 154–5.

[53] Bindman (1982) *op. cit.*

relations than to take no action at all, particularly when, as often appeared to be the case, the speech in issue had been delivered as part of an election campaign. Bindman did however point to greater judicial support for prosecutions.[54]

The 1986 legislation

Racial hatred remains the focus of the 1986 legislation, contained in Part III of the Public Order Act. Part III creates several related race hate offences, although holding hateful opinions or thoughts *per se* remains quite lawful. A modified version of section 5A of the 1936 Act appears in section 18. The crime now includes behaviour as well as words, and has been made an arrestable offence. The Attorney-General's consent is still required for prosecution, the offence remains triable either way, and the maximum penalty remains two years plus a fine.

The 1986 Act was promoted by a government whose ideological preferences on most matters were quite distinct from those of the first and third Wilson governments. One might therefore assume that abhorrence of racial violence crosses the party political divide, although whether that merely points to a consensus to be ineffective is perhaps the larger question.

The Act seems merely to repeat past formulae. The legislation does define 'racial', but does not make clear what is meant by hatred. A. H. T. Smith offers the *Shorter Oxford Dictionary* definition, which embraces 'active dislike, detestation, enmity, ill will, malevolence'. All those concepts could seemingly be met by thoughts which never leave a person's head.

There is no doubt that section 6, section 5A, and section 18 would all have been facially invalid as overbroad or void for vagueness had they been enacted by a state legislature in the USA. From a symbolic perspective, that inconsistency is unfortunate. Symbolic difficulties might be countered by the practical consideration that Britain is seeking to achieve concrete results that are beyond the competence of American governments. However, the particular achievement of the British legislation appears to be that it couples an abstract threat to freedom of thought and expression with a negligible impact on the concrete problem it purports to address. As phrased in principle, and as applied in practice, the offence of incitement to racial hatred smacks of a tokenistic response, within which neither preserving freedom of expression nor safeguarding black citizens from racism are accorded sufficient status. The second strand of British law dealing with race hate crimes is perhaps more legitimate in constitutional

[54] Citing *R* v. *Relf and Cole*, Court of Appeal 12 Mar. 1979, unreported.

terms than the free-standing statutory offence, but there is little evidence to suggest that it is any more effective.

Sentence enhancement

As Martin Wasik argues in chapter twelve, no British government has been prepared to introduce and maintain a systematic, rule bound framework with which to structure the exercise of the judiciary's sentencing discretion. Should a government ever wish to do so, it would seem likely that the question of how the courts should respond to crimes committed solely or primarily for racist reasons would provoke considerable discussion. At present however, the sentencing implications of racist motive remain an *ad hoc*, individuated feature of the criminal justice process. It is clear that racist motive may be viewed by our courts as an aggravating factor at the sentencing stage when offenders have been convicted of existing substantive offences, although there appear to be few examples of this. Moreover there is no explicit legislative basis for awarding an increased sentence to punish racist motive. In *R* v. *Cushen and Spratley*[55] the Court of Appeal approved a three month sentence for racially motivated threatening behaviour which did not result in actual violence. The black victim had been approached by a gang of white youths who had shouted 'Let's get the black bastard.' It is not entirely clear however if the aggravating factor in this case was gang violence or racial hatred. In the more recent decision of *R* v. *Alderson*,[56] the accused was one of a gang of white youths who had entered a restaurant in Durham and attacked several Jordanian students after previously calling them 'Pakis' and 'coloured bastards'. Alderson was sentenced to thirty months after pleading guilty to a charge of violent disorder. The sentencing judge had described the racist motive as a 'seriously aggravating feature', a conclusion with which the Court of Appeal was not willing to interfere.[57]

There may be some temptation to assume that if we wish to attach additional sanctions to racially motivated crimes, such *ad hoc* judicial intervention may be the most appropriate way to proceed. The imagery of sentencing as part of the judicial function might suggest to the wider public that enhanced punishments were devoid of party political content—and perhaps even to the untutored eye devoid of any political content at all—and therefore more legitimate than legislation, which is open to charges of having been fostered by particular interest groups. Recent developments in sentencing policy and practice have perhaps undermined that particular

[55] 25 Apr. 1978. This case appears to be unreported anywhere, including Lexis. It is noted at [1978] *Crim. LR* 571–2.

[56] 11 Cr. App. R (S) 301.

[57] See also *R* v. *Ribbins, Duggan and Ridley* (CA), *The Guardian* 28 Nov. 1994.

argument,[58] but even if that had not been the case, there are powerful arguments for addressing the issue of racist crime through legislative rather than judicial innovation.

A judicial response to individual cases lacks the symbolic power of legislation, particularly if it attracts bipartisan support, to signal explicit societal disapproval of certain types of behaviour. Moreover, there is no guarantee that judicial discretion in sentencing will not be informed by the judges' no doubt divergent opinions on the gravity of racism as a social evil.

Consequently, if one accepts that this problem demands a Parliamentary rather than judicial response, the next question that arises is whether, from the perspective of maxmizing the legitimacy of legal responses to racist violence, an explicit statutory scheme of sentence enhancement is a more viable device than the creation of free-standing offences. In an attempt to answer this question, section III considers recent events in the United States, specifically the Supreme Court judgments in *RAV* v. *St. Paul* and *Wisconsin* v. *Mitchell.*

HATE CRIMES AND THE FIRST AMENDMENT

As suggested above, opinion is likely to be divided on the question of whether the Court's tolerance of racist speech and action in *Terminiello* and *Brandenburg* contributed to the 'spirit-murder' of America's black and Jewish communities.[59] There would however seem little doubt that the thirty plus States which have enacted hate crimes laws have found that public policy argument at least partially persuasive. It is now also possible to begin to form a clear picture of the compatibility of such legislation with First Amendment requirements.

Race hate violence as a discrete crime

The legislative initiative in issue in *RAV* v. *St. Paul*[60] was a St. Paul city by-law which criminalized the placing on private property of any object (including a burning cross or swastika) when the placer knew or had reasonable grounds to know that the object would arouse 'anger, alarm or resentment in others on the basis of race, colour, creed, or gender'.[61] The

[58] See the chapter by Wasik in this volume.

[59] Although it may well be that such a division is founded on racial lines, if only because members of a dominant ethnic group are simply unable to appreciate the nature of the social reality experienced by victim groups; see Williams *op. cit.* and Massaro *op. cit.*, 231–41.

[60] (1992) 120 L Ed. 2d. 305.

[61] St. Paul, Min. Legis. Code s. 292,02 (1990).

petitioners were white youths who had been convicted under the ordinance after having placed a burning cross in the back garden of a neighbouring black family. The Minnesota Supreme Court upheld the conviction,[62] on the basis that insofar as the ordinance affected 'speech' it encompassed only socially valueless 'fighting words' under the *Chaplinsky*[63] formula, and so made no incursion into protected First Amendment territory.

For a fragmented Supreme Court, Scalia J's majority opinion held that the ordinance contravened the First Amendment. The thrust of his argument was that the ordinance enacted a system of content based discrimination against different types of speech. This conclusion rested on a controversial interpretation of the 'fighting words' doctrine. Scalia J argued that 'fighting words' were not neccesarily a worthless form of speech, but that they could on occasion be 'quite expressive indeed'. As such, they merited some First Amendment protection, sufficient to ensure that government regulation did not entail viewpoint discrimination. Scalia J used the examples of libel and obscenity to illustrate his argument. So, for example, government could regulate libellous or obscene speech, but not only those libels or obscenities critical of government. Similarly, a State could regulate all fighting words, but not just those fighting words intended to convey the speaker's opinions about particular political matters. The latter course would raise the spectre that 'government may effectively drive certain ideas or viewpoints from the marketplace'.[64]

Such selectivity was however apparent on the face of the St. Paul ordinance. Scalia J observed that: 'Displays containing abusive invective, no matter how vicious or severe, are permissible unless they are addressed to one of the specified disfavoured topics'.[65] By singling out 'race, colour, creed, and gender' as the basis for prohibited expression, St. Paul had disadvantaged bigots whose bigotry rested on those grounds compared with bigots whose bigotry stemmed from hatred based on, *inter alia*, a victim's sexual orientation or political affiliation. Such people could not be prosecuted under the ordinance.

Following the logic of this argument, the majority opinion did not place hate crimes entirely beyond the reach of State or municipal regulation: the ordinance would have been acceptable if it had ended without specifying any basis at all for the 'anger, alarm, or resentment' occasioned by the placing of the object.[66]

[62] *In re Welfare of RAV* (1991) 464 N.W. 2d. 507.

[63] (1942) 315 US 568.

[64] At 320, quoting *Simon & Shuster Inc.* v. *Members of NY State Crime Victims Board* 116 L Ed. 2d. 476.

[65] (1992) 120 L Ed. 2d. 305, 323.

[66] *Id.*, 326. For a helpful, if lengthy introduction to the conceptual basis of the overbreadth doctrine see Note 'The First Amendment Overbreadth Doctrine' (1970) 83 *Harvard LR* 844.

Sceptics might wonder if so expansive a statute would have been facially overbroad. This was indeed the basis on which the four concurring Justices found the ordinance unconstitutional. White J observed that the Minnesotan Supreme Court had misinterpreted *Chaplinsky* in holding a conviction could be sustained if the accused's action raised 'anger, alarm, or resentment'. This was fatally overbroad, for it would 'criminalize expressive conduct that causes only hurt feelings, offence, or resentment'.[67] Following *Terminiello* v. *Chicago*, White J concluded that preventing hurt feelings was not a substantive evil that any tier of government could address through penal legislation.

The concurring judgments also took issue with Scalia J's use of the fighting words doctrine. Stevens J decribed Scalia's judgment as 'an adventure in a doctrinal wonderland'.[68] White J argued that fighting words were *per se* unprotected, not because of the mode in which they were delivered, but because they were 'a class of speech that conveys an overriding message of personal injury and imminent violence'.[69] Consequently, there was no scope for the Court to search for viewpoint discrimination within fighting words regulation—all fighting words existed entirely outside the 'market place of ideas'.

White J characterized the majority opinion as producing an entirely new First Amemdment concept, which he labelled an 'underbreadth' doctrine. He suggested that Scalia J's opinion demanded that government should seek to control more speech than was necessary to achieve its desired objectives. This seemed quite inconsistent with accepted First Amendment principles. Moreover, White J suggested that the majority's concern was adequately met by the equal protection clause of the Fourteenth Amendment. State limits on speech or expressive conduct had to rest on a rational, legitimate basis. Selection based on factors such as political affiliation would not pass the equal protection test. But White J saw no reason for doubting that controlling racist violence against minority groups provided such a foundation.[70]

RAV attracted little attention here. Tony Bradley was fiercely critical of the decision in a short article in *Public Law*.[71] Bradley suggested that in Britain, which was fortunate enough to be spared 'the full rigours of First Amendment jurisprudence',[72] such manifestly racist behaviour would not have escaped criminal sanction.

This is an overly harsh criticism both of the Court and of the First Amendment itself. Notwithstanding Scalia J's innovative analysis of fighting words theory, St Paul's ordinance was poorly phrased given the then existing reach of the overbreadth doctrine. Furthermore, the Court's

[67] *Id.*, 338. [69] *Id.*, 334. [68] *Id.*, 341. [70] *Id.*, 333.
[71] 'Free Expression and Acts of Racial Hatred' [1992] *PL* 357. [72] *Id.*, 359.

more recent judgment in *Wisconsin* v. *Mitchell*[73] indicates that the outcome of *RAV* owed more to the city's legislative shortcomings than to the Court's indifference to racist violence or its mechanical adherence to an absolutist view of the First Amendment.

Racist motive as 'crime plus'—*Wisconsin* v. *Mitchell*

Wisconsin's legislative response to an upsurge of racial and religious violence in the State was to enact a sentence enhancement statute. If the perpetrator of a felony intentionally selects the victim '**because of** her race, religion, colour, disability, sexual orientation or ancestry',[74] the sentencing court may increase the sentence awarded by up to $5,000 or five years imprisonment.[75]

Both state and federal legislatures in the United States have, as Martin Wasik observes in chapter twelve below, addressed the policy underpinnings and practical implications of sentencing in a considerably more systematic way than the British Parliament. To an extent, such deliberations are a constitutional necessity. The Supreme Court has intervened significantly since 1970 into the procedures surrounding capital sentencing,[76] and has also made clear that the substance of legislative policy choices are subject to a proportionality requirement imposed by the Eighth Amendment.[77] In respect of non-capital issues, however, legislatures enjoy rather greater autonomy.[78] The question placed before the Court in *Wisconsin* v. *Mitchell* was the extent to which that autonomy was constrained with regard to hate crimes by the provisions of the First Amendment.

Mitchell was one of several black youths who had been watching the movie *Mississippi Burning*, which contains several scenes of white racists making violent attacks on black citizens. When the group moved outside, Mitchell asked them: 'Do you all feel hyped up to move on some white people?' On noticing a white teenager, Gregory Reddick, walking nearby, Mitchell then said to his peers: 'You all want to fuck somebody up? There goes a white boy; go get him.' In the ensuing assault, Reddick was beaten unconscious and suffered permanent brain damage. Mitchell was convicted of aggravated battery, an offence carrying a two year sentence. However

[73] (1993) 124 L Ed. 2d. 436.

[74] Emphasis added, for reasons which will become apparent below.

[75] Wisconsin Stats. 1989–90, s. 939.645.

[76] *Furman* v. *Georgia* (1972) 408 US 239: *Gregg* v. *Georgia* (1976) 428 US 153: *Woodson* v. *North Carolina* (1976) 428 US 280.

[77] *Coker* v. *Georgia* (1977) 433 US 485.

[78] Although proportionality would also appear to be a requirement of non-capital sentencing; see *Weems* v. *United States* (1910) 217 US 349.

the jury found the victim selection to have been racially motivated, with the result that Mitchell's sentence was raised to four years.

The Wisconsin Supreme Court[79]

The majority on the State Supreme Court concluded that the hate crimes statute contravened the First Amendment. At the heart of the majority judgment, delivered by Heffernan CJ, was the assumption that the statute was directed at 'pure thought', a category of expression that is invariably beyond any form of governmental regulation. In an opinion heavily influenced by academic writings,[80] the majority held that the process of selecting a victim was not 'conduct' as the State contended, but was rather a purely intellectual exercise, part of the defendant's 'intent':

> The hate crimes statute enhances the punishment of bigoted criminals because they are bigoted. The statute is directed solely at the subjective motivation of the actor—his or her prejudice. Punishment of one's thought, however repugnant the thought, is unconstitutional.[81]

Heffernan CJ found support for this analysis in the Supreme Court's *RAV* judgment. The Wisconsin statute, no less than the St. Paul ordinance, evinced a 'special hostility towards . . . particular biases. . . . This is precisely what the First Amendment forbids'.[82] The majority further concluded that the statute contravened the First Amendment because of its indirect 'chilling effect' on free speech. Heffernan CJ suggested that the awareness of the Wisconsin statute would deter individuals from expressing bigoted beliefs, or joining bigoted groups, (which was not in itself unlawful) since such speech or action might subsequently be invoked as evidence to sustain the prosecution's claims that a crime which he/she might later commit was racially motivated.

Nor did the majority consider that the State's case was assisted by its reference to the undoubted constitutionality of anti-discrimination statutes, embracing such matters as employment conditions or access to public facilities. Heffernan CJ sought to distinguish 'anti-bigotry' laws (the subject of the hate crimes law) from 'anti-discrimination' laws, on the basis that the latter addressed the physical act of conduct, (i.e. the failure to hire or promote a person) while the former dealt only with the mental act of selection.

The majority reached its conclusions with 'great regret', for it found itself in complete agreement with the legislature's wish to prevent hate crimes, which it described as 'disgraceful and deplorable'. Evil as such

[79] 485 N. W. 2d. 807 (Wis 1992).
[80] Especially by Gellman's article, cited at n. 4 *supra*.
[81] 485 N.W. 2d. 807, 815. [82] *Id.*, 815.

crimes were however, they amounted to a lesser evil than would be done by upholding the suppression of free speech which the statute imposed.

Heffernan CJ's reasoning did not commend itself to all of his colleagues. Abrahamson J questioned the wisdom of the Act as a means to achieve the legislators' desired objective, but nevertheless considered the law to be consistent with First Amendment protections. Abrahamson J construed the statute as a restraint on conduct, not upon belief. In her view, the Act's use of the words 'because of' demanded that the State demonstrate a 'tight nexus between the selection of the victim and the underlying crime'.[83] An individual could be a bigot, and he/she could commit a crime, but 'these two facts, standing alone, do not subject that individual to punishment under section 939.645'.[84] The sentence enhancement could only be applied if the State could demonstrate a direct causal link between bigotry, selection of the victim, and commission of the crime. As such, the Wisconsin law could have no substantial chilling effect on the expression of bigotry; evidence of abstract belief or past associations would not be admissible at trial.[85]

Bablitch J's dissent was expressed in rather more forthright terms. In his view, the statute did not enact a hate speech law, nor even a hate crime law. It was simply a law against discrimination—'discrimination in the selection of a crime victim'.[86] Bablitch J discerned no merit in the majority's assumption that the statute was directed against bigoted thought. Rather it was targeted at individuals who gave such beliefs tangible effect: 'It punishes the act of discriminatory selection plus criminal conduct, not the thought or expression of bigotry'.[87] Consequently he saw no basis for the majority's attempt to distinguish hate crime laws from anti-discrimination laws. The latter did not, as the majority claimed, punish failure to hire a person, but failure to hire **because of** that person's racial status. Bablitch J thus made common cause with Abrahamson J on the question of the need for a direct evidentiary link between bigotry, victim selection, and commission of the crime.

He found authoritative support for this position in the Supreme Court's judgment in *Dawson* v. *Delaware*.[88] Dawson was a white prisoner who had murdered a black fellow inmate. After he had been found guilty, the

[83] 485 N.W. 2d. 818. [84] *Id.*

[85] There is little case-law on this point. Abrahamson J's argument is strengthened when one recalls the disquiet now voiced over the evidentiary regime approved by the trial and appellate courts in the *Rosenberg* litigation. Both courts permitted the prosecution to dig deep into the accuseds' pasts to present their membership of left-wing organizations and their vocal and written support of leftist causes as evidence of their motive to act as Soviet spies; see P. Quint, 'Towards First Amendment Limitations on the Introduction of Evidence: the Problem of *US* v. *Rosenberg*' (1977) 86 *Yale LJ* 1622: Baker *op. cit.* 456–60.

[86] *Id.*, 819. [87] *Id.*, 820. [88] (1992) 117 L Ed. 2d. 309.

prosecution introduced evidence at the sentencing stage, to persuade the court to impose a capital sentence, that the accused belonged to a white supremacist group known as the Aryan Brotherhood. The Supreme Court found that the sentencing court's acceptance of this evidence violated the First Amendment, for Dawson's political affiliations had not been shown to have any direct bearing on the selection of his victim. Bablitch J saw no reason to doubt that the Wisconsin legislation required such a direct causal link, and that the link had been established in Mitchell's case.

Bablitch J's method, as well as his conclusion, merits some comment. Some academic critiques have suggested that the legal process cannot deal adequately with hate crimes because the majority of its personnel (and here one includes legislators, judges, attorneys, and police officers) are unable to understand the enormity of the loss suffered by members of the victim group. The type of argument propounded by Patricia Williams has been labelled 'outsider jurisprudence' as a means to convey what one might term the 'otherness' of the issue being addressed.[89] Bablitch J made some effort to view the problem from an outsider perspective. In what one might characterize as an imaginative extension of the Brandeis brief, he began his judgment by quoting from a Lorna Dee Cevantes poem, entitled 'Races':[90]

> *everywhere the crosses are burning,*
> *sharp shooting goose-steppers around every corner,*
> *there are snipers in the schools . . .*
> *(I know you don't believe this.*
> *You think this is nothing but faddish exaggeration.*
> *But they are not shooting at you).*

Oliver Wendell Holmes famously remarked that 'the life of the law is experience not logic'. But if one looks at the majority judgment in *Mitchell*, one wonders if logic provides too attractive a shelter for judges who simply lack certain kinds of experience. It is perhaps easier for a predominantly white, upper middle class male élite to empathize with the abstract concern of the racist's entitlement to free speech than with the concrete concern of minority citizens to be free of fear of violence and intimidation in their everyday lives. That Bablitch J elevated the experience of a minority woman to the forefront of his judgment is perhaps more than simply an excursion into tokenism. To borrow Holmes' aphorism, this judgment seems to recognize that the 'experience' from which the law appears is a multifaceted concept, and accepts that lawmakers should at least try to view the legal landscape from hitherto unfamiliar vantage points.

[89] Matsuda *op. cit.*
[90] *Contemporary Chicana Poetry* (Los Angeles, 1986).

Whether such efforts at empathy would commend themselves to British courts is a matter for speculation. But when Wisconsin appealed *Mitchell* to the federal Supreme Court, the judicial methodology the Court adopted was in no sense unconventional. A unanimous bench nevertheless found itself in agreement with Bablitch J's conclusions.

The United States Supreme Court[91]

Delivering the sole judgment, Rehnquist CJ began his analysis by accepting that the State's characterization of victim selection as 'conduct' rather than 'speech' was 'literally correct'. This did not settle the First Amendment question however, since many forms of conduct are considered as speech for First Amendment purposes. While physical assault could never assume this status, the Wisconsin statute nevertheless seemed to present a First Amendment difficulty, for the same criminal conduct may be more heavily punished if the victim is selected because of his race or other protected status than if no such motive obtained'.[92]

Rehnquist CJ continued by observing that this apparent difficulty did not withstand closer evaluation. Central to his conclusion was a distinction between 'motive' and 'abstract belief'. Rehnquist CJ noted that trial judges in both state and federal jurisdictions had traditionally been permitted to take account of many factors in deciding how severely to punish a particular offence. A defendant's motive was one such factor which could either aggravate or mitigate the crime; many States for example had decided that pursuit of monetary gain was a legitimate aggravating factor when deciding if murder should be punished by execution.

However this discretion could not be stretched to encompass 'abstract beliefs',[93] a point that the Court had already confirmed in *Dawson*. Rehnquist CJ reinforced this point by contrasting *Dawson* with the Supreme Court's decision in *Barclay* v. *Florida*,[94] which held that it was proper for a trial court to enhance a murder sentence because the defendant's membership of the Black Liberation Army and his stated desire to engage in a race war had been shown to have led directly to selection of a white man as his victim.

This is perhaps a rather misleading analogy. While *Barclay* and *Dawson* undoubtedly have a substantial First Amendment dimension, they might more appropriately be placed in the stream of case-law assessing the adequacy of the States' various responses to *Furman* v. *Georgia*,[95] the landmark 1972 decision in which the Supreme Court held that the Eighth Amendment precluded the imposition of the death penalty unless

91 (1993) 124 L Ed. 2d. 436.

92 *Id.*, 445.

93 (1993) 124 L Ed. 2d. 436, 435.

94 (1983) 77 L. Ed. 2d. 1134.

95 (1972) 408 US 238.

States adopted far more precise procedures for capital sentencing than had thitherto been observed.

The suggestion that the Court may have been searching for an expedient precedent for upholding Mitchell's conviction is reinforced when one considers that Rehnquist CJ did not offer a principled rationale through which one can separate 'motive' and 'abstract belief'. Rather he rooted the distinction in Bablitch J's argument that the Wisconsin statute could not be distinguished from anti-discrimination laws, whose constitutionality was beyond question. Both types of measure were examples of 'a permissible content neutral regulation of conduct'.[96] The St. Paul ordinance overturned in *RAV* could be distinguished from the Wisconsin statute, on the basis that the former was targeted at speech or 'messages', while the latter addressed only conduct. This distinction between speech and conduct also appeared to be assumed rather than established through reasoned argument.

The Court saw no reason to question the legitimacy of the State's conclusion that hate crimes merited additional sanctions. Perhaps surprisingly, the source Rehnquist CJ invoked to support this conclusion was a passage in *Blackstone's Commentaries*: 'it is but reasonable that among crimes of different natures those should be most severely punished, which are the most destructive of the public safety and happiness'.[97] The Court also found little merit in the argument that the statute might chill free speech. It was simply 'too speculative' to assume that an individual would suppress his/her bigotry on the basis that such expression could at some future date result in the imposition of a harsher sentence for a crime not yet committed and probably not yet planned.

CONCLUSION

The differing fates of the St. Paul and Wisconsin initiatives perhaps offer some useful guidance for the British Parliament. Several senior members of the British judiciary have recently suggested that they are becoming increasingly prepared to accord persuasive authority to the constitutional values of other democratic nations when dealing with ambiguous statutory or common law provisions which impact upon civil liberties issues.[98] Much of this movement towards the 'internationalization' of public law is focused on the European Convention of Human Rights. However, the British courts have lately also begun to cast their eyes towards the First

[96] *Id.*, 446. [97] *Id.*, 447.
[98] Browne-Wilkinson *op. cit.*: Laws *op. cit.*

Amendment as an interpretive aid when faced with ambiguous areas of the common law.[99]

Parliament would no doubt be reluctant to accept that it should allow American constitutional law to shape the substantive scope of legislation directed at Britain's social problems.[100] However from a policy perspective, paying explicit attention to First Amendment jurisprudence would offer several advantages to British legislators. The Supreme Court's unanimous condemnation of a free-standing offence of racial violence in *RAV* v. *St. Paul*, and its unanimous approval of a sentence enhancement statute in *Mitchell*, suggest that the latter approach offers a more readily defensible strategy if one is concerned to signal strong societal disapproval of such crimes, while simultaneously minimizing the scope for racist criminals to claim that they are being 'martyred' because their civil right to free expression is being infringed. The Supreme Court's stance in *Mitchell* provides a powerful symbolic statement to refute charges that attaching greater penalties to crimes motivated by racism infringes the racist's civil liberties.

But even this more 'constitutionally defensible' response to the problem of escalating racial violence is by no means unproblematic. Parliament would, for example, face difficult choices over which offences should be selected for sentence enhancement. Perhaps more problematic is the question of how substantially existing penalties should be increased. Most controversial of all is the evidentiary question of how tight a causal link one should require between abstract belief and criminal action before triggering any increased sanction. Patricia Leopold suggested in 1977 that Parliament could defuse civil liberties based opposition to the incitement to hatred crime by introducing an evidentiary regime that allowed the prosecution to invoke matters such as the accused's previous opinions on racial issues, any subscriptions he might have to racist publications, and his membership of political organizations to establish a racist motive.[101] Such a test would be far too expansive to satisfy the First Amendment; it clearly lacks the tight causal nexus required by Abrahamson and Bablitch JJ in *Mitchell*. Unless Parliament was to make racist opinions *per se* criminal, an offence which allowed all such beliefs to be admissible as evidence of criminality would have an obvious chilling effect on lawful expression. And

[99] See *Derbyshire County Council, supra*. For comment on the case see E. Barendt 'Libel and Freedom of Speech in English Law' [1993] *PL* 449.

[100] Although there seems to be something of a tradition whereby British race relations legislation somewhat belatedly accepts American experience as a valid influence on British policy; see J. Solomos, 'Equal Opportunities Policies and Racial Inequality: the Role of Public Policy' [1989] *Public Administration* 79.

[101] (1977) *op. cit.*

it seems most unlikely that any Parliament would take the radical step of making racist thought and sentiment *per se* a crime.

Nor should one assume, even if Parliament could produce a measure whose details commanded cross-party support, that the wider public would embrace its spirit. If one returns, momentarily, to the American context, the Rodney King trial stands as compelling testimony to the resistance of white juries even to acknowledge, still less to punish, racially motivated violence perpetrated by members of their own ethnic group. It would perhaps be rash to assume that British juries would be immune to such sentiments. It also seems quite plausible to suggest that a jury which had already found an assailant guilty of a serious criminal offence would conclude that he/she had been 'punished enough', and decline to conclude that he/she was also motivated by racist belief. Moreover, such highly publicized acquittals could actually undermine the social policy objectives that the law was purportedly intended to achieve, by confirming that racism is not 'really criminal' at all.[102]

That it appears difficult to draft from scratch a measure that is both symbolically legitimate and effective in practical terms perhaps lends some weight to the argument that Parliament should do nothing at all. However legislative inaction over this issue would also send a powerful message—namely that the government is unconcerned by violent racist assaults on Britain's non-white citizens. Given that all three major parties claim unequivocally to condemn racist violence, and now that the Wisconsin legislature and the US Supreme Court have provided a model statute which (as long as one does not examine Rehnquist CJ's judgment too closely) surmounts the most rigorous of civil liberties hurdles, one would have thought that the Parliamentary stage was set for a prompt statutory response to this already severe and apparently worsening social problem. The Major government appears however resolutely to have set its face against any such initiative of its own, despite being urged to take new measures by the Home Affairs Select Committee. The Committee Chairman, Sir Ivan Lawrence, criticized the government in terms that suggested Mr Howard might usefully undergo an introduction to 'outsider jurisprudence':

> I am not sure that the government fully appreciates the extent of the problem. There is an obvious growth in the number of racist attacks and in the fear among ethnic minorities in Britain. . . . [I]t is time to build up our defences against the cancer of racism which is eating at the very fabric of our society.[103]

[102] See e.g. the argument raised about civil liability under race relations legislation by P. Fitzpatrick, 'Racism and the Innocence of Law' (1986) 13 *JLS* 119.

[103] The *Guardian* 1 Apr. 1994.

The Cabinet evidently considered the defences adequate however, even going so far as to have a back-bencher talk out a modest extension of the 1986 Act proposed in a Bill introduced by Hartley Booth MP. One wonders how many more black citizens will suffer the fate of Qaddus Ali before our government learns this most basic of lessons from America.

12

Changing Patterns in Sentencing Policy

MARTIN WASIK*

THE British have long had an ambivalent attitude towards the importation of American ideas on criminal justice. The hostile attitudes evinced by Lords Reid and Ackner which were remarked upon in the opening chapter are by no means an exclusively judicial phenomenon.[1] From time to time, politicians find it similarly easy to deride a particular proposal for sentencing change, solely on the basis of its being 'American'. Ian Loveland has explored in chapter eleven just such a governmental reaction in respect of crimes involving racist violence. Yet a number of penal experiments which have developed in the United States have later been adopted, or at least mooted, in England. Curfew and electronic monitoring of offenders, and weekend imprisonment, are examples.[2] The most important recent trend is the move towards privatization of prison services, an American initiative[3] which has taken root here in recent statutory provisions. In this essay, however, we are less concerned with specific initiatives such as these, but with developments across the broad spread of sentencing policy.

In that context, one point must certainly be mentioned at the outset. Over the period of time considered in this essay—the last twenty years or

* I am grateful to Andrew von Hirsch for his helpful comments on an earlier draft. Responsibility for the views expressed here is, however, mine alone.

[1] See 12–14 above.

[2] On curfew and electronic monitoring of offenders see Home Office Research Study No. 120, *Electronic Monitoring: The Trials and their Results* (London, 1990). The relevant provisions, in Criminal Justice Act 1991, s.13, were brought into force in 1995. For equivalent provisions in the US see J. Byrne, S. Lurigio, & J. Petersilia (eds.), *Smart Sentencing Part II* (California, 1992). On weekend imprisonment see Home Office, *Intermittent Confinement* (London, 1984) and Editorial 'For intermittent custody or against perpetual proliferation?' [1984] Crim. LR 517.

[3] For an account of these developments in the United States see L. Savas, 'Privatization and Prisons' (1987) 40 *Vanderbilt Law Review* 88; D. Evans, 'Private Prisons' (1987) 36 *Emory law Journal* 253; and R. Porter, 'The Privatisation of Prisons in the United States' (1990) 29 *Howard Journal* 65. In England the relevant law is now contained in the Criminal Justice Act 1991, Part IV and the Criminal Justice and Public Order Act 1994, Part VIII. See M. Wasik & R. Taylor, *Blackstone's Guide to the Criminal Justice and Public Order Act 1994* (London: 1995) ch. 6 and the essay by Genevra Richardson in the present volume, which brings the discussion up to date.

so—both the United States and England have experienced more or less unremitting rises in their remand and sentenced custodial populations.[4] This single unpalatable fact, to a greater or lesser extent, lies behind the range of policy initiatives described in this chapter. There have been various legislative efforts to control the size of the custodial population, by the manipulation of early release arrangements, by the introduction of more community-based sentencing alternatives, and by exhortations to sentencers to impose fewer and shorter custodial sentences, but all these have achieved only a limited impact on the problem. Living conditions in prisons have improved only slowly and in some places they have deteriorated. Frictions within the system have continued, with not infrequent explosions of inmate violence and destruction. The stock governmental response, of course, is to build new prisons to try to relieve pressure on the older institutions, and this response seems set to remain an important plank in criminal justice strategy on both sides of the Atlantic.[5] The prohibitive expense involved in commissioning and running new institutions has, however, given governments pause. This, together with the prevailing political orthodoxy of privatization and profit, accounts for the emerging emphasis on private sector developments in criminal justice.

Right-wing policy makers, in common with many sentencers, argue simply that increased lawbreaking requires increased use of custodial sentencing, and that it is the responsibility of governments to provide prison places for those that the courts choose to punish by deprivation of liberty. The opposing view, however, is that the jails contain many people who should not be there (such as the mentally disordered, petty offenders, and money order defaulters), and many who are serving sentences which, on any sensible estimate, are too long. The policy of expanding the prison estate is, on this view, hopelessly mistaken since it simply confirms sentencers in their long-held beliefs and encourages them to fill the new spaces as soon as they are made available. If real headway is ever to be made on the issues of prison overcrowding and prison conditions then, it is said, this must be done by a much more radical restructuring of sentencing powers.

Against this background, a comparison of the sentencing reforms which have taken place in the United States and in England over the last twenty

[4] With 1.3 m. Americans in prison, the rate of incarceration in the US is approximately 519 per 100,000. This rate has increased by 22% since 1989 and is about five times higher than those of most industrialized nations ((1994) 5(5) *Overcrowded Times*, 9). In the UK the prison population currently stands at around 50,000 and the incarceration rate is approximately 93 per 100,000 (compared with 84 in France, 63 in Sweden and 49 in the Netherlands). The population is currently rising sharply, after a fall during 1992.

[5] A. Rutherford, *Prisons and the Process of Justice* (London, 1986); A. Bottoms, 'Limiting Prison Use: Experience in England and Wales' (1987) 26 *Howard Journal* 177.

years reveals some interesting and important parallels. There is no doubt that developments in this field in England have been influenced by what has occurred in America but, as we shall see, practical reforms have taken place in rather different ways.

THE BACKGROUND: LAWLESSNESS IN SENTENCING

In both the United States and England, the long-established pattern in sentencing has been the setting by the legislature of high statutory maxima for most offences, whilst allowing a considerable degree of discretion to sentencers, and to parole authorities. This discretion can be seen in a context where, in the past, there was very little real debate over what the aims of sentencing were, or should be.[6] There was a reliance, although not often clearly articulated, upon a range of utilitarian sentencing objectives—mainly deterrence, reform, and incapacitation of the offender. Judges and parole boards seem to have been accorded such wide discretion because it was assumed that they were best placed to match an appropriate sentence to the needs of the offender or to achieve the protection of the public. This resulted, in both countries, in substantial sentencing disparity, and in high incarceration rates. This state of affairs was the subject of an important book by the American Judge Marvin Frankel in 1992,[7] in which he described sentencing as 'a wasteland in the law' operating in 'an arbitrary, random, inconsistent and unspoken fashion'. He stressed the importance of determining priority within sentencing aims, generating rules to regulate the weighing of mitigating and aggravating factors, and requiring sentencers to give full reasons for the sentences which they imposed.

Since the time of publication of that book, in both countries there has been a trend towards much greater legislative involvement in sentencing, and there has been a reduction in the discretion accorded to sentencers and to parole boards. In the United States there has developed a wide range of techniques for the reduction of sentencers' discretionary powers, mainly through the implementation of voluntary and presumptive systems of sentencing guidelines.[8] In addition to the Federal Sentencing Guidelines

[6] See A. Ashworth, 'Structuring Sentencing Discretion', in A. von Hirsch & A. Ashworth (eds.), *Principled Sentencing* (Boston, 1992), 257. In England see L. Radzinowicz & R. Hood, *History of the English Criminal Law: The Emergence of Penal Policy* (London, 1986), 755–8; and D. Thomas, *Constraints on Judgment* (Cambridge, 1978).

[7] M. Frankel, *Criminal Sentences: Law Without Order* (New York, 1972). See also M. Frankel, 'Lawlessness in Sentencing' (1972) 41 *Cincinnati Law Review* 1.

[8] M. Tonry, 'Sentencing Guidelines and Sentencing Commissions—the Second Generation', in M. Wasik & K. Pease, *Sentencing Reform* (Manchester, 1987), 23.

(which came into effect in 1987), the majority of states now have sentencing guidelines in one form or other. Legislatures have also placed restrictions upon parole discretion. Several states, such as Minnesota and Oregon, have removed the previously highly discretionary element in parole release. Others, such as Washington and Maine, have gone further and have abolished the supervised licence period entirely. In England, the Criminal Justice Act 1991 ushered in a more or less comprehensive framework for the structuring of sentencing discretion by judges and magistrates. The same Act amended early release laws, in line with the proposals of the Carlisle Report, so as to produce a closer relationship (and to narrow the gap) between the sentence imposed by the judge and the period actually to be served by the offender.[9] The 1991 Act, and subsequent developments, are considered further, below.

During the same period of time there have been important developments in the practice and procedure of sentencing. Again the objective has been to counter the traditional highly flexible and discretionary approach. In both countries we have seen the development of clearer procedural rules on the admission of evidence about the offender subsequent to his or her guilty plea or conviction. The principal danger here is that offenders (particularly those pleading guilty) may be accorded no proper opportunity to challenge factual allegations in the prosecution case, or to dispute information contained in the antecedent or pre-sentence reports. In England, prompted by the writings of Dr. David Thomas,[10] change has come about through a series of Court of Appeal decisions produced under Lord Lane CJ's direction during the late 1970s and early 1980s, the most important of which was *Newton*.[11] These cases have established that where the prosecution and defence versions of the facts are at variance such that the sentencer's adoption of one rather than the other would make a significant difference to the sentence, the prosecution must establish its version of the facts beyond reasonable doubt. In the United States comparable due process concerns have been addressed, although in that country attention has mainly been upon the extent to which pre-sentence reports prepared on an offender and which contain material which is

[9] Carlisle Committee Report, *The Parole System in England and Wales*, Cm. 532 (London, 1988). For discussion see Ashworth, 'The Criminal Justice Act 1991' in C. Munro & M. Wasik (eds.), *Sentencing, Judicial Discretion and Training* (London, 1992), 77; Wasik & Taylor *op. cit.*

[10] D. Thomas, 'Establishing a Factual Basis for Sentencing' [1970] *Crim. LR* 80; and D. Thomas 'Form and Function in the Criminal Law' in P. Glazebrook (ed.), *Reshaping the Criminal Law* (London, 1978), 21. See also R. Fox & D. O'Brien, 'Fact Finding for Sentencers' (1975) 10 Melbourne University LR 163.

[11] (1982) 4 Cr. App. R (S) 388. The relevant authorities are fully considered in *Blackstone's Criminal Practice*, D16.2 *et seq.*

prejudicial to him, might be challenged.[12] Closely associated with the right to challenge the prosecution case is perhaps the most fundamental sentencing principle of all: that the offender should be sentenced only on the basis of matters which have been specifically proved, or have been admitted. Thus, even where the judge is personally convinced that on the evidence the jury should have convicted the offender of a greater offence, the sentence must loyally reflect the conviction for the lesser offence which they have returned.[13] Such a proposition would seem to be a basic requirement of due process, yet the American Federal Sentencing Guidelines have adopted a version of 'real offense' sentencing, whereby the sentence to be passed may properly be based not just on the offence of conviction but on other, often unsubstantiated, allegations made against the offender. Uncharged conduct need not be proved beyond reasonable doubt and, indeed, a court may increase an offender's sentence for acts in respect of which the defendant has been formally exonerated.[14]

In both the United States and England there has been much debate amongst academics over the more rigorous development of sentencing principles, and the application of those principles to practical sentencing issues. A substantial and sophisticated literature has now developed in this area.[15] These theoretical concerns have, however, rarely been sustained in any coherent way amongst the politicians, policy makers, or criminal law practitioners, many of whom still seem to regard sentencing as an area of discretion *par excellence*. It is true that politicians have seized upon ideas which have emerged from the debate but, in general, these ideas have been employed merely as tokens or slogans, and largely subverted to party political ends. The modern intellectual debate over sentencing principles, which is now a worldwide concern, began in earnest in the United States in the mid-1970s. It was prompted in part by the problems of disparity and incoherence in sentencing principle which have been mentioned above. The reform process received further impetus from the growing realization amongst liberals that the unchecked pursuit of utilitarian sentencing aims

[12] See D. Goldman & P. Mullenix, 'A Hidden Issue in Sentencing: Burdens of Proof for Disputed Allegations in Pre-Sentence Reports' (1978) 66 *Georgetown LR* 1515; Note, 'Constitutional Rights During the Sentencing Proceeding' (1978) 69 *J. of Criminal Law and Criminology* 362; M. Tonry, 'Criminal Law: the Missing Element in Sentencing Reform' (1982) 35 *Vanderbilt LR* 607.

[13] e.g. *Hazelwood* (1984) 6 Cr. App. R (S) 52; *Baldwin* (1989) 11 Cr. App. R (S) 139.

[14] G. Heaney, 'The Reality of Guidelines Sentencing: No End to Disparity' (1991) 28 *American Criminal LR* 161, 209: 'Under the Guidelines, however, sentencing judges are routinely required to sentence offenders for "relevant conduct" which has not been charged in an indictment or information and which was not admitted in a guilty plea or proved at trial.' See further W. Wilkins & J. Steer, 'Relevant Conduct: the Cornerstone of the Federal Sentencing Guidelines' (1990) 41 *South Carolina LR* 495.

[15] See, e.g., M. Forst (ed.), *Sentencing Reform* (Beverley Hills, 1982); & von Hirsch and Ashworth (eds.), *op. cit.*

had resulted in the imposition of many indeterminate sentences. These (often in practice, extremely long) sentences had been imposed for crime control reasons, and were obviously disproportionate to the offences for which they had been passed. At around the same time, summaries of empirical research became available which seriously undermined many of the claims which had been made for the success of criminal rehabilitative programmes.[16] The rehabilitative ethic, which had been dominant for decades, went sharply into decline. The effective relegation of reform as a prime penal objective created a vacuum which was soon occupied by rival penal philosophies. Now the two dominant approaches became grouped around, on the one hand, deterrence and incapacitation and, on the other hand, desert.[17]

Deterrence and incapacitation are both utilitarian sentencing aims, in that they offer strategies whereby sentencers may seek to influence the occurrence of future lawbreaking, whether by the offender or by others. Deterrence theory assumes that offenders make rational decisions about their offending, and will weigh the advantage to them of committing offences against the severity of punishment to be exacted in the event of their being caught. The moral objections, and empirical uncertainties, which surround deterrence are too well known to require detailed repetition here. The main moral objection lies where the sentencer's efforts to create the necessary fear of the penalty generate a punishment of exceptional severity for an individual offender: 'exemplary sentencing'. On deterrence grounds, the future benefit to society is taken to outweigh the injustice done to the individual. General deterrent effects are, however, very difficult to demonstrate empirically, and it seems clear that deterrent effects are very patchy in their effects across different crimes and different offender personalities. Even if the 'success' of an exemplary sentence could be demonstrated empirically, there remains the moral sticking point of whether, even so, it can ever be justifiable to use an individual offender in such a way, as a means to achieving a particular social effect. Incapacitation restrains the offender, usually through the use of imprisonment, so that he or she becomes incapable, for a period of time, of offending in the community again. Incapacitative strategies are usually associated with a prediction that the offender is likely to reoffend, so that long custodial sentences may be justified here on the ground of both short-term and long-term prevention. These predictions are typically based upon such factors as

[16] T. Brody, 'Research into the Aims and Effectiveness of Sentencing' (1978) 17 *Howard J. of Criminal Justice* 133. See more generally F. Allen, *The Decline of the Rehabilitative Ideal: Penal Policy and Social Purpose* (New Haven, 1981).

[17] For much fuller accounts, and for extracts from key writings see von Hirsch & Ashworth *op. cit.* chs. 2 & 3. Also R. Duff & D. Garland (eds.), *Punishment* (Oxford, 1994).

the offender's lifestyle and personality, and his or her previous convictions. The problems which beset the incapacitative strategies are again empirical and ethical. Prediction of future lawbreaking is a very unreliable technique, and inevitably involves the longer-than-normal incarceration of some offenders who, if released at their due date, would not in fact have re-offended. The rate of 'false positives' is higher when forecasts of serious criminality such as violent crime are attempted, since these offences are, in statistical terms, comparatively rare. Claims that certain groups of offenders can be more reliably targeted, through 'selective incapacitation', have turned out to have been overstated. Further, even if the predictions were accurate, and the proportion of false positives was low, there remains the ethical dilemma of balancing the benefit to society of keeping large numbers of offenders out of circulation, against holding people in prison on the basis of crimes which they are expected to commit, but which they have not in fact committed.

Utilitarian sentencing goals stand in contrast to desert theory, which requires that in the distribution of punishment sentencers should achieve proportionality of sentence, judged primarily in accordance with the seriousness of the current offence. Crime seriousness thus becomes the driving factor in sentencing. In a sentencing system modelled on desert principles, this objective is given priority over the various utilitarian goals mentioned above. Deterrence and incapacitation become relevent as sentencing objectives only insofar as they can be achieved by the imposition of a sentence proportionate to the seriousness of the offence. An important aspect of desert sentencing is the focus on the seriousness of past offending. This requires the theory to give prime attention to issues such as the ranking of different forms of harm, gradations of offender culpability, and the development of a scheme of commensurability between offence and penalty.[18] Unlike the utilitarian sentencing strategies, it should be appreciated that desert theory holds out no promise to reduce overall levels of offending, by the offender or by others, in consequence of the imposition of sentence. Fairness in sentencing is treated as the paramount aim of sentencing policy, and as an exercise largely distinct from the development of various societal strategies of crime control.

From the late 1970s onwards there was intense activity in sentencing and parole reform in the United States. Tonry[19] reports that by 1981 guidelines projects of various kinds had been set up in twenty-three states, and by 1985 this figure had risen to forty. These efforts towards reform achieved a mixed degree of success. By the latter date fifteen states had developed parole guidelines, a further nine had made release on parole 'automatic',

[18] See further A. von Hirsch, *Past or Future Crimes* (Manchester, 1986).
[19] (1987) *op. cit.*

three states had developed and promulgated presumptive sentencing guidelines (a number of others had tried, but failed) and in a handful of other states judges had developed their own persuasive guidelines. The sentencing guidelines which have attracted the most attention (apart from the Federal Guidelines, which came a little later) are those developed by the state of Minnesota. Tonry has described the work of the Minnesota Sentencing Guidelines Commission as 'probably the most significant development in sentencing policy and practice in the English-speaking world since the establishment of parole boards'.[20] These guidelines are a landmark for a number of reasons. One reason is the explicit and carefully considered choice of a guiding rationale for a sentencing scheme. In Minnesota's case, this was desert. Some other guidelines (most notably, the Federal Guidelines) have not adopted a guiding rationale. Their decision not to do so is a crucial one. It would appear to gloss over the important differences between utilitarian and desert approaches to sentencing. These require resolution, which can only be achieved within the context of a stated rationale. It is very difficult to address detailed questions of disparity between cases unless there is agreement upon the rationale against which such disparity can be evaluated.[21] A second feature of interest in the Minnesota guidelines is that they were designed so as to achieve a level of custodial sentencing which was just within the state's resources to manage. This strategy was initially highly successful, but seems since to have been eroded, as a result of later amendments to the guidelines.[22] The approach is also, of course, controversial in principle, since there is no particular reason to assume that a state's custodial capacity at the time when guidelines are written is its optimum capacity.

Desert principles have become influential in England during the last ten years. The views of American theorists, including Andrew von Hirsch, the author of *Doing Justice*,[23] became better known in England as a result of a conference on sentencing guidelines held at Manchester University in 1986, the proceedings of which were published in the following year.[24]

[20] Tonry (1987) *op. cit.*, 44. See further A. von Hirsch, K. Knapp, & M. Tonry, *The Sentencing Commission and its Guidelines* (Boston, 1987) ch. 1. See also D. Parent, *Structuring Criminal Sentences: The Evolution of Minnesota's Sentencing Guidelines* (St. Paul, Minnesota, 1988); R. Frase, 'Sentencing Reform in Minnesota: Ten Years On' (1991) 75 *Minnesota LR* 727.

[21] See A. Von Hirsch, 'Federal Sentencing Guidelines: the United States and Canadian Schemes Compared' (New York University School of Law, Occasional Paper No. 4, from the Center for Research in Crime and Justice).

[22] See R. Frase, 'Implementing Commission-Based Sentencing Guidelines: the Lessons of the First Ten Years in Minnesota' (1993) 2 *Cornell J. of Law and Policy* 279, 329–33; A. von Hirsch, 'Sentencing Guidelines and Penal Aims in Minnesota' (1994) 13(1) *Criminal Justice Ethics* 39.

[23] A. Von Hirsch, *Doing Justice: The Choice of Punishments* (New York, 1976).

[24] Wasik & Pease *op. cit.*

While there had been some earlier discussion in England on contrasting 'justice' and 'welfare' models in juvenile courts, for adult offenders the watershed came in 1990 with the publication by the government of a White Paper, *Crime, Justice and Protecting the Public*.[25] This policy document specifically endorsed desert (and rejected deterrence) as the proper foundation for the mainstream of sentencing practice in England.[26] It envisaged a scale of penalty severity, running from discharges in the lowest tier, up through fines and community sentences to custodial sentences. Each upward move by a sentencer to impose a more severe sentence would require justification in terms of the seriousness of the offence, the reasons for such decision being articulated in open court and explained to the offender. Community sentences were to be viewed as a range of punishments and sentences in their own right, rather than as 'alternatives' to custody.[27] The government was also at last prepared (after years of prevarication) to introduce into magistrates' courts a system of unit fines on the continental European model.[28] Whilst much of the White Paper was couched in desert terms, there were some important compromises with the guiding philosophy. The most significant, perhaps, was the continuation of the government's policy of 'bifurcation' in sentencing, which required that while property offenders should receive proportionate disposals, offenders convicted of violent or sexual offences would be eligible to serve substantial custodial terms, on the grounds of public protection. Another compromise was to make available to the courts a greater number of community sentence combinations (such as community service plus probation, and probation plus fine), a move which seemed to reflect older ideas of tailoring specific forms of sentence to achieve rehabilitative effects rather than the coherent grading of community penalties on desert lines.

TECHNIQUES FOR CHANGE

In the United States, the most far-reaching sentencing reform has been implemented through the work of the various State and Federal Sentencing Guidelines Commissions.[29] An early proposal for a sentencing commission

[25] Cm. 965 (London, 1990). For comment see A. Ashworth, 'The White Paper on Criminal Justice and Sentencing' [1990] *Crim. LR* 217; M. Wasik & A. von Hirsch, 'Statutory Sentencing Principles: the 1990 White Paper' [1990] 53 *MLR* 508.

[26] At paras 1.6, 2.2 & 2.3.

[27] M. Wasik & A. von Hirsch, 'Non-Custodial Penalties and the Principles of Desert' [1988] *Crim. LR* 555; A. von Hirsch, M. Wasik, & J Greene, 'Punishments in the Community and the Principles of Desert' (1989) 20 *Rutgers LJ* 595.

[28] See D. Moxon *et al.*, *Unit Fines: Experiments in Four Courts*, Home Office Research and Planning Unit Paper 59 (London, 1990); B. Gibson, *Unit Fines* (Winchester, 1990).

[29] See the sources cited at n. 7 above.

can be found in the writings of Frankel. His suggestion was for a highly prestigious 'national commission charged with permanent responsibility for the study of sentencing, corrections and parole, the formulation of laws and rules to which the results of such study might lead and the actual enactment of rules subject to congressional veto'. He envisaged that the commissioners would act as 'philosopher-statesmen', and he suggested a membership of lawyers, judges, criminologists, sociologists, penologists and (rather radically) present or former prison inmates.

The Guidelines Commissions which have been created in the United States have occupied a role somewhere between the state legislatures and the sentencing practitioners. They have drawn their membership from political life, legal practice, and academic institutions. Sentencing commissions are authorized by statute to describe detailed norms (mainly in relation to the imposition and duration of sentences of imprisonment) which become law either automatically or after submission to the legislature for approval. Judges are bound then to follow the norms, unless they can provide detailed reasons in an individual case for departure. Departures are subject to appeal. The commissions are standing bodies which, once the guidelines have been produced, retain a continuing review and advisory role. On the face of it, the sentencing commission model is a promising one for enhancing the quality and consistency of justice delivered by the criminal courts. It would be a mistake to think that the American sentencing guidelines are indistinguishable one from another. There has now developed a substantial literature on the techniques of sentencing guidelines, and there are numerous different models. Some of the schemes come close to prescribing the sentencing outcome for the judge, although even the Minnesota guidelines (which are probably the most prescriptive of all) still leave scope for the judge to take account of relevant aggravating and mitigating factors. Others merely specify rather broad penalty bands within which sentencers remain free to operate. Commissions have experienced varying success in having their proposals enacted. As a key component of success, commentators have noted the importance of the personnel involved. Obviously, much depends upon the competence and sense of commitment of the commissioners,[30] but while this is important, equally if not more important is the sensitivity of these individuals to local conditions, and their ability to guide their reform proposals around the pitfalls of state politics.

In England there is no sentencing commission, nor anything approaching comparison with such a body. A proposal that there should be established a Sentencing Council, which might exercise functions comparable to that of

[30] See R. Frase, 'The Role of the Legislature, the Sentencing Commission and Other Officials under the Minnesota Sentencing Guidelines' (1993) 28 *Wake Forest LR* 345.

a sentencing commission, was advanced by Professor Ashworth in his book *Sentencing and Penal Policy* in 1983. The Council would be 'charged with the task of developing and keeping under review a corpus of coherent sentencing guidance for the Crown Courts and magistrates' courts'.[31] This suggestion has received widespread support,[32] but it has also attracted powerful critics.[33] The government set its face against it in the 1990 White Paper, prefering to build a 'partnership' between government, which would determine what sentencing policy should be, and the courts, which would apply it. Interpretation and guidance, when required, would be supplied by the Judicial Studies Board.[34] During the passage through Parliament of the Bill which became the Criminal Justice Act 1991 the opposition moved an amendment to the Bill, which would have established a Sentencing Council, but they were defeated. The main argument against the sentencing council seems to have been that it would create a rival to the Court of Appeal which, for many years, has provided general appellate review and guidance in sentencing cases. In his proposal, Professor Ashworth attempted to rebut this argument, explaining that 'The council would be concerned with policy, not with individual cases, which would remain in the hands of the courts subject to appeal'. Sir Frederick Lawton, a former Lord Justice of Appeal, commented bluntly in an article published at the time that 'Parliament, having decided what the sentencing policy should be, would be well advised to leave the Court of Appeal to implement the policy'.[35] This is the view which, in England, has prevailed.

Appellate review of sentencing is much more firmly entrenched in England than in the United States. The Court of Appeal has regarded the promulgation of sentencing guidance as one of its key roles since the Court was established in 1907. This stands in contrast to the United States, where traditionally sentencing decisions have been unregulated by appellate review. Recently, however, this has begun to change. One of the important developments introduced in Minnesota and by other jurisdictions which have generated presumptive guidelines, has been a system of meaningful appellate review. This has resulted in the development of case-law to place flesh on the bones of the statutory guideline structure.[36] While appellate guidance is a very valuable tool, such guidance standing alone is inadequate as the main instrument of sentencing policy. Firstly, case-law

[31] See *Sentencing and Criminal Justice* (London, 1992), 321 *et seq.*, where the discussion is taken further.

[32] From e.g., the Labour Party, the Penal Affairs Consortium and JUSTICE.

[33] It was opposed by Dr Thomas (in an article in *The Times*, 13 Feb. 1990) and by Sir Frederick Lawton (in an article in *The Times*, 8 Jan. 1991).

[34] White Paper (1990), para 2.20. See further Lord Justice Glidewell, 'The Judicial Studies Board', in Munro & Wasik *op. cit.*

[35] Lawton, *op. cit.*

[36] See the article by Frase, cited at n. 30. Also D. Boerner, *Sentencing in Washington* (Seattle, 1985).

is bound to collect in those areas of sentencing practice where there is most at stake for the individual appellant.[37] Thus, there are numerous decisions in England on the imposing of long custodial sentences for very serious offences, but other areas of sentencing practice have hardly been the subject of appellate guidance at all. The main gaps are in relation to sentencing for the less serious offences (such as theft, deception, handling stolen goods, and the lesser varieties of assault or sexual offences), the proper principles applicable to the use of community sanctions (there is, for example, no effective guidance on the number of hours of community service which should be given for particular offences) and, more generally, those matters which form the day-to-day sentencing concerns of the magistrates' courts. This absence of guidance is clearly not the fault of the Court of Appeal—it cannot advise in respect of matters which do not come before it. Secondly, while case-law is an excellent device for supplying the details to an existing underlying structure, it is unlikely in itself to be capable of providing that structure. Appellate judges are under considerable time pressure and their decisions, which are normally given *ex tempore*, generally turn on the particular facts. Even in its so-called 'guideline judgments' in which, when dealing with one or more individual cases, the Court of Appeal takes the opportunity to consider issues of sentencing policy, comments are confined to remarks about the sentencing range for the particular offence concerned, and rarely address matters of general principle. For a while there was a realistic hope in England that the 1991 Act would supply the necessary sentencing structure. The Court of Appeal in general, and the Lord Chief Justice in particular, were, however, openly hostile to much of the sentencing policy which lay behind the Act.[38] The government took note of various expressions of judicial disapproval, and changed certain key provisions of the 1991 Act by amendments made in the Criminal Justice Act 1993.[39]

In the absence of a Sentencing Council, and following the demise of the Advisory Council on the Penal System,[40] there exists no standing forum in England in which sentencing policy may be fully debated and ideas generated. It falls outside the remit of the Law Commission and the Criminal Law Revision Committee. Important work in the sentencing

[37] Although the possibility of appeal by the prosecution from a Crown Court sentence thought to be too lenient was introduced in the Criminal Justice Act 1988, s. 35 & s. 36.

[38] M. Wasik, 'England Repeals Key Provisions of 1991 Sentencing Reform Legislation' (1993) 4(4) *Overcrowded Times* 1.

[39] A. Ashworth & B. Gibson, 'The Criminal Justice Act 1993: Altering the Sentencing Framework' [1994] *Criminal LR* 101.

[40] The last report of which, ironically, made the most systematic attempt in England in recent years to advocate the introduction of sentencing guidelines, by the radical revision of statutory sentencing maxima: Advisory Council on the Penal System, *Sentences of Imprisonment: A Review of Maximum Penalties* (London, 1978).

sphere is carried out by the Home Office Research Unit, and by various University departments or individual academics. Penal reform and pressure groups such as the Howard League, NACRO and the Prison Reform Trust, all turn out well-researched documents on sentencing and, from time to time, commission independent reports into various aspects of sentencing. The impact of all this worthy effort is, however, haphazard and unclear. The impression gained in recent years (and confirmed by a reading of Hansard during the passage of the Criminal Justice and Public Order Act 1994) is that sentencing policy is now more likely to be affected by a single controversial (and untypical) case given effective treatment in the media, than it is by any amount of thorough and well-informed research. The 1990 White Paper on sentencing was an exception, since that clearly was influenced by a body of published academic writings in the United States and in England but, once the White Paper proposals were implemented, several of its key proposals were watered down, or substantially compromised.[41]

In the United States the Sentencing Commissions thus far all seem to have opted for numerical sentencing grids, apparently based upon the pioneering work by Wilkins and others on parole guidelines,[42] which took that approach. These grids are two-dimensional tables of prescribed sentences, the vertical axis being the offence score (which grades the seriousness of the offence committed) and the horizontal axis being the offender score (which grades the offender's criminal record). Across the grid is drawn a dispositional 'in-out' line, above which are prescribed custodial sentences of varying duration and below which are other suggested sanctions. The preference for employing numbers, rather than words, in such guidelines can be traced, once again, to Frankel's book.[43] He proposed there that 'numerical weights or ranges [sh]ould be assigned—as, for example, to the relative gravity of the offence, and to the defendant's past criminal record'. In England the numerical approach has never seriously been contemplated—and it provides another example of a development on the other side of the Atlantic which has been rejected here with a pejorative 'American' label. Here, as in other jurisdictions such as Sweden and Canada, guidance by words rather than numbers has been seen as more appropriate. The English line has, in the main, been to structure the **approach** to sentencing, and to channel sentencing discretion,

41 See n. 38.

42 D. Gottfredson, L Wilkins, & L Hoffman, *Guidelines for Parole and Sentencing* (Lexington, 1978); L Wilkins, *The Principles of Sentencing Guidelines* (Lexington, 1980); I. Blalock, 'Parole Guidelines', in Forst *op. cit.*

43 Above, n. 7.

rather than to specify presumptive sentences.[44] The relevance to sentence of an offender's criminal record may be given here as an example to illustrate the two approaches. Under the American sentencing guidelines schemes sentencers have been provided with a computed numerical score for the offender, determined on the basis of factors determined by the Commission. Thus, for example, the 'criminal history score' would be enhanced where the offender has offended frequently in the past, or where the new offence is similar to previous offending, but would be reduced where the offender has no convictions, or is lightly convicted, or where previous convictions are very old or are dissimilar to the new offence. In contrast, section 29 of the Criminal Justice Act 1991 (in its original form, before its substitution by the Criminal Justice Act 1993) dealt with this matter by making a general statement of principle qualified by an exception. The general principle was that normally the fact that an offender had previous convictions did not, in itself, make a new offence committed by him more serious. The exception was that such record could be relevant where it revealed to the court an aggravating factor of the new offence. This section prompted a great deal of criticism from practitioners (much of which was ill informed), and section 29 has now been repealed and replaced by a more loosely-worded provision.[45]

A comparison between drafting sentencing guidelines by numbers, and by words, has been made by von Hirsch.[46] In his article the author stresses that if the drafting of guidelines by words is to prove successful, it is essential that this be done by a body sufficiently skilled to draft the standards, and that a Bill produced in the normal way would yield much less satisfactory results. This has, unfortunately, been borne out by the English experience with the 1991 Act. Von Hirsch also says that the successful implementation of written sentencing principles requires responsive lower courts. The reaction of legal practitioners and lay magistrates to the 1991 Act reforms was, unfortunately, largely negative and hostile.[47] He also notes that sentencing principles in words are

[44] *Sentencing Guidelines* issued by the Magistrates' Association (latest edition Sept. 1993) offer guidance on the thought process which should lead to the sentencing decision, including the identification of likely aggravating and mitigating factors, but also indicate 'entry point' sentences. These merely point to 'custody' or to 'community sentence', but where a fine is the entry point sentence a 'guideline fine' (which reflects the average seriousness of an offence of the type) is suggested. There are no equivalent published guidelines for Crown Court sentencers.

[45] See M. Wasik & A. von Hirsch, 'Section 29 Revised: Previous Convictions in Sentencing' [1994] *Crim. LR* 409; I. Brownlee, 'Taking the Straitjacket Off: Persistence and the Distribution of Punishment in England and Wales' (1994) 14 *Legal Studies* 295.

[46] A. von Hirsch, 'Guidance by Numbers or Words? Numerical Versus Narrative Guidelines for Sentencing', in Wasik & Pease *op. cit.*, 46.

[47] The author can attest to this from personal experience, having taken part in the compulsory training for sentencers which was required before implementation of the 1991 Act.

demanding of appellate courts, which must be faithful to the spirit of the legislation. In the first batch of cases decided by the Court of Appeal after the 1991 Act came into force, the reaction was largely discouraging. The Court gave the impression that it was interpreting the provisions of the Act wherever possible so as to maximize judicial discretion. The Lord Chief Justice stated that the desert-based concept of 'seriousness' in the Act still required courts to give consideration to deterrence,[48] that the prevalence of offending was relevant to seriousness,[49] and that while sentencers must 'comply with their statutory duty', the procedural requirements should 'not be treated as a verbal tightrope for judges to walk'.[50] In a number of other recent decisions, the Court of Appeal has elected to mark the threshold of seriousness between custodial and community sentences (defined in the Act as being that point at which an offence is 'so serious that only a custodial sentence can be justified') at a remarkably low level.[51] This has had the effect of placing many offenders at real risk of a custodial sentence who would not have been at such risk before the Act. It also, incidentally, maximizes the discretion vested in sentencers to impose or to withhold custody in the light of matters in mitigation personal to the offender. In one final set of recent decisions the Court has been making the most of its powers under the Act to dispense with desert principles, and to impose longer-than-normal sentences on offenders convicted of violent or sexual crimes.[52]

[48] In *Cunningham* (1993) 14 Cr. App. R (S) 444, the Lord Chief Justice said, 447, 'Does [the 1991 Act] permit the sentencing judge to take the need for deterrence into account? In our judgment, it does. The purposes of a custodial sentence must primarily be to punish and to deter. Accordingly, the phrase "commensurate with the seriousness of the offence" must mean commensurate with the punishment and deterrence which the seriousness of the offence requires'. Later, 448, however, Lord Taylor accepted that this wording would 'prohibit . . . adding any extra length to the sentence . . . simply to make a special example of the defendant'.

[49] *Id.*, 448.

[50] *Baverstock* (1993) 14 Cr. App. R (S) 471, 475.

[51] One example is *Keogh* (1994) 15 Cr. App. R (S) 279. The offender pleaded guilty to obtaining by deception from a shop goods to the value of £35. The Court of Appeal upheld a sentence of one month's imprisonment and said that 'right thinking members of the public . . . would not feel justice had been done by the passing of any sentence other than a custodial one' (281). Keogh was subject to a suspended prison sentence at the time of the deception but the Court of Appeal made it quite clear that the deception, standing alone, merited custody. Another example is *Fenton* (1994) 15 Cr. App. R (S) 682, where one motorist pleaded guilty to common assault on another motorist, by pushing him in the chest. The drivers had confronted each other after one had overtaken the other and both had stopped their cars to argue. The Court of Appeal said that seven days imprisonment was appropriate.

[52] In *Bowler* (1993) 14 Cr. App. R (S) 78 the defendant pleaded guilty to indecent assault, having put his hand up a young girl's skirt. In the light of the offender's record of eight very similar offences, the Court of Appeal upheld a sentence of six years' imprisonment, which was passed to protect female members of the public in the future from being occasioned serious psychological harm by the offender.

POLICY AND PRACTICE

A comparison of sentencing developments in the United States and in England displays in both countries a fundamental tension. On the one hand there is the aspiration of academic lawyers (and some policy makers) to develop a more principled approach to sentence decision making. On the other hand there is the desire of most sentencing practitioners for the widest possible range of sentencing options to be made available, and for them to be given wide discretion to choose in each case the sentence which seems appropriate in all the circumstances of the case—'give us the tools and let us get on with the job'. The practitioners' response reflects in part a natural human reluctance to be shorn of powers which have been formerly enjoyed, since the role and authority of any official is diminished when their discretion is reduced or eliminated. This can be seen in the United States, where many of the sentencing guideline schemes have been the subject of vehement criticism from practitioners. This has especially been the fate of the Federal Guidelines, which seem to have been almost universally reviled by those required to use them.[53] It is significant that prosecutors, who have acquired by a side wind rather **greater** discretionary powers following the implementation of presumptive statutory sentencing guidelines, have distanced themselves from these criticisms. The general lack of enthusiasm of practitioners for guideline systems probably also stems from the continuing belief of many of them in the individualized approach to sentencing. Many sentencers are ambivalent about the desert model. They may well agree the importance of offence seriousness in sentencing, but they continue to see the sentencing exercise as an opportunity to influence future events, by the pursuit of one utilitarian goal or another. Since desert theory is concerned essentially with past crimes, rather than with future conduct, sentencers may well come to believe that the adoption of desert principles in sentencing tends to diminish and undermine their own status and position.

A significant difference between sentencing reforms in the United States and England has been the respective roles played by the sentencers themselves. In the United States, it seems that judges have been poorly organized and politically weak, unable to exercise much influence on the tide of legislative reform for which few in fact have had any enthusiasm.[54] A consideration of the respective influence of judges and legislature in the

[53] See M. Tonry, 'The Failure of the US Sentencing Commission's Guidelines' (1993) 39 *Crime and Delinquency* 131.

[54] M. Tonry, 'Judges and Sentencing Policy—the American Experience', in Munro & Wasik *op. cit.*

sentencing field tends to lead on to arguments of constitutionality and the separation of powers. Indeed, it was argued in the United States that the Federal Sentencing Guidelines were unconstitutional, but this claim was eventually rejected by the Supreme Court.[55] In England and Wales the constitutionality point is also raised from time to time, but it seems to have very little merit, and much of the heat has gone out of the argument.[56] In comparison to the American position, in England the judiciary forms a powerful lobby, and there have been several recent instances of judicial activism forcing the government to change its course on criminal justice policy. One example is the action taken by senior judges during the 1980s to sink a governmental proposal for the introduction of 'automatic' parole to alleviate prison overcrowding. More recently, it is clear that Lord Chief Justice Taylor's extrajudicial comments in a speech to the Law Society of Scotland, in which he openly declared his antipathy to key elements of the Criminal Justice Act 1991, were highly effective in causing the government to amend key provisions of that Act.[57] As a member of the House of Lords in its legislative capacity, Lord Taylor clearly also had considerable influence on the final shape of several of the provisions in the Criminal Justice and Public Order Act 1994. The Magistrates' Association has also been functioning recently as an effective pressure group, such as in forcing the abolition of the unit fine system and by hastening a governmental retreat over key provisions in the Police and Magistrates' Courts Act 1994. There has been an increasing willingness on the part of judges generally to comment on sentencing matters in public. Lord Taylor has appeared on a special edition of *Question Time* on television, as a panellist answering questions on criminal justice from a studio audience. Individual judges have begun to respond to criticism of sentences imposed by them, by writing to newspapers to explain why the particular decision was reached,[58] a development unthinkable a few years ago.

There can be little doubt that criminal justice policy in general, and sentencing policy in particular, is now more highly charged and highly politicized than ever. The climate in England has changed considerably in

[55] *Mistretta* v. *US* (1989) 109 S Ct. 647.

[56] For discussion see C. Munro, 'Judicial Independence and Judicial Functions', in Munro & Wasik *op. cit.*, 13.

[57] See 'Judges and Sentencing', *J. of the Law Society of Scotland*, Apr. 1993, 129. His Lordship referred to the Act as an 'ill-fitting strait-jacket' and told practitioners in Scotland that they were fortunate that the relevant provisions did not apply in that jurisdiction.

[58] When, e.g., Mr Justice Drake was criticized in the press for imposing a sentence of five years' imprisonment for manslaughter on a 25 year-old ex-soldier who had attacked and killed a 17 year-old man who had chased and tried to detain him after seeing him stealing from a shop, the judge responded by stating in a letter to *The Times* that in his view guidelines issued by the Court of Appeal, which he had endeavoured to follow, were too low: *The Times*, 19 Mar. 1994.

the five years since the government produced its White Paper. The Labour Party, which has traditionally employed a moderate voice in criminal justice matters has, with the elevation of Tony Blair to the posts of Shadow Home Secretary and now Labour Party leader, adopted the new strategy of challenging the Conservatives' reputation as the 'Party of Law and Order'. Labour's slogan is to be 'tough on crime, and tough on the causes of crime', and this has seen Mr Blair, in television interviews, employing increasingly bellicose remarks, and apparently agreeing with the sentiments of members of the public calling for more severe sentences for offenders and for the return of corporal punishment. The Criminal Justice and Public Order Act 1994 is a measure full of repressive developments in sentencing,[59] as well as in the fields of public order and the rules of criminal evidence, but much of the Bill was weakly opposed, or not opposed at all, by the Labour Party in the House of Commons. The most vociferous objections to the Bill came from members (of all political persuasions) of the unelected chamber, the House of Lords. Short-termism for party political advantage is perhaps the greatest enemy of a rational and humane criminal justice and sentencing policy. In the United States and, to some extent in England, efforts have been made by the right wing to subvert desert principles, by trying to employ 'desert' merely as a synonym for 'severity'. But most right-wingers really place their ultimate faith in deterrence and incapacitation, and positively oppose the parsimony in punishment which desert principles presuppose. When the current Home Secretary, Mr Howard, makes his repeated declarations that 'Prison works', he is certainly announcing his faith in the value of incapacitation.

With the benefit of hindsight, the 1990 White Paper seems an even more remarkable document than it did at the time. The sentencing changes to the Criminal Justice Act 1991 brought about by the 1993 Act amendments have been widely seen as a political U-turn, a bowing to pressure from practitioners, and representing a sacrifice of coherent criminal justice principles for reasons of political expedience. This is certainly true of the cynical abandonment of unit fines.[60] It is also being borne out in respect of the other changes made to the 1991 Act, and the general interpretation given to the provisions of that Act by the Court of Appeal. There is no doubt at all that the impact of all these changes will be to further escalate current increases in the sentenced custodial population.[61] Emergency

[59] It introduces a new custodial sentence (the 'secure training order') for 12–14 year olds and extends powers of long-term detention to 10–13 year-olds. For a full account see Wasik & Taylor *op. cit.*

[60] Ironically, various unit fine schemes now seem to be taking root in the US: J. Greene, 'Structuring Criminal Fines' (1988) 13 *Criminal Justice Journal* 37; and J. Greene, 'Day Fines: Monetary Sanctions Apportioned to Income', in von Hirsch & Ashworth *op. cit.*

[61] See R. Morgan, 'Punitive Policies and Politics Crowding English Prisons' (1994) 5(3) *Overcrowded Times* 1.

arrangements have been put in place for the provision of additional prison accommodation, including the use of prison ships.[62] The Home Office is known to be planning for a population of over 56,000 by the year 2000.[63] This impending crisis in custodial provision takes us full circle to one of the key factors which prompted the sentencing reform movement, discussed in this essay, in the first place.

[62] Criminal Justice and Public Order Act 1994, s.100. Floating prisons, or 'maritime detention centres' have also been used in the US, but it is not clear whether this particular idea is best regarded as an import to, or an export from, the UK. The *Maidstone* was, for example, used as a prison ship in Belfast Lough in the 1970s.

[63] Home Office Statistical Bulletin 16/94.

Bibliography

Ackerman B., 'Constitutional Politics, Constitutional Law' (1989) 103 *Harvard LR* 407.

—— *We the People. Volume I: Foundations* (Cambridge, Mass, 1991).

Adamany D. and Agree G., *Political Money: a Strategy for Campaign Financing in America* (Baltimore, 1975).

Adeji C., 'Human Rights Theory and the Bill of Rights Debate' [1995] 58 *MLR* 17.

Advisory Council on the Penal System, *Sentences of Imprisonment: a Review of Maximum Penalties* (London, 1978).

Albert L., 'Standing to Challenge Administration: an Inadequate Surrogate for Claims for Relief' (1974) *Yale LJ* 425.

Alder J., 'Hunting the Chimera—the End of *O'Reilly v Mackman*' (1993) 13 *Legal Studies* 183.

Alderman G., 'Book Review' [1993] *PL* 548.

Alexander H., *Money in Politics* (Washington DC, 1972).

Alexandrowicz C., *An Introduction to the History of the Law of Nations in the East Indies* (Oxford, 1967).

Allan T. R. S., 'Parliamentary Sovereignty: Lord Denning's Dexterous Revolution' (1983) 3 *OJLS* 23.

—— 'Law, Convention and Prerogative: Reflections Prompted by the Canadian Constitutional Case' (1986) 45 *CLJ* 305.

—— *Law, Liberty and Justice* (Oxford, 1993).

Allen F., *The Decline of the Rehabilitative Ideal: Penal Policy and Social Purpose* (New Haven, 1981).

Allison J., 'The Procedural Reason for Judicial Restraint' [1994] *PL* 452.

Althusser L., 'Ideology and Ideological State Apparatuses', in Althusser L., *Essays in Ideology* (London, 1984).

Aman A., 'Administrative Law in a Global Era' (1988) 73 *Cornell LR* 1101.

Angell E., 'The *Amicus Curiae*: American Development of English Institutions' (1987) 16 *ICLQ* 1016.

Armin Trept P., 'Extension of the EC Procurement Regime to Public Services Contracts: an Overview of the Services Directive' [1993] *PPLR* 1.

Arrowsmith S., 'Protecting the Interests of Bidders for Public Contracts' (1994) 53 *CLJ* 104.

Ashworth A., 'The White Paper on Criminal Justice and Sentencing' [1990] *Crim LR* 217.

—— 'Structuring Sentencing Discretion', in Von Hirsch A. and Ashworth A., (eds.) *Principled Sentencing* (Boston, 1992).

—— 'The Criminal Justice Act 1991', in Munro C. and Wasik M. (eds.) *Sentencing, Judicial Discretion and Training* (London, 1992).

Ashworth A. and Gibson B., 'The Criminal Justice Act 1993: Altering the Sentencing Framework' [1994] *Crim LR* 101.

Atiyah P. and Summers R., *Form and Substance in Anglo-American Law* (Oxford, 1987).
Bagehot W., *The English Constitution* (London, 1963).
Bailyn B., *The Ideological Origins of the American Revolution* (Cambridge, Mass, 1967).
Baker L., *Holmes and Brandeis: a Dual Biography* (New York, 1986).
Baldwin R., 'Why Rules Don't Work' [1990] 53 *MLR* 321.
Baldwin R. and Hawkins K., 'Discretionary Justice: Davis Reconsidered' [1984] *PL* 570.
Baldwin R. and McCrudden C. (eds.), *Regulation and Public Law* (London, 1987).
Ball M., 'Constitutions, Courts, Indian Tribes' (1987) 1 *American Bar Foundation Research Journal* 3.
Ball S. and Bell S., *Environmental Law* (London, 1994, 2nd ed).
Bamforth N., 'The Scope of Judicial Review: Still Uncertain' [1993] *PL* 239.
Baram M., *Alternatives to Regulation* (Lexington Mass, 1982).
Barendt E., *Freedom of Speech* (Oxford, 1987).
—— 'Libel and Freedom of Speech in English Law', [1993] *PL* 449.
—— *Broadcasting Law* (Oxford, 1993).
—— 'Press and Broadcasting Freedom: Does Anyone Have Any Rights to Free Speech?' [1993] *CLP* 63.
Baudrillard J., *The Transparency of Evil: Essays on Extreme Phenomena* (London, 1993).
Beard C., *An Economic Interpretation of the Constitution* (New York, 1913).
Becker C., *The Declaration of Independence: a Study in the History of Political Ideas* (New York, 1958).
Becker T. and Feeley M. (eds.), *The Impact of Supreme Court Decisions* (London, 1973, 2nd ed).
Beloff M., 'Judicial Review 2001: a Prophetic Odyssey' [1995] 58 *MLR* 144.
Bender P., 'The Canadian Charter of Rights and Freedoms and United States Bill of Rights: a Comparison' (1983) 28 *McGill LJ* 811.
Bentley A., *The Process of Government* (Chicago, 1908).
BeVier L., 'Money and Politics: a Perspective on the First Amendment and Campaign Finance Reform' (1985) 73 *Calif LR* 1045.
Bhabba H., *The Location of Culture* (London, 1994).
Bindman G., 'Incitement to Racial Hatred' (1982) *NLJ* 299.
—— 'Bringing Race Bigots to Book' *The Guardian*, October 30 1994.
Bingham, Sir Thomas, 'Should Public Law Remedies Be Discretionary?' [1991] *PL* 64.
—— 'There Is a World Elsewhere: the Changing Perspectives of English Law' (1992) 41 *ICLQ* 513.
—— 'The European Convention on Human Rights—Time to Incorporate' (1993) 109 *LQR* 390.
Birkinshaw P., Harden I. and Lewis N., *Government by Moonlight* (London, 1990).
Bishop W., 'A Theory of Administrative Law' (1990) 19 *J of Legal Studies* 489.
Blalock I., 'Parole Guidelines', in Forst *infra*.
Boerner D., *Sentencing in Washington* (Seattle, 1985).

Bogdanor V., 'Britain and the European Community', in Jowell J. and Oliver D. (eds.) (1994) *infra.*

Borrie, Sir Gordon, 'The Regulation of Public and Private Power' [1989] *PL* 522.

Boyle A., 'Sovereignty, Accountability and the Reform of Administrative Law', in Richardson G. and Genn H. (eds.) *Administrative Law and Government Action* (Oxford, 1994).

Bracken H., 'Philosophy and Racism' 8 *Philosophia* 241.

Bradley A., 'Free Expression and Acts of Racial Hatred' [1992] *PL* 357.

Brennan W., 'Why Have a Bill of Rights?' (1989) 9 *OJLS* 425.

Brest P., 'The Misconceived Quest for Original Understanding' (1980) 60 *Boston LR* 204.

Bridges L., Game C., Lomas O., McBride J. and Ranson S., *Legality and Local Politics* (Birmingham, 1987).

Brilmayer L., 'The Jurisprudence of Article III: Perspectives on the "Case or Controversy" Requirement' (1979) 93 *Harvard LR* 297.

Brody T., 'Research into the Aims and Effectiveness of Sentencing' (178) 17 *Howard J of Criminal Justice* 133.

Browne-Wilkinson, Lord, 'The Infiltration of a Bill of Rights' [1992] *PL* 397.

Brownlie I., 'Taking the Straitjacket Off: Persistence and the Distribution of Punishment in England and Wales' (1994) 14 *Legal Studies* 295.

Bryden P., 'Public Interest Intervention in the Courts' (1987) 66 *Canadian Bar Review* 490.

Bushnell S., 'The Use of American Cases' (1986) 35 *U of North Brunswick LJ* 157.

Byrne J., Lurigio S. and Petersilia J. (eds.) *Smart Sentencing Part II* (California, 1992).

Caldeira G. and Wright J., 'Organised Interests and Agenda-Setting in the US Supreme Court' (1988) 82 *American Political Science Review* 1109.

—— '*Amici Curiae* Before the Supreme Court. Who Participates, When and How Much?' (1990) *Journal of Politics* 782.

Campbell T., 'Rationales for Freedom of Communication' Conference Paper presented in Canberra, August 1993.

Cane P., 'The Function of Standing Rules in Administrative Law' [1980] *PL* 303.

—— 'Statutes, Standing and Representation' [1990] *PL* 307.

—— *An Introduction to Administrative Law* (Oxford, 1992, 2nd ed).

Cantor M., 'The Writ of Habeas Corpus; Early American Origins and Development', in Hyman H. and Levy L. (eds.) *Freedom and Reform. Essays in Honour of Henry Steele Commager* (New York, 1967).

Cappelletti M., 'Alternative Dispute Resolution Processes Within the Framework of the Worldwide Access to Justice Movement' [1993] 56 *MLR* 282.

Carty A., *The Decay of International Law?* (Manchester, 1986).

Cerullo K., 'Sociopolitical Control and the Structure of National Symbols: an Empirical Analysis of National Anthems' (1989) 68 *Social Forces* 76.

Cervantees L., *Contemporary Chicana Poetry* (Los Angeles, 1986).

Chayes A., 'The Role of the Judge in Public Law Litigation' (1976) 89 *Harvard LR* 1281.

Clagget B. and Bolton J., '*Buckley v Valeo*, Its Aftermath and Its Prospects: the Constitutionality of Government Restraints on Political Campaign Financing' (1976) 29 *Vanderbilt LR* 1327.

Cohen F., *The Legal Conscience: Selected Papers of Felix S. Cohen* (New Haven, 1960).

Commager H., *The Empire of Reason* (New York, 1977).

Cooper J. and Dhavan R., *Public Interest Law* (Oxford, 1986).

Cortner R., 'Strategies and Tactics of Litigants in Constitutional Cases' (1968) 17 *J of Public Law* 287.

Corwin E., 'The Higher Law Background of American Constitutional Law Part II' (1929) *Harvard LR* 365.

—— 'The Constitution as Instrument and as Symbol' (1936) 30 *American Political Science Review* 1071.

—— 'The Worship of the Constitution', in Loss R. (ed.) *Corwin on the Constitution* (Ithaca, NY, 1981).

Cosgrove R., *Our Lady the Common Law: An Anglo-American Legal Community, 1870–1930* (New York, 1987).

Cotterrell R., 'Prosecuting Incitement to Racial Hatred' [1992] *PL* 378.

—— 'Law's Community: Legal Theory and the Image of Legality' (1992) 19 *JLS* 405.

—— 'Judicial Review and Legal Theory', in Richardson G. and Genn H. (eds.) *Administrative Law and Government Action* (Oxford, 1994).

—— *Law's Community: Legal Theory in Sociological Perspective* (Oxford, 1995).

—— 'Some Aspects of the Communication of Constitutional Authority, in Nelken D. (ed.) *Law and Communication* (Aldershot, forthcoming).

Craig P., *Administrative Law* (London, 1989, 2nd ed).

—— *Public Law and Democracy in Britain and the USA* (Oxford, 1990).

—— 'Legitimate Expectations: a Conceptual Analysis' (1992) 108 *LQR* 79.

—— *Administrative Law* (London, 1994, 3rd ed.).

Cranston R., 'Reviewing Judicial Review' in Richardson G. and Genn H. (eds.) *Administrative Law and Government Action* (Oxford, 1994).

Dahl R., *Dilemmas of a Pluralist Democracy* (New Haven, 1982).

Daintith T., 'Political Programmes and the Content of the Constitution', in Finnie J. et al (eds.) *Edinburgh Essays in Public Law* (Edinburgh, 1992).

Daintith T. and Sah M., 'Privatisation and the Economic Neutrality of the Constitution' [1993] *PL* 465.

Dallen R., 'An Overview of European Community Protection of Human Rights with Some Special References to the UK' [1990] 27 *CMLR* 761.

Dauses M., 'The Protection of Fundamental Rights in the Community Legal Order' (1985) 10 *ELR* 398.

Davis K., 'The Future of Judge-Made Public Law in England: a Problem of Practical Jurisprudence' (1961) 61 *Col LR* 201.

—— *Discretionary Justice* (Illinois, 1991, 2nd ed).

Denvir J., 'Towards a Political Theory of Public Interest Law Litigation' (1976) 54 *U of North Carolina LR* 1133.

Derrida J., 'White Mythology Metaphor and Text in History', in Derrida J., *Margins of Philosophy* (Chicago, 1982).

DeSmith S. and Brazier R., *Constitutional and Administrative Law* (London, 1989).

Devlin P., *The Enforcement of Morals* (Oxford, 1965).

Diamond P., 'Dishonourable Defences: the Use of Injunctions and the EC Treaty—Case Study of the Shops Act 1950' [1991] 54 *MLR* 72.

Dickey A., 'Prosecutions Under the Race Relations Act 1965 s.6' [1968] *Crim LR* 489.

Dickinson J., *Administrative Justice and the Supremacy of the Law in the United States* (Cambridge, Mass, 1927).

DiIulio J., *Courts, Corrections and the Constitution* (New York, 1990).

Douglas M., *Purity and Danger: an Analysis of Concepts of Pollution and Taboo* (Harmondsworth, 1970).

Douglas W., *The Court Years* (New York, 1980).

Doyle L., 'Racism: West Europe's Mounting Death Toll' *The Independent* January 13 1994.

Duff R. and Garland D. (eds.), *Punishment* (Oxford, 1994).

Dumbauld E., *The Constitution of the United States* (Norman, Oklahoma).

Durham J., *A Certain Lack of Coherence: Writings on Art and Cultural Politics* (J. Fisher ed.) (London 1993).

Dworkin R., *Taking Rights Seriously* (London, 1977).

—— *Law's Empire* (London, 1986).

—— *A Matter of Principle* (Oxford, 1986).

—— 'What is Equality? Part 3: the Place of Liberty' (1987) 73 *Iowa LR* 1.

—— *Life's Dominion* (London, 1993).

Dyk, T., 'The Supreme Court's Role in Not Shaping Administrative Law' (1992) *Administrative LR* 429.

Easterbrook F., 'The Supreme Court 1983, Foreword: the Court and the Economic System' (1984) 88 *Harvard LR* 4.

Edwards J., *The Attorney-General, Politics and the Public Interest* (London, 1984).

Elkind J., *The Impact of American Law on English and Commonwealth Law* (St. Paul, Minnesota, 1978).

Ely J., *Democracy and Distrust* (Cambridge, Mass, 1980).

Epstein L., *Conservatives in Court* (Knoxville, 1985).

—— *Political Parties in the American Mold* (Madison, Wis., 1986).

Epstein L. and Kobylka J., *The Supreme Court and Legal Change* (Chapel Hill, 1992).

Erickson N., 'Historical Background of "Protective" Labour Legislation: *Muller v Oregon*', in Weisberg D. (ed.) *Women and the Law: the Social Historical Perspective* (Cambridge, Mass, Vol 2, 1982).

Errera R., 'In Defence of Civility: Racial Incitement and Group Libel in French Law', in Coliver S. (ed.) *Striking a Balance* (London, 1992).

Eskridge W. and Peller G., 'The New Public Law Movement: Modernism as a Postmodern Cultural Form' (1991) 89 *Michigan LR* 707.

Evans D., 'Private Prisons' (1987) 36 *Emory LJ* 253.

Ewing K., *The Financing of Political Parties in Britain* (Cambridge, 1987).

—— *Money, Politics and the Law: a Study of Electoral Campaign Finance Reform in Canada* (Oxford, 1992).

Farina C., 'Statutory Interpretation and the Balance of Power in the Administrative State' (1989) 89 *Col LR* 452.

Feeley M., 'Hollow Hopes, Flypaper and Metaphors', 17 *Law and Social Inquiry* 715.

Fiemeger M., 'Consent Decrees in Prison and Jail Reform' (1993) *J of Criminal Law and Criminology* 1024.

Figgis J., *The Divine Right of Kings* (Cambridge, 1913, 2nd ed).

Fisher L., *Constitutional Rights: Civil Rights and Civil Liberties* (New York, 1990).

Fishkin J., *Democracy and Deliberation: New Directions for Democratic Reform* (New Haven, 1991).

Fiss O., 'Free Speech and Social Structure' (1986) 71 *Iowa LR* 1405.

—— 'Why the State?' (1987) *Harvard LR* 781.

—— 'State Activism and State Censorship' (1991) 100 *Yale LJ* 2087.

Fitzgerald P., 'An English Bill of Rights' (1982) 70 *Georgetown LJ* 1229.

Fitzpatrick P., 'Racism and the Innocence of Law' (1986) 13 *JLS* 119.

—— *The Mythology of Modern Law* (London, 1992).

—— ' "We Know What It Is When You Do Not Ask Us": Nationalism as Racism', in Fitzpatrick P. (ed.) *Nationalism, Racism and the Rule of Law* (Aldershot, 1995).

Fleishman J., 'Freedom of Speech and Equality of Political Opportunity: the Constitutionality of the Federal Election Campaign Act 1971' (1973) 51 *North Carolina LR* 389.

Foley M., *The Silence of Constitutions* (London, 1989).

Forst M. (ed.), *Sentencing Reform* (Beverley Hills, 1992).

Forsyth C., 'The Provenance and Protection of Legitimate Expectations' (1988) 47 *CLJ* 238.

Foucault M., *The History of Sexuality Vol 1 : an Introduction* (Harmondsworth, 1981).

Fox R. and O'Brien D., 'Fact Finding for Sentencers' (1975) 10 *Melbourne ULR* 163.

Frankel M., *Criminal Sentences: Law Without Order* (New York, 1972).

—— 'Lawlessness in Sentencing' (1972) 41 *Cincinnati LR* 1.

Frase R., 'Implementing Commission-Based Sentencing Guidelines: the Lessons of the First Ten Years in Minnesota' (1993) 2 *Cornell J of Law and Policy* 279.

—— 'The Role of the Legislature, the Sentencing Commission and Other Officials under the Minnesota Sentencing Guidelines' (1993) 28 *Wake Forest LR* 345.

Fredman S. and Morris G., 'The Cost of Exclusivity: Public and Private Re-examined' [1994] *PL* 69.

Freedland M., 'Government by Contract and Private Law' [1994] *PL* 86.

Frickey P., 'Marshalling Past and Present: Colonialism, Constitutionalism and Interpretation in Federal Indian Law' (1994) 107 *Harvard LR* 381.

Fried C., 'The New First Amendment Jurisprudence: a Threat to Liberty', in Stone G., Epstein R. and Sunstein S. (eds.) *The Bill of Rights in the Modern State* (Chicago, 1992).

Fuller L., 'Reason and Fiat in Case Law' (1946) 54 *Harvard LR* 376.

—— 'The Form and Limits of Adjudication' (1978) 92 *Harvard LR* 353.

Galanter M., 'Why the "Haves" Come Out Ahead: Speculations on the Limits of Legal Change' (1974) *Law and Society Review* 225.
—— 'Reading the Landscape of Disputes' (1983) 31 *U of Calif LR* 225.
—— 'The Radiating Effects of Courts', in Boyum K. and Mather L. (eds.) *Empirical Theories of Courts* (New York, 1983).
—— 'Law Abounding: Legalisation Around the North Atlantic' [1992] 55 *MLR* 1.
Galligan D., *Discretionary Powers* (Oxford, 1990).
Ganz G., 'Allocation of Decisionmaking Functions' [1972] *PL* 215.
—— *Administrative Procedures* (London, 1974).
—— *Quasi-Legislation* (London, 1986).
Geddes A., 'Locus Standi and EC Environmental Matters' (1992) 4 *J Env Law* 29.
Gellman S., 'Sticks and Stones Can Put You in Jail, but Can Words Increase Your Sentence?' (1991) 39 *UCLA LR* 333.
Gershwer L., 'Informational Standing under NEPA: Justiciability and the Environmental Decisionmaking Process' (1993) 93 *Columbia LR* 996.
Ginson B., *Unit Fines* (Winchester, 1990).
Gibson D., *The Law of the Charter* (Toronto, 1986).
Glendon M., *Rights Talk: the Impoverishment of Political Discourse* (New York, 1991).
Glidewell, Lord Justice, 'The Judicial Studies Board', in Munro C. and Wasik M. (eds.) *Sentencing, Judicial Discretion and Training* (London, 1992).
Goerlich H., 'Fundamental Constitutional Rights: Content, Meaning and General Doctrines', in Karpen U. (ed.) *The Constitution of the Federal Republic of Germany* (Baden-Baden, 1988).
Goldberg S., Green E. and Sander F., *Dispute Resolution* (Boston, 1992, 2nd ed).
Goldman D. and Mullinex P., 'A Hidden Issue in Sentencing: Burdens of Proof for Disputed Allegations in Pre-Sentencing Reports' (1978) 66 *Georgetown LR* 1515.
Gong G., *The Standard of 'Civilization' in International Society* (Oxford, 1984).
Goodrich P., 'Fate as Seduction: the Other Scene of Legal Judgment', in Norrie A. (ed.) *Closure or Critique* (Edinburgh, 1993).
Gottfredson D., Wilkins L. and Hoffman L., *Guidelines for Parole and Sentencing* (Lexington, 1978).
Gottlieb S., 'The Dilemma of Election Campaign Finance Reform' (1989) *Hofstra LR* 301.
Gough J., *Fundamental Law in English Constitutional History* (Oxford, 1955).
Gravells N., 'Disapplying an Act of Parliament Pending a Preliminary Ruling: Constitutional Enormity or Common Law Right?' [1989] *PL* 568.
Green L., 'Claims to Territory in Colonial America', in Green L. and Dickason O. (eds.) *The Law of Nations and the New World* (Alberta, 1988).
Greene J., 'Structuring Criminal Fines' (1988) 13 *Criminal Justice Journal* 37.
—— 'Day Fines: Monetary Sanctions Apportioned to Income', in von Hirsch A. and Ashworth A. (eds.) *Principled Sentencing* (Boston, 1992).
Greenawalt K., 'O'er the Land of the Free: Flag Burning as Speech' (1991) 38 *UCLA LR* 925.
Grey T., 'Do We Have an Unwritten Constitution?' (1975) 27 *Stanford LR* 703.

—— 'The Origins of the Unwritten Constitution: Fundamental Law in American Revolutionary Thought' (1978) 30 *Stanford LR* 843.
—— 'The Constitution as Scripture' (1984) 37 *Stanford LR* 21.
Grief N., 'The Domestic Impact of the ECHR as Mediated through Community Law' [1991] *PL* 555.
Griffith J., 'The Political Constitution' [1979] 42 *MLR* 1.
—— 'Judicial Decision-Making in Public Law [1985] *PL* 564.
—— *The Politics of the Judiciary* (London, 1991, 4th ed.).
Grosz S., 'Pergau Be Damned' (1994) 144 *NLJ* 1708.
Grotious H., *De Jure Belli ac Pacis I* (Sijthoff, 1919).
Hakman N., 'Lobbying the Supreme Court—an Appraisal of "Political Science Folklore" ' (1966) 35 *Fordham LR* 15.
Handler J., Hollingsworth E. and Erlanger H., *Lawyers and the Pursuit of Legal Rights* (New York, 1978).
Hansard Commission on the Legislative Process, *Making the Law* (London, 1993).
Harden I., 'Defining the Range of Application of the Public Sector Procurement Directives in the UK' [1992] *PPLR* 362.
Harding C., 'Who Goes to Court in Europe? An Analysis of Litigation Against the EC' (1980) 5 *ELR* 354.
Harlow C., 'Remedies in French Administrative Law' [1977] *PL* 277.
—— ' "Public" and "Private" Law: Definition Without Distinction' [1980] 43 *MLR* 241.
—— 'Public Interest Law: the State of the Art', in Cooper and Dhavan, *supra*.
—— '*Gillick*: a Comedy of Errors' [1986] 49 *MLR* 768.
—— 'Towards a Theory of Access for the European Court' (1993) 12 *Yearbook of European Law* 213.
—— 'Changing the Mindset: the Place of Theory in English Law' (1994) *OJLS* 419.
Harlow C. and Rawlings R., *Law and Administration* (London, 1984).
—— *Pressure Through Law* (London, 1992).
Harring S., *Crow Dog's Case: American Indian Sovereignty, Tribal Law, and United States Law in the Nineteenth Century* (New York, 1994).
Hart, H. L. A., *The Concept of Law* (Oxford, 1961).
—— *Law, Liberty and Morality* (Oxford, 1963).
Hart H. L. A. and Sacks A., *The Legal Process: Basic Problems in the Making and Application of Law* (Cambridge, Mass, 1958).
Hartley T., *Foundations of European Community Law* (Oxford, 1994, 3rd ed.).
Harvie R. and Foster H., 'Ties That Bind? The Supreme Court of Canada, American Jurisprudence, and the Revision of Canadian Criminal Law under the Charter' (1990) 28 *Osgoode Hall LJ* 729.
Hayek F., *The Constitution of Liberty* (London, 1960).
Heaney G., 'The Reality of Guidelines Sentencing: No End to Disparity' (1991) 28 *American Crim LR* 161.
Heard A., *The Costs of Democracy* (Chapel Hill, NC, 1960).
Hegel G., *Philosophy of Right* (Oxford, 1952).
Heinz J., Laumann E., Nelson R. and Salisbury R., *The Hollow Core: Private Interests in National Policymaking* (Chicago, 1993).
Hogg P., 'A Comparison of the Canadian Charter of and Freedoms with the

American Bill of Rights', in Tarnopolsky W. and Beuadouin G. (eds.) *The Canadian Charter of Rights and Freedoms* (Toronto, 1982).
—— 'The Charter of Rights and American Theories of Interpretation' (1987) 25 *Osgoode Hall LJ* 87.
Home Office, *Intermittent Confinement* (London, 1984).
—— *Electronic Monitoring: the Trials and Their Results* (London, 1990).
—— *Racially Motivated Crime: a British Crime Survey Analysis* (London, 1994).
Horowitz D., *Courts and Social Policy* (Washington, 1977).
Howe M., *Holmes-Laski Letters Volumes I and II* (London, 1953).
Hulme P., 'The Spontaneous Hand of Nature: Savagery, Colonialism and the Enlightenment', in Hulme P. and Jordanova L. (eds.) *The Enlightenment and its Shadows* (London, 1990).
Hutchinson A., 'Mice Under a Chair: Democracy, Courts and the Administrative State' (1990) 50 *U of Toronto LJ* 374.
Hutchinson A. and Jones M., '*Wheeler*-dealing: an Essay on Law, Politics and Speech' (1988) 15 *JLS* 263.
Ibbs Report, *Improving Management in Government: the Next Steps* (London, 1988).
Institute for Public Policy Research, *The Constitution of the United Kingdom* (London, 1991).
Jabbari D., 'Critical Theory in Administrative Law' 14 *OJLS* 189.
Jaconnelli J., *Enacting a Bill of Rights* (Oxford, 1980).
Jaffe L., *English and American Judges as Lawmakers* (Oxford, 1969).
Jensen M., Meckling W. and Holderness C., 'Analysis of Alternative Standing Doctrines' (1986) 6 *IRLE* 205.
Jowell J., 'The Legal Control of Administrative Discretion' [1973] *PL* 178.
—— 'The Rule of Law Today' in Jowell and Oliver (eds.) (1994) *infra*.
Jowell J. and Lester A., 'Beyond *Wednesbury*: Substantive Principles of Administrative Law' [1987] *PL* 368.
—— 'Proportionality: Neither Novel nor Dangerous', in Jowell J. and Oliver D. (eds.), *New Directions in Judicial Review* (London, 1988).
Jowell J. and Oliver D. (eds.), *The Changing Constitution* (Oxford, 1994, 3rd ed).
Kahn-Freund O., 'On Uses and Misuses of Comparative Law' (1974) 37 *MLR* 1.
—— 'Common Law and Civil Law—Imaginary and Real Obstacles to Assimilation', in Cappelletti M. and Kohnstamm M. (eds.) *New Perspectives for a Common Law of Europe* (Leyden, 1978).
Kant I., *Kant's Political Writings* (H. Reiss ed.) (Cambridge, 1970).
Katz J., *Poor People's Lawyers in Transition* (New Brunswick, 1982).
Kay S., 'The Implications of Prison Privatisation on the Conduct of Prisoner Litigation under 42 USC s. 1983' (1987) 40 *Vanderbilt LR* 867.
Kelsen H., *The Pure Theory of Law* (Berkeley, Cal., 1967).
—— 'The Function of a Constitution', in Tur R. and Twining W. (eds.) *Essays on Kelsen* (Oxford, 1986).
Kennedy D., 'Form and Substance in Private Law Adjudication' (1976) 89 *Harvard LR* 1685.
Kessler M., *Legal Services for the Poor* (Westport, 1987).

—— 'Legal Mobilisation and Social Reform: Power and the Politics of Agenda Setting' (1990) *Law and Society Review* 121.

Koch J., 'Making Room: New Direction in Third Party Intervention' 48 *U of Toronto LR* 151.

Kommers D., *The Constitutional Jurisprudence of the Federal Republic of Germany* (Durham, NC, 1989).

Koopmans J., 'European Public Law—Reality and Prospects' [1991] *PL* 53.

Krislov S., 'The Amicus Curiae Brief: From Friendship to Advocacy' (1963) 72 *Yale LJ* 694.

Lathers V., 'Associational and Third Party Standing and Federal Jurisdiction under *Hunt*' (1978) *Iowa LR* 121.

Law Commission No. 40, *Remedies in Administrative Law* (London, 1970).

—— No. 73, *Report on Remedies in Administrative Law* (London, 1976).

—— No. 121, *Privity of Contract: Contracts for the Benefit of Third Parties* (London, 1991).

—— No. 126, *Administrative Law, Judicical Review and Statutory Appeals* (London, 1993).

—— No. 226, *Administrative Law, Judicial Review and Statutory Appeals* (London, 1994).

Laws, Sir John, 'The Problem of Jurisdiction', in Supperstone M. and Goudie J. (eds.) *Judicial Review* (London, 1992).

—— 'Is the High Court the Guardian of Fundamental Constitutional Rights' [1993] *PL* 59.

—— 'Judicial Remedies and the Constitution' (1994) 57 *MLR* 213.

Lee H., 'The Australian High Court and Implied Fundamental Guarantees' [199?] *PL* 606.

Lee S., 'Bicentennial Bork, Tercentennial Spycatcher: Do the British Need a Bill of Rights?' (1988) 49 *U Pitt LR* 777.

Leopold P., 'Incitement to Hatred—the History of a Controversial Offence' [1977] *PL* 389.

Lerner M., 'Constitution and Court as Symbols' (1937) 46 *Yale LJ* 1290.

Lester A., 'Fundamental Rights: the United Kingdom Isolated' [1984] *PL* 46.

—— 'The Overseas Trade in the American Bill of Rights' (1988) 88 *Columbia LR* 537.

—— '*Amici Curiae*: Third Party Interventions Before the European Court of Human Rights', in Matscher F. and Petzold H. (eds.) *Protecting Human Rights: the European Dimension* (Berlin, 1990, 2nd ed).

—— 'European Human Rights and the British Constitution', in Jowell J. and Oliver D. (eds.) (1994) *supra.*

—— 'Discrimination: What Lawyers Can Learn from History' [1994a] *PL* 224.

—— 'No Place for a Politician to Hide' *The Guardian* 22 Nov 1994.

Levinson S., *Constitutional Faith* (Princeton NJ, 1988).

Levit K., 'Campaign Finance Reform and the Return of *Buckley v Valeo*' (1993) 103 *Yale LJ* 469.

Levitsky J., 'The Europeanisation of the British Legal Style' (1994) 42 *Am J of Comp Law* 347.

Levy L., *Emergence of a Free Press* (New York, 1985).

—— 'Introduction—the Making of the Constitution', in Levy L. (ed.) *The Making of the Constitution* (New York, 1987).

Lewis N., 'The Citizens Charter and Next Steps: a New Way of Governing' (1993) *Political Quarterly* 316.

Lily J. and Knepper P., 'An International Perspective on the Privatisation of Corrections' (1992) 31 *Howard J of Criminal Justice* 174.

Linton M., *Money and Votes* (London, 1994).

Livok R., 'Science, Law and Safety Standards: a Case Study of Industrial Disease' (1979) 6 *JLS* 172.

Locke J., *The Second Treatise on Government* (1690).

Lockhart W., Kamisar Y. and Choper J., *Constitutional Law* (Minnesota, 1975, 5th ed.).

Logan C., *Private Prisons* (New York, 1990).

Loughlin M., *Public Law and Political Theory* (Oxford, 1992).

—— 'The Limits of Judicial Review', in Birks P. (ed.) *Frontiers of Liability* (Oxford, Vol 1, 1994).

—— 'The Pathways of Public Law Scholarship', in Wilson G. (ed.) *Frontiers of Legal Knowledge* (Warwick, 1995).

Loveland I., 'Legal Rights and Political Realities: Government Responses to Homelessness in Britain' 16 *Law and Social Inquiry* 249.

—— 'Positive Discrimination and Fair Electoral Representation in the United States' [1994a] *PL* 332.

—— 'Taking Lessons from America?' (1994b), *Legal Studies* 22.

—— *Constitutional Law* (London, forthcoming).

Lowenstein D., 'On Campaign Finance Reform: the Root of All Evil Is Deeply Rooted' (1989) 18 *Hofstra LR* 301.

Lyons D., *Ethics and the Rule of Law* (Cambridge, 1984).

MacCormick N., 'A Political Frontier of Jurisprudence: John Chipman Gray on the State' (1981) 66 *Cornell LR* 973.

—— *Legal Right and Social Democracy* (Oxford, 1982).

Maier P., 'John Wilkes and American Disillusionment with Britain' (1963) *William and Mary Quarterly* 373.

Main J., 'The Anti-Federalists', in Ollman B. and Birmbaum J. (eds.), *The United States Constitution* (New York, 1990).

Manfredi P., 'The Canadian Supreme Court and American Judicial Review: United States Constitutional Jurisprudence and the Canadian Charter of Rights and Freedoms' (1992) 86 *American J of Comparative Law* 213.

Markesinis B., 'Comparative Law—A Subject in Search of an Audience' [1990] 53 *MLR* 1.

Markesinis B. (ed.), *The Gradual Convergence* (Oxford, 1994).

Marshall G., *Constitutional Conventions* (Oxford, 1984).

Mashaw J., *Bureaucratic Justice* (New Haven, 1983).

—— *Due Process in the Administrative State* (New Haven, 1985).

Matsuda M., 'Public Response to Racist Speech: Considering the Victim's Story' (1989) *Michigan LR* 2320.

McAfee W., 'Tennessee's Private Prison Act 1986: A Historical Perspective with Special Attention to California's Experience' (1987) 40 *Vanderbilt LR* 851.

McCann M., 'Reform Litigation on Trial' 17 *Law and Social Inquiry* (1992) 715.

—— *Rights at Work: Pay Equity Reform and the Politics of Legal Mobilisation* (Chicago, 1994).

McDonald D., 'Public Imprisonment by Private Means' (1994) 34 *Brit J Crimin* 29.

Merry S., *Getting Justice and Getting Even: Legal Consciousness Among Working Class Americans* (Chicago, 1990).

Mclinden J., *Amicus Curiae: an American Model for the New Zealand Court of Appeal* (mimeo, Auckland, 1992).

Michelman F., 'Foreword: Traces of Self Government' (1986) 100 *Harvard LR* 17.

—— 'Law's Republic' (1988) 97 *Yale LJ* 1493.

—— 'The Rule of Law as a Law of Rules' (1989) 56 *U of Chicago LR* 1175.

Mill J. S. M., *On Liberty* (first published in 1859).

Miller K., *Doubles: Studies in Literary History* (Oxford, 1987).

Minnow, M., *Making All the Difference: Inclusion, Exclusion and American Law* (Cornell, 1990).

Mnookin R. and Kornhauser L., 'Bargaining in the Shadow of the Law: The Case of Divorce' (1979) 88 *Yale LJ* 951.

Morgan R., 'Punitive Policies and Politics Crowding English Prisons' (1994) 5(3) *Overcrowded Times* 1.

Mount F., *The British Constitution Now* (London, 1992).

Moxon D., *et al.*, *Unit Fines: Experiments in Four Courts*, Home Office Research and Planning Unit Paper 59 (London, 1990).

Munro C., 'What is a Constitution?' [1983] *PL* 567.

—— 'Judicial Independence and Judicial Functions', in Munro C. and Wasik M. (eds.), *Sentencing, Judicial Discretion and Training* (London, 1992).

Nairn T., *The Enchanted Glass: Britain and its Monarchy* (London, 1988).

Nichol G.R., 'Rethinking Standing' (1984) 72 *Calif LR* 68.

Nicholson M., 'Campaign Financing and Equal Protection' (1974) 26 *Stanford LR* 815.

Nimmer M., 'The Right to Speak from *Times* to *Time*: First Amendment Theory Applied to Libel and Misapplied to Privacy' (1968) 56 *Calif LR* 935.

—— 'The Meaning of Symbolic Speech Under the First Amendment' (1969) 17 *UCLA LR* 29.

Nonet P. and Selznick D., *Law and Society in Transition: Towards Responsive Law* (California, 1978).

Noorani A., 'Rights and Wrongs: Issues of Libel and Press Freedom', *Frontline* 30 December 1994, 100–2.

O'Connor K. and Epstein L., '*Amicus Curiae* Participation in US Supreme Court Litigation: An Appraisal of Hakman's "Folklore" ' (1981) 16 *Law and Society* 311.

Oliver, D., 'Is *Ultra Vires* the Basis of Judicial Review?' [1987] *PL* 543.

—— 'Law, Politics and Public Accountability. The Search for a New Equilibrium' [1994] *PL* 238.

Olsen S., 'The Political Evolution of Interest Group Litigation', in Gambitta R., May M. and Foster J. (eds), *Governing Through Courts* (Beverley Hills, 1981).

Osborne D. and Gaebler T., *Reinventing Government* (Reading, Mass., 1992).
Pagden A., *European Encounters with the New World* (New Haven and London, 1993).
Pallister D. and Chaudhary V., 'Killer Attacks Detective at Old Bailey' *The Guardian* 19 November 1993.
Palmer R., *The Age of the Democratic Revolution: A Political History of Europe and America, 1760–1800* (Princeton, New Jersey, 1959).
Pannick D., 'Who is Subject to Judicial Review and in Respect of What?' [1992] *PL* 1.
Parent D., *Structuring Criminal Sentences: The Evolution of Minnesota's Sentencing Guidelines* (St. Paul, Minnesota, 1988).
Partington M., 'Race Relations Act 1965: a Too Restricted View' [1967] *Crim LR* 497.
Perritt Jnr. H., 'The Electronic Agency and the Traditional Paradigms of Administrative Law' (1992) 44 *Administrative LR* 79.
Perry M., *The Constitution in the Courts: Law or Politics?* (New York, 1994).
Pierce R., '*Chevron* and Its Aftermath: Judicial Review of Agency Interpretation of Statutory Provisions' (1988) 41 *Vanderbilt LR* 301.
Playfair E., 'INTERIGHTS—An International Human Rights Law Centre' [1994] *PL* 573.
Plucknett T., 'Bonham's Case and Judicial Review' (1926) 39 *Harvard LR* 30.
Pocock J. G. A., *The Ancient Constitution and the Feudal Law*, extended ed. (Cambridge, 1987).
Poggi G., *The Development of the Modern State: A Sociological Introduction* (London, 1978).
Polyviou P., *The Equal Protection of the Laws* (London, 1980).
Porter R., 'The Privatisation of Prisons in the United States' (1990) 29 *Howard Journal* 65.
Post R., 'On the Popular Image of the Lawyer: Reflections in a Dark Glass' (1987) 75 *Calif LR* 379.
—— 'Theories of Constitutional Interpretation' in Post (ed.) *Law and the Order of Culture* (Berkeley, Cal., 1991).
Postema G. J., *Bentham and the Common Law Tradition* (Oxford, 1986).
Powe L.A., *American Broadcasting and the First Amendment* (California, 1987).
—— *The Fourth Estate and the Constitution* (California, 1991).
Powell H., 'Rules for Originalists' (1987) 73 *Virginia LR* 659.
Power M., *The Audit Explosion* (London, 1994).
Prosser T., *Test Cases for the Poor* (London, 1983).
Purdue M., 'The Scope of Fact-Finding in Judicial Review', in Hand G. and McBride J. (eds.) *Droit Sans Frontiers* (Birmingham, 1991).
Purdum T.S., 'Trying a Constructional Tack to Curb Campaign Spending' *New York Times* 21 October 1994.
Quint P., 'Towards First Amendment Limitations on the Introduction of Evidence: the Problem of *US* v. *Rosenberg*' (1977) 86 *Yale LJ* 1622.
Rabban D., 'The Original Meaning of the Free Speech Clause of the First Amendment', in Simmons R. (ed.) *The US Constitution—the First Two Hundred Years* (Manchester, 1988).

Radzinowicz L. and Hood R., *History of the English Criminal Law: The Emergence of Penal Policy* (London, 1986).
Raskin J.B., 'Challenging the "Wealth Primary"' *The Nation* 21 November 1994.
Rasmussen H., 'Why is Article 173 Interpreted Against Private Plaintiffs' (1980) 5 *ELR* 112.
Rawlings H. F. *Law and the Electoral Process* (London, 1988).
Rawlings R., 'The Eurolaw Game: Some Deductions from a Saga' (1993) 20 *JLS* 309.
—— 'Legal Politics: the United Kingdom and the Ratification of the Treaty on European Union (Part One)' [1994] *PL* 254.
—— 'Legal Politics: the United Kingdom and the Ratification of the Treaty on European Union (Part Two)' [1994] *PL* 367.
Rawls J., *A Theory of Justice* (New York, 1977).
—— *Political Liberalism* (New York, 1993).
Raz J., *The Morality of Freedom* (Oxford, 1986).
Redman M., 'Archaeology and Development' [1990] *JPL* 87.
Reich C., 'The New Property' (1964) 73 *Yale LJ* 733.
Resnik J., 'Managerial Judges' (1982) 96 *Harvard LR* 374.
Rhodes S., 'Prison Reform and Prison Life' (1992) 26 *Law and Society Review* 189.
Richards A., *Toleration and the Constitution* (New York, 1986).
Richardson G., *Law, Process and Custody* (London, 1993).
—— 'Prisoners and the Law: Beyond Rights', in McCrudden C. and Chambers G. (eds.), *Individual Rights and the Law in Britain* (Oxford, 1994).
Rivera-Ramos E., *The Legal Construction of American Colonialism: An Enquiry into the Constitutive Force of Law* (Ph.D. Dissertation, University College London, 1993).
Robbins I., 'The Legal Dimensions of Private Incarceration' (1989) 38 *Am U LR* 531.
Roberts D. M., 'Notice Pleading and Standing' (1980) 65 *Cornell LR* 390.
Roche J. P., 'The Convention as a Case Study in Democratic Politics' in Levy L. W. (ed.) *Essays on the Making of the Constitution* (New York, 1987, 2nd ed.).
Rohr M., 'Fighting for the Rights of Others: the Troubled Law of Third Party Standing and Mootness in the Federal Courts' (1981) 35 *U of Miami LR* 393.
Rose D., 'Racist Wave Sweeps East End' *The Observer* 13 February 1994.
Rose-Ackerman S., 'Progressive Law and Economics and the New Administrative Law' (1988) 98 *Yale LJ* 341.
Rosenberg G., 'Hollow Hopes and Other Aspirations: A Reply to Feeley and McCann' 17 *Law and Social Inquiry* (1992) 761.
Rutherford A., *Prisons and the Process of Justice* (London, 1986).
Sabato L., *PAC Power: Inside the World of Political Action Committees* (New York, 1985).
Sapir E., 'Symbols' in Seligman E. R. A. (ed.) *Encyclopedia of the Social Sciences* Vol 14 (New York, 1934).
Sarat A., '"The Law is all Over": Power, Resistance and the Legal Consciousness of the Welfare Poor' (1990) 2 *Yale Law J of Law and Humanities* 343.
Savas L., 'Privatization and Prisons' (1987) 40 *Vanderbilt LR* 88.

Sax J., *Defending the Environment: A Strategy for Citizen Action* (New York, 1971).
Scanlon T., 'A Theory of Freedom of Expression' (1972) 1 *Philosophy and Public Affairs* 214.
Scalia A., 'Judicial Deference to Administrative Interpretations of Law' (1989) *Duke LJ* 511.
Scarman LJ, *Report on the Red Lion Square Disorders of June 15 1974* (Cmnd. 5919, 1975).
Schauer F., 'Social Foundations of the Law of Defamation' (1980) 1 *J of Media Law and Practice* 3.
—— *Free Speech: A Philosophical Enquiry* (Cambridge, 1982).
Scheingold S., *The Politics of Rights: Lawyers, Public Policy and Political Change* (New Haven, 1974).
Schuck P., 'The New Ideology of Tort Law' (1988) 92 *The Public Interest* 93.
Schwartz B., 'Wade's New Edition and its Relevance for Americans' (1990) 42 *Administrative LR* 67.
Schwartz B. and Wade H. W. R., *Legal Control of Government: Administrative Law in Britain and the United States* (London, 1972 and Oxford, 1978).
Schwarze J., 'Tendencies Towards a Common Administrative Law in Europe' (1991) 16 *ELR* 3.
Schwarze J., 'Developing Principles of European Administrative Law' [1993] *PL* 229.
Scott J. B., *The Spanish Origin of International Law: Francisco de Vitoria and his Law of Nations* (Oxford, 1934).
Scott K.E., 'Standing in the Supreme Court—a Functional Analysis' (1973) 86 *Harvard LR* 645.
Sedler R.A., 'Standing to Assert *Jus Tertii*' (1974) *Harvard LR* 423.
—— 'The Assertion of Constitutional *Jus Tertii*: a Substantive Approach' (1982) 70 *Calif LR* 1308.
Sedley S., 'The Sound of Silence: Constitutional Law Without a Constitution' (1994) 110 *LQR* 270.
Seidle F. L. and Seidle K. Z., 'Party Finance, the Election Expenses Act, and Campaign Spending in 1979 and 1980', in Penniman H. (ed.) *Canada at the Polls in 1979 and 1980: A Study of the General Elections* (Washington DC, 1981).
Seth V., *A Suitable Boy* (London, 1993).
Shapiro M., 'APA: Past, Present, Future' (1986) 72 *Virginia LR* 447.
Shapiro S. and Glicksman R., 'Congress, the Supreme Court and the Quiet Revolution in Administrative Law' (1988) *Duke LJ* 819.
Shattuck P. and Norgren P., *Partial Justice: Federal Indian Law in a Liberal Constitutional System* (Providence, 1991).
Shaw M., *International Law* (Cambridge, 1986).
Sheppard R. and Valpy M., *The National Deal: The Fight for a Canadian Constitution* (Toronto, 1982).
Sherry S., 'The Founders' Unwritten Constitution' (1987) 54 *U of Chicago LR* 1127.
Simon D., 'Associational Standing and Due Process: the Need for Adequate Representation Scrutiny' (1981) 61 *Boston ULR* 174.

Skelly Wright J., 'Politics and the Constitution: Is Money Speech? (1976) 85 *Yale LJ* 1001.
—— 'The Bill of Rights in Britain and America: a Not Quite Full Circle', (1981) 55 *Tulane LR* 291.
—— 'Money and the Pollution of Politics: Is the First Amendment an Obstacle to Political Equality?' (1982) 82 *Columbia LR* 609.
Smith A., *Offences Against Public Order* (London, 1986).
Smith J. and Hogan B., *Criminal Law* (London, 7th ed., 1992).
de Smith S. A., *Judicial Review of Administrative Action* (London, 1959) and (London, 4th ed., 1980).
Smolla R., *Free Speech in an Open Society* (New York, Knopf, 1992).
Snyder F., 'The Effectiveness of European Community Law: Institutions, Processes, Tools and Techniques' [1993] 56 *MLR* 19.
Solomos J., 'Equal Opportunities Policies and Racial Inequality: the Role of Public Policy' (1989) 67 *Public Administration* 79.
Sorabjee S., 'Obliging Government to Control Itself: Recent Developments in Indian Administrative Law' [1994] *PL* 39.
Sorauf F., *Inside Campaign Finance. Myths and Realities* (New Haven, 1992).
Stapleton J., 'Minimum Directives: Do Not Be Misled' (1994) 110 *LQR* 213.
Stewart R., 'The Reformation of American Administrative Law' (1975) 88 *Harvard LR* 1667.
Stone C., 'Should Trees Have Standing?' (1972) 45 *So Cal LR* 450.
Street H., 'Book Review' 59 *Yale LJ* 590 (1950).
Stumpf H., *American Judicial Politics* (New York, 1988).
Sturm S., 'Resolving the Remedial Dilemma: Strategies of Judicial Intervention in Prisons' (1990) 138 *U of Penn LR* 805.
Sullivan K., 'Foreword: the Justices of Rules and Standards' (1992) 106 *Harvard LR* 56.
Sunkin M., Bridges L. and Meszaros G., *Judicial Review in Perspective* (London, 1993).
Sunkin M. and Le Sueur A., 'Can Government Control Judicial Review?' (1991) *CLP* 161.
Sunstein C., 'Beyond the Republican Revival' (1988) 97 *Yale LJ* 1539.
—— 'Constitutionalism after the New Deal' (1988) 101 *Harvard LR* 421.
—— 'Standing and the Privatization of Public Law' (1988) 88 *Columbia LR* 1432.
—— 'Law and Administration After *Chevron*' (1990) 90 *Columbia LR* 2072.
—— 'Free Speech Now', in Stone G., Epstein R. and Sunstein C. (eds.) *The Bill of Rights in the Modern State* (Chicago, 1992).
—— 'What's Standing After *Lujan*? Of Citizen Suits, "Injuries" and Article III' (1992) 91 *Michigan LR* 163.
—— *The Partial Constitution* (Cambridge, Mass., 1993).
—— 'Political Equality and Unintended Consequences' (1994) 94 *Columbia LR* 1390.
Taggart M., 'Corporatization, Contracting and the Courts' [1994] *PL* 351.
Taylor LCJ, 'Judges and Sentencing' *J. of the Law Society of Scotland* April 1993, 129.
Thomas D., 'Establishing a Factual Basis for Sentencing' [1970] *Crim LR* 80.

—— *Constraints on Judgment* (Cambridge, 1978).
—— 'Form and Function in the Criminal Law', in P. Glazebrook (ed.) *Reshaping the Criminal Law* (London, 1978).
Thompson B., *Textbook on Constitutional and Administrative Law* (London, 1993).
Thompson E.P., *Whigs and Hunters* (London: Penguin edition, 1990).
Thorne S., 'Dr Bonham's Case' (1938) 54 *LQR* 543.
Tonry M., 'Criminal Law: The Missing Element in Sentencing Reform' (1982) 35 *Vanderbilt LR* 607.
—— 'Sentencing Guidelines and Sentencing Commissions—the Second Generation', in Wasik M. and Pease K., *Sentencing Reform* (Manchester, 1987).
—— 'Judges and Sentencing Policy—the American Experience', in Munro C. and Wasik M. (eds.) *Sentencing, Judicial Discretion and Training* (London, 1992).
—— 'The Failure of the US Sentencing Commission's Guidelines' (1993) 39 *Crime and Delinquency* 131.
Travis A., 'Howard Fears "BNP Martyrs" ' *The Guardian* 14 October 1993.
Tribe L. H., *Constitutional Choices* (Cambridge, Mass., 1985).
—— *American Constitutional Law* (Mineola, NY, 2nd ed., 1988).
Truman D., *The Governmental Process* (New York, 1951).
Turner V., *The Forest of Symbols: Aspects of Ndembu Ritual* (Ithaca NY, 1967).
Tushnet M., *The NAACP's Legal Strategy Against Segregated Education, 1925–1950* (Chapel Hill, 1987).
Tyler T., *Why People Obey the Law* (New Haven, 1990).
Vile M., *Constitutionalism and the Separation of Powers* (Oxford, 1967).
Vose C., 'The National Consumers' League and the Brandeis Brief' (1957) 1 *Midwest J of Political Studies* 267.
—— *Caucasians Only: The Supreme Court, the NAACP and the Restrictive Covenant Cases* (Berkeley, 1959).
Wade C. C. S., *Introduction to the Study of the Law of the Constitution* (London, 9th ed., 1959).
Wade H. W. R., *Administrative Law* (Oxford, 1961).
Wade H. W. R. and Forsyth C., *Administrative Law* (Oxford, 7th ed., 1994).
Walker N., 'The Middle Ground in Public Law' in W. Finnie *et al.* (eds.), *Edinburgh Essays in Public Law* (Edinburgh, 1991).
—— 'Law Under Pressure' [1994] 57 *MLR* 130.
Wasik M., 'England Repeals Key Provisions of 1991 Sentencing Reform Legislation' (1993) 4(4) *Overcrowded Times* 1.
Wasik M. and von Hirsch A., 'Non-Custodial Penalties and the Principles of Desert' [1988] *Crim LR* 555.
—— 'Statutory Sentencing Principles: the 1990 White Paper' [1990] 53 *MLR* 508.
—— 'Section 29 Revised: Previous Convictions in Sentencing' [1994] *Crim LR* 409.
—— and Taylor R. *Blackstone's Guide to the Criminal Justice and Public Order Act 1994* (London, 1995).
Weber M., *Economy and Society* (Berkeley, Cal., 1978).
Wecht D., 'Breaking the Code of Deference: Judicial Review of Private Prisons' (1987) 96 *Yale LJ* 815.

Wedderburn, *The Worker and the Law* (London, 3rd ed., 1986).
Westlake J., 'John Westlake on the Title to Sovereignty', in Curtin P. (ed.) *Imperialism* (London, 1971).
Whelan J., 'An Introduction to the US Federal Government System of Contracting' [1992] *PPLR* 207.
White F., Harden I. and Donnelly K., 'Audit, Accounting Officers and Accountability: The Pergau Dam Affair' [1994] *PL* 526.
White M., *The Philosophy of the American Revolution* (London, 1982).
Wilkins L., *The Principles of Sentencing Guidelines* (Lexington, 1980).
Wilkins W. and Steer J., 'Relevant Conduct: The Cornerstone of the Federal Sentencing Guidelines' (1990) 41 *So Carolina LR* 495.
Williams D., 'Racial Incitement and Public Order', *Crim LR* 320.
Williams P., 'Spirit-Murdering the Messenger: the Discourse of Fingerpointing as the Law's Response to Racism' (1987) 42 *U Miami LR* 127.
Williams R., *The American Indian in Western Legal Thought: The Discourses of Conquest* (New York, 1990).
Woolf H., 'Public Law—Private Law: Why the Divide? A Personal View' [1986] *PL* 220.
—— 'Judicial Review: A Possible Programme for Reform' [1992] *PL* 221.
—— *Protection of the Public—A New Challenge* (London, 1994).
Wunder J., '*Retained By the People*': *A History of American Indians and the Bill of Rights* (Oxford, 1994).
Zemans F., 'Legal Mobilisation: The Neglected Role of the Law in the Political System' (1983) 77 *American Political Science Review* 690.

Index